OXFORD MONOGRAPHS IN INTERNATIONAL LAW

General Editor: PROFESSOR VAUGHAN LOWE
Chichele Professor of Public International Law in the University of Oxford and Fellow of All Souls College, Oxford

Diplomatic Protection

OXFORD MONOGRAPHS IN INTERNATIONAL LAW

The aim of this series is to publish important and original pieces of research on all aspects of international law. Topics that are given particular prominence are those which, while of interest to the academic lawyer, also have an important bearing on issues that touch upon the actual conduct of international relations. Nonetheless, the series is wide in scope and includes monographs on the history and philosophical foundations of international law.

RECENT TITLES IN THE SERIES

The Decolonization of International Law
Matthew Craven

Investment Treaty Arbitration and Public Law
Gus Van Harten

Diplomatic Protection
Chittharanjan F. Amerasinghe

The 'War on Terrorism', Human Rights, and Non-Discrimination
Daniel Moeckli

The Immunity of States and their Officials in International and Criminal Law andInternational Human Rights Law
Rosanne Van Alebeek

Defining Terrorism in International Law
Ben Saul

Peremptory Norms in International Law
Alexander Orakhelashvili

Differential Treatment in International Environmental Law
Lavanya Rajamani

International Organizations and their Exercise of Sovereign Powers
Dan Sarooshi

The Fair and Equitable Treatment Standard in the International Law of Foreign Investment
Ioana Tudor

Jurisdiction in International Law
Cedric Ryngaert

The Interpretation of Acts and Rules in Public International Law
Alexander Orakhelashvili

Targeted Killing in International Law
Nils Melzer

Diplomatic Protection

CHITTHARANJAN F. AMERASINGHE

BA, LLB, Ph D, LLD (Cambridge, UK),
LLM (Harvard), Ph D (Ceylon);
Member, Institut de Droit International;
Former Judge, UN Administrative Tribunal, and
Registrar, World Bank Administrative Tribunal,
Full Professor and Honorary Professor of Law,
University of Ceylon, Colombo.

OXFORD
UNIVERSITY PRESS

This book has been printed digitally and produced in a standard specification in order to ensure its continuing availability

OXFORD
UNIVERSITY PRESS

Great Clarendon Street, Oxford OX2 6DP
United Kingdom

Oxford University Press is a department of the University of Oxford. It furthers the University's objective of excellence in research, scholarship, and education by publishing worldwide.

Oxford is a registered trade mark of Oxford University Press in the UK and in certain other countries

Reprinted 2012

British Library Cataloguing in Publication Data
Data available

Library of Congress Cataloging in Publication Data
Data available

ISBN 978-0-19-921238-5

Contents—Summary

Contents

Table of Cases

Table of Abbreviations

A.D.	see AD
AALCC	Asian African Legal Consultative Committee
AC	Law Reports of the House of Lords (UK)
ACHR	American Convention on Human Rights
AD	Annual Digest of Public International Law Cases
AFDI	Annuaire Francais de droit international
AIDI	Annuaire de Institut de droit international
AJIL	American Journal of International Law
All ER	All England Law Reports (UK)
ASIL	American Society of International Law
BFSP	British Foreign State Papers
BIT	Bi-lateral Investment Treaty
BYIL	British Yearbook of International Law
CCR	Crown Court Reports (UK)
Cmd.	Command Papers (UK)
COE	Council of Europe
Collection	Collection of Decisions of the European Commission of Human Rights
CTC	see UNCTC
DCF	Discounted Cash Flow
DRC	Democratic Republic of Congo
E.C.H.R.	see ECHR
ECHR	European Court of Human Rights
ECJ	European Court of Justice
EComHR	European Commission of Human Rights
EEC	European Economic Community
EPIL	Encyclopedia of Public International Law
ETS	European Treaty Series
FCSC	Foreign Claims Settlement Commission (US)
FRG	Federal Republic of Germany
FRY	Federal Republic of Yugoslavia
GA	General Assembly of the UN
GAOR	GA of the UN, Official Records
GATT	General Agreement on Trade and Tariffs
GB	Great Britain
Hackworth, Digest	Hackworth, Digest of International Law (1943)
Hague Recueil	Académie de droit international: Recueil des cours
HLS	Harvard Law School
HRC	Human Rights Committee (UN)
HRJ	Human Rights Journal
IACHR	Inter-American Court of Human Rights

IAComHR	Inter-American Commission on Human Rights
IBRD	International Bank for Reconstruction and Development
ICC	International Chamber of Commerce
ICJ Pleadings	ICJ Pleadings, Oral Arguments and Documents
ICJ	International Court of Justice
ICLQ	International and Comparative Law Quarterly
ICSID	International Centre for Settlement of Investment Disputes
ICTY	International Criminal Tribunal for the Former Yugoslavia
IDA	International Development Association
IJIL	Indian Journal of International Law
ILA	International Law Association
ILC	International Law Commission
ILM	International Legal Materials
ILR	International Law Reports
IOLR	International Organizations Law Review
Iran–US CTR	Iran–US Claims Tribunal Reports
ITLOS	International Tribunal for the Law of the Sea
JDI	Journal de droit international
LN	League of Nations
LNTS	League of Nations Treaty Series
LQR	Law Quarterly Review
La Fontaine	La Fontaine, Pasicrisie Internationale
MIGA	Multilateral Investment Guarantee Agency
MIT	Multilateral Investment Treaty
Moore, Digest	Moore, A Digest of International Law (1906)
Moore, International Arbitrations	Moore, History and Digest of the International Arbitrations to Which the United States Has Been a Party (1898)
NAFTA	North American Free Trade Agreement
NATO	North Atlantic Treaty Organization
New LR	New Law Reports (Ceylon)
NILR	Netherlands International Law Review
OECD	Organization for Economic Cooperation and Development
OJ	Official Journal (EEC)
ÖZÖR	Österreichische Zeitschrift für Öffentliches Recht
PCIJ	Permanent Court of International Justice
QB	Queen's Bench Division Reports (UK)
QBD	Queen's Bench Division Reports (UK)
RAI	Receuil des arbitrages international (La Pradelle—Politis)
RBDI	Reveue Belge de droit international
RDI	Revue de droit international
RDILC	Revue de droit international et législation comparé
Receuil TAM	Receuil de Tribunaux Arbitrales Mixtes
RGDIP	Revue générale de droit international public
RHDI	Revue Hellénique de droit international
SCOR	Security Council of the UN, Official Records

TAM	Tribunaux Arbitrales Mixtes
TGS	Transactions of the Grotius Society
UK	United Kingdom
UKTS	United Kingdom Treaty Series
UN	United Nations Organization
UNCC	United Nations Compensation Commission
UNCITRAL	United Nations Commission on International Trade Law
UNCTC	UN Commission on Transnational Corporations
UNGA	GA of the UN
UNRIAA	United Nations Reports of International Arbitral Awards
UNTS	UN Treaty Series
UNYB	United Nations Yearbook
US For. Rel.	US Foreign Relations
US	United States of America
USA	see US
VJIL	Virginia Journal of International Law
VRS	Army of the Republika Srpska
WTO	World Trade Organization
YBILC	Yearbook of the International Law Commission
ZAORV	Zeitschrift für ausländisches öffentliches Recht und Völkerrecht

1

Prologue

General Observations

The law relating to diplomatic protection in reality crystallized as part of international law long after the Peace of Westphalia (1648), which gave birth to the nation State and modern international law. It was comparatively recently—not until the early part of the nineteenth century—that the institution of diplomatic protection asserted itself in the field of international law and jurisprudence. The birth and maturing of this institution for all practical purposes coincided particularly with the gaining of independence by the, largely Spanish, European colonies of America. The observation is pertinent that the practical conditions responsible for its nascence and development did not appear in full force until this time or even some time later. More will be said about the development and history of this institution in Chapter 2. Suffice it to note here that from the early nineteenth century to the present this institution had certain features which permit a conceptual description of diplomatic protection, which will be done fully in Chapter 3.

By way of explanation, diplomatic protection of aliens and their property may correctly be described as an institution in the international legal system. An institution in a legal system may be defined as an established law, custom, usage, organization, or other element in the political or social life of the subjects of that legal system.[1] Insofar as diplomatic protection embodies a set of rules and principles which relate to the elements in the political and social life and relationships of States which are subjects of the international legal system, and to the organization of those elements in a comprehensible and unified conceptual whole, it fits into the concept of a legal institution. The totality of the rules and principles focusing on the implementation of diplomatic protection constitute the institution, because it is an identifiable corpus within the legal system and subsists in that system as such.

[1] *Oxford English Dictionary; Black's Law Dictionary* (2004) 813. The term 'institution' had several meanings, even in a legal context, as the latter reference shows. The use of the term to refer to diplomatic protection is different from its use to describe international organizations, for instance.

Diplomatic protection is concerned basically and in broad terms with the subject of injuries to aliens. There are primary rules on this subject, ie the rules governing the treatment of the person and property of aliens, breach of which gives rise to responsibility on the part of the respondent State to the national State of the injured person. Certain secondary rules, ie rules that relate to the conditions that must be met for the bringing of a claim and to the remedies available, are at the core of the institution of diplomatic protection. Diplomatic protection is concerned with the settlement of disputes and thus relates in principle to secondary rules. While diplomatic protection is triggered by the breach of primary rules, the institution itself does not purport to cover all of these rules, though some which may be regarded as primary, such as those relating to the attribution or imputing of unlawful acts or omissions to the respondent State, are ambivalent in this regard and are inextricably involved with the pertinent secondary rules. Whether there has been a substantive violation of international obligations relating to the treatment, as such, of persons who are aliens is left to the law of the treatment of aliens. The conditions which govern the taking of action by a State vis-à-vis the offending State in respect of that violation of international law are at the heart of the pursuit of remedial measures following the violation and constitute the law relating to diplomatic protection.

However, now it appears that not all secondary rules are regarded by some as necessarily and specifically covered by the term 'diplomatic protection'. The rules relating to reparation are sometimes regarded as peripheral to the now accepted concept of diplomatic protection, although they relate to remedial action. They are so regarded, because most of them apply across the board in situations where a State incurs responsibility under international law.[2] In fact they do belong to the corpus of rules relating to diplomatic protection.

The attribution or imputation to the respondent State of acts or omissions by persons or organs, constituting the violation of international obligations which may be regarded as part of the primary rules, relate also in a sense to objective or passive capacity or the capacity to be sued or be at the receiving end of the exercise of diplomatic protection. Such attribution or imputation may thus be regarded as relevant to diplomatic protection, even if such attribution or imputation may not be included as such in some modern conceptions of diplomatic protection.

Moreover, in a converse sense, subjectively or actively the nationality of the alien is in reality, as will be seen, relevant to the substantive violation of international law insofar as the alien must have the nationality of the claimant State, at the time of the impeached act or omission, in order that there may be a violation of the respondent State's international obligations vis-à-vis the claimant State. Nationality is thus a necessity for substantive responsibility to

[2] These general rules relating to reparation have been included in the ILC's Draft Articles on State Responsibility: Articles 34 to 39 and commentary thereon in Crawford, *The International Law Commission's Articles on State Responsibility* (2002) 67–8, 211–41.

be attributed to the respondent State in respect of the claimant State. Yet the same nationality also gives the claimant State procedural capacity to exercise diplomatic protection and, consequently, the issue of nationality is relevant to diplomatic protection.

As a result of the above realities, rules of reparation—which have usually been dealt with in the context of State responsibility in general—will be examined here, insofar as they are particularly relevent, as an important part of diplomatic protection as an institution. The issue of attribution or imputability of conduct to the respondent State which objectively makes it possible to cite that State as respondent in a dispute will also be included in the study. Nationality of the alien, as relevant to the claimant State's standing in a dispute, will form an important part of the study.

In discussing the subject of diplomatic protection care must be taken not to criticize the *lex lata* merely for the sake of criticizing it or to allow whims and fancies to enter into the process. Nor is it a matter of being original in suggesting changes in the law but rather how the law should be evaluated realistically, in terms of its development and underpinnings, and changes be made accordingly. Above all it must be recognized that the institution has become what it is after close to two centuries of distinct development and concentrated attention on it. In making an effort to have the institution conform to modern needs, it must be borne in mind that there are limits to what can be done to change the institution itself and that the institution, as it has developed and now subsists, does have an important function to perform in international society and international relations. By and large the *lex lata* may not be significantly out of step with modern society and its legitimate needs.

As for the literature on the subject, since the celebrated dictum of Vattel in the mid-eighteenth century which will be addressed in the next chapter, there has been precious little attention paid to the subject until the late nineteenth century. It was really towards the end of the nineteenth century and in the early twentieth century that more concentrated discussion about it took place both in general treatises and in monographs, though the latter were perhaps concerned as well with the substantive law relating to the treatment of aliens.[3] These discussions were also associated with the law of State responsibility in general, while the subject of the treatment of aliens and their diplomatic protection was by and large a stepping stone to, and an instrument enabling, the consideration of the general law of State responsibility. A significant milestone in that era was Brochard's *Diplomatic Protection of Citizens Abroad* published in 1915. Since then there have been summary and limited excursions into aspects

[3] General works of this era include Bluntschli, *Das modern Völkerrecht der civilisirten Staaten als Rechtsbuch dargestellt* (3rd edn 1878); Calvo, *Le droit international théorique et pratique* (5th edn 1896); Moore, *Digest of International Arbitrations* (1898); Moore, *Digest of International Law* (1906). A monograph, the first of its kind apparently, on the subject was Tcharnoff, *Le droit de protection exercé par un état à l'ègard de ses nationaux residant à l'étranger* (1898).

of the law of State responsibility for injuries to aliens, including the diplomatic protection of aliens,[4] sometimes associated with the law of State responsibility in general and apart from treatment of the subject in general treatises on international law.[5] Meanwhile, in the 1950s, not long after the ILC was created, that UN organ turned its attention to the subject of State responsibility. More will be said about its efforts at codification in Chapters 3 and 6. However, at this point suffice it to note that the study of State responsibility in general was inextricably linked with issues of diplomatic protection and to some extent mired in the controversies surrounding the latter subject. Hence, as will be seen, it was not until the beginning of the twenty-first century that the ILC was able to conclude its work on both diplomatic protection and State responsibility in general.

Scope of this Work

The object of this work is to describe and consider the conditions for the exercise of diplomatic protection as a remedial measure. Following this introductory chapter are chapters on the history of the institution (Chapter 2), on the essence of diplomatic protection (Chapter 3), on violations of international law (Chapter 4), on arrangements not covered by the concept of diplomatic protection (Chapter 5), on the unsuccessful attempts at codification leading up to the work done by the ILC (Chapter 6), on the basic interests underlying diplomatic protection (Chapter 7), on how the human rights factor has not rendered the institution obsolete (Chapter 8), and on the duty or absence of a duty of national States to protect (Chapter 9).

Chapter 10 deals with nationality as a condition for the exercise of diplomatic protection, while Chapter 11 considers the exhaustion of local remedies as an additional condition. These two conditions are critical for the exercise of diplomatic protection and are in reality at the heart of the institution.

[4] See, eg Eagleton, *Responsibility of States in International Law* (1928), which dealt more or less entirely with injuries to aliens, though its title referred to State responsibility in general; C F Amerasinghe, *State Responsibility for Injuries to Aliens* (1967); Lillich (ed), *International Law of State Responsibility for Injuries to Aliens* (1983).

[5] Examples of these general works from the early and mid-twentieth century are Anzilotti, *Corso di diritto internazionale* (1928); Rousseau, *Droit international public* (1953); Oppenheim, *International Law* (8th edn 1955); Dahm, *Völkerrecht* (1958), 3 vols. Select bibliographies on State responsibility in general and for injuries to aliens and on diplomatic protection published after 1950 are to be found in C F Amerasinghe, *State Responsibility for Injuries to Aliens* (1967) 306–14; Ago, 'Fourth Report to the ILC on State Responsibility', 2 YBILC (Part I, 1972) 152–60; Spinedi, 'Bibliography on the Codification of State Responsibility by the United Nations, 1973–1985', in Spinedi and Simma (eds), *United Nations Codification of State Responsibility* (1987) 395 ff; Crawford, 'First Report to the ILC on State Responsibility', UN Doc A/CN.4/490/ Add 7, and *The International Law Commission's Articles on State Responsibility* (2002) 368–80.

Chapter 12 explores the effect of the Calvo Clause. Chapter 13 considers the 'clean hands' (*mains propres)* doctrine as possibly applicable to diplomatic protection as a remedial measure. Chapter 14 deals with the attribution (or imputation) to the host or respondent State of violations of substantive primary rules, which relates to its objective capacity to be a respondent. Chapter 15 will consider the elements of the secondary rules relating to remedies which are relevant to diplomatic protection. Chapter 16 deals with the influence of human rights law on the law of diplomatic protection, while Chapter 17 discusses the effect on the law of diplomatic protection of investment treaties and of international investment law. Chapter 18 draws together a number of concluding observations.

Important Sources and References

While Article 38 of the Statute of the ICJ refers to judicial decisions and legal commentators as equally important sources of international law,[6] in international law today it has come to be accepted that judicial decisions of all international tribunals, but especially of the ICJ, have a special relevance and a particular importance and force. This is in addition, of course, to State practice, treaties, and general principles of law. Thus, the consideration of judicial decisions has been given particular emphasis in this work as also creating or reflecting State practice giving rise to customary law and general principles of law, both of which are primary legal sources of equal force. Legal commentators are generally referred to, as it is accepted should be the case, for what they say is the law rather than for what they say the law should be. However, where a change in the law is discussed, they may be cited for what they say the law ought to be. Care has been taken in every instance to cite the most useful and relevant commentators while avoiding references which would overburden and possibly obfuscate the discussion. What is to be found in this work is not an encyclopedia of references but ones which have been judiciously and sometimes sparingly selected. The work is to be read not only as a presentation of the law and how it works but also as a discussion of how it may be developed in its application and how it may be improved where it is weak or outmoded.[7]

[6] They are described as subsidiary sources but have come to be regarded, nevertheless, as very important.

[7] The six reports, with addenda, on diplomatic protection by Dugard, as special Rapporteur of the ILC, have been very helpful in the preparation of my work: see UN Docs. A/CN.4/506 (2000), A/CN.4/506/Add.1 (2000), A/CN.4/514 (2001), A/CN.4/523 (2002), A/CN.4/523/Add.1 (2002), A/CN.4/530 (2003), A/CN.4/530/Add.1 (2003), A/CN.4/538 (2004), A/CN.4/546 (2005). There must also be mentioned, among UN documents, particularly some of the many Special Rapporteurs' Reports to the ILC on State Responsibility and many of the Reports of the ILC to the GA over a long period from 1956 to the present, especially those made after diplomatic protection was taken up for

A Basic Premise

A basic premise in this work is that diplomatic protection of the persons and property of nationals abroad still survives as an institution which has a place in the legal system of international society. On the one hand, it cannot be suggested that because diplomatic protection grew up in a colonial climate and that most states currently members of international society were not party to its creation and development, it cannot be regarded as an institution which is relevant to and covers the post colonial independent States.[8] On the other hand, it cannot be accepted that it is outmoded simply because firstly, there are already arrangements which give individuals access to international tribunals under treaties and conventions and, secondly, because it is based on a 'fiction' that it is a State which is injured when its nationals abroad are injured. As for the first point, it will be seen later that there are situations in which nationals abroad who are injured by States may be left without a remedy but for the right of their national States to protect them. Moreover, as to the second point, even though this protection is based on what has come to be called a fiction, it is a valuable source of protection which has not outlived its usefulness. However, a consequence of the fundamental relevance of the 'fiction' is that the legal capacity of the national State must be recognized, at any rate procedurally, in terms of remedial action and of

study by the ILC, beginning with the Report of 1998 1–13 (paras 56–110). Earlier works of interest other than those referred to in the chapters which follow are to be found in the bibliography at the end of Geck, 'Diplomatic Protection', 1 EPIL (1992) 1065–7 and at the end of Dolzer, 'Diplomatic Protection of Foreign Nationals', ibid 1069–70. Some of the material available sometimes espouses a particular interest and may appear to be somewhat less objectively 'judicious': eg Lillich, 'Editorial Comment on Diplomatic Protection of Nationals Abroad', 69 AJIL (1975) 359–65; Lillich (ed), *International Law of State Responsibility for Injuries to Aliens* (1983) *passim,* especially 1–7, 26–9, 321–45. Also worth particularly noting is the Summary of the Discussion in the Sixth Committee of the GA on Diplomatic Protection, soon after the ILC began its work specifically on diplomatic protection: UN Doc. A/CN.4/496 (1999) paras 52–76.

Some remarks on the ILC's treatment of the connected subjects of State responsibility and diplomatic protection will be made in chapter 6 below.

Also noted, as a textual source, is the resolution of the ILA on Diplomatic Protection of Persons and Property (Rs No. 5/2006) adopted at its 72nd conference in Toronto in 2006 (<http://www.ila-hq.org>) and the reports to its committee on the subject and the reports to the plenary of such committee (see ILA, *Report of the 69th Conference* (2000) 604 ff; ILA, *Report of the 70th Conference* (2002) 228 ff; ILA, *Report of the 72nd Conference* (2006) <http://www.ila-hq.org>). All the reports and work connected with the ILA lean unusually heavily towards protecting the interests of the alien, to the extent sometimes of obliterating the balance in the institution of diplomatic protection and consequently attacking its foundation as an inter-State concept.

[8] Questions have been raised about the current relevance of the law of State responsibility for injuries to aliens for ex-colonial States: see Guha Roy, 'Is the Law of State Responsibility for Injuries to Aliens Part of Universal International Law?', 55 AJIL (1961) 863. As a consequence similar questions would have had to be asked about diplomatic protection as a remedial process for the redress of injuries to aliens.

secondary rules and as important in the formation of the rules relating to diplomatic protection. A basic assumption in the discussion of the law that follows is that the 'fiction' cannot entirely be ignored, though changes may usefully be made by working around it. It may be said that, though a person—natural or juridical—suffers the primary injury, it is through, and because of, a legal relationship between States that his interests have come to be and can be protected. More particularly the remedial process involved in the protection of the person's interests is dependent on States for it to work.[9]

[9] The 'fiction', which originated with Vattel, is discussed in Chapter 2 herein and is referred to in later chapters.

2

History and Development of Diplomatic Protection

Diplomatic protection, as contrasted with such areas of international law as the law of the sea or acquisition of territory, is a comparatively young creature in international law. As far as the sources reveal, there are no recorded examples of its possible exercise prior to the late eighteenth and early nineteenth century, although the institution is believed to have been referred to by Vattel in a work published in 1758.[1] Grotius, writing in the previous century after the Peace of Westphalia when the nation State came to be established, does not deal with it particularly in his writings.

There is no recorded evidence, for example in classical Greek or Roman history, the history of South Asia (India), the history of China, or the early history of any other area, of a sovereign or ruler taking up against another sovereign ruler, on the basis of a law governing his relations with the latter, the cause of a subject or the equivalent where the claim was that such subject had been ill-treated by the latter. There were city-states, kingdoms, principalities, fiefdoms and the like in which subjects owed allegiance to and had obligations to rulers, princes, kings, or lords but no evidence that as between such entities the latter protected those who lived in territories under their control against each other in this way. This is so, even though there may be evidence of some kind of law, however embryonic, recognized as governing the relations between sovereigns, lords or rulers, in early times in many parts of the world.[2] Even in medieval Europe there is no recorded evidence of such an event. It is not till much later and, indeed, after a considerable lapse of time after the rise of the nation State subsequent to the Peace of Westphalia, when a more developed relationship between subject and sovereign or ruler had taken root, that even legal commentators and scholars referred to what was the beginning of the institution of 'diplomatic protection'.

In any case the law developed when it did after the period of colonization had begun and had established itself as a way of life for the European nations. It was

[1] Emmerich Vattel, *The Law of Nations, or the Principles of Natural Law* (1758), Book II, Chapter VI: see 3 *Classics of International Law* (1916) 136.

[2] See C F Amerasinghe, 'The Historical Development of International Law—Universal Aspects', 38 *Archiv des Völkerrechts* (2001) 367 ff *passim*.

applicable only among the States of Europe and America, omitting in its application entities outside that narrow world. The observation had been made with regard to the law of diplomatic protection that prior to the mid-eighteenth or early nineteenth century the practical conditions that were responsible for its development did not appear in full force and,

> By that time the conceptual framework of international law had been fairly well crystallized. The fundamental doctrines of the juristic system had been worked out against the background of a more or less static world of localized and isolated communities ruled over by personal sovereigns. In the nineteenth century, that background changed radically, and along with it the practical needs to be served by a legal system. However, the basic conceptual structure of the system remained almost unchanged. Hence we find that the early history of the legal institution of diplomatic protection is very largely represented by its attempts to deal with a new set of practical needs and conflicts of interests in terms of old doctrines and standards developed to fit the requirements of a different type of civilization.[3]

Grotius, writing on international law in 1625 soon after the Renaissance and the age of discovery, entailing more complex relationships between nation States, had begun, addressed those relations between States but paid no attention to the position of the individual, particularly as an alien.[4] This was probably because States were not concerned with the position of the individual, frequent interaction between States and individuals as aliens having only just begun. Nor do other authors, such as Suarez[5] and Pufendorf,[6] have anything to say on the subject.

Grotius and his immediate successors had little, if anything, to say with regard to the legal obligations of a State toward foreigners and foreign property interests within its borders, at least in time of peace. New States that arose out of the disintegration of the Holy Roman Empire were very largely self-supporting economic units. At that time the preoccupations were with different problems from those with which the world was faced later and particularly in the nineteenth century and thereafter. Problems which arose later were unknown to the early writers and could not be foreseen by them.

Grotius wrote of the legal relations of personal sovereigns in their dealings with each other, not of the relations between abstract States. For him sovereigns were human beings subject to a moral order in their mutual relations in virtually the same manner in which private individuals were then subject to an authoritative moral order.[7] The system of political order and authority represented in the Holy

[3] Dunn, *The Protection of Nationals* (1932) 46.

[4] Grotius, *De jure belli et pacis libri tres* (1625).

[5] *De legibus, ac Deo legislatore* (1612) and other works in *Selections from Three Works of Fransisco Suárez, SJ* (1944), Volumes 1 & 2.

[6] Pufendorf, *Elementorum jurisprudentae universalis libri II* (1672) and other works. For references to the works of Pufendorf see O'Connell, 2 *International Law* (1970) 1303–4 (Table of General Treatises on International Law).

[7] See Pound, 'Philosophical Theory and International Law,' 1 *Bibliotheca Visseriana* (1923) 76.

Roman Empire was disintegrating, together with the dissolution of the Empire, and threatened to be supplanted by anarchy and general disorder. The concept of absolute sovereignty of the monarch over his subjects, as propounded by political theorists such as Bodin, was regarded as the best means of preventing strife and chaos in the internal life of the new nation States.

Because absolute freedom of the monarch in his external relations with other States would lead to chaos and constant war, a system of restraints was developed upon the external actions of absolute monarchs in the interest of peace for the community at large. Grotius was content to believe that these monarchs were subject both to a higher law based on natural reason and to a customary law voluntarily accepted. This conception, also reflected in the philosophical beliefs of the time, supplanted gradually the system of universal authority embodied in the Holy Roman Empire. Naturally, Grotius did not reflect on the subject of the protection of the citizen abroad, primarily because the citizen for the most part stayed at home, and Grotius had little or nothing to say about it.

The Early Beginnings

Vattel was the first of the authorities on international law to give attention to the subject of protection of aliens, their property interests and diplomatic protection. His thinking and statements gave rise more or less to the institution, because he was the first to provide a doctrinal basis for it. When he wrote his work entitled *The Law of Nations, or the Principles of Natural Law,* about a century and a quarter after Grotius's principal work appeared, international life had expanded considerably. Colonization of other parts of the world outside Europe had been successful and foreign trade had become an important element in the economic systems of a number of States. However, in spite of the frequency of travel and trading relations the impact of industrialization had not yet been felt.

Vattel without hesitation propounded the thesis that an injury to an individual is an injury to his State. He wrote:

> Whoever ill-treats a citizen indirectly injures the State, which must protect that citizen. The sovereign of the injured citizen must avenge the deed and, if possible, force the aggressor to give full satisfaction or punish him, since otherwise the citizen will not obtain the chief end of civil society, which is protection.[8]

This thesis became the substantial basis for the practice of diplomatic protection of citizens abroad. When taken by itself, its terms seem sufficiently broad to cover all types of injuries to foreigners now customarily included under this heading. Vattel was writing for a homogeneous international society of European Christian States possessing a common civilization and a common moral code.

[8] Op cit (note 1 above) 136.

He, therefore, probably did not find it necessary to establish the fact that certain kinds of treatment of foreigners should be regarded as wrongful or injurious. He could probably assume with success that there would be fairly general agreement throughout the community on this matter. His concern was, thus, essentially to establish the kind of wrongs that fell within the province of the law of nations.[9]

Vattel did refer to the relations existing between foreigners and the State of their sojourn and the extent of the responsibility of the latter towards the former, but his concern there was 'not so much to show what humanity and justice call for in our treatment of foreigners', but 'to lay down the rules of the Law of Nations on this subject, rules whose object is to secure the rights of both parties and to prevent the peace of Nations from being disturbed by the disputes of individuals'.[10] He begins with the proposition, on the other hand, that, because the lord of the territory may forbid entrance into it whenever he thinks proper, he may undoubtedly fix the conditions on which admittance will be allowed, and that, if he grants foreigners access to his dominions, it is presumed that he does so only on the implied condition that they will be subject to the local laws. In that context he referred to disputes between foreigners, or between a foreigner and a citizen, stating that they should be settled by the local courts.[11] There was no reference to disputes between the foreigner and the sovereign as such. But Vattel's approach to the problem did provide a useful basis for those who sought then and later to uphold and extend the practice of diplomatic protection, even though he was dealing specifically and only with denials of justice by the local courts. He said:

> Sovereignty following upon ownership gives a Nation *jurisdiction* over the territory which belongs to it. It is the part of the Nation, or of its sovereign, to enforce justice throughout the territory subject to it, to take cognizance of crimes committed therein, and of the differences arising between the citizens.
>
> Other Nations must respect this right; and as the administration of justice necessarily requires that every sentence, pronounced in due form and by the court of last resort, be regarded as just and executed as such, when once a case in which foreigners are involved has been decided in due form, the sovereign of the litigants may not review the decision. To undertake to inquire in to the justice of a definitive sentence is an attack upon the jurisdiction of the court which passed it. Hence a sovereign should not interfere in the suits of his subjects in foreign countries nor grant them his protection, except in cases where justice has been denied or the decision is clearly and palpably unjust, or the proper procedure has not been observed, or finally, in cases where his subjects, or foreigners in general, have been discriminated against.... The principle may be accepted without any reference to the merits of the particular case which turned on the facts involved.[12]

Ironically and by the same token, Vattel's views were later used by opponents of a wide concept of injury to an alien to support a narrow view of denial of justice by a State as the only substantive basis for the exercise of diplomatic protection.

[9] See ibid 139–50.
[10] Ibid 144.
[11] Ibid.
[12] Ibid 146.

Vattel gave expression to the concept of exclusive territorial jurisdiction, yet he also implied that a sovereign had responsibilities towards foreigners whom he allowed to come to his territory. Thus, Vattel stated that a sovereign, in allowing foreigners the right of entry, 'agrees to protect them as his own subjects and to see that they enjoy, as far as depends on him, perfect security'.[13] Vattel did not, however, go into details with regard to this responsibility. Clearly, the responsibilities were substantive for the treatment of foreigners.

In regard to the property interests of foreigners, which again relate to the substantive law and the breach of which would generate a reason for diplomatic protection, Vattel repeated the proposition that an injury to a citizen is an injury to his State. He asserted that the property of an individual does not cease to belong to him because he happens to be in a foreign country and that it still forms part of the aggregate wealth of his nation.[14]

While the above statements of Vattel are frequently cited as authority for the entrenchment of the institution of diplomatic protection, as has been said,

> in making them, he was thinking of a different set of problems from those which we face at the present time. He wrote of a world in which foreign property interests offered but few problems in national or international affairs. He viewed the state primarily in terms of personal sovereignty rather than of territorial jurisdiction. His personification of the state as an organic unity made up of the sovereign and his subjects (from which he derived his thesis that an injury to a citizen is an injury to the state) undoubtedly served a useful purpose in the juristic evolution of the modern state, but it is not easy to apply to the modern world of extensive international trade and intercourse, and easy and frequent changes of allegiance.[15]

Whether Vattel's views on the treatment of aliens arose from State practice he had observed or whether they were theories based on factual premises he had observed is not clear. There is no recorded evidence to support the former possibility. Moreover, he did not specifically address the aspects of remedial action resulting from the maltreatment of foreigners which constitute the modern institution of diplomatic protection.

At the close of the eighteenth century, however, there occurred an event which gave considerable impetus to the development of diplomatic protection as remedial action and as a branch of international law. That was the inclusion in the Jay Treaty of 1794, between the USA and Great Britain, of provisions for the establishment of arbitration commissions to settle, among other things, the claims of British subjects for confiscated debts and the reciprocal claims growing out of the alleged illegal seizure of US vessels by British cruisers, and the capture of British vessels by French ships armed in the ports of the USA.[16] This action

[13] Ibid 145.

[14] Ibid 146. See further ibid 148 on immovable property particularly.

[15] Dunn, op cit (note 3, above) 52.

[16] The decisions of these commissions are to be found in Moore, 1–4 *International Adjudications* (1929–33). There are on record several legal opinions given in the nineteenth century by the

not only inaugurated the modern era of international arbitration but introduced a means of settling disputes which came to be resorted to with increasing frequency in the diplomatic protection by States of citizens abroad. It is to be noted that the earliest arbitral decisions involving the exercise of diplomatic protection were intended to settle disputes between the USA and Great Britain, and did not involve the Latin-American States which gained independence in the nineteenth century. Their involvement at the butt-end of diplomatic protection did take place subsequently and was significant both in terms of numerical quantity and importance of disputes. What is more, these first attempts at diplomatic protection resorted to the Claims Commission which gave the alien standing before international tribunals.

The Nineteenth and Early Twentieth Centuries

It was in the early nineteenth century that the development of a body of law governing the treatment of aliens really began and with it the use of the remedial institution of diplomatic protection. The primary incentive for this was the growth of a variety of means of communication and the introduction of mechanical technology and industrialization which resulted in individuals traveling to all parts of the world in search of raw materials and thereafter to sell manufactured products. There appeared large numbers of foreigners and extensive foreign property interests within the territorial jurisdiction of all States. This gave rise to numerous conflicts of interest, controversies, and disputes over the exercise of jurisdiction in relation to such foreigners.

The opening up of the western hemisphere to international trade was of special importance. There was a large new area both rich in raw materials and other resources needed for the economic life of Europe and opening up vast markets for European goods. The populations of the new States in North and South America which had acquired independence recently were, in general, made up of ruling classes of white émigrés of European extraction and large indigenous groups of Native Americans, where such survived. The forms of government adopted in these States were based on European models, and on the political theory of individualism and representative government. In many ways these forms of government were found to be ill-adapted to the needs of the new States. As a result, in large areas of the western hemisphere political disorder and revolutions were prevalent for a considerable length of time.

The recognized international society of States of the eighteenth century had been wholly European in character. The legal relations which that society had built up were produced by the European culture of the time. In the course of the

UK government's legal advisers on the matter of the treatment of British subjects by foreign States: see McNair (ed), 2 *International Law Opinions* (1956) 32 ff, 101 ff, 197 ff.

nineteenth century the society of States expanded beyond the European continent westward. At the same time the European model which had governed the relations between the members of this society continued to prevail. The concept of justice found in the accepted legal norms for European States spilled over into the wider sphere of the international society of the nineteenth century. In the economic sphere, particularly, this concept derived its content from the capitalistic individualism prevalent in Europe at that time. The notions of individual liberty, the sacredness of private property even as against the actions of governments, and the sanctity of contracts had a special place in this sphere. Of course, colonies in Asia and Africa were not included as international persons in the society of States.

The new States in the western hemisphere generally incorporated these concepts in their legal systems (which they had borrowed largely from European sources). Where that was not the case, as in the Far East and in certain States of the Near East, inter-State relations were conducted on the special basis of extraterritoriality. As for conditions of order and stability which were required to make the European system work satisfactorily, these had not yet been established in many States of the new society of States. Thus, there were continual clashes of interest and frequent accusations of unjust treatment of foreigners.

With time and with the building up of a body of precedents, it became customary to frame demands as claims of legal right, flowing from breach of international law, and the practice was encouraged by the inclusion in treaties of provisions requiring the protection of the lives and property of the nationals of each contracting party in the territory of the other. By the middle of the nineteenth century, governments had begun consistently to treat questions of protection of nationals abroad as legal questions which justified interposition by appeal to principles of international law, from whatever source they may be derived. The settlement of disputes of this nature was gradually becoming subject to legal methods and the institution of diplomatic protection for all practical purposes took root. However, there developed a disagreement between the larger and smaller powers as to the justifiable scope of diplomatic protection. The occasions for the exercise of diplomatic protection arose far more often in the newer and more unsettled countries of Latin America than in the old established countries of Europe or elsewhere. It has been observed that:

> The continued state of political disorder in many South American countries gave rise to a steady stream of complaints of injuries to foreigners, and to occasional resort to armed intervention to enforce demands for redress. The repeated failure of local governmental institutions to function in the expected manner led to a general loss of confidence in those institutions among foreigners, and to an increasing readiness to resort to diplomatic protection. In any event, the demands and claims filed by other countries against the Latin-American states far exceeded the claims which these countries had against other countries.
>
> The impression soon spread in Latin America that diplomatic protection was a practice which strong countries only resorted to against weaker countries, and never against each

other. This seems to infer an inferior position for the states against which demands were regularly made. Furthermore, the nineteenth century was an era of expansionism among the great powers, and there was a constant fear among the smaller powers that complaints regarding the lack of protection of foreign interests would be used as excuses for terrestrial conquest. These things led to the growth of a school of thought in Latin America which was vigorously opposed to the extension of the practice of diplomatic protection and which sought to confine it to the narrowest possible limits.[17]

Calvo, an Argentinean scholar, in 1868 expressed strong opposition to 'intervention' on behalf of citizens or of their property interests abroad. From the independence and equality of States he concluded that aliens were entitled to the same kind of treatment as natives *and no better*, and that, as long as the local institutions of justice were open to them on the same basis as to natives, there could be no basis for an international complaint. He stated that the decisions of the local courts with regard to aliens were final, and could not be called into question by the aliens' own States. He sought to demonstrate that such were the principles observed by European States in their relations with each other, but not in their relations with Latin American States. This view, supported throughout Latin America, became known as the Calvo Doctrine. To a great extent Latin American States subsequently on the general subject of diplomatic protection tended to adopt, whether successfully or unsuccessfully, the Calvo Doctrine in their foreign policy.

Throughout the late nineteenth and early twentieth centuries diplomatic protection had an important place in the relations between States, and especially between the larger powers on the one hand and the smaller and newer States on the other. Claims for pecuniary compensation for injuries to foreigners began constantly accumulating against certain Latin American States. Such claims appear to have been used often to bring pressure to bear on indebted States for the attainment of other ends. They also provided the immediate justification for armed intervention in several instances; for example, the French interventions in Mexico in 1838 and 1861, the intervention of Germany, Great Britain, and Italy in Venezuela in 1902–03, and American interventions in Santo Domingo in 1904 and in Haiti in 1915.

While the Latin American States reacted adversely to the practice of diplomatic protection short of the use of force relatively more than other States, it is very possible that, had the practice of diplomatic protection not developed as an international legal institution, some Latin American States would have had to pay much higher penalties than they did for the injuries and losses sustained by aliens in their territories. The institution did not operate always in the manner in which Latin American writers approved, but, on the other hand, it served to delay or eliminate resort to forceful action by stronger States when their nationals were alleged to have been mistreated in the territories of weaker States. The legal institution of diplomatic protection which could in the last resort lead to a peaceful

[17] Dunn, op cit (note 3, above) 55–6.

settlement of disputes by arbitration, if not by negotiation, unquestionably served as a substitute for territorial conquest, while bringing the Latin American States within the pale of international trade and intercourse. While the results obtained were not what these countries might have desired, the probable alternatives would have been far less desirable.

The recourse to international arbitration, even though under pressure, for the settlement of claims for compensation for injuries to aliens, which began with the Jay Treaty in 1794, became increasingly frequent in the nineteenth and early twentieth century. Arbitration produced a large body of judicial precedents which eventually found their way into the legal treatises, though most of the litigation involved Latin American States. Some examples of widespread arbitration of outstanding claims may be given: those of the USA and Mexico under the conventions of 1839, 1848, 1868 and 1923; the Venezuelan arbitrations of 1903, in which the claims of ten countries against Venezuela were settled by arbitration; the arbitrations of the United States with Great Britain under the conventions of 1853, 1871 and 1908, with Spain in 1871, with France in 1880, with Colombia in 1864 and 1874, with Chile in 1892, with Costa Rica in 1860, with Ecuador in 1862, with Peru in 1863 and 1868, and with Venezuela in 1888. These arbitrations were generally conducted as judicial proceedings, the members of the tribunals acting as judges and supporting their decisions by reference to rules and principles of international law. The process of arbitration which gave rise to judicial settlement became a recognized feature of diplomatic protection well into the twentieth century and beyond where negotiations, of course, failed.

The writings of legal scholars based on arbitrations and on other judicial decisions also aided greatly in the development of jurisprudence on diplomatic protection. By the close of the nineteenth century scholars were beginning to interest themselves in the theory and practice relating to the international responsibility of States for injuries to aliens within their borders and diplomatic protection of aliens as such.[18]

The Late Twentieth Century and Thereafter

In the twentieth century, especially after the Second World War, the institution of diplomatic protection was finally accepted as part of the international

[18] The following nineteenth century and early twentieth century works may be cited as examples: Heilborn, *Das System des Völkerrechts entwickelt aus der völkerrechtlichen Begriffin* (1896); Triepel, *Völkerrecht und Landesrecht* (1899); Tcharnoff, *Le droit de protection exercé par un état à l'égard de ses nationaux résidant à l'étranger* (1898); Anzilotti, *Teoria generale della responsabilita dello Stato nel diritto internazionale* (1902); Moore, *International Law Digest* (1906); Borchard, *Diplomatic Protection of Citizens Abroad* (1915); Eagleton, *The Responsibility of States in International Law* (1928); Decencière-Ferrandière, *La responsabilité internationale des Etats à raison des dommages subis par des étrangers* (1925); Dunn, *The Protection of Nationals* (1932); Dunn, *The Diplomatic Protection of Americans in Mexico* (1933).

legal system. The quarrelling and disputation has been not about the *existence* of the institution of diplomatic protection which involves remedial action and the application of secondary as opposed to primary rules, but about difficulties with the aspects of the institution, such as the local remedies rule, and the substantive content of the rules relating to the treatment of aliens the breach of which may give rise to diplomatic protection.

There were several Claims Commissions which decided disputes involving claims by aliens established after the First World War.[19] Moreover, the PCIJ also was faced with disputes involving diplomatic protection.[20] The trend in the decisions of international tribunals showed that the institution of diplomatic protection was firmly established, whatever the disputes about the rules governing it and about the rules relating to the substantive law of State responsibility for injuries to aliens.[21]

After the Second World War, the spate of nationalizations of foreign property, particularly in Eastern Europe, generated much diplomatic action by western States in protection of their nationals.[22] There were several lump-sum settlements reached in connection with these cases. The disagreements among legal commentators on the universal applicability of and the content of the substantive law governing the treatment of aliens by States[23] did nothing to quell the assertion by States of their right to exercise diplomatic protection of their nationals abroad. This was so, even though the disagreements generally pitted less-developed countries, among them those that had just secured independence from colonial domination, against more developed countries. While problems relating to that substantive law may still remain and require solution, the right to diplomatic protection as such and the fact that there is a law governing the institution does not appear to have been questioned. Indeed, the ICJ has in four leading cases for all intents and purposes accepted the fact that diplomatic protection is a viable institution. These are the *Nottebohm Case (Preliminary Objections)*,[24] the *Barcelona*

[19] See the digest of cases in Coussirat-Coustère and Eisemann, 2 *Repertory of International Arbitral Jurisprudence* (1989) 375–647.

[20] Eg, the *Mavrommatis Palestine Concessions Case* (1924), PCIJ Series A No 2; *German Interests in Polish Upper Silesia Case (Preliminary Objection)* (1925), PCIJ series A No 6.

[21] For a discussion in general of this area of the law during the post-First World War period, apart from Eagleton's and Dunn's works mentioned earlier, see Lillich (ed), *State Responsibility for Injuries to Aliens* (1983) *passim*.

[22] On these nationalizations and the problems created by them see, *inter alios*, C F Amerasinghe, *State Responsibility for Injuries to Aliens* (1967) 121 ff, and authorities there cited; and C F Amerasinghe, 'The Quantum of Compensation for Nationalized Property' in Lillich (ed), 3 *The Valuation of Nationalized Property in International Law* (1975) 91 ff. See also the discussion of the law of expropriation prior to 1970 and the authorities cited in O'Connell, 2 *International Law* (1970) 776 ff.

[23] See the debate singularly brought to the fore in Guha Roy, 'Is the Law of Responsibility of States for Injuries to Aliens a Part of Universal International Law', 55 AJIL (1961) 863.

[24] 1953 ICJ Reports 11.

Traction Co Case (Preliminary Objections),[25] the *ELSI Case*,[26] and the *Diallo Case (Prelimary Objections)*.[27] Furthermore, there have been cases where States in the exercise of diplomatic protection have established arbitral tribunals along the lines of the earlier claims commissions to decide disputes involving aliens. Such is the Iran-United States Claims Tribunal.[28]

Nevertheless, dissatisfaction with some of the rules governing diplomatic protection, such as the local remedies rule, have, it must be noted, given rise to several developments where either the right to diplomatic protection is renounced by States in favour of other means of settling disputes which are considered more effective or aliens do not seek diplomatic protection, at least provisionally, by agreeing to another means of settlement with the host or respondent State. Under the ICSID Convention, which was agreed upon by States in 1965 and came into effect soon after, national States agree not to exercise diplomatic protection in investment disputes while the aliens and the host States enter into arbitration under the auspices of ICSID as a means of settling such disputes.[29] This is provisional, insofar as the same article also permits diplomatic protection to be exercised on certain conditions and certain eventualities taking place. The arbitrations under the ICSID Convention are international arbitrations, where States have agreed in advance by becoming parties to the Convention to accept arbitration between them and aliens, provided the latter are nationals of a contracting party to the Convention and the two parties to the dispute have specifically agreed to arbitration in order to settle the dispute. States may also agree under BITs to a similar kind of arbitration in matters of alien treatment which is meant to replace the exercise of diplomatic protection.[30]

The second phenomenon is that resort to local remedies is initially avoided by the alien entering into an arbitration agreement with the host State for the settlement of disputes without any intervention by the national States. Such an arbitration proceeding in reality takes the place of local remedies and is generally governed by private international law subject to any applicable rules of public international law.[31] It is a substitute for resort to local remedies which induces the alien not to seek the diplomatic protection of his national State and is regarded as inuring to the benefit of the alien.

[25] 1964 ICJ Reports 5.

[26] 1989 ICJ Reports 15.

[27] 2007 ICJ Reports 17 ff. See also the *Arrest Warrant of 11 April 2000 Case*, 2002 ICJ Reports 17 ff <http://www.icj-cij.org>.

[28] For the documents establishing this tribunal see 1 *Iran-US CTR* (1983) 3 ff.

[29] Article 27.

[30] On this subject see C F Amerasinghe, *Local Remedies in International Law* (2nd edn, 2004) 267 ff.

[31] See, for example, the *LIAMCO (Liamco v Libya) Arbitration* (1977), 62 ILR 140; the *TEXACO (Texaco v Libya) Arbitration* (1977), 53 ILR 389; and the *Sapphire-NIOC Arbitration* (1963), 35 ILR 136.

These developments in the sphere of settlement of disputes between aliens and host States, while signalling a certain dissatisfaction with the efficacy of the process of diplomatic protection on the part of aliens and of their national States in their dealings with other States, has not diluted the availability of the institution, as, among other things, the attempts at codification discussed in Chapter 6 will show. The institution is now well established on a firm foundation in international law—so much so that States of which aliens are nationals and which played an important part in the development of the institution (a development resisted to some extent by Latin American States at one time and by developing nations in the latter part of the twentieth century, and later by aliens themselves for whom the institution was in effect founded) have now to find means of circumventing it. The institution, it has been recognized by the international community of States, is a useful one—even if it is to become an institution of last resort or just a possible alternative. That even developing countries resort to it as host States in their relations with aliens and other States is illustrated by the *Diallo Case*, filed before the ICJ in 1998 by the Republic of Guinea against the Democratic Republic of Congo.[32] Moreover, now with nationals of developing States themselves investing in other States (see Malaysia, India and Singapore) and the ease of travel and of cross-border movement of persons, developing States may very well find themselves in a position not only to avail their nationals of diplomatic protection against other countries but to find that it is a needed institution.

The short point is that there have been changes in the condition of international society. In the nineteenth and early twentieth centuries diplomatic protection was seen as a weapon wielded by wealthy nations against the poorer or less developed nations, particularly those in the western hemisphere. As colonized nations gained independence in the early part of the second half of the twentieth century, diplomatic protection came to be associated more generally with a tussle between developed and less developed States connected particularly with foreign investment by nationals of developed States. In fact, later, especially with the liberalization of travel, the movement of investment relatively freely between States, and the possibility of doing business abroad for nationals of all States, the emphasis on diplomatic protection as a means only to protect the nationals of the richer developed States must, indeed, have waned and States seem in general to regard the institution, appropriately constructed as a legal institution, as one which could benefit them—regardless of whether they are poor or rich. Even if this observation is questioned, the inescapable fact remains that in the modern era, when nationals of developed States are not the only ones to cross frontiers by travel and invest or do business in foreign countries, diplomatic protection has become an institution whose force and usefulness have not been spent and which can be resorted to both by the wealthy and the not so wealthy in the appropriate

[32] <http://www.icj-cij.org>, 2007 ICJ Reports.

circumstances. It is an institution which, rather than being abandoned, needs to be rationalized and developed.[33]

The ICJ has recognized diplomatic protection in several cases, as will be seen, and most recently in the *Diallo Case (Preliminary Objections),* in agreement with the description of diplomatic protection by the ILC in its 2006 Draft Articles which state:

diplomatic protection consists of the invocation by a State, through diplomatic action or other means of peaceful settlement, of the responsibility of another State for an injury caused by an internationally wrongful act of that State to a natural or legal person that is a national of the former State with a view to the implementation of such responsibility. (Article 1 of the draft Articles on Diplomatic Protection adopted by the ILC at its Fifty-eighth Session (2006), ILC Report, doc. A/61/10, p.24).[34]

[33] The point was made by me for the first time in my treatise, *State Responsibility for Injuries to Aliens* (1967) 4–5. See subsequently Lillich, 'The Diplomatic Protection of Nationals Abroad: An Elementary Principle of International Law under Attack,' 69 AJIL (1975) 359; Przetacznik, 'The Protection of Individual Persons in Traditional International Law (Diplomatic and Consular Protection)', 21 *ÖZÖR* (1971) 113. The *Diallo Case,* now before the ICJ, is an example of a dispute involving diplomatic protection between two (African) developing nations.

[34] 2007 ICJ Reports para 39 (<http://www.icj-cij.org>).

3

Diplomatic Protection in Context

Definition

The institution of diplomatic protection, as legally conceived, covers largely certain procedural aspects relating to secondary remedial obligations and rights of the protection of aliens. The law refers in this respect to the enforcement of State responsibility by peaceful means and consists of secondary rules, the substantive or primary rules being left to be determined by the law relating to the treatment of aliens. As generally conceived in practice and theory, but often not clearly articulated, diplomatic protection incorporates principally certain specific customary secondary rules relating to the capacity to espouse or institute claims and to the exhaustion of local remedies, though in order to trigger the remedial rules, the law of alien treatment enshrines rules which give the complainant State a substantive right, the violation of which is of importance for the law relating to the secondary or remedial rights.

Before the advent of the human rights conventions after the Second World War there were technically no procedures as such available to the individual under international law to contest his treatment by his own State. But, if certain rights of an individual—relating to treatment according to an international minimum standard and comparable to current human rights–had been violated abroad by a foreign State, the individual's national State could intervene to protect him against the wrongs which he had suffered. Though theoretically the institution of diplomatic protection was universal, in practice it was mainly the powerful western States that exercised this privilege. It was those States which most often had nationals abroad and most readily intervened to protect their nationals who were not treated in accordance with the ordinary standards of civilization set by those States themselves.[1] Inevitably diplomatic protection of this kind came to be seen by developing nations, particularly in Latin America, as a discriminatory exercise of power rather than as a method of protecting the lawful rights of aliens.

As will be seen, diplomatic protection or intervention was based on the theory that an injury to a national abroad constituted an injury to his national State

[1] The *Roberts Claim (US v Mexico, 1926)*, 4 UNRIAA 77; the *Neer Claim (US v Mexico, 1926)*, 4 UNRIAA 60.

itself. This substantive aspect had important consequences.[2] For instance, at one level, it provided a justification for military intervention or 'gunboat' diplomacy while, at another level, it allowed the US and European powers to reject Latin American attempts to compel foreigners doing business in Latin America to waive or renounce the procedure of diplomatic protection, on the ground that the national could not waive a right that belonged to the State.[3] The latter aspect of the law still survives.

The substantive aspect also influenced, for example, the legal position which prevails that the State claimant cannot be controlled internationally with regard to the disposal of the damages or compensation received, whether it be after negotiations or after litigation. This is so, even though the injury suffered by the individual national is the basis for the calculation of damages or compensation to be paid to the claimant State, in those cases where the damages or compensation is not paid directly to the alien pursuant to the judgment of an international tribunal.

The right to protect aliens as such, which should begin with negotiations with the host State, was often exercised by the use of force. To mention some examples, the Anglo-Boer war from 1899 to 1902 was justified by Great Britain as an intervention to protect its nationals who owned the gold mines of Witwatersrand; US military intervention in Latin America, on the ground of defending its nationals, has continued until recent times, as shown by the interventions in Grenada in 1983[4] and Panama in 1989.[5] Non-military action, mainly in the form of demands for compensation for injuries inflicted on the persons or property of aliens, was almost exclusively pursued by powerful States;[6] so much so it was often only the settlement of claims by arbitration that saved Latin American States (as weaker States receiving foreigners) from military intervention to enforce such claims.[7]

[2] For a brief account of and history of the institution of diplomatic protection see Dugard, 'First Report on Diplomatic Protection,' (ILC), UN Doc. A/CN4/506 5 ff. This work is a useful reference point.

[3] Shea, *The Calvo Clause: A Problem of Inter-American and International Law and Diplomacy* (1955).

[4] See 78 AJIL (1984) 200.

[5] See 84 AJIL (1990) 545.

[6] See the separate opinion of Judge Padilla Nervo in the *Barcelona Traction Co Case*, 1970 ICJ Reports at 246.

[7] Dunn, *The Protection of Nationals* (1932) at 58. The use of force to protect nationals who are allegedly wronged—this is slightly different from the protection of nationals in the face of danger from civil war, for instance—raises other problems. It has not been mentioned in the ILC's final Draft Articles on Diplomatic Protection, although the rapporteur in his 'First Report to the ILC' did propose an Article on the subject: UN Doc. A/CN4/506 16 ff. The use of force is strictly not a matter of diplomatic protection which by its very name involves the use of peaceful remedies. However, some legal commentators use the term 'diplomatic protection' to embrace 'consular action, negotiation, mediation, judicial and arbitral proceedings, reprisals, retorsion, severance of diplomatic relations, economic pressure, and, the final resort, the use of force'. See ibid 15, citing, among others, early writers such as Dunn and Borchard. The 2006 Draft Articles of the ILC, on the other hand, make it quite clear in Article 1 that the term covers only peaceful means of settlement.

Developments, particularly the human rights treaties which will be further discussed in Chapters 8 and 16, have led some to argue that for a variety of reasons diplomatic protection is obsolete and that the right of a State to assert its own right when it acts on behalf of its national is an outdated fiction which should be discarded—except, perhaps, in cases in which the real *national* interest of the State is affected.[8] In passing, it may be observed that in any case to rely on the argument that an institution which is based on a fiction should be dismissed simply because it is based on a fiction, is a mistake. An institution like diplomatic protection which serves a purpose is not to be dismissed simply on the ground that it is premised on a fiction and cannot stand up to logical scrutiny. Most legal systems have fictions. Moreover, diplomatic protection, it will be seen, rather recognizes a mixture of interests and is not based on fictions as such.[9]

There has been some debate over a variety of aspects of the institution—for example, as to whose rights are asserted when a State exercises diplomatic protection in respect of a national—but it is a generally accepted rule of customary international law that States have the right to protect their nationals abroad. For this purpose, although the State in which the wrong was perpetrated has territorial jurisdiction over the alien, the State of nationality retains its personal jurisdiction over its national, even while he or she is residing in another State.[10] The classical formulation of this position concerning the consequences of the personal jurisdiction of the State of nationality was made by the PCIJ in the *Mavrommatis Palestine Concessions Case*:

> It is an elementary principle of international law that a State is entitled to protect its subjects, when injured by acts contrary to international law committed by another State, from whom they have been unable to obtain satisfaction through the ordinary channels. By taking up the case of one of its subjects and by resorting to diplomatic action or international judicial proceedings on his behalf, a State is in reality asserting its own right—its right to ensure, in the person of its subjects, respect for the rules of international law.[11]

The State of nationality, according to the traditional view, acts on its own behalf because an injury to the individual as a national is an injury to the State itself. The right of the State of nationality to exercise protection in this way has been

[8] García Amador, 'State Responsibility. Some New Problems', 94 Hague Recueil (1958) 437–9, 472; García Amador, 'Second Report to the ILC', 2 YBILC (1957) 112–16. Bennouna, 'Preliminary Report on Diplomatic Protection', UN Doc. A/CN.4/484, paras 34–7, also advances an argument based on the existence of human rights mechanisms.

[9] Furthermore, the life of the law is not logic, perhaps, but experience. See Holmes, 'The Path of the Law', 10 Harvard Law Review (1897) 476 ff.

[10] Leigh, 'Nationality and Diplomatic Protection', 20 ICLQ (1971) 453.

[11] (1924), PCIJ Series A, No. 2, 12. The origin of this theory is traced to Vattel writing in 1758: 'Whoever ill-treats a citizen indirectly injures the State, which must protect that citizen.' (*The Law of Nations*, 136.)

confirmed both by judicial decisions[12] and by legal commentators.[13] Part of the right has been codified in Article 3 of the 1961 Vienna Convention on Diplomatic Relations and in Article 5 of the 1963 Vienna Convention on Consular Relations, although these provisions cover a wider range. The former refers to the function of diplomatic and consular missions in:

> protecting in the receiving State the interests of the sending State and of its nationals, within the limits permitted by international law.[14]

To the extent that the provision covers protection by diplomatic or consular missions after an injury to a national in the receiving State has been committed, the provision codifies diplomatic protection.

The general agreement on the right of the State to exercise diplomatic protection has led to definitions of diplomatic protection in terms which reflect the traditional State-centered position. In 1915 a legal commentator explained that, 'Diplomatic protection is in its nature an international proceeding, constituting "an appeal by nation to nation for the performance of obligations of the one to the other, growing out of their mutual rights and duties".'[15] Another writer has stated that 'diplomatic protection can be defined as a procedure for giving effect to State responsibility involving breaches of international law arising out of legal injuries to the person or property of the citizen of the State'.[16] C de Visscher defined diplomatic protection as 'a procedure by which States assert the right of their citizens to a treatment in accordance with international law'.[17] One rapporteur of the ILC described diplomatic protection as 'a mechanism or a procedure for invoking the international responsibility of the host State'.[18] The same rapporteur, in explanation, continued, 'diplomatic protection has been regarded from the outset as the corollary of the personal jurisdiction of the State over its population when elements of that population, while in foreign territory, have suffered injury in violation of international law'.[19] The most recent rapporteur of the

[12] *Panevezys-Saldutiskis Railway Case,* (1939) PCIJ Series A/B, No. 76 16, 17; the *Nottebohm Case,* 1955 ICJ Reports, 24.

[13] Joseph, *Nationality and Diplomatic Protection—The Commonwealth of Nations* (1969) 1; Leigh (note 10 above) 453; Geck, 'Diplomatic Protection', 1 *EPIL* (1992) 1046.

[14] Article 3(1)(b) of the 1961 Vienna Convention on Diplomatic Relations of States. The 1963 Vienna Convention on Consular Relations contains a very similar but somewhat more specific provision. Article 51 states:

> Consular functions consist in:
> (a) Protecting in the receiving State the interests of the sending State and of its nationals, both individuals and bodies corporate, within the limits permitted by international law;...
> (e) Helping and assisting nationals, both individuals and bodies corporate, of the sending State.

The 1967 European Convention on Consular Functions endorses this principle in Article 2(1): ETS No. 61.

[15] Borchard, *The Diplomatic Protection of Citizens Abroad* (1915) 354, quoting US Secretary of State Blaine, and 357.

[16] Joseph (note 13 above) 1. Refer also Leigh (note 10 above) 453.

[17] 'Cours Général de Principes de Droit International Public', 86 Hague Receuil (1954) 507.

[18] Bennouna (note 8 above) 4.

[19] Ibid.

ILC on the subject of diplomatic protection in his report to the ILC explained the concept as 'action taken by a State against another State in respect of an injury to the person or property of a national caused by an internationally wrongful act or omission attributable to the latter State'.[20]

The ILC itself in Article 1 of its final Draft Articles submitted to the GA in 2006 stated unequivocally that:

> diplomatic protection consists of the invocation by a State, through diplomatic action or other means of peaceful settlement, of the responsibility of another State for an injury caused by an internationally wrongful act of that State to a natural or legal person that is a national of the former State with a view to the implementation of such responsibility.[21]

This definition, which is satisfactory, purports to describe the main elements of diplomatic protection, while indicating the scope of the mechanism for the protection of nationals injured abroad. It takes into account several considerations and has specific objectives,[22] which are discussed below.

Basic Content of the Concept

Diplomatic protection as a concept may be explained as follows:

(i) Under international law, a State is responsible for injury to an alien caused by its wrongful act or omission. Diplomatic protection is the procedure

[20] Article 1(1) of his draft: Dugard, 'First Report on Diplomatic Protection' (2000), UN Doc. A/CN.4/506, 11.

[21] *Report of the ILC, 2006* 16. The definition was approved and adopted by the ICJ in the *Diallo Case (Preliminary Objections)*: 2007 *ICJ Reports* para 39 (<http://icj-cij.org>). The ILC's treatment of State responsibility for injuries to aliens and its corollary, diplomatic protection, was at the beginning of its work rather confused, inter alia, with State responsibility in general. The first rapporteur on State responsibility, García Amador, included a number of draft articles on this subject in his reports presented from 1956 to 1961. The subsequent codification of State responsibility in 2001 paid little attention to diplomatic protection and the final Draft Articles on this subject expressly state that the two topics central to diplomatic protection—nationality of claims and the exhaustion of local remedies—would be dealt with more extensively by the Commission in a separate undertaking (*Official Records of the GA, Fifty-sixth Session, Supplement No. 10*) (UN Doc. A/56/10), commentary on Article 44, footnotes 722 and 726). Nevertheless, there was a connection between the Draft Articles on State responsibility and the final Draft Articles on diplomatic protection. While many of the principles contained in the Draft Articles on State responsibility were considered by the ILC as relevant to diplomatic protection, they were not repeated in the final Draft Articles on diplomatic protection. This applied in particular to the provisions dealing with the legal consequences of an internationally wrongful act. A State responsible for injuring a foreign national is obliged to cease the wrongful conduct and to make full reparation for the injury caused by the internationally wrongful act. This reparation may take the form of restitution, compensation or satisfaction, either singly or in combination. All these matters were dealt with in the Draft Articles on State responsibility (*Report of the ILC to the GA, 2004* 24–5). Articles on Diplomatic Protection were confined rules governing the admissibility of claims, ie to the elaboration of rules on the nationality of claims and the exhaustion of local remedies (*Report of the ILC, 2006* 23).

[22] See commentary on Article 1 of the final Draft Articles on diplomatic protection submitted by the ILC to the GA: ibid 24–8.

employed by the State of nationality of the injured person to secure protection of that person and to obtain reparation for the internationally wrongful act inflicted. The concept covers only the rules governing the circumstances in which diplomatic protection may be exercised and the conditions that must be met before it may be exercised. The internationally wrongful acts that give rise to the responsibility of the State for injury to an alien are not included in the concept. The concept aims at maintaining the distinction between primary and secondary rules and strictly covers only the latter.[23]

(ii) The definition makes it clear that the right of diplomatic protection belongs to the State, the injured individual as such not having any right. In exercising diplomatic protection the State adopts in its own right the cause of its national arising from the internationally wrongful act of another State. This formulation follows the language of the ICJ in the *Interhandel Case* where it was stated that the applicant State had 'adopted the cause of its national'[24] whose rights had been violated. The legal interest of the State in the exercising of diplomatic protection derives from the injury to a national resulting from the wrongful act of another State, which is conceived as wrongful vis-à-vis the former State. It will be suggested later in this work that this view of diplomatic protection may be adjusted so as to accommodate the additional right of the injured alien.

(iii) In most circumstances it is upon the link of nationality between the State and the injured person that the exercise of diplomatic protection is based. The term 'national' in the definition covers both natural and juridical or legal persons. Where appropriate, the law as relating to natural persons needs to be treated separately from that relating to juridical or legal persons.

(iv) The definition makes clear the point that what is covered is the exercise of diplomatic protection by a State and not with the protection afforded by an international organization to its agents, which was recognized by the ICJ in the *Reparation Case*[25] as a right of the organization.

(v) The definition covers the protection of nationals not engaged in official international business on behalf of the State. These officials are protected by other rules of international law and instruments such as the Vienna Convention on Diplomatic Relations of 1961[26] and the Vienna Convention on Consular Relations of 1963.[27] The protection of such officials is the consequence of a direct injury to the State and is not considered merely diplomatic protection of nationals.

[23] The Draft Articles of the ILC on State Responsibility (for Internationally Wrongful Acts) maintains the same distinction: see *Official Records of the General Assembly, Fifty-sixth Session, Supplement No. 10* (UN Doc. A/56/10) para 77.

[24] 1959 ICJ Reports 37. See also the *Mavrommatis Palestine Concessions Case* (1924), PCIJ Series A No. 2.

[25] 1949 ICJ Reports 174.

[26] 500 UNTS 95.

[27] 596 UNTS 261.

(vi) The definition, while implying the rules relating to nationality of claims by referring to the protection of nationals, does not specifically incorporate the requirement of exhaustion of local remedies. Such a reference, it may be argued, is not necessary in an explanation which seeks to define. However it must be recognized that the element of exhaustion of local remedies is a basic premise of diplomatic protection, as will be seen in Chapter 11.

(vii) Most importantly diplomatic protection must be exercised by lawful and peaceful means. Several judicial decisions draw a distinction between 'diplomatic action' and 'judicial proceedings' when describing the action that may be taken by a State when it resorts to diplomatic protection.[28] The definition goes further than incorporating this distinction by subsuming judicial proceedings under 'other means of peaceful settlement'. 'Diplomatic action' covers all the lawful procedures employed by a State to inform another State of its views and concerns, including protest, request for an inquiry, or for negotiations aimed at the settlement of disputes. 'Other means of peaceful settlement' embraces all forms of lawful dispute settlement, from negotiation, mediation, and conciliation, to arbitral and judicial dispute settlement. What is included goes beyond simple 'diplomacy'. The use of force, prohibited by Article 2(4) of the UN Charter, however, is not a permissible method for the exercise of the right of diplomatic protection. The action taken must be *peaceful,* and clearly includes judicial proceedings. It is in the *Panavezys-Saldutiskis Railway Case* that the PCIJ explicitly distinguished between 'diplomatic action' and 'judicial proceedings',[29] making a distinction repeated by the ICJ in the *Nottebohm Case*[30] and by the Iran-United States Claims Tribunal in *Case No. A/18.*[31] But this distinction is unnecessary and not a useful one, and has been abandoned by the ILC.

The Use of Force

Legal writers, however, generally draw no distinction between peaceful action and the use of force but have often used the term 'diplomatic protection' to embrace consular action, negotiation, mediation, judicial and arbitral proceedings, reprisals, retorsion, severance of diplomatic relations, economic pressure

[28] The *Mavrommatis Palestine Concessions Case* (1924), PCIJ Series A No. 2; the *Panevezys-Saldutiskis Railway Case* (1939), PCIJ Series A/B, No. 76, 16; the *Nottebohm Case,* 1955 ICJ Reports 24.

[29] (1939), PCIJ Series A/B No. 76, 16.

[30] 1955 ICJ Reports 24.

[31] (1984), 5 *Iran-US CTR* 261.

and, even in the final resort, the *use of force*.[32] In 1932 it was stated in respect of the term diplomatic action that:

It embraces generally all cases of official representation by one Government on behalf of its citizens or their property interests within the jurisdiction of another, for the purpose, either of preventing some threatened injury in violation of international law, or of obtaining redress for such injuries after they have been sustained...

What ordinarily happens in the case of protection is that the Government of an injured alien calls the attention of the delinquent Government to the facts of the complaint and requests that the appropriate steps be taken to redress the grievance... the term 'diplomatic protection' is here used as a generic term covering the general subject of protection of citizens abroad, *including those cases in which other than diplomatic means may be resorted to in the enforcement of obligations*...

it should be noted that we are here concerned only with representations of demands that are made (expressly or impliedly) under a claim of right. Governments often take action in behalf of their citizens abroad which is not based on any assertion of international obligation and does not fall within the category of protection in a technical sense.[33]

The description includes the use of force.

One rapporteur of the ILC, on diplomatic protection, on the other hand, while recognizing the wide range of actions open to a State in the exercise of the right of diplomatic protection, stated that:

The State retains, in principle, the choice of means of action to defend its nationals, while respecting its international commitments and preemptory norms of international law. In particular, it may not resort to the threat or use of force in the exercise of diplomatic protection.[34]

There is here an exclusion of the use of force.

The restrictions on the means of action open to the protecting State are governed by general rules of international law, particularly those relating to countermeasures as defined in the Draft Articles of the ILC on State Responsibility.[35] The use of force as the ultimate means of protecting nationals has in the past frequently been considered part of the topic of diplomatic protection. This requires some explanation.

History, including the recent past,[36] is replete with examples of cases in which the pretext of protecting nationals has been used as a justification for military intervention. The writings of the Argentine jurist, Calvo, who sought

[32] Borchard (note 15 above) 439 ff; Geck (note 13 above) 1061–3; Weiss, 'Diplomatic Protection of Nationals and International Protection of Human Rights', 4 HRJ (1971) 645.

[33] Dunn (note 7 above) 18 ff (my emphasis).

[34] Bennouna (note 8 above) 4. For Dugard's treatment of the subject in his reports to the ILC see his 'First Report to the ILC' (note 7 above) 15 ff.

[35] Articles 47–50 (note 23 above).

[36] See the intervention in 1983 by the US in Grenada, 78 AJIL (1984) 200, and the intervention in 1989 in Panama by the US, 84 AJIL (1990) 494, 545.

to restrict the right of diplomatic protection, were a response to military interventions in Latin America.[37] The Drago Doctrine of 1903,[38] which sought to outlaw military intervention for the recovery of contract debts owed to foreign nationals, was a response to the action taken by Italy, Germany, and Great Britain against Venezuela in 1902 following its failure to pay contractual debts owed to the nationals of those States. This resulted in the Porter Convention of 1907 Respecting the Limitation of the Employment of Force for the Recovery of Contract Debts (Convention II of the 1907 Hague Peace Conference), which in Article 1 required States 'not to have recourse to armed force for the recovery of contract debts claimed from the Government of another country as being due to its nationals'. That this prohibition on the use of force was not absolute was made clear by the qualification to the Article that 'this understanding is not, however, applicable when the debtor State refuses or neglects to reply to an offer of arbitration or, after accepting the offer, prevents any *compromis* from being agreed on, or, after the arbitration, fails to submit to the award.'[39] This history, coupled with the prohibition on the use of force contained in Article 2(4) of the UN Charter, has led many more recent writers to assert that the use of force is prohibited as a means of diplomatic protection.[40]

Article 2(4) of the UN Charter contains a prohibition on the use of force. The use of force to recover contract debts appears to be prohibited by Article 2(4) and Article 51 of the UN Charter. Beyond that there is extensive debate on the extent of the prohibition of the use of force, whether in self-defence or otherwise. The threat or use of force as a reprisal in protecting nationals is difficult to justify. The only possible justification is if it can be characterized as self-defence. There is no suggestion that defence of nationals may be categorized as humanitarian intervention.[41] The right of self-defence in international law was formulated well before 1945. It required action taken in self-defence to be an immediate and necessary response to a situation threatening a State's security and vital interests. Moreover, the response was to be kept within the bounds of proportionality. The scope of the right was wide and included both anticipatory self-defence and intervention to protect nationals.[42] On one interpretation of Articles 2(4) and 51 of the Charter, this right of self-defence still exists in its broadest extension.[43] Some

[37] For the Calvo Clause see Shea (note 3 above) and Chapter 12 herein.

[38] *Papers Relating to the Foreign Relations of the United States, 1903* 1–5.

[39] *The Hague Conventions and Declarations of 1899 and 1907* (1915) 89.

[40] See García Amador, 'First Report on State Responsibility', 2 YBILC (1956) 221; Bennouna (note 8 above) 4.

[41] Some writers draw no clear distinction between protection of the nationals of the injuring State (humanitarian intervention) and intervention by a State to protect its own nationals: see Ronzitti, *Rescuing Nationals Abroad through Military Coercion and Intervention on Grounds of Humanity* (1985); Verway, 'Humanitarian Intervention', in Cassesse (ed), *The Current Regulation of the Use of Force* (1986) 57.

[42] Bowett, *Self-Defence in International Law* (1958) 96ff.

[43] C F Amerasinghe, 'Dispute Settlement by International Organizations,' 43 IJIL (2003) 416ff.

writers[44] argue that Article 51 contains a complete and exclusive formulation of the right of self- defence, which limits it to cases in which an armed attack has occurred against a State, while others maintain that the phrase 'inherent right' in Article 51 preserves the pre-Charter customary right.[45] In the *Nicaragua Case* the ICJ gave support to the latter view when it held that 'Article 51 of the Charter is only meaningful on the basis that there is a "natural" or "inherent" right of self-defence, and it is hard to see how this can be other than of a customary nature, even if its present content has been confirmed and influenced by the Charter'.[46] The ICJ confirmed this approach in the *Legality of the Threat or Use of Nuclear Weapons Opinion* when it declared that some of the constraints on the resort to self-defence 'are inherent in the very concept of self-defence' while others are specified in Article 51. Moreover, it said, 'The submission of the exercise of the right of self-defence to the conditions of necessity and proportionality is a rule of customary international law.'[47]

It would appear that the totality of the customary law right of self-defence has survived, be it under Article 2(4) or Article 51. It may, therefore, be difficult to argue that the Charter's prohibition of the use of force internationally extends to the protection of nationals abroad.[48] Such contention is made more difficult by the amount of State practice since 1945 in support of military intervention to protect nationals abroad in time of emergency[49] and the failure of courts[50] and political organs[51] of the United Nations to condemn such action. There is, however, a prevailing view that the right to use force in the protection of nationals has been greatly abused[52] in the past and that it is a right that lends itself to abuse.[53] The right may, therefore, have to be narrowly

[44] Brownlie, *International Law and the Use of Force by States* (1963) 272 ff; Verdross and Simma, *Universelles Völkerrecht: Theorie und Praxis* (1984) 905.

[45] Bowett (note 42 above) 87 ff; Waldock, 'The Regulation of the Use of Force by Individual States in International Law', 81 Hague Receuil (1952) 496 ff.

[46] 1986 ICJ Reports at 94.

[47] 1996 ICJ Reports 245.

[48] Bowett (note 42 above) 87 ff; Dinstein, *War, Aggression and Self-Defence* (1994) 222; Dahm, *Völkerrecht* (1961) 209. *Pace* Brownlie (note 44 above) 289 ff; Ronzitti (note 41 above).

[49] Jennings and Watts (eds), 1 *Oppenheim's International Law*, 440–2.

[50] In the *United States Diplomatic and Consular Staff in Tehran Case,* 1980 *ICJ Reports* 18, the ICJ, in a judgment on the merits, declined to pronounce on the legality of the unsuccessful US attempt to rescue hostages in the exercise of its inherent right of self-defence. Two individual judges, Morozov, at 57, and Tarazi, at 64, concluded that the rescue operation was not lawful. See on this case, D'Angelo, 'Resort to Force by States to Protect Nationals: The US Rescue Mission to Iran and its Legality under International Law', 21 VJIL (1981) 485.

[51] In the instances in which force has been used to rescue or protect nationals the SC has not reached a decision in favour of or against the interventions. Consequent upon the Entebbe raid in 1976 a resolution condemning Israel was not put to the vote: UN Doc. S/12139 (1976), 15 ILM 1227.

[52] The criticisms of the military interventions of the US in Grenada and Panama: 84 AJIL (1990) 545; Nanda, 'US Forces in Panama: Defenders, Aggressors or Human Rights Activists? The Validity of United States Intervention in Panama under International Law', 84 ibid (1990) 494.

[53] Borchard (note 15 above) 331, 447; García Amador (note 40 above) 216; Guha Roy, 'Is the Law of Responsibility of States for Injuries to Aliens a Part of Universal International Law?'

formulated to make it clear both that it may not be invoked merely to protect the property of a State's nationals abroad[54] and that it may only be invoked in emergencies to justify the rescue of foreign nationals. The 1976 forcible intervention by Israeli commandos, at Entebbe airport[55] in Uganda, may serve as a model for such a rescue operation. This approach seems to reflect State practice more accurately than an absolute prohibition on the use of force (which is impossible to reconcile with actual State practice) or a broad right to intervene (which is impossible to reconcile with the protests that have been made by the injured State and third States on the occasion of such interventions). From a policy perspective it is wiser to recognize the existence of such a right, but to prescribe severe limits, than to ignore its existence, which will permit States to invoke the traditional arguments in support of a broad right of intervention and lead to further abuse.[56]

However, the use of force to protect nationals is generally for the elimination of future damage or injury and certainly does not focus on reparation for injury already caused. The use of force is not considered as a permissible form of reprisal for injuries to aliens. Diplomatic protection, on the other hand, is aimed at securing redress through remedial and peaceful action. Hence, while the use of force to protect nationals from injury may be permitted in certain circumstances by international law, it is not to be regarded strictly as the exercise of diplomatic protection.

These considerations on the use of force to protect nationals aside, it should be noted that the ILC in its draft has correctly confined the use of the term diplomatic protection to peaceful means of settlement in the exercise of protecting nationals. It is not only convenient but the proper use of language to follow this course. The use of force to protect nationals, when it is legal, need not and should not be described as 'diplomatic' protection.

55 AJIL 863; Lillich, *The Human Rights of Aliens in Contemporary International Law* (1984) 14–15.

[54] Shaw, *International Law* (1997) 793; Jennings and Watts (eds) (note 49 above) 441.

[55] See 1976 *UNYB* 315–20; Margo, 'The Legality of the Entebbe Raid in International Law', 94 SALJ (1977) 306; Boyle, 'The Entebbe Hostage Crisis', NILR (1982) 32. The attempted rescue of hostages by the US in Tehran in 1979 may also be mentioned.

[56] In practice the right to use force in the protection of nationals has been asserted also to protect non-nationals, where they are threatened together with nationals of the protecting State: see Jennings and Watts (eds) (note 49 above) 442. In an emergency situation it will be both difficult and unwise to distinguish sharply between nationals and non-nationals. There should be no objection to the protecting State rescuing non-nationals exposed to the same immediate danger as its nationals, provided the preponderance of the threatened persons are nationals of that State. Where the preponderance of threatened persons are non-nationals the use of force might conceivably be justified as a humanitarian action but not as self-defence in the protection of nationals. Humanitarian intervention as such is not a subject included in this study. On the use of force to protect nationals and their property and by way of humanitarian intervention see C F Amerasinghe, 'The Conundrum of Recourse to Force to Protect Persons', 3 IOLR (2006) 7.

Alternative Arrangements

The right violated, as was explained earlier, is that of the State, even though it is the individual who suffers the primary injury and in respect of whom the law is violated. This is the traditional and accepted view, even though individuals may make claims before international tribunals with, of course, the agreement of their national States. When a State of which the injured person is a national makes such arrangements, it does so in the exercise of diplomatic protection and thereby recognizes together with the respondent State the right to judicial settlement of its national, in place of its own remedial rights. International law does not preclude the express or implied agreement by a national State not to intervene or not to continue to intervene directly in a dispute by referring the settlement of disputes to other means in the implementation of its own right to protect diplomatically.[57]

Now, recognizing this position, Article 16 of the final Draft Articles of the ILC provides that:

> The rights of States, natural persons, legal persons or other entities to resort under international law to actions or procedures other than diplomatic protection to secure redress for injury suffered as a result of an internationally wrongful act, are not affected by the present draft articles.[58]

The customary international law rules on diplomatic protection that have evolved, and the more recent principles governing the protection of human rights particularly, complement each other and, ultimately, may be regarded as serving a common goal—the protection of human rights.[59] States, including the State of nationality and States other than the State of nationality of an injured individual, have a right to protect the individual under, as the case may be, either customary international law or a multilateral or bilateral human rights treaty or other treaty. Natural persons or other entities, such as non-governmental organizations, also may resort under international law to actions or procedures other than diplomatic protection to secure redress for injury suffered as a result of an internationally wrongful act.

A State may protect a non-national against the State of nationality of an injured individual or a third State in inter-State proceedings under the International

[57] The arrangements made pursuant to the ICSID Convention of 1965 (575 UNTS (1996) 159; 4 ILM (1965) 352) are pertinent. Under this Convention aliens are given rights to appear in arbitration proceedings with States as the other parties, while their national States have agreed to forego much of the initial right to exercise diplomatic protection, at least until a later stage in the settlement of the dispute (Article 27 of the Convention).

[58] *Report of the ILC, 2006* 21. For the commentary on which what follows is based, see ibid 86–9. The reference is evidently to *peaceful* means of protection.

[59] See Dugard (note 20 above), paras 22–32, and Chapter 8 herein.

Covenant on Civil and Political Rights,[60] the International Convention on the Elimination of All Forms of Racial Discrimination,[61] the Convention against Torture and Other Cruel, Inhuman and Degrading Treatment or Punishment,[62] the European Convention on Human Rights,[63] the American Convention on Human Rights,[64] and the African Charter on Human and People's Rights.[65] The same conventions allow a State to protect its own nationals in inter-State proceedings. Moreover, customary international law allows States to protect the rights of non-nationals by protest, negotiation and, if a jurisdictional instrument so permits, legal proceedings. Thus, the decision of the ICJ in the 1966 *South West Africa Cases (Second Phase)*[66] holding that a State may not bring legal proceedings at all to protect the rights of non-nationals is today seen as such as bad law and has been expressly repudiated by the ILC in its Articles on State Responsibility.[67] Further, Article 48 of these Articles permits a State other than the injured State to invoke the responsibility of another State if the obligation breached is owed to the international community as a whole (*erga omnes*).[68] Thus, the individual may be endowed with rights and remedies to protect himself against the injuring State, whether the individual's State of nationality or another State, in terms of international human rights conventions. This is most frequently achieved by the right to petition an international human rights monitoring body.[69]

Individual rights under international law may also arise outside the framework of human rights protection. In the *La Grand Case (Merits)* the ICJ held that Article 36 of the Vienna Convention on Consular Relations 'creates individual rights, which by virtue of Article 1 of the Optional Protocol, may be invoked in this Court by the national State of the detained person';[70] and in the *Avena Case* the Court further observed 'that violations of the rights of the individual under Article 3 may entail a violation of the rights of the sending State, and that violations of the rights of the latter may entail a violation of the rights of the individual'.[71] A saving clause was inserted in Article 33 of the ILC's Articles on State Responsibility to take account of this development in

[60] Article 41, 999 UNTS 171.
[61] Article 11.
[62] Article 21, 1465 UNTS 85.
[63] Article 24.
[64] Article 45.
[65] Articles 47–54, 1520 UNTS 217 ff.
[66] 1966 ICJ Reports 6.
[67] *Official Records of the GA, Fifty-sixth Session, Supplement No. 10* (UN Doc. A/56/10), commentary to Article 48, footnote 766.
[68] Ibid.
[69] The Optional Protocol to the ICCPR, 999 UNTS 171; Article 14 of the International Convention on the Elimination of All Forms of Racial Discrimination; Article 22 of the Convention against Torture and Other Cruel, Inhuman and Degrading Treatment.
[70] 2001 ICJ Reports 494.
[71] (2004) 26, para 40, <http://www.icj-cij.org>.

international law.[72] It is apparent, though, that the protection afforded under such provisions is not diplomatic protection in the technical sense, although it may involve diplomats.

The actions or procedures referred to in Article 16 of the final ILC Draft Articles on Diplomatic Protection include those available under both universal and regional human rights treaties as well as any other relevant treaty—for example, some treaties on the protection of investment. Article 16 does not deal with domestic remedies. This Draft Article is primarily concerned with the protection of human rights by means other than diplomatic protection. It does, however, also embrace the rights of States, natural persons, and other entities conferred by treaties and customary rules on other subjects, such as the protection of foreign investment. The Draft Articles are without prejudice to such rights that exist under procedures other than diplomatic protection.

Article 16 makes it clear that the rights that States, individuals, or other entities may have to secure redress for injury suffered as a result of an internationally wrongful act by procedures other than diplomatic protection are not prejudiced. Where, however, a State resorts to such procedures, it does not per se, because of that fact, abandon its right to exercise diplomatic protection in respect of an individual, if that individual should be a national.[73]

Article 17 of the ILC Draft Articles provides that the Articles on diplomatic protection do not apply:

> to the extent that they are inconsistent with special rules of international law, such as treaty provisions for the protection of investments.[74]

Foreign investment is largely regulated and protected by bilateral investment treaties (BITs).[75] The number of BITs has grown considerably in recent years and today there are a considerable number of such agreements in existence. An important feature of the BIT is its procedure for the settlement of investment disputes. Some BITs provide for the direct settlement of the investment dispute between the investor and the host State before either an ad hoc tribunal or a tribunal established by the International Centre for Settlement of Investment Disputes (ICSID) under the Convention on the Settlement of Investment

[72] The Article reads, 'This part is without prejudice to any right, arising from the international responsibility of a State which may accrue directly to any person or entity other than the State' (note 67 above), para 76.

[73] In the *Selmouni Case*, Application No. 25803/94, Judgment of 28 July 1999, ECHR, 1999-V, 149, the Netherlands intervened in support of a national's individual complaint against France before the European Court of Human Rights. This did not preclude the Netherlands from making a claim in the exercise of diplomatic protection on behalf of the injured individual—had it chosen to do so.

[74] (note 58 above) 21. For what follows see the commentary to the Article, ibid 89–90.

[75] See the *Barcelona Traction Co Case*, 1970 ICJ Reports at 47 for an acknowledgement of this. The NAFTA may also be mentioned in connection with arrangements to protect aliens as investors or traders.

Disputes between States and Nationals of Other States.[76] Other BITs provide for the settlement of investment disputes by means of arbitration between the State of nationality of the investor (corporation or shareholder) and the host State over the interpretation or application of the relevant provision of the BIT. The dispute settlement procedures provided for in BITs and by the ICSID offer greater advantages to the foreign investor than the customary international law system of diplomatic protection, as they give the investor direct access to international arbitration, they avoid the political uncertainty inherent in the discretionary nature of diplomatic protection, and may result in the investor securing a judgment which is enforceable directly in a domestic court. Where the dispute resolution procedures provided for in a BIT or by the ICSID are invoked, diplomatic protection is in most cases excluded.[77]

Article 17 makes it clear that the Draft Articles do not apply to the alternative, special regime for the protection of foreign investors provided for in bilateral and multilateral investment treaties. However, it acknowledges that some treaties do not exclude recourse to diplomatic protection altogether. Hence the provision is formulated so that the Draft Articles do not apply 'to the extent that' they are inconsistent with the provisions of a BIT (or MIT). To the extent that the Draft Articles remain consistent with the BIT (or MIT) in question, they continue to apply. Covered also by the Article are provisions of treaties such as those relating to investments in treaties of friendship, commerce and navigation. In the *Diallo Case (Preliminary Objections)* before the ICJ the plaintiff State argued in favour of a change in the customary international law relating to the protection of shareholders of corporations by 'substitution', relying on treaties, such as the ICSID Convention, and the *compromis* governing certain arbitrations. The Court pointed out quite clearly that it could not agree that such a change had taken place, stating:

> The fact invoked by Guinea that various international agreements, such as agreements for the promotion and protection of foreign investments and the Washington Convention, have established special legal régimes governing investment protection, or that provisions in this regard are commonly included in contracts entered into directly between States and foreign investors, is not sufficient to show that there has been a change in the customary rules of diplomatic protection; it could equally show the contrary. The arbitrations relied on by Guinea are also special cases, whether based on specific international agreements between two or more States, including the one responsible for the allegedly unlawful acts regarding the companies concerned (see, for example, the special agreement concluded between the American, British and Portuguese Governments in the *Delagoa* case or the one concluded between El Salvador and the United States of America in the *Salvador Commercial Company* case) or based on agreements concluded directly between

[76] 575 UNTS 159.

[77] See Article 27(1) of the ICSID Convention.

a company and the State allegedly responsible for the prejudice to it (see, for example, the *Biloune* v *Ghana Investment Centre* case).[78]

Clearly, the Court did not consider the treaties and *compromis* as being based on consistent practice backed by the required *opinio iuris* which could result in a change in the law. Rather to the contrary, it regarded such developments as special cases to be dealt with separately and on their merits.

There may also be special arrangements as a *lex specialis* for the protection of persons in the context of the EU.[79]

[78] 2007 ICJ Reports, para 90 (<http://www.icj-cij.org>).

[79] Stein, 'Diplomatic Protection under the European Union Treaty', in ILA, *Report of the Seventieth Conference* (2002) 277.

4

The International Law Violated

As already pointed out, diplomatic protection is exercised, properly, by the national State, in the case of a violation of international law in respect of the person or property of an alien. It is international law that governs the question whether such a violation of international law has taken place, though international law may refer to national law for determining whether a violation of international law has occurred. The rules relating to such violation of international law are primary rules concerning the treatment of aliens the breach of which could lead to the exercise of diplomatic protection. Diplomatic protection occurs at the stage of a dispute after the violation of such primary rules.

The injury to person or property when caused by the State is to be characterized as a violation of international law in any case by the application of what has come to be known as the international minimum standard applicable to the treatment of aliens. Tortious acts are the ones generally to which this standard is applicable. The international minimum standard is applied over and above the content of the national law of the host State to determine a violation of international law. That is to say, a tortious act so characterized by the national law of the host State would also be a violation of international law. It is where the national law fails to meet the international minimum standard that international law will be called in aid to characterize the injury as a violation of international law. Tortious acts may be committed by the State in respect of the person of the alien, such as arrests, physical injury, torture or improper imprisonment, or they may involve the property of the alien, when, for example, the acts cause physical damage to property or in the case of improper deprivation of property.

The primary rules of international law on the treatment of aliens have a broad coverage and include rules which deal both with personal injury and with injuries in respect of property. The treatment of foreign investment is also dealt with by these primary rules. Multilateral and bilateral treaties, such as investment treaties, may contain rules dealing with the treatment of aliens. Where such rules apply they take the place of the customary rules based on the international minimum standard.

It is also to be noted at this point that, most importantly, the standard applicable to acts of the host State is determined primarily by any treaty to which the two States concerned are parties. In the absence of such treaties the minimum standard of international law has come to be influenced by the conventional law governing human rights. Particularly the UN international conventions on political, civil, economic, and social rights and the European and American conventions on human rights have now, it is strongly arguable, had an effect on the international minimum standard for the treatment of aliens. National States would not be ruled out of court for founding an argument relating to the treatment of their nationals on such treaties on the basis that, where appropriate, the definition of wrongs contained in those treaties reflect customary international law and are an indication of the international minimum standard for the treatment of aliens. In this connection it is important to note that in the *Diallo Case (Preliminary Objections)* the ICJ recently stated:

> Owing to the substantive development of international law over recent decades in respect of the rights it accords to individuals, the scope *ratione materiae* of diplomatic protection, originally limited to alleged violations of the minimum standard of treatment of aliens, has subsequently widened to include, *inter alia* internationally guaranteed human rights.[1]

As pointed out by me elsewhere,[2] a State breach of contract with an alien is not per se a violation of international law, although there has been an interference with the alien's rights by the State. In such cases, as in the case of injury caused the alien by private individuals, there has to be a denial of justice by or in respect of the courts of the host State in order that an international wrong occur. This denial of justice also is to be determined by the application of an international standard. The standard requires, for example, a manifestly unjust judgment, where resort to the courts has been had, or denial of access to the courts by the host State.

The implication of a denial of justice in certain circumstances has led to some confusion arising from the need on the part of the alien to exhaust local remedies.[3] The exhaustion of local remedies is a condition precedent for the exercise of diplomatic protection, as will be seen. A word needs to be said about the violation of international law, denial of justice, and exhaustion of local remedies.

From the point of view of denial of justice a tendency may be observed to accept in principle that there is a distinction between, for example, the situation where the initial injury is a private wrong or the alien is a defendant in a proceeding, and that in which the State commits a wrong which may be equated to an internationally wrongful 'delict' or 'tort' (better described as a *fait internationalement illicite*

[1] 2007 ICJ Reports, para 39 (<http://www.icj-cij.org>). It would seem to be more appropriate to describe the impact of human rights developments as widening and implementing the scope of the international minimum standard rather than adding to it. It is, however, correct to state that human rights standards are included in 'the scope *ratione materiae* of diplomatic protection', on the understanding that this is a reference to the international law relating to the treatment of aliens.

[2] See C F Amerasinghe, *Local Remedies in International Law* (2004), Chapter 5.

[3] The exhaustion of local remedies as a condition for the exercise of diplomatic protection is discussed in Chapter 11 below and in detail in C F Amerasinghe (note 2 above) Chapter 7 ff.

in French or *lecho internacionalemente ilícito* in Spanish) against the alien. Cases such as the *Interhandel Case*[4] support the view that, where the alleged wrong of this nature is committed by, or is attributable to, the State, this amounts at once to a violation of that State's international obligations vis-à-vis the alien. On the other hand, where the alleged initial wrong is, for example, a private one for which the State is not responsible or which is not attributable to the State because of an act or omission on its part, or where the alien is a defendant in a case, there is no violation of its international obligations in respect of the alien by the State until some further act or omission attributable to the State has taken place. Such act or omission occurs when a subsequent wrong is perpetrated during the judicial process or the process of settlement of the dispute concerned. This is usually some act or omission of the judiciary which may properly be characterized as a denial of justice. For example, if access to the courts or to the available procedures is obstructed or if a manifestly unjust judgment is given against the alien, whether he be the plaintiff or the defendant, such denial of access or unjust judgment which is attributable to the State is the violation of international law vis-à-vis the alien on which an international claim may be based by the alien's national State.[5] The difference between the two situations is that in the one the alleged initial wrong does not by itself generate a violation of international law, while in the other it does.

In the one situation no additional act or omission connected with the administration of justice is necessary to generate an international wrong, while in the other the international cause of action is precisely the defect in the administration of justice. If this defect is described as a denial of justice, it is this denial of justice that generates a violation of international law in respect of the alien. Where the alleged initial wrong is directly attributable to the State and is an international wrong, this should not and cannot be characterized as a denial of justice, although it is a violation of international law, so that it is not a denial of justice that generates a violation of international law.[6]

Recognition must be given to the truth that it is always a State's violation of international law which gives rise to international responsibility, whether that violation is a denial of justice in the narrow sense or not. On the other hand, such a denial of justice not only gives rise to responsibility, where it is the initial State

[4] 1959 ICJ Reports 11. There are earlier cases such as the *Neer Case* (*US* v *Mexico*), 4 UNRIAA 60 (1926), and *Janes Case* (*US* v *Mexico*), 4 UNRIAA 82 (1926), which recognize the importance of the kind of initial wrong involved.

[5] The *Neer Case* and the *Janes Case* cited at note 3 above.

[6] 'Responsibility' arises internationally, in strict terms, at the time at which a violation of international norms takes place. As pointed out above, the international legal violation may take place before resort to the local justice system is had. That the responsibility cannot be enforced by resort to diplomatic or legal action at an international level before local remedies have been exhausted does not alter the fact that international responsibility has been incurred. A further point that may emerge is that the existence of the distinction noted above between the initial international wrongs warrants the restriction of the term denial of justice to no more than acts or omissions committed in the course of the administration of justice or the settlement of a dispute that has already arisen.

violation of international law, but will in certain circumstances also compound responsibility by creating an additional violation of international law, ie where the initial State violation of international law is something other than, and prior to, that denial of justice.

Given the difference in situations generating a breach of international norm, it becomes easier to understand how the rule that local remedies must be exhausted will operate in each case. Clearly, where the alleged initial wrong is attributable to the State and is an international wrong, the exhaustion of local remedies will take place in respect of the wrong and will be concerned with rectifying that wrong. The rule would then require that remedies be exhausted up to the highest level. The whole of the dispute settlement procedure relates properly to the application of the rule in this case. It would be important to recognize that, consequent upon the exhaustion of remedies, it is sufficient merely that the initial international wrong remain inadequately redressed for the violation of international law to persist and generate a situation that can be subjected to an international claim or to diplomatic protection. There is clearly no requirement that in the process of settling the dispute anything such as a 'denial of justice' in any appropriate sense by the organ or organs responsible for settling the dispute be committed, it being understood that the initial violation of international law, which continues to remain unredressed and therefore subsists, should not and cannot be described as a denial of justice.

In these circumstances, therefore, it is not appropriate to say that there must be an exhaustion of local remedies resulting in a denial of justice, for this would mean that something more than the absence of satisfactory redress for the initial wrong (such as denial of access to the courts, undue delay in settling the dispute or the rendering of a manifestly unjust judgment) would be required to give rise to a claim based on diplomatic protection. The fact that the process of internal remedies results in a decision which is contrary to international law or is in violation of the international obligations of the host State cannot appropriately be characterized as a denial of justice, although it is sufficient eventually to give rise to an international claim based on diplomatic protection. It is to be noted that in respect of the final decision in the process of exhausting local remedies there is no need for proof that that decision was 'manifestly unjust' in any sense of that term in order to give rise to international responsibility. It is sufficient that the decision is inconsistent with the host State's international obligations for a diplomatic claim to be made or international legal action to be taken. What is required in short is that after the exhaustion of local remedies the final decision taken is simply not one which an international tribunal in prospect would take in the case concerned. The fact that the final decision is one which could reasonably be reached by any impartial court deciding the case does not relieve the host State of, or discharge, its responsibility, for instance, on the ground that there had not been a denial of justice.

Where the initial wrong is not a violation of international law by the host State, for example, where it is a private wrong or where the alien is made a defendant, or where the State is guilty of a simple breach of contract with the alien, resort or an attempted resort to local remedies must take place or local remedies must be activated before an international wrong which is a violation of the host State's international obligations can occur. It is only where such *resort, attempted resort,* or *activation* results in an act or omission which is a violation of international law that international responsibility will be incurred, the original wrong not being per se capable of giving rise to responsibility as such. The violation of international law which subsequently takes place may usually be described as a denial of justice. In whatever terms it is described, and whether it is, for example, an act of the executive interfering with the judicial process or denying access to remedies or a failure to make remedies available or an improper act of the judiciary which renders the process tainted or a manifestly unjust judgment pertaining to the substance of the case, this 'malfunctioning' of the judicial process is the international wrong which generates international responsibility. If any such malfunctioning of the judicial process, which is to be determined according to the norms of international law, may conveniently be described as a denial of justice, then the international wrong generating responsibility is properly called a *denial of justice.*[7]

This is, however, not the end of the matter in this particular event. The rule of local remedies is then applicable to this international wrong and the claimant must in accordance with the requirements of that rule *exhaust* (and not merely *resort to*) the means of local redress in respect of that so-called *denial of justice* up to the highest level.[8] Thus, it is true to say that in the above circumstances there must be an exhaustion of local remedies—in addition to there being a denial of justice after *resort* to local remedies—before an international claim may properly be made, although international responsibility would have arisen once there has been a so-called denial of justice. It is important to emphasize that the international wrong, in respect of which responsibility arises and local remedies must be exhausted, is the denial of justice, although the measure of the injury done to the alien may in the appropriate case be the initial wrong which did not per se give rise to international responsibility.[9] It is the denial of justice which occurred after the *resort* to local remedies or after such initial *resort* was improperly not made possible, which persists and which has not been remedied after local remedies have ultimately been *exhausted* that is, nevertheless, the cause of action in

[7] Where 'denial of justice' is so defined as not to cover all the substantive obligations of the host State connected with the administration of justice, it is possible that the international wrong generating international responsibility will be an act or omission relating to the administration of justice which is not described as a denial of justice but which is, nevertheless, connected with the administration of justice. Local remedies may have to be exhausted in relation to this wrong.

[8] See the *Ziat, Ben Kiran Case* (*Great Britain* v *Spain*), 2 UNRIAA 731 (1924) *per* arbitrator Huber. However, this is only the general principle. There may be certain wrongs which may be termed 'denials of justice' in respect of which no exhaustion of local remedies need take place: see C F Amerasinghe (note 2 above) Chapter 7.

[9] The *Neer Case* (*US* v *Mexico*), 4 UNRIAA 60 (1926).

respect of which responsibility arose and in respect of which an international claim may be made. The failure of redress for the initial denial of justice after *exhaustion* of local remedies makes an international claim legitimate and appropriate, though it is the initial denial of justice after *resort* alone, real or imputed, to local remedies that gives rise to international responsibility.

Three simple examples will illustrate how these principles operate:

- First, where the host State confiscates the property of an alien (without any compensation), or tortures him, this is a violation of the host State's international obligations. Local remedies must be exhausted to redress the wrong. If the wrong remains unredressed or inadequately remedied after such exhaustion, a diplomatic or international judicial claim may be made in respect of the original confiscation or torture. No additional denial of justice in the process of exhausting remedies is required. It is sufficient that exhaustion of remedies has resulted in a decision which perpetuates the violation of international law, which was caused by the original confiscation or act of torture, and does not restore the rights of the alien recognized by international law. Diplomatic protection is exercisable at this point, after the exhaustion of local remedies.
- Second, where, for example, the alien's property is destroyed by a private citizen, or a private citizen commits a breach of contract vis-à-vis the alien, or there is a simple breach by the State of a State contract with the alien,[10] this does not as such cause a violation of the host State's international obligations, although there may be injury to the alien. The alien must *resort* to (not *exhaust* at this stage) local remedies and it is only if, in having such recourse, there is some act or omission amounting to what may be described as a *denial of justice* that an international wrong attributable to the host State will have been committed. Such a denial of justice may arise, for instance, because of procedural abuses by the courts, or a manifestly unjust judgment. A mere adverse decision will not be a denial of justice or an international wrong. While the denial of justice generates international responsibility on the part of the host State, the alien must then *exhaust* (not merely *resort* to) local remedies in respect of that denial of justice up to the highest level before his national State may espouse a diplomatic claim or take international legal action, ie exercise the right of diplomatic protection, which would then be also connected with international 'liability' in a technical or formal sense. After the exhaustion of local remedies, all that is required for international 'liability' to arise, while 'responsibility' would continue, is that the initial denial of justice not be corrected. There is no need for a further aberration in the administration of justice. It is in respect of, and to correct, the denial of justice that local remedies must be exhausted.Further after the unsuccessful exhaustion of local remedies the initial destruction of

[10] On the breach by the State of a State contract with an alien and the relationship between such breach and resort to local remedies in terms of a violation of international law see C F Amerasinghe (note 2 above) Chapter 5.

property or breach of contract may well be the measure of the wrong done to the alien, even though the wrong done is the denial of justice.

- Third, where the alien is prosecuted for a crime, the initial international wrong in respect of the prosecution will occur only when there has been a miscarriage of justice as a result of some defect in the process of administering justice. This occurrence, which may be described as a *denial of justice*, will generate international responsibility. A mere adverse decision will not generate such responsibility, because there would not be a violation of international law. The alien will have to exhaust local remedies up to the highest level in respect of that denial of justice before a diplomatic or international legal claim may be made on his behalf, ie the right of diplomatic protection may be exercised. All that is required for such a claim to be made is that the initial denial of justice or its effect must persist without having been remedied after local remedies have been exhausted. There is no need for the exhaustion of local remedies to result in an additional denial of justice beyond the original denial of justice.

Two consequences emerge from the situations described above. First, in the case where the initial international wrong is the malfunctioning of the judicial process (a *denial of justice*, so-called), the activation of local remedies before the occurrence of the international wrong does not pertain to the exhaustion of local remedies or to the operation of the rule of local remedies. The operation of local remedies up to the point of the commission of an international wrong is required in order that an international wrong generating international responsibility for the host State may arise and is not an integral part of the rule. What follows after the 'denial of justice' is the result of the genuine application of the rule of local remedies and is the exhaustion of local remedies required by that rule. There must be *resort* to remedies in order for an international wrong and responsibility to arise from a denial of justice, and *exhaustion* of remedies after that denial of justice in order for the complaint to be espousable or actionable at an international level, ie by the exercise of the right of diplomatic protection.

Secondly, if, subsequent to the occurrence of the 'denial of justice' which constitutes the international wrong from which responsibility arises, and in the course of exhaustion of local remedies in respect of this denial of justice, more instances of the malfunctioning of the judicial process or local remedies occur, these would compound the basic international wrong. Such additional occurrences would not be required for the admissibility of a claim or its espousal after local remedies have been exhausted, as already noted, but they would certainly constitute additional wrongs for which the host State would be responsible.

While statements have often been made to the effect that the exhaustion of local remedies resulting in a denial of justice is a condition precedent to the institution of a diplomatic claim, the above analysis, which, it is believed, accurately reflects what now happens in practice, shows that this kind of statement can lead to misunderstanding and confusion and does not correctly describe the modern developments in international law. Where the basis for international responsibility is a so-called denial of justice, international responsibility will continue to exist, international 'liability' will additionally arise, the right of diplomatic protection may be exercised, and an international claim will lie or may be espoused after the exhaustion of local remedies according to the requirements of the rule, because that denial of justice subsists or has been inadequately redressed. Where the basis of international responsibility is a violation of the international obligations of the host State other than a denial of justice, all that is required for an international claim to lie or to be espoused subsequent to the incidence of international responsibility is the simple failure to obtain adequate redress after the exhaustion of local remedies.

5

Arrangements Excluded from the Concept of Diplomatic Protection

There are some areas which involve action by diplomats or consular officers or involve direct protection of individuals who may or may not be foreigners but are not included in the concept of diplomatic protection. This is apart from those arrangements for protection of aliens which have been concluded in treaties or conventions and which give the aliens themselves power to litigate against States before arbitral tribunals created by those instruments, such as the systems created under the ICSID Convention or some bilateral treaties.[1] There is also the matter of staff protection by international organizations which may conflict with diplomatic protection proper and is not covered by diplomatic protection.

A Critical Distinction—Diplomatic and Consular Action

'Diplomatic protection' is to be distinguished from consular action or action by a State's diplomats in regard to nationals of the State, where there has been no ostensible violation of international law in the treatment of such nationals.[2] Thus, for example, ambassadors and consuls of a State in foreign States, assisting nationals with trade, investments, or purchases of property, or visiting nationals in prison to ensure that their rights are not violated or to enable them to secure legal representation, do not act in the exercise of the national State's international law right to afford 'diplomatic protection' to nationals against foreign States. These acts are performed in the course of diplomatic or consular action in regard to nationals in foreign States pursuant to rules of international law relating to the functions of diplomats and consuls, whether they flow from conventions or customary law. They do not as such depend on a violation of international law by

[1] The impact of multilateral and bilateral treaties on the law of diplomatic protection proper is discussed in Chapter 17 below.

[2] See Dunn, *The Protection of Nationals* (1932) 18 ff, Bennouna, 'Preliminary Report on Diplomatic Protection' (ILC), UN Doc. A/CN.4/484, 4.

the foreign host State in respect of the national nor are they adversarially directed at the host State. As has been stated:

> diplomatic or consular actions to obtain concessions or other government contracts for nationals from the receiving State, or the arrangement of legal defence for a justly imprisoned national are not diplomatic protection in our sense; they are usually neither directed against the other State nor based on a real or alleged violation of international law.[3]

Protection by States of Diplomatic and Consular Officers and Other Agents

States have a right to exercise protection in respect of their diplomats and consular officers and their families, when they are injured. This right has been recognized generally in customary international law and is now codified as a result of the Vienna Convention on Diplomatic Relations 1961[4] and the Vienna Convention on Consular Relations 1963.[5] Customary law had for long recognized that the right to protect such persons in cases in which they were injured or their property was damaged was not only vested in the State but was owned by the State as a direct benefit. The injury was construed as a 'direct' injury to the State, regardless of whether the officer was a national of the State, and the injury to the individual being only incidental. This was so even though the injury to the individual could be considered in determining reparation to the injured State. In the *United States Diplomatic and Consular Staff in Tehran Case*[6] the ICJ implicitly endorsed this general position and did not deny it.

Apart from diplomatic and consular officers and their families, there are other State agents, such as heads of State and members of foreign offices,[7] and even some miscellaneous agents,[8] in respect of whom States have certain rights and the right to protect whom is both vested in the State and is regarded as based on a direct injury to the State like injury to diplomatic and consular officers and their families. The direct rights involved have long been acknowledged in customary international law.

In all these cases States do not exercise diplomatic protection, although the injury to the individual may be taken into account in calculating damages. A State asserts a direct right belonging to it based on a direct injury to it to which

[3] Geck, 'Diplomatic Protection', 1 EPIL (1992) 1046.

[4] 500 UNTS 95. For more on the Convention see Denza, *Diplomatic Law* (1976) and Dembinski, *The Modern Law of Diplomacy* (1988) particularly 153–61, 183–90, 201–21; Jennings and Watts (eds), 2 *Oppenheim's International Law* (1992) 1053–1131.

[5] 596 UNTS (1963) 261. The Convention came into force in 1967. On the Convention see Lee, *Vienna Convention on Consular Relations* (1966), Jennings and Watts (eds), (note 4 above), 1132–53.

[6] 1980 ICJ Reports 3, passim.

[7] See Jennings and Watts (eds), (note 4 above), Chapter 9.

[8] See Jennings and Watts, 2 ibid, Chapter 12.

the injury to the individual is only incidental. It is a right based on interference with a State's dignity or functioning in discharge of its official functions.[9] In those circumstances a State is not itself as such injured in the person of its national in the Vattelian sense but it is subjected to interference in the execution of its sovereign functions.

Rights of International Organizations in Regard to their Staff

Developments after the Second World War and the creation of the UN have led to:

(i) the recognition of the international personality of international organizations;[10]
(ii) the responsibility of States or other organizations for violations of the law *to* international organizations;[11]
(iii) the right of international organizations to protect their staff, the violation of which produces international responsibility to the organization concerned.[12]

Whenever international personality is attributed to an international organization, it is a legal person separate from and additional to its member States, and is not simply an aggregation of those States. It constitutes a distinct entity with functions, rights and duties of its own. While it has duties, there are counterpart obligations owing to it by, inter alia, States, the performance of which the organization has a right to expect and, if necessary, to require. This principle was referred to by the ICJ in the *Reparation Case* when it stated that there was an 'undeniable right of the Organization to demand that its Members shall fulfil the obligations entered into by them in the interest of the good working of the Organization'.[13] The Court emphasized that the effective working of the organization and the accomplishment of its task required that the undertakings of Member States be strictly observed. For that purpose the ICJ thought it 'necessary that, when an infringement occurs, the Organization should be able to call upon the responsible State to remedy its default, and in particular, to obtain from the State reparation for the damage that the default may have caused'.[14]

[9] The Convention on the Prevention of Crimes against Internationally Protected Persons, Including Diplomatic Agents, of 1973 (13 ILM (1974) 41) codifies some of the rights States enjoy in respect of internationally protected persons: see on this convention Bloomfield and Fitzgerald, *Crimes against Internationally Protected Persons* (1975).

[10] C F Amerasinghe, *Principles of the Institutional Law of International Organizations* (2005), Chapter 3.

[11] On this see C F Amerasinghe, ibid 390 ff.

[12] See C F Amerasinghe, ibid 393 ff.

[13] 1949 ICJ Reports 184.

[14] Ibid 183.

That international organizations can possess rights under conventional law cannot be doubted. Thus, under the headquarters agreements or constitutions of organizations it was clearly envisaged that organizations would have rights vis-à-vis States. When organizations enter into treaties the same order would prevail. This was implicitly recognized in the *WHO Agreement Case*,[15] where the obligations of international organizations were specifically in issue and were affirmed. The rights of the UN under international agreements were recognized by the ICJ in the *PLO Observer Mission Case*.[16] But there are also undoubtedly obligations owed to international organizations by States primarily under customary international law, based on the analogy of the responsibility of States to each other. For example, States may have to conduct themselves actively or passively in such a way that they do not injure or damage the interests of international organizations, whether such obligations are based on risk, negligence or on absolute liability, as the case may be. The existence of obligations of international organizations at customary international law was referred to in the *WHO Agreement Case*[17] by the ICJ, it being reasonable to infer that conversely the organizations had rights as well. As an international person, an international organization may be expected to have such international rights.

The rights of organizations may cover an unlimited area depending on their capacity to enter into treaties and agreements and on the practical circumstances and situations in which they are placed and operate. It is not possible or necessary to identify all the rights that organizations may have. To some extent they may correspond to those that States have, but what is the source of these rights is a question. It is not clear whether they are generated by analogy with States (general principles of law) or by customary law. They certainly have the rights to have loans repaid under and in accordance with loan agreements or aid agreements, for example, as is clearly the case with loans and credits made by the IBRD and the IDA. They also have rights in respect to protection by States in which they have offices, whether under agreement or under general international law. In the *Reparation Case* the ICJ thought that it could not be disputed that the UN had rights relating to damage to its property and other interests.[18]

Attention has been paid particularly to the right of protection for their staff members that organizations have vis-à-vis States, since the advisory opinion of the ICJ in the *Reparation Case*. There the principle issue was whether the UN had the capacity to bring a claim against a State for injury caused to one of its staff members. In the opinion the ICJ, without discussing the matter in detail, took the view that States had obligations vis-à-vis the UN in regard to the protection from injury of its staff members in the course of performing their duties.[19]

[15] 1980 ICJ Reports 90. The case concerned the rights of the parties vis-à-vis each other under an international agreement relating to the location of an office of the WHO.

[16] 1988 ICJ Reports 13.

[17] 1980 ICJ Reports 90.

[18] 1949 ICJ Reports 184. Other organizations, it may be inferred, have similar rights.

[19] Ibid 181 ff.

The exact content of the duty to protect or keep free from injury or damage was, however, not discussed, but it may be inferred that this was one owed under general international law and would correspond to that owed by States to other States in respect of the latter's officials.

In regard to the protection of staff, Article 100 of the UN Charter provides in effect that members of the staff of the UN are not to seek or receive instructions from governments or other authorities, that their responsibility is to the organization they serve, and that the member States are not to seek to influence them in the discharge of this responsibility. The constitutions of many other international organizations have similar provisions. Even if such provisions are not included in some constitutions, what is stated in them is implicit in the position of the staff of international organizations as international civil servants. In the *Reparation Case*, the ICJ declined to assimilate the legal bond resulting from the stipulations of the Charter between the UN, on the one hand, and the Secretary-General and the staff, on the other, to the bond of nationality existing between a State and its nationals. However, the Court derived certain consequences from the position of the international civil servant in his relationship with his organization:

> In order that the agent may perform his duties satisfactorily, he must feel that this protection is assured to him by the Organization, and that he may count on it. To ensure the independence of the agent, and, consequently, the independent action of the Organization itself, it is essential that in performing his duties he need not have to rely on any other protection than that of the Organization... In particular, he should not have to rely on the protection of his own State. If he had to rely on that State, his independence might well be compromised, contrary to the principle applied by Article 100 of the Charter. And lastly, it is essential that—whether the agent belongs to a powerful or to a weak State; to one more affected or less affected by the complications of international life; to one in sympathy or not in sympathy with the mission of the agent—he should know that in the performance of his duties he is under the protection of the Organization.[20]

The Court had already concluded that the organization was a distinct international person as a consequence of which Member States not only owed duties to it but were subject to being reminded, if need be, of certain obligations. Consequently, the independence of the organization became particularly important. However, the independence of the organization depended on the independence of the staff. For this reason the latter assumed special juridical significance. Thus, it was a logical conclusion that the organization's right vis-à-vis members, particularly, of the organization to protect and demand protection of its staff in the performance of duties, was implicit. It must be noted, nevertheless, that the Court's view also implied, first, that an international official does not cease to owe allegiance to his own country in his personal capacity; second, that in his official capacity and in the performance of his functions his first allegiance was to his organization; and, third, that in case of conflict the latter allegiance must prevail.

20 Ibid 182.

An important question concerns the right of organizations to assert their claims at international law, where their international rights have been infringed and responsibility to them has been incurred. In the *Reparation Case* the ICJ concluded that, as in the case of claims by States, the foundation of any international claim by an international organization must be a breach of an obligation owed to it on the international plane by the defendant State:

> It cannot be doubted that the Organization has the capacity to bring an international claim against one of its Members which has caused injury to it by a breach of its international obligations towards it . . . As the claim is based on the breach of an international obligation on the part of the Member held responsible by the Organization, the Member cannot contend that this obligation is governed by municipal law, and the Organization is justified in giving its claim the character of an international claim.[21]

The Court stated that in the case of an international organization this capacity flowed from its purpose and functions, as specified or implied in its constituent documents and developed in practice. In the case of the UN its functions were of such a character that they could not be effectively discharged, unless the organization were regarded as having been endowed with capacity to bring international claims when necessitated by the discharge of its functions.[22] The Court pointed out that: 'It cannot be supposed that . . . all the members of the Organization, save the defendant State, must combine to bring a claim against the defendant for the damage suffered by the Organization.'[23] The UN, as an organization, had the capacity to bring claims against States broadly in two categories of cases: (i) where, by reason of the wrongful act of the State in question, the organization itself had suffered direct loss or damage to its property, assets, finances or interests; and (ii) in respect of the personal loss or damage caused to or suffered by a servant or agent of the organization in the course of his duties, arising out of such an act, and additional to any damage caused to the organization itself by the same act. The Court referred to the inconvenience that would result, if the organization were not endowed with their corporate capacity in the matter.

Capacity in the first type of case is easy to concede because it is really a necessary attribute of the corporate character of the organization and its possession of international personality. However, the position in regard to the second category is less obvious for two reasons: firstly, because the servant or agent of the organization would also be the national of some State which prima facie was entitled to claim on his behalf; and, secondly, because a claim by the organization on his behalf might seem at first sight to be at variance with the rule, normally applicable in the case of claims made by States in respect of persons, that only the State of which the injured party is a national can bring a claim on his behalf. The Court met these difficulties by invoking two basic principles.

[21] Ibid 180. [22] Ibid.
[23] Ibid 180–1.

The first was a positive one, that the special relationship between the organization and its servants required, for the effective discharge of the functions of the latter and through them the discharge of the organization's own functions, and for the effective preservation of the independence of both, that the organization should have the capacity to extend protection to its servant, and in case of need to bring a claim on his behalf. The second principle of relevance was that the rules concerning the nationality of claims applied only to those cases where the nationality of the injured person formed the sole basis for the legal wrong done to the claimant State, entitling it to make a claim, and that they did not preclude claims by entities of which the injured person was not a national where another basis justifying such a claim existed.

On the first of these points the Court introduced the problem by stating that the Charter did not expressly confer upon the UN the capacity to include, in its claim for reparation, damage caused to the victim or to persons entitled through him and that, therefore, an enquiry must first be made into whether the provisions of the Charter concerning the functions of the UN, and the part played by its agents in the performance of those functions, implied for the organization power to afford its agents the limited protection that would consist in the bringing of a claim on their behalf for reparation for damage suffered in such circumstances.[24] The work of the UN necessitated the dispatch of important missions to be performed in disturbed parts of the world, involving for the members of the mission unusual dangers to which ordinary persons were not exposed.[25] Further, the circumstances might also be such that a claim for any injury done to an agent of the organization in the performance of such a mission could not appropriately be brought by his national State or that the latter would not feel disposed to do so. Efficiency and independence of the staff required their protection.[26] The Court's conclusion was, therefore, that: 'Upon examination of the character of the functions entrusted to the Organization and of the nature of the missions of its agents, it becomes clear that the capacity of the Organization to exercise a measure of functional protection of its agents arises by necessary intendment out of the Charter.'[27]

On the second issue of the absence of the nationality link, the Court explained why the special relationship between the organization and its servants or agents which did not depend on a nationality link made it possible for the organization to make a claim not merely for the loss or damage caused to itself, but in respect also of the personal loss or damage caused to the servant or agent himself.[28] The question was why, in bringing a claim in respect of a breach of an international obligation owed to itself, the organization should be able to do anything more

[24] Ibid 182.
[25] Ibid 183.
[26] Ibid.
[27] Ibid 184.
[28] Ibid 181–2.

than claim for the damage caused directly to itself, *qua* organization, and why it should be entitled also to make a claim on behalf of the agent personally. The national State of an injured alien could bring a claim on behalf of its national because it is regarded as having suffered injury in the person of its national in addition to having suffered a breach of an obligation owed to it. But in the case of an international organization the international obligation was something other than the general international law obligation to afford certain treatment to aliens. The obligation arose from the nature, functions, and requirements of an international organization which normally make it necessary that its agents be able to look to it, and not to any State, even their national State, for protection while carrying out their duties on behalf of the organization. There was a duty to afford protection to agents of the UN in the performance of their functions which arose as a general inference both from the Charter and from certain related instruments. Not only were these general undertakings of the Members but Article 2(5) of the Charter required them to render the UN 'every assistance'.[29] Thus, the breach of an obligation owed to the organization gave the organization, like the national State of an injured party, its own right in making the claim, even though the claim was in respect of personal damage to the agent or his defendants.[30]

Having established that the tie of nationality was not crucial to the right of an organization to bring a claim on behalf of one of its servants, the Court, further, concluded, as a logical corollary, that the fact that the injured party was a national of the defendant State did not affect the right to claim. Because the action of the organization was in fact based not upon the nationality of the victim but upon his status as agent of the organization, it did not matter whether he was a national of the State to which the claim was addressed. Thus, the fact of the possession of the nationality of the defendant State by the agent did not constitute any obstacle to a claim brought by the organization for a breach of obligations towards it occurring in relation to the performance of his mission by the agent.[31]

The conclusion of the ICJ is explicable by reference to the fact that the reason why a claim cannot be brought by a State of which the injured party is a national, when he is also a national of the defendant State, is that, because the treatment accorded by the latter to the injured party constitutes action on the domestic plane, as he is a national of the latter, irrespective of any other nationality he may possess, there has been no conduct on the international plane which could give rise to an international claim. There has been no violation of an international obligation in these circumstances, because the injured party is not an alien vis-à-vis the defendant State and the latter could not have

[29] Ibid 183.

[30] Ibid 184.

[31] Ibid 186. The reasoning and conclusions of the ICJ in this case are of general application to all organizations. This is reasonable.

committed a breach of rules relating to the treatment of aliens which is what normally gives rise to an international claim on behalf of an individual. The situation may be contrasted with that in which the basis of the international claim is not an obligation relating to the treatment of aliens as such but an obligation designed to protect local nationals against certain kinds of treatment at the hands of their own State, such as arises from human rights or minorities provisions in treaties. In such cases the claim is not based on the injury suffered by the claimant State in the person of its national, arising out of a breach of the general international law obligation to treat aliens in a certain way. It is based on a separate right, generally arising from a treaty, that exists independently of the issue of nationality. A claim by an international organization for an injury done to one of its agents in the performance of his functions is of a similar kind. The claim does not arise from the breach of general international law obligation to treat aliens in a certain way. But it is based on a breach of certain obligations owed to the organization by member States arising in consequence of the terms of its constitutive instrument and possibly by analogy with general rules of international law.

The ICJ also dealt with the question of conflicting claims by an international organization on behalf of its agent and by his national State in connection with the same events. International tribunals were already familiar with the problem of a claim in which two or more national States were interested and knew how to protect the defendant State in such a case.[32] The general rule (to which there may be exceptions)[33] was that priority was not assigned to one or the other and that neither was compelled to refrain from bringing an international claim: 'There is no rule of law which assigns priority to the one or to the other, or which compels either... to refrain from bringing an international claim.'[34]

As regards the relationship with non-Member States, the Court found that in principle the UN had capacity to bring an international claim against non-Member States in respect of injuries done to its agents. Because the international personality of the organization, though in origin the creation of the Charter, existed as an independent objective fact, and therefore existed vis-à-vis non-members also together with the attributes and incidents deriving from the Charter and from the character and functions of the organization as thereby created, along with it went the capacity to bring international claims.[35]

The right of international organizations to bring claims involving staff is not based on diplomatic protection as such but is based on attributing to organizations a direct right relating to their functioning as organizations with international personality.

[32] Ibid.
[33] The *Nottebohm Case*, 1955 ICJ Reports 22.
[34] 1949 ICJ Reports at 185.
[35] Ibid. Here also the findings of the court may be applied generally.

Protection of Individuals under Treaties

Individuals may be covered by a system of protection created by treaties. The treaties may or may not create particular substantive rights but become significant because of the procedural structures created for invoking remedies. Under these treaties protection by a State may not depend on nationality of the protecting States. Such treaty arrangements include treaties for the protection of minorities and the current human rights conventions. The protection given by States to individuals pursuant to such treaty arrangements are not describable as diplomatic protection but it is specific to such arrangements.

Moreover, as will be seen in later chapters of this work, there are conventional arrangements which have supplanted diplomatic protection, at least to some extent, or have modified or qualified the coverage of diplomatic protection. Such are the arrangements under the ICSID Convention and pursuant to many bilateral investment treaties.

6

Codification of the Law of Diplomatic Protection

The Earliest Attempt

After the First World War the necessity of order and security in the international world was realized more keenly than ever. Thus, the post-war period was characterized by serious efforts to reorganize the existing body of international law, in order to make its rules clear and certain, and, where possible, to give definite expression to the obligation to observe these rules by having codifying conventions. The belief had been widely held that much of the existing disorder and conflict was due to the lack of clear and fixed rules.

Diplomatic protection was a prime target in the field of codification. It was argued that, because of the extensive jurisprudence that had developed in the field, it would be comparatively easy to codify the subject. There were diligent and well-planned efforts on the part of governments and of scholars to codify it but eventually without success. It emerged that there was disagreement on the subject as well as to some extent a lack of agreement on the purpose of the institution of diplomatic protection itself. In establishing the rules of law on the subject, the great powers saw the purpose of the rules as maintaining conditions favourable to international investment, trade, and intercourse, while the States of Latin America, particularly, on the other hand, had little, if any, interest in the security and protection of foreigners. The latter were concerned with drafting rules which would safeguard the independence of small States in administering their own territories. This underlying conflict of approach made obtaining acceptance of any well defined formulation of rules of law highly unlikely.

The most important effort at codification involving States was made under the auspices of the League of Nations.[1] In September 1924 the Assembly of the LN adopted a resolution requesting the Council of the LN to convene a committee of experts with a view to the 'progressive codification' of international law. This committee, which was established in due course, drew up reports on seven subjects which it regarded as sufficiently ripe for codification. One of these subjects was

[1] See Dunn, *The Protection of Nationals* (1932) 62ff for an account of this attempt at codification.

the 'Responsibility of States in respect of injury caused in their territory to the person or property of foreigners'. The rapporteur on this subject was Guerrero, an El Salvadorian. Not surprisingly his report reflected very definitely the Latin-American viewpoint on the subject.

In his report,[2] Guerrero reflected the usual theoretical basis of the right of diplomatic protection, ie that every individual has certain fundamental rights, namely the right to life, the right to liberty, and the right to own property, which States had recognized and had mutually undertaken to ensure the possibility of enjoying. On account of these rights Guerrero stated that nationality sank into the background because the rights belonged to man as a human being and were not, therefore, subordinate to the will of the State. This was in essence a description of the minimum standard of justice which, again according the usual theory, all States were obliged to observe in their treatment of aliens within their borders.

However, Guerrero sought to deprive this customary theory of its force and effect by qualifying it in a manner supported by Latin-American authorities. He was of the view that in no case was a State obliged to accord to foreigners any more favourable treatment than it accorded to its own nationals. Guerrero did not add the usual proviso made by authorities outside of the Latin American States that this national standard of treatment was acceptable as an appropriate discharge of a State's obligations in respect of foreigners only when such treatment was not below the international minimum standard as found in the practice of 'civilized' States generally. This proviso left it open to foreign States to contend that the laws and institutions of, or their application by, a particular State were not in keeping with the international minimum standard.

As has been observed,

> Guerrero sought further to limit the scope of the exercise of diplomatic protection in his definition of 'denial of justice.' While he recognized this ground as a basis of international responsibility, he did it in such a manner as to limit it to cases which virtually never happen in practice. In the first place, he advanced the usual thesis that a foreigner must seek his protection only in the laws and courts of the country of his sojourn (i.e., if he sustains an injury he must seek redress in the local courts). Guerrero then deduced from the principle of equality of states that the decisions of the local courts on any matter covered by local law must be regarded as final and in conformity with that law, even though the decision in a particular case represented a mistake in judgment, or could be looked upon as 'unjust,' or even 'manifestly unjust.'
>
> In brief, Guerrero concluded that no international recourse was admissible against a judgment of a local court, however mistaken or unjust it might seem. Even an abnormal delay in the administration of justice where a foreigner was involved could not, under his theory, provide a basis for international responsibility. Only where a state refused

[2] The report was produced and signed by Guerrero only, although there was another member, who was indisposed, on the committee entrusted with drafting it. For the report see 20 *AJIL, Supplement II* 177–203.

to foreigners access to its courts on the same terms as to its own nationals, or where the courts refused to proceed with an action brought by a foreigner, could international responsibility arise. Inasmuch as practically all states afford access to their courts to foreigners on the same terms as to nationals, and also provide judicial remedies for injuries sustained by individuals at the hands of the government or of its officials, it can be readily seen that Guerrero's thesis, while logically deducible from accepted general principles, would have restricted the exercise of diplomatic protection to occasions which seldom if ever arise in practice.[3]

The Assembly of the LN in September 1927 decided to submit three subjects to a first international law conference for the codification of international law. One of these was the responsibility of states for damage done in their territory to the person or property of foreigners. A Preparatory Committee was appointed, and this committee prepared and sent to the various governments for their consideration a 'List of Points' on this subject. The list was in the form of a detailed questionnaire.

Some thirty governments replied to the questionnaire regarding Responsibility of States, including, however, only one Latin American State, Chile. These replies were analyzed by the Preparatory Committee and 'Bases of Discussion' were drawn up on the points covered, to serve as starting points of discussion by the proposed conference. The scope of international responsibility marked out in these bases of discussion was much broader than that admitted in Guerrero's report, and did not give recognition to the Calvo Doctrine[4] as contended for by the Latin American States.

Forty-seven States (including the United States and seven other States not members of the League of Nations) were represented at the First Conference for the Codification of International Law convened at The Hague in March 1930, at which the subject of Responsibility of States was considered. After prolonged discussions the Conference finally adjourned without adopting any convention on the subject of State responsibility. The Third Committee, which was charged with the consideration of this subject, merely adopted on first reading ten articles of a proposed convention, which in substance embodied twelve of the thirty bases of discussion drawn up by the Preparatory Committee, but reached no agreement on the final bases of discussion which could be referred to by the general conference for action.

The main points on which the Committee could not agree related to the inclusion of a rule that foreigners were entitled to no more than equal treatment with native citizens and on the inclusion of a definite standard of 'due diligence' in the prevention of injuries to foreigners. The disagreement reflected the main difference of opinion between the powers concerned with preserving conditions favourable to international trade, commerce, and intercourse on the one hand

[3] Dunn (note 1 above) 63–4, referring to Guerrero's report (note 2 above) 190–3.

[4] This doctrine was explained in Chapter 2 above. See also Chapter 12 below.

and those concerned with establishing their complete independence of action within their own territories on the other. It related, in substance, to the international standard for the treatment of foreigners to which all States would be required to conform and which would prevent each State from virtually fixing its own standard.

So long as this difference, which was fundamental, existed, it was unlikely that unanimous agreement could be reached on any definite formulation of rules of law. While this was a matter of substantive law, rather than one relating to remedial rules governing diplomatic protection as such, the conference failed to adopt any rules on the subject before it. Clearly, because there was disagreement on the fundamentals of the substantive primary rules, the question of codifying the remedial rules relating to diplomatic protection could not even be considered.

It may be noted that the subject considered by the Third Committee did not in fact cover the rules relating to diplomatic protection as defined in Chapter 1 above. These are remedial or secondary rules which come into effect when a host State has injured an alien. The subject considered related to the rules determining the substantive obligations owed by the host State in respect of the treatment of aliens.[5]

Consideration by the ILC

In 1948 the United Nations General Assembly established the International Law Commission, as a step towards fulfilling the Charter mandate of 'encouraging the progressive development of international law and its codification'.[6] The ILC's initial step was to draw up a work programme, which included the subject of State responsibility.[7]

[5] Between the two world wars there were some private attempts to codify the whole gamut of the law relating to the responsibility of States for the treatment of aliens: eg the project drawn up in 1927 by the International Commission of Jurists appointed in conformity with a resolution of the Third Pan American Conference in 1906. Among the efforts of private organizations in this direction should be noted also the projects of the Institute of International Law, adopted at Lausanne in 1927, and of the American Institute of International Law submitted to the International Commission of Jurists at Rio de Janeiro in 1927. These latter are printed as Appendices 3 and 5 to the Report of the Harvard Research in International Law on *The Law of Responsibility of States for Damage Done in Their Territory to the Person or Property of Foreigners* (1930). There was also a draft convention prepared by the Research in International Law of the Harvard Law School for the First Conference on the Codification of International Law: Dunn, (note 1 above) 205 ff. Diplomatic protection as such was, inter alia, dealt with in this draft. This draft was updated later. Some Latin American bodies also produced drafts connected with the responsibility of States for injuries to aliens: García Amador, 'First Report on State Responsibility' to the ILC, 2 YBILC (1956) 226–7.

[6] UN Charter, Art. 13 (a); G.A. Res. 174 (II) of 21 November 1947. For a concise description of the ILC's work on State Responsibility see Crawford, *The International Law Commissions Articles on State Responsibility* (2002) 1 ff.

[7] *YBILC* (1949) 281.

Work began in 1956 with García Amador of Cuba as Special Rapporteur. It covered State responsibility for injuries to aliens and their property. The concern was with the substantive rules of international law on the subject and not particularly on diplomatic protection. García Amador submitted six reports between 1956 and 1961, but the ILC hardly discussed them. The main reason for this was the divisiveness of the general debate held in 1957 which suggested that there was no agreement as to how to proceed. Some sought to limit the topic to diplomatic protection; others thought the rules of diplomatic protection outmoded.[8] An initial decision which was made had the effect of limiting the topic to 'civil' injuries to aliens.[9] But the rapporteur was criticized by others for not including, inter alia, 'penal' reprisals.[10] Little progress was made and finally his proposals were never discussed individually.[11]

In 1962 an inter-sessional subcommittee of the ILC chaired by Roberto Ago (Italy) recommended that the ILC should redraw the boundaries of the topic so as to focus on 'the definition of the general rules governing the international responsibility of the State'.[12] By this was meant the rules of general application concerning States responsibility, applicable not only to diplomatic protection as meaning responsibility for injuries to aliens but also to other fields (human rights, disarmament, environmental protection, the law of the sea etc.). By inference, the point was not to elaborate the substantive rules themselves or the specific obligations of States arising from them. These would differ, inter alia, from treaty to treaty and from State to State. Rather the focus was to be on the framework or matrix of rules of responsibility, identifying whether there has been a breach by a State of law and what were its consequences. The subcommittee added that:

> there would be no question of neglecting the experience and material gathered in special sectors, specially that of responsibility for injuries to the person or property of aliens; and... that careful attention should be paid to the possible repercussions which new developments in international law may have had on responsibility.[13]

In 1963 the ILC approved this reconceptualization of the topic and appointed Ago as Special Rapporteur. Between 1969 and 1980 he produced eight reports, together with a special addendum to the eighth report. During that time, the ILC provisionally adopted thirty-five articles, together making up Part One of the proposed Draft Articles ('Origin of State Responsibility'). There was, among other things, a detailed treatment of the rules of attribution and the general justification or excuses for an internationally wrongful act (under the title 'Circumstances precluding wrongfulness'). Ago's structure for the five chapters

[8] 1 *YBILC* (1957) 154–72.

[9] 1 *YBILC* (1956) 246.

[10] 1 *YBILC* (1957) 169.

[11] 1 ibid 181. In their final form they are recorded in 2 *YBILC* (1961) 46–54; see also García Amador, Sohn and Baxter, *Recent Codification of State Responsibility for Injuries to Aliens* (1974).

[12] 2 *YBILC* (1963) 228.

[13] Ibid.

of Part One proved conclusive, but there was no similar structure for the remaining part or parts. Evidently these would concern reparation; he made it clear they should also include countermeasures. The consequences of 'international crimes of State', a concept introduced in one Article, would presumably be spelled out. But these were little more than vague hints, not formal proposals.

In 1979 Wilhelm Riphagen (Netherlands) was appointed Special Rapporteur. Between 1980 and 1986, he presented seven reports, containing a complete set of Draft Articles on Part Two ('Content, forms and degrees of international responsibility') and Part Three ('Settlement of disputes') together with commentaries. Owing to the priority given to other topics, however, only five Articles from his Part Two were provisionally adopted during this period. By far the most important of these was an Article including an extended definition of 'injured State'.

In 1987, Riphagen not having been re-elected to the ILC, Gaetano Arangio-Ruiz (Italy) was appointed in his place. In the period 1988–1995, he presented seven reports. The Drafting Committee dealt with the remainder of Parts Two and Three in the quinquennium 1992–1996, enabling the ILC to adopt the text with commentaries on first reading in 1996. The Draft Articles of 1996 thus consisted of three tranches, Part One (Articles [1]-[35], adopted in the period 1971 to 1980 under Ago), a few articles in Part Two, Chapter I, adopted in the period to 1986 under Riphagen, and the residue dealing with reparation, countermeasures, the consequences of 'international crimes' and dispute settlement, adopted in the period 1992–1996 under Arangio-Ruiz.

During these years no attempt was made to reconsider any issues raised by Part One except the article referring to international crimes of State. Even then, once it had been decided to retain the concept of international crimes, the actual language was left undisturbed; only the addition of a footnote revealed the fundamental lack of consensus.[14] Nor for that matter were Riphagen's five articles in Part Two reconsidered. Following disagreements within the ILC on a number of questions—in particular, the relations between State responsibility and the powers of the Security Council—Arangio-Ruiz resigned as Special Rapporteur. Not having been renominated by Italy, he ceased to be a member of the ILC the same year. For these and other reasons, the coordination of articles in the different Parts, rather obviously lacking, was left to the second reading. The articles did contain sections on diplomatic protection in the narrow sense as defined in Chapter 1.

At its forty-ninth session in 1997 the ILC adopted a provisional timetable with the aim of completing the second reading by the end of the quinquennium, ie by 2001. Three major unresolved issues were tentatively identified as requiring special consideration: international crimes, the regime of countermeasures, and

[14] 2 *YBILC* (1996) 63.

the settlement of disputes.[15] This was an obvious enough list, but as events were to prove it included only some among many unresolved issues. For the present purpose, suffice it to indicate how the project stood in 1996 in terms particularly of its handling of diplomatic protection in the narrow sense.

There was a limited article on exhaustion of local remedies, which was analyzed within the specific framework of a breach of a certain kind of obligation (Ago's draft). Generally, however, the draft available in 1996 showed an outcome consistent with a universal approach to the problem of State responsibility, freeing it from particular categories of rules such as those concerning diplomatic protection and injuries to aliens. There was 'a contextual approach which avoids the imposition of across-the-board rules of substance and allows such questions to be solved for the purpose of each particular rule or even each particular case'.[16]

James Crawford, who was appointed Special Rapporteur, revised and completed work on the draft codification on State responsibility by 2001. The second reading took place and the ILC submitted the draft to the GA. The draft dealt with State responsibility in general including a section on reparation and an Article 44 which contained a requirement that the rules relating to nationality of claims and exhaustion of local remedies should be observed where appropriate.[17] This article was the first relating to diplomatic protection as remedial action produced on a second reading by the ILC. The Commission, moreover, had succeeded in distinguishing among State responsibility in general, the substantive law of State Responsibility for Injuries to Aliens, and diplomatic protection as remedial action.

At almost the same time as Crawford was appointed Special Rapporteur for State Responsibility the ILC decided to prepare a draft code on diplomatic protection. Mohamed Bennouna was appointed Special Rapporteur in 1997 and produced a preliminary report on the subject in 1998.[18] The report addressed certain basic questions concerning diplomatic protection. Bennouna resigned from the ILC soon after and John Dugard took over as Special Rapporteur. Dugard produced five reports (with addenda) with draft articles on the subject[19] which were considered by the Commission and by 2004 a first reading of nineteen articles was completed. The articles dealt entirely with the aspects of diplomatic protection and were a thorough study of the subject as far as they went. However, there was no reference to special rules relating to damages in cases of diplomatic protection. In 2005, after the nineteen drafted articles had been referred in

[15] *Report of the ILC*, 1997, UN Doc. A/52/10 paras 30, 161.
[16] See Crawford (note 6 above) 13.
[17] Crawford, ibid 67–8 and 70.
[18] UN Doc. A/CN.4/484.
[19] See UN Doc. A/CN.4/506 and Add. (2000); UN Doc. A/CN.4/515 (2001); UN Doc. A/CN.4/523 and Add. (2002); UN Doc. A/CN.4/530 and Add. (2003); UN Doc. A/CN.4/538 (2004); UN Doc. A/CN.4/546 (2005).

2004 to the GA,[20] Dugard prepared a sixth report on the relevance of the clean hands doctrine to diplomatic protection,[21] in which he concluded that it had no relevance. The second reading of the articles was completed in 2006 and the completed articles were sent to the GA.[22]

The drafted articles are as complete as can be found, even if one may not agree with everything in them. They are also drafted in such a manner as to leave open a few highly controversial matters. This draft will be considered in this work.

It may be noted that matters relevant to diplomatic protection have been dealt with by the ILC in two separate codification drafts. The final product on State responsibility with Crawford as Special Rapporteur referred to the rules on nationality of claims and exhaustion of local remedies (Article 44), which are at the heart of diplomatic protection, while not dealing with them in detail. That draft also treated, inter alia, the attribution of acts to the State and reparation. The articles on these last two subjects were based to a large extent on material relating to diplomatic protection as remedial action. Dugard's work as Special Rapporteur examined in detail most aspects of diplomatic protection as remedial action, while omitting consideration of attribution of acts to the State and reparation which had been considered in the work on State responsibility.[23] These features must be kept in mind, because in dealing with diplomatic protection as remedial action, elements relating to it are to be found in both sets of ILC articles.[24]

[20] *Report of the ILC*, 2004 73 ff. The ILC had at about the same time submitted the Draft Articles to governments for their comments.

[21] UN Doc. A/CN.4/546 (2005).

[22] *Report of the ILC*, 2006 13 ff.

[23] There is a question mark in regard to the ILC's treatment of lawful excuses to wrongfulness as a matter for State responsibility, the content of which concerns secondary norms. It is unnecessary to discuss the question here. Suffice it to note the problem by asking whether such lawful excuses should really be regarded as part of the substantive law relating to international wrongs rather than as relating to secondary norms or remedial action.

[24] Private work, such as the 1961 Harvard Draft on State Responsibility, the 2006 Resolution 5/2006 on Diplomatic Protection of the ILA, and the resolutions of the Institut de droit international connected with State responsibility and diplomatic protection (eg the resolution adopted in 1965 on 'The National Character of an International Claim Presented by a State for Injury Suffered by an Individual', *AIDI, Resolutions 1957–1991* (1992) 55 ff), is not to be considered as involving official attempts at codification nor is comparable to such official attempts at codification.

7

The Clash of Interests in Diplomatic Protection

While the protection of aliens by their national States in one form or another may predate the eighteenth century, it was not until the time of Vattel that a clear attempt was made to explain diplomatic protection. In 1758 Vattel rationalized the position by stating that '*Quiconque maltraite un citoyen offense indirectement l'État, qui droit protéger ce citoyen*'.[1] He further explained that 'the sovereign of the injured citizen must avenge the deed and, if possible, force the aggressor to full satisfaction or punish him, since otherwise the citizen will not obtain the chief end of civil society, which is protection'.[2]

Although, as will be seen in Chapter 9, the duty of the national State to protect a national against the wrongdoing State has never been accepted as such, the principle that the right infringed in cases where an alien suffers illegal injury at the hands of a State is the right of the alien's national State and not the right of the alien himself, apparently deriving as it does from the theory that States alone are subjects of international law, has been recognized in several international judicial decisions. Starting with the *Mavrommatis Palestine Concessions Case,* the PCIJ stated that:

> It is an elementary principle of international law that a State is entitled to protect its nations, when injured by acts contrary to international law committed by another State, from whom they have been unable to obtain satisfaction through the ordinary channels. By taking up the case of one of its subjects and resorting to a diplomatic action or international judicial proceedings on his behalf, a State is in reality asserting its own rights—its right to ensure, in the person of its subjects, respect for the rules of international law.[3]

The point at issue in the case was whether the dispute, which originated in an injury to a national of the claimant State, was a dispute involving the Mandatory,

[1] *Le droit des gens* (1758), Book II, Section 71.

[2] *The Law of Nations or the Principles of Natural Law* (1758) in Fenwick (trans), *Classics of International Law* (1916) 136. Earlier, Grotius had written what appears to have foreshadowed Vattel's bold and outright formulation; *De Jure Belli ac Pacis* (1625), Book II, Chapter 17, para 20, and Chapter 21, para 2. However, it was not until Vattel that the particular formulation referred to here was articulated.

[3] (Jurisdiction), PCIJ Series A No 2, 12 (1924).

the defendant State, and another State member of the League of Nations for the purposes of Article 26 of the British Mandate over Palestine. It was held that the dispute in issue was such a dispute for the reasons stated, even though it arose from an injury to a private individual.

Later, in the *Panavezys-Saldutiskis Railway Case,* which concerned the expropriation of a concession given to an Estonian company by the Lithuanian Government, the PCIJ, in dealing with the preliminary objection based on the nationality of claims rule, confirmed this view stating that 'In the opinion of the Court, the rule of international law on which the first preliminary objection is based is that in taking up the case of one of its nationals, by resorting to diplomatic action in international judicial proceedings on his behalf, a State is in reality asserting its own right, the right to ensure in the person of its national respect for the rules of international law'.[4] In the *Serbian Loans Case,*[5] where the dispute arose from the failure to service certain loans taken by the Serbian government from French bondholders, and in the *Chorzów Factory Case,*[6] which concerned the expropriation of alien property, the same principle was held to be applicable. In the former case the application of the principle resulted in the finding that the dispute before the court was one between States. In the latter case the court applied the principle concluding that the damage caused the claimant State was not identical with that which its national had suffered, a consideration which was relevant to the calculation of damages.

The ICJ has also affirmed the principle in several cases. In the *Reparation Case,* it said of the rule inhering in the institution of diplomatic protection that such protection must be exercised by the national State of the alien:

> In the third place, the rule rests on two bases. The first is that the defendant State has broken an obligation towards the national State in respect of its nationals. The second is that only the party to whom an international obligation is due can bring a claim in respect of its breach.[7]

The principle was mentioned only incidentally in this case in the process of establishing another rule of international law, that international organizations too had rights of protection in respect of their officials in connection with the performance of their duties, such rights belonging to the organization and not to the official.[8] The principle was reaffirmed by the ICJ in the *Nottebohm Case,*[9] where limitations were placed upon the link of nationality between the individual and

[4] PCIJ Series A/B No 76, 16 (1938).
[5] PCIJ Series A No 20 (1929).
[6] Merits, PCIJ Series A No 17 (1928).
[7] 1949 ICJ Reports 181.
[8] See also Judge Badawi in a Dissenting Opinion: 1949 ICJ Reports 206. Judge Badawi expressly stated that the national State of the alien does not assert a claim as a '*répresantant legal de la victime*' and thus defends not the right of the alien on his behalf but its own right.
[9] 1955 ICJ Reports 24.

his national State, and implicitly in the *Barcelona Traction Co Case,*[10] where again the application of the nationality of claims rule was in issue.

There are several decisions of other international tribunals in which the principle has been recognized. Thus, in *Administrative Decision No. V* of the US-German Claims Commission it was stated that 'the nation is injured through injury to its national and it alone may demand reparation'.[11]

These cases cover injuries arising from the alleged violation of customary international law as well as of treaties involving obligations undertaken vis-à-vis aliens. There is no reason to distinguish between customary international law and treaties with regard to the basic principle, that it is the right of the alien's national State that is infringed when an injury is done to an alien per se as a result of which diplomatic protection is exercised. It would be incorrect, therefore, to say that, where the substantive obligation is contained in a treaty the corresponding right is that of the national State, whereas in the case of an obligation under customary international law, the right is enjoyed not by the national State but by the alien himself.

The principle is also supported by opinions expressed by State legal advisers and in official correspondence. Thus in 1912 the Solicitor for the Department of State of the US said, 'It should, in the first place, be observed that by espousing a claim of its national for injuries inflicted by a foreign government the espousing government makes the claim its own'.[12] In the *Finnish Ships Arbitration* the UK government espoused the same view of diplomatic protection.[13] Many rapporteurs and draft codifications have unhesitatingly conceded that this principle underlies the doctrine of diplomatic protection.[14]

There has been a growing dissatisfaction with this avowed basis of the law of diplomatic protection. Not only has it been attacked because of the purely logical inconsistencies the present law on the subject reveals, but it has been severely criticized by legal commentators on the ground that it is incompatible with the modern conception of fundamental human rights and freedoms.[15]

[10] 1970 ICJ Reports 4. See also the *Interhandel Case,* 1959 ICJ Reports 27, where it was said that the applicant State adopted the cause of its national.

[11] US v Germany, 7 UNRIAA 140 (1924), per Umpire Parker. See also *Administrative Decision No. II* (US v Germany), 7 UNRIAA 26 (1923); the *Finnish Ships Arbitration* (Finland v Great Britain), 3 UNRIAA 1485 (1934); the *Spanish Zone of Morocco Case* (Great Britain v Spain), 2 UNRIAA 640 (1923); and the *Dickson Car Wheel Co Claim* (US v Mexico), 4 UNRIAA 678 (1931).

[12] Hackworth, 5 *Digest,* 488. See also the letter of Secretary of State Frelinghuysen of 11 February 1884, Moore, 6 *International Law* 616.

[13] *Finnish Ships Arbitration* (Finland v Great Britain), 3 UNRIAA 1485 (1934).

[14] García Amador, 'First Report on State Responsibility', 2 YBILC (1956) 192; the Guerrero Report adopted by the Sub-Committee of the League of Nations Committee of Experts, 2 YBILC (1956), Annex 1, 222; the Harvard Draft Convention of 1961, 2 YBILC (1956), Annex 9, 229; now Dugard, 'First Report on Diplomatic Protection' (ILC), UN Doc A/CN.4/506 5 ff, and Article 1 of the Draft Articles of the ILC on Diplomatic Protection and commentary on that Article, para 3.

[15] O'Connell, 2 *International Law* (1970) 1115; and García Amador (note 14 above) 199 ff.

While the basic principle must be recognized, and it is evident that many consequences which have been reflected in the current law of diplomatic protection flow from it, the law, as it has developed, has taken into account a variety of interests, thus confirming my view that the law is the result of compromises or of choices made from among the competing interests on the basis of different policies. It cannot be denied that the interests of the alien's national State (which owns the right involved as a complainant) and those of the host State (which is under the obligation as a defendant, in respect of the alien, as a result of the right-duty relationship between those two entities) are not the only interests which have shaped the current law. Although the formal incidence of rights and obligations may be established for the current law, the law has been shaped also by the influence of other conflicting interests involved. This factor is of importance in discussing particularly the role of nationality in diplomatic protection. For this reason, a brief overview of how the different interests have affected some of the rules relating to the law of diplomatic protection is given here.

The State of Nationality

The interests of the national State have been responsible for certain important and well-established rules in the law of diplomatic protection. Some examples are given here.

(i) The rule that the injured alien must have the nationality of the claimant State at the time of the injury[16] flows from account being taken of the national State's interest. Nationality at the time of the injury is the bond which creates rights in respect of the individual at international law. The modification introduced by the *Nottebohm Case*,[17] which in a certain limited circumstance required a genuine link between alien and national States, may also in a way be explained by reference to the genuine interest of the claimant State.

(ii) There is a rule that a Calvo Clause, which is an agreement between host State and alien by which the alien agrees not to seek the protection of his national State in the event of an injury suffered at the hands of the host State, does not have the unqualified effect of depriving the national State of the alien of its right of applying international remedies to violations of international law committed in respect of the alien.[18] This rule can only stem from the idea that the interests affected when an alien is injured are those of his national State.

[16] See the *Panavezys-Saldutiskis Railway Case*, PCIJ Series A/B No 76 (1938); the *Reparation Case*, 1949 ICJ Reports 181; the *Nottebohm Case*, 1955 ICJ Reports 23; Hyde, 2 *International Law* (1945), 893; O'Connell, (note 15 above) 1116 and the authorities there cited at note 17.

[17] 1955 ICJ Reports 4.

[18] The *North American Dredging Co Case* (US v Mexico), 4 UNRIAA 29 (1926); Shea, *The Calvo Clause* (1955) 217; Hyde (note 16 above) 994; O'Connell, (note 15 above) 1151.

(iii) It is an accepted rule that the damage for which reparation must be made is the damage to the alien's national State which is not identical with that which its national has suffered, so that the reparation ordered in a given case need not be simply equivalent to the loss suffered by the alien.[19] This rule also reflects consideration of the interests of the national State.

(iv) The reason that the national State has complete control over the disposition of the proceeds of a claim and is not even obliged to hand them on to the individual whose claim it has espoused[20] is that the claim has a public character based on the interests of the national State.

(v) The rule that the national State may waive, compromise or discontinue the presentation of the claim irrespective of the wishes of the alien[21] is also derived from the same interests.

(vi) That the alien may appear as a claimant in proceedings against the host State, resulting from an injury to him, only with the agreement of his national State, also reflects concern for the interests of the national State.

(vii) Multiple claims may be instituted by national States, where the alien has more than one nationality other than that of the defendant State. This is a recognition that the interests of all national States *qua* national States are protected, regardless of other considerations.

Such rules, which reflect the basic principle that the State does not appear as a representative or on behalf of the alien whose claim it espouses, but defends its own rights, are designed directly to protect the interest of the national State of the alien which alone may assert a claim.

The Defendant State

Some of the rules applicable in the area of diplomatic protection are designed to protect the interests of the defendant State. The interests of the defendant State must naturally and legitimately be considered, as opposed to the interests of the claimant State. A few examples which demonstrate this position are given here:

(i) The rule, as it was, that the alien must not have the nationality of the defendant State both at the time of injury and continuously up to the time of the

[19] The *Chorzów Factory Case (Merits)*, PCIJ Series A No 17, 28 (1928).

[20] *Frelinghuysen v US ex rel. Key,* 110 US 63 (1884); *US ex rel. Boynton v Blaine,* 139 US 306 (1891); *Heirs of Oswald v Swiss Government,* 3 AD (1925–6) 244; *US v La Abra Silver Mining Co Case,* 175 US 423 (1899); *Great Western Insurance Co v US,* 19 Ct.Cl. 206 (1884); Hackworth, (note 12 above) 763 ff; and Feller, *The Mexican Claims Commissions* (1935) 84 and the authorities there cited at note 6. In *Administrative Decision No V* (US v Germany), 7 UNRIAA 152 (1924), the Umpire recognized this rule, while stating that in reality States distribute the proceeds of awards on the basis that the interests of individuals are involved.

[21] Moore, (note 12 above) 1012 ff; Borchard, *The Diplomatic Protection of Citizens Abroad* (1915) 366 ff; Whiteman, 1 *Damages in International Law* (1937), 282.

award,[22] is a concession to the defendant State. Even though the alien may be a national of the defendant State at the relevant time, there is technically a violation of the right of the other State whose nationality the alien enjoys.

(ii) The rule that local remedies must be exhausted before an international claim may be espoused recognizes the defendant State's interest, by affording such State the opportunity to redress the initial wrong committed. If the substantive rights of the alien's national State are violated, it is logically that State which must have the right to pursue immediately a claim against the defendant State, whether at the national, diplomatic, or international judicial level. The fact that the defendant State is given an opportunity to redress the wrong through its own judicial facilities which the alien must first exhaust reflects a concession to the interests of the defendant State.

(iii) In general, where a choice of interest is made between a defendant which is a national State and other national States in favour of the former, the policy behind that choice is the protection of the interests of the defendant State.[23]

(iv) Where multiple claims may be instituted by national States which do not include the defendant State, it is an accepted proposition that there cannot be more than a single recovery of damages or compensation. This is a recognition of the defendant State's interests in not being penalized more than once, though technically and logically each national State has suffered an injury and merits being compensated.

(v) The practice of dispute settlement by resort to Claims Commissions and arbitral bodies, before which aliens have standing to bring claims themselves on the understanding that it is only the injury to them that will be compensated and not the total injury to the alien's national State, also to some extent puts the interests of the defendant State before those of the national State. The national State qua national State is not given complete recognition, or the best interests of the alien in having multiple sources of protection are overlooked in favour of other interests, although in certain cases the rules purport to give the alien the best protection possible through a single source.

The Injured Alien

Certain rules relating to diplomatic protection that have evolved and been applied in practice display an approach which stresses the important position of

[22] Jessup, *A Modern Law of Nations* (1956) 100; and Van Panhuys, *The Role of Nationality in International Law* (1959) 73 ff. The exact rule has been the subject of discussion, although what is reflected above seems to be the better view. See also *Award No. 31-157-2*, 2 Iran-US CTR 160 ff (1983), where the rule was rejected. For a discussion of this rule, see below. Dugard, 'First Report on Diplomatic Protection' (ILC), UN Doc A/CN.4/506, 44 ff, proposes a change in this rule for codification and development on the basis of effective and dominant nationality. It is possible to disagree with his reasoning.

[23] See the discussion below in Chapter 10 of the nationality rules.

the individual in this context. They can only be explained on the premise that the law is basically interested in protecting the rights and interests of aliens themselves. In such cases, the law has not paid much attention to the principle that the right infringed is that of the national State. In a sense the law is interested in protecting directly the basic human rights of aliens:

(i) There are certain exceptions to the rule that the alien must have the nationality of the claimant State at the time of the injury. It is possible that a State may espouse the claim of an alien who is not its national as a result of an agreement made before or after the injury with the defendant State. In the same way, aliens may be under the special protection of a State, generally with the agreement of the host State, although they are not nationals of the former State.[24] In these cases, it cannot be said that the law merely protects the rights of a particular State. Some allowance is being made for the protection of the rights of aliens through representation.

(ii) The exception to the application of the local remedies rule that the alien must not be caused undue hardship in exhausting local remedies recognizes the interests of the alien.[25]

(iii) The injury suffered by the alien is used as a scale for the calculation of damages. Although the ultimate reparation may involve more than the actual loss to the alien,[26] the damage suffered by the alien is the basis for the award of reparation. Such damages awarded may include both damages for material loss and for moral injury suffered by the alien. Although the economic assets of an individual may, by a fiction, be regarded as part of the wealth of his national State, international law does not really treat such assets as being actually the property of the national State. As regards damage through personal injury including moral suffering, it would be difficult to regard the national State as having suffered such damage even by a legal fiction. Thus, it is clear that the law is here paying heed to the interest of the alien rather than that of his national State.

Such rules, and some of the rules already discussed above, demonstrate that international law recognizes also the nature of the claim as a private claim belonging to the alien, in contradistinction to the recognition given to the public nature of the claim, which has been asserted to be the real basis of diplomatic protection.

[24] The *Reparation Case,* 1949 ICJ Reports 181.

[25] See C F Amerasinghe, *Local Remedies in International Law* (2004) 200 ff, particularly 203. The rule of local remedies itself recognized the host State's interests. Some Articles on the rule, formulated for the ILC, are discussed in Dugard, 'Second Report on Diplomatic Protection', UN Doc A/CN.4/506 (2001) and Dugard, 'Third Report on Diplomatic Protection', A/CN.4/523 (2002). On the rule in general see C F Amerasinghe.

[26] See the *Chorzów Factory Case (Merits),* PCIJ Series A No 17 28 (1928).

Choices Among Competing Interests

The evolution of the rules relating to diplomatic protection shows that logic has taken a second place and the competing interests involved have been taken into account and one or the other of them has been given recognition, so much that, while a place has been given to the basic principle that it is the right of the alien's national State that lies at the heart of the institution of diplomatic protection as it has developed, other interests have also been considered in the formulation, based on distinct policies, of some of the applicable rules. In particular, the interests of the injured alien have not been ignored, although it has often been stated that formally it is not the alien's rights that have been violated but those of his national State. The fact that the alien is per se involved in the situation has resulted in the formation of certain rules. Moreover, the interests of the host State (the defendant) have sometimes been given preference as opposed to the formal rights of the national State or the interests of the alien. Competition among these interests has been resolved in practice in relation to specific rules by choices in favour of one or the other, without any apparent order or scheme referable to a hierarchy of social policy values. Pragmatism, apparently, has governed. Thus, it is not possible to assert with any conclusiveness that one or the other of these interests is necessarily superior to any of the others. According to the traditional view, the interests of the national State of the alien generally or primarily provide the framework on which the law of diplomatic protection is built, and this is the formal mould in which the law is cast, although it may not be proper to describe it as the sole basis of the law of diplomatic protection.

The interests of the alien and of the host State are strong elements in determining the precise content of certain rules, so that they too merit consideration as a material basis of the law of diplomatic protection. In the event of competition among the various interests in an area where the rules are not clear, as noted above, it is difficult categorically to state which might or should be given preference, although it may be possible to assert that the formal structure of the law of diplomatic protection, resting as it does on the interests of the injured national State, may be given a prominent position in determining the result. However, the criticism may be cogent that the interests of the injured alien should be given particular recognition, especially in the context of modern developments in the law of human rights which are the result of increased concern for the protection of the individual. In the final analysis, as a matter of substance, the institution of diplomatic protection relates basically to a conflict situation involving host State and aliens, although formally the mould in which the law is cast may be limited to a relationship between two sovereign States. The fact that particularly the interests of the alien have shared in shaping the law demonstrates that the formal basis of the law has not always determined the direction of the law. However, the interests of the host or defendant State have called for recognition in addition to those of the injured alien. It may also be noted at this point that development of the law of diplomatic protection, whether for the purpose of codification or otherwise, especially by the ILC, tends rightly to take the form of raising the level of recognition given to the interests of the injured alien in securing international protection.[27] The comment may be made, however, that it is a mistake to ignore, to the extent of erasing, the relevance of the interests of the respondent State. To do so undermines one of the underpinnings of the institution of diplomatic protection. A much more balanced approach is required.

The argument has been made that on account of the development of the law relating to human rights protection, the focus of the law of diplomatic protection as a remedial process has changed and gives a distinct priority to the interests of the injured alien. There are available to him remedial procedures which will enable him to secure the protection of his substantive rights in respect of treatment as an alien which are now tantamount to human rights recognized as flowing from customary rules of international law or general principles of law.[28] A consequence of this view is that the interests of the alien in securing protection for the violation of substantive rights, even though these constructively belong to his national State, merit recognition in every situation to the exclusion of the interest of the respondent or host State. While there is no evidence that the current international law has adopted this stance, it is possible, as pointed out earlier, that the interests of the alien, because of the substantive human rights factor, have been given an *important* place—though not in total priority—in the development of the law of diplomatic protection which relates to remedial procedures. On the other hand, there has not been a complete disregard of the interests of the respondent State. It may be suggested that for the future the important place given now to the interests of the alien as an individual, and not merely as an alien, should not be disregarded in the development of the law of diplomatic protection. Indeed, as will be seen later, a measure of development of the law may be recommended by recognizing that the alien's rights as well as the national State's rights are infringed, where injuries are inflicted on him in violation of international law, so that he personally has the right to a remedy.

It is also doubtful whether it is appropriate that the interests of the host or respondent State should be eclipsed. Rather is it desirable that a suitable balance be found between the two sets of interests when in given circumstances there is a conflict between the two. Even in the systems of human rights protection, the development and application of the rule of local remedies, for example, has

[27] Some of the rulings of the Iran-US Claims tribunal show a tendency to take further account of the relationship between the alien and the host State and consequently to value more the interests of the alien; see *Award No. 31-157-2*, 2 Iran-US CTR 160 ff (1983). In these decisions, the role played by the interests of the national State of the alien seems to be under-emphasized, although formally the dispute settlement machinery was set in motion by an agreement between the host State and the national State of the aliens and was in essence in the exercise of diplomatic protection.

[28] Dugard in his reports to the ILC stresses this human rights aspect of diplomatic protection. There are others who do the same.

been based on appreciable recognition being given to the interests of the host or respondent State.[29] It is thus not a good argument to say as an outright policy goal that at all costs the alien's resort to an international forum, with or without the intervention of his national State, must be facilitated and encouraged, whether what is in issue is the application of, for example, the rule of local remedies, the nationality rules, or the clean hands doctrine. To hold otherwise would change the whole character of the institution of diplomatic protection. It is a different matter to view as obsolete and ready to be replaced by a different remedial procedure the institution of diplomatic protection as currently structured. On the other hand, the fact is that in the present state of the international legal system the institution of diplomatic protection as it is being developed does afford valuable protection for aliens in the absence of universal procedures for the enforcement of human rights as such.

The International Community

Finally, it would be unwise and improper to overlook the fact that the international community has a residual interest in having disputes involving States and aliens settled without escalation. This interest is not a dominant one, though. It could, however, for instance, have had an influence on the current development of the local remedies rule with the exceptions that have been recognized in its application. In a sense this interest may be largely nebulous but its relevance may need to be kept in mind, if only residually. At the same time it must be emphasized that it is not as important as the other interests involved in situations where diplomatic protection may be exercised.

[29] See C F Amerasinghe (note 25 above) 203 ff.

8

The Human Rights Factor—The Claimed Obsolescence of Diplomatic Protection

In the post-Second World War period there have been significant changes not only in international life and society but in international law's approach to the individual. The human rights of the individual not only in the civil and political areas but also in the social and economic fields have come to be regarded as important. While more than 150 of some 190-odd States are today parties to human rights conventions of one kind or another, in some cases the individual, whether alien or national, may bring complaints about the violation of his human rights to the attention of international bodies such as the United Nations Human Rights Committee, the European Court of Human Rights, the Inter-American Court of Human Rights, and the African Commission on Human and Peoples' Rights.

The relevance of the modern recognition of the human rights of the individual is twofold. First, the emergence of this recognition both under the UN Charter provisions and through conventions has caused questions to be raised about the need for the institution of diplomatic protection in respect of aliens. The argument is that aliens, like any other individual, can resort to the protection given to them under the Charter and human rights conventions and do not need the institution of diplomatic protection. Second, the question may be asked whether the substantive law on State responsibility for injuries to aliens has come under the influence of the development of human rights standards so that the content of the international minimum standard for the treatment of aliens, which relates to primary rights and duties, has been upgraded.

The second question, which may very well have to be answered in the affirmative, strictly does not concern the institution of diplomatic protection, which consists of a remedial procedure. Modern developments, both under conventional and customary law, in human rights do point towards an upgrading of the rights of aliens. However, these concern primary rights and not remedial procedures.

The first issue does concern diplomatic protection as a remedial procedure and is dealt with here. The developments, particularly the human rights treaties, have led some to argue that diplomatic protection is obsolete: the equality-of-treatment-with-nationals-standard and the international minimum standard of treatment of aliens, it is said, have been replaced by an international human rights standard, which accords to national and alien the same standard of treatment—a standard incorporating the core provisions of the Universal Declaration of Human Rights; the individual is now a subject of international law with standing to enforce his or her human rights at the international level; the right of a State to claim on behalf of its national should be restricted to cases where there is no other method of settlement agreed on by the alien and the injuring State; in such a case the claimant State acts as agent for the individual and not in its own right; and the right of a State to assert its own right when it acts on behalf of its national is an outdated fiction which should be discarded—except, perhaps, in cases in which the real *national* interest of the State is affected.[1]

In passing, it may be observed that in any case, to rely on the argument that an institution which is based on a fiction should be dismissed simply because it is based on a fiction, is a mistake. An institution like diplomatic protection which serves a purpose is not to be dismissed simply on the ground that it is premised on a fiction and cannot stand up to logical scrutiny. Most legal systems have fictions. Moreover, diplomatic protection, it will be seen, rather recognizes a mixture of interests and is not based on fictions as such.[2]

The suggestion that developments in the field of international human rights law of a procedural nature have rendered diplomatic protection obsolete, on the other hand, is more serious. The first Special Rapporteur of the International Law Commission on the subject of State responsibility, stated that the traditional view of diplomatic protection that allowed the State to claim on behalf of its injured national belongs to an age in which the rights of the individual and the rights of the State were inseparable and that now the position is completely different. He argued that aliens, like nationals, enjoy rights simply as human beings and not by virtue of their nationality, and concluded that the alien had been internationally recognized as a legal person, independently of his State, and was a true subject of international rights.[3] A necessary implication of this reasoning is that the individual, now a subject of international law, with rights and duties under international law, should, other than in exceptional cases, look after himself when he ventures abroad.

It may be that the individual has in certain circumstances become a subject of international law with rights recognized by the law as a consequence of being endowed with these rights by States under customary or conventional law. But it is also true that, while the individual may have rights as a subject under

[1] García Amador, 'State Responsibility. Some New Problems' (1958 II) 94 Hague Receuil 437–9, 472; García Amador, 'Second Report to the ILC', 2 YBILC (1957) 112–16. Bennouna, 'Preliminary Report on Diplomatic Protection', UN Doc A/CN.4/484, paras 34–7, also advances an argument based on the existence of human rights mechanisms.

[2] Furthermore, the life of the law is not logic, perhaps, but experience. For this idea see Holmes, 'The Path of the Law', 10 Harvard Law Review (1897) 476 ff.

[3] García Amador (note 1 above), Hague Receuil 421.

international law, his remedies are limited and this is of significant importance. While the European Convention on Human Rights may offer real remedies to many Europeans and those in European states, it is difficult to accept the argument that the American Convention on Human Rights or the African Charter on Human and Peoples' Rights have achieved the same degree of success. Moreover, the majority of the world's population, situated in Asia, is not covered by a regional human rights convention. To observe that universal human rights conventions, particularly the International Covenant and Political Rights, provide individuals with effective remedies for the protection of their human rights is inaccurate. Only a few individuals in the limited number of States which accept the right of individual petition to the monitoring bodies of these conventions have obtained or will obtain satisfactory remedies from these conventions. Universal and regional human rights conventions do extend protection to all individuals—national and alien alike—within the territory of States parties. But there is no multilateral convention that seeks to provide the alien with remedies for the protection of his rights, though in the field of foreign investment alone the multilateral ICSID Convention may to some extent do so.

It is observed that the GA of the UN adopted in 1985 the Declaration on the Human Rights of Individuals Who are not Nationals of the Country in which They Live.[4] This instrument expressly sought to extend the rights contained in the Universal Declaration of Human rights to aliens. That was a substantive matter. But the Declaration provided no machinery for its enforcement. On the other hand, it reiterated the right of the alien to get in touch with his consulate or diplomatic mission for the purpose of protection. Thus, it was recognized that the institution of diplomatic protection not only survived but was largely a remedial process relating to secondary rights and obligations. The current position is that aliens as individuals have practically no remedies under international law, in the absence of a human rights treaty, except through the intervention of their national States.

A development conceivably concerned with the relevance and survival of diplomatic protection as an institution in the modern era of human rights protection was the formulation of the International Convention on the Protection of the Rights of All Migrant Workers and Members of their Families[5] which was adopted in 1991 by the GA of the UN. The convention sought to establish a Charter of rights for migrant workers. There was a provision for a monitoring body similar to the UN Human Rights Committee and for an optional right of individual petition. That this institution of protection did not replace the rights of diplomatic protection was emphasized by Article 23, which provided that 'Migrant workers and members of their families shall have the right to have

[4] General Assembly Resolution 40/144, annex.

[5] See General Assembly Resolution 45/158, 30 ILM (1991) 1517. On this Convention see Cholewinski, *Migrant Workers in International Human Rights Law* (1997).

recourse to the protection and assistance of the consular or diplomatic authorities of their State of origin or of a State representing the interests of that State whenever the rights recognized in the Present Convention are impaired…'. This Convention has not yet been brought into force by the required number of ratifications, which, moreover, suggests that States are not ready to extend special and individual remedial rights to migrant workers. Further, a point of importance is that the right of workers to seek diplomatic protection from their national States was expressly left untouched.

It is important to recognize that at any given point in time, even though the formal mould of diplomatic protection was and is a relationship between States, the true essence of the law of diplomatic protection was and is substantively regard for the interests of individuals. This is so, although the category of individuals is restricted essentially to those with an alien nationality, excluding in principle the nationals of the defendant State. State practice, international case law, and legal commentators have not articulated this truth as such, but may have explained, when given a chance, the foundations of the rule in a more limited manner. Moreover, while in the past the substantive rights of the individual which were respected may have been limited in comparison to what modern human rights conventional (and, perhaps, customary) law now protects, the law of diplomatic protection was based on the notion that in effect the interests (and, in reality, the rights) of the individual deserved and required protection. In a sense, there was in diplomatic protection an incipient law of human rights protection. The basic concerns in the two areas are really very similar,[6] although legal articulation of those concerns in the law of diplomatic protection may have been different and in a manner indirect and rudimentary.

This recognition of human rights as deserving protection which was not articulated in this way, however, is not related in any direct way to the growth of modern human rights law which is conceivably broader both substantively and procedurally. On the substantive side, modern human rights law, which grew in the latter half of the twentieth century, may influence the content of the substantive rights (or interests) of aliens determined by an international minimum standard which is the basis for such rights in the law relating to the treatment of aliens. Yet, clearly, the awareness of the need to respect the (human) rights or interests of individuals (in the persons of aliens only) long pre-dated the modern law of human rights. Nor was it connected particularly with the interaction between developed and developing States which can be traced fully to the post-Second World War era, even though Latin American States were involved in the application of the law in the nineteenth century.

[6] This point was made systematically for the first time in history by me in 1967 in my *State Responsibility for Injuries to Aliens* (1967) 11 ff. García Amador had touched on the matter of human rights protection in (note 1 above), Hague Receuil, and 2 YBILC (note 1 above) but only to use it as a means to dismissing diplomatic protection as superfluous. There was a difference in his observations on the relevance of human rights.

It would, therefore, be wrong to deny or gloss over the essential similarity, unarticulated though it was, of the fundamental purpose and basis of the law of diplomatic protection and modern human rights law. At the same time, it is necessary to recognize that the practical approach to both the substantive and the remedial aspects of human rights protection, which has derived in one way or another from conventional instruments, may be different from that taken to such aspects in the law of diplomatic protection as such, regardless of some similarity of purpose and basis.

Substantively, international human rights law does not consist of human rights conventions only. In fact there is a whole body of conventions and customs, including the remedial institution of diplomatic protection, that together comprise international human rights law. The International Covenant on Civil and Political Rights, the European Convention on Human Rights, the American Convention on Human Rights, the African Charter on Human and Peoples' Rights and other universal and regional human rights instruments are important, particularly as they extend protection to both alien and national in the territory of States parties.[7] But the remedies in most of these instruments are weak. Diplomatic protection, only available to protect individuals against a foreign State on the other hand, is based on customary rules of international law which apply universally and, potentially, offer a very effective remedy. It is possible that States in general may treat a claim of diplomatic protection from another State more seriously than an individual's complaint against its conduct to a human rights monitoring body.[8]

Contemporary international human rights law accords to nationals and aliens the same protection which may, on the one hand, now exceed the international minimum standard of treatment for aliens set by western powers in an earlier era. But it does not follow that these developments have rendered obsolete the traditional procedures recognized by customary law in connection with the treatment of aliens.[9] Although individuals today enjoy more international remedies for the protection of their rights than before, diplomatic protection remains an important remedial procedure for what is in reality now the protection of human rights. As long as the State remains the dominant actor in international relations, the espousal of claims by States for the violation of the rights of their nationals

[7] For example, Article 2(1) of the International Covenant on Civil and Political Rights requires parties 'to respect and to ensure to all individuals within its territory' the rights recognized in the Covenant. See, also Article 1 of the European Convention on Human Rights; Article 2 of the African Charter on Human and Peoples Rights.

[8] A complaint from an individual under the European Convention on Human Rights backed by a foreign government is likewise likely to carry more weight: see *Soering v UK,* ECHR Series A, No 161 (1989) (West Germany intervening); *Selmouni v France,* Application No 25803/94, Judgement of 28 July 1999 (Netherlands intervening); *Denmark v Turkey,* Application No 34382/97, Judgement of 8 June 1999.

[9] In the *Barcelona Traction Co Case,* 1970 ICJ Reports 165, Judge Jessup said: 'The institution of the right of diplomatic protection is surely not obsolete although new procedures are emerging.'

remains a most effective remedy for the protection of human rights,[10] though the area affected may be limited. The crux of the matter is that, as the substantive and procedural law now stands in the international legal system and considering the present state of international society, it would be foolhardy to abandon the institution of diplomatic protection. As has been said,

> It cannot be denied, . . . , that diplomatic protection has always been abused, and that the stronger States are in a better position in the performance of diplomatic protection. Thus, the fault lies primarily in too harsh practices and not in the institution itself. . .
>
> As far as human rights are developed and strengthened, diplomatic protection may lose some of its significance. However, human rights will probably not be able to supersede diplomatic protection in its entirety.
>
> As long as diplomatic protection cannot be replaced by any better remedies, it is necessary to keep it, because it is badly needed, and its advantages outweigh its disadvantages in any case.[11]

The acid test for the recognition of diplomatic protection as a useful and viable institution may be whether, where a human rights remedial procedure is also available, an injured alien would rather appeal to his national State for diplomatic protection. There is no clear answer in the abstract to this question. That the availability of alternative or cumulative remedies gives the alien greater protection, however, must be and is generally conceded. The practice in the human rights area is not to deny the existence of a remedy through diplomatic protection, even though an alternative remedy through human rights procedures is available.

[10] For the ideas in the above two paragraphs with which I agree see Dugard, 'First Report on Diplomatic Protection' (ILC), UN Doc A/CN.4/506, 5 ff.

[11] See Przetacznik, 'The Protection of Individual Persons in Traditional International Law (Diplomatic and Consular Protection)', 21 ÖZÖR (1971) 113.

9

A Duty to Protect?

As already pointed out, in 1758 Vattel rationalized diplomatic protection by stating that, 'Whoever ill-treats a citizen indirectly injures the State, which must protect that citizen'.[1] He further explained that 'the sovereign of the injured citizen must avenge the deed and, if possible, force the aggressor to full satisfaction or punish him, since otherwise the citizen will not obtain the chief end of civilized society, which is protection'.[2]

Vattel's thesis not only asserted the rights of the national State of the alien to protect its national, but implied that there was an obligation resting upon the alien's national State to protect him. Vattel conceived of the right of protection as inhering in the national State of the alien and did not envisage the injury done to the alien as creating any right vesting in the alien at international law to a remedy *from* the host State. A consequence was that the injury done to the alien was regarded as being a violation of an obligation owed by the host State to the alien's national State. Formally, this explanation was the result of the theory that the individual had no rights at international law.[3] On the other hand, it is not clear what Vattel meant by the duty to protect a national abroad which he stated rested upon the national State of the alien. Assuming he was correct in postulating a duty of protection—and this is not certain in the light of subsequent developments in diplomatic protection, the practice of reprisals prior to his time, and the practice of diplomatic protection even during his time—a question to be answered is to whom was the duty owed, particularly if the alien as an individual had no rights recognized by international law. Vattel did not venture to answer this question, nor was the issue seriously faced by the authorities who

[1] *The Law of Nations or the Principles of Natural Law* (1758), Book II, Section 71, in Fenwick (trans), *Classics of International Law* (1916) 136.

[2] Ibid 136. Earlier, Grotius had written what appears to have foreshadowed Vattel's bold and outright formulation: *De Jure Belli ac Pacis* (1625), Book II, Chapter 17, para 20, and Chapter 21, para 2. However, it was not until Vattel that the particular formulation referred to here was articulated.

[3] This theory was supported by GF Martens, for instance, in the early nineteenth century in 1 *Précis du droit des gens moderne de l'Europe* (1831) 224 ff. In the latter half of the nineteenth century and in the early twentieth century, writers such as Pradière-Fodéré, Calvo, Tcharnoff, Triepel, Moore, Anzilotti, Hallek, Phillimore, Wheaton, Arias, and Oppenheim threw in their support for this view. Later, Fauchille, Holland, Borchard, Décencière-Ferrandière, Eagleton, Dunn, Freeman, Ralston, Brierly, and García Amador, for example, made the same assumption in dealing with diplomatic protection.

followed him. However, the right and duty of States to protect their nationals abroad against a host State was strongly asserted later, in discussing diplomatic protection, by legal commentators, among them Fauchille,[4] Oppenheim,[5] and Holland.[6]

Be that as it may, later and now, the accepted doctrine of diplomatic protection gives a State the right to protect its national but does not place it under an obligation to do so. Consequently, the national of the State which has suffered injury abroad has no right to diplomatic protection under international law. Borchard made the position clear, stating in 1915 that:

> Many writers consider diplomatic protection a duty of the State, as well as a right. If it is a duty internationally, it is only a moral and not a legal duty, for there is no means of enforcing its fulfillment. Inasmuch as the State may determine in its discretion whether the injury to the citizen is sufficiently serious to warrant or whether political expediency justifies the exercise of the protective forces of the collective in his behalf—for the interests of the majority cannot be sacrificed—it is clear that at international law there is no legal duty incumbent upon the State to extend diplomatic protection. Whether such a duty exists towards the citizen is a matter of municipal law of his own country, the general law being that even under municipal law the State is under no legal duty to extend diplomatic protection.[7]

He further made it clear that the injured individual (national) had no rights, which meant that the State did not owe him a duty of protection in international law:

> It is hardly correct... to speak of the citizen's power to invoke the diplomatic protection of the Government as a 'right' of protection.... At best, therefore, it is an imperfect right... Being devoid of any compulsion, it resolves itself merely into a privilege to ask for protection. Such duty of protection as the Government may be assumed to owe to the citizen in such cases is a political and not a legal one, responsibility for the proper execution of which is incurred to the people as a whole, and not to the citizen as an individual.[8]

This position was approved most importantly by the ICJ in the *Barcelona Traction Case* in 1970, where it stated that:

> within the limits prescribed by international law, a State may exercise diplomatic protection by whatever means and to whatever extent it sees fit, for it is its own right that the State is asserting. Should the national or legal person on whose behalf it is acting consider that their rights are not adequately protected, they have no remedy in international law. All they can do is resort to international law, if means are available, with a view to furthering their cause or obtaining redress...

[4] *Traité de droit international public* (1922), Part I, 884 and 922 ff.

[5] *International Law* (1905) 375 ff.

[6] *Lectures on International Law* (1933) 165 ff.

[7] Borchard, *The Diplomatic Protection of Citizens Abroad* (11915) 29. The writers cited by Borchard include Grotius and Vattel.

[8] Ibid. 356.

The State must be viewed as the sole judge to decide whether its protection will be granted, and to what extent it is granted, and when it will cease. It retains in this respect a discretionary power the exercise of which may be determined by considerations of a political or other nature, unrelated to the particular case.[9]

The rapporteur of the ILC on diplomatic protection made an analysis which revealed a body of evidence which he interpreted as showing that the law was moving in a different direction.[10] Most writers now accept the traditional position[11] although there has been some opposition to it. C de Visscher, for example, stated that 'the absolute discretion left to the State in the exercise of protection goes ill with the principle that the treatment due to aliens is a matter of international law'.[12]

While diplomatic protection may be seen as a means for the furtherance of the international protection of human rights, it is not possible to describe diplomatic protection as an individual human right. Two human rights instruments concerned with the right of aliens support this view. The 1985 United Nations General Assembly Declaration on the Human Rights of Individuals Who are not Nationals of the Country in Which They Live[13] and the 1991 International Convention on the Protection of the Rights of All Migrant Workers and Members of their Families[14] both affirm the right of the alien to have recourse to his diplomatic or consular mission for protection but place no explicit duty on the State of nationality to protect him.[15]

Recent discussions in the Sixth Committee of the GA illustrate the divergence of views on this issue. Most speakers[16] considered that the decision whether or not to exercise diplomatic protection was the sovereign prerogative of the State with

[9] 1970 ICJ Reports 44. The UK Court of Appeal, citing the *Barcelona Traction Co Case,* has acknowledged that international law did not impose a *duty* upon a State to exercise diplomatic protection in respect of 'a citizen who is suffering or threatened with an injury in a foreign State': the *Abbasi Case* [2002], 42 ILM (2003) 375.

[10] Dugard, 'First Report on Diplomatic Protection', UN Doc A/CN.4/506, 28 ff. Dugard's report provides very useful material on the subject of this chapter. I have relied on it extensively here for the source material.

[11] Greig, *International Law* (1976) 523; Geck, 'Diplomatic Protection', 1 EPIL (1992) 1059–60; Jennings and Watts (eds), 1 *Oppenheim's International Law* (1992) 427; and references therein.

[12] *Theory and Reality in Public International Law* (1957) 275. See also Orrego Vicuna, 'The Changing Law of Nationality of Claims' in ILA, Report of the Sixth-ninth Conference (2000) 646.

[13] Article 10, GA Rs 40/144, Annex.

[14] Article 23, 30 ILM (1991) 1517.

[15] See also for this view of protection, Skubiszewski, 'Introduction' in Lauterpacht and Collier (eds), *Individual Rights and the State in Foreign Affairs* (1977) 10; Warbrick, 'Protection of Nationals Abroad: Current Legal Problems', 37 *ICLQ* (1988) 1004.

[16] Sepulveda (Mexico) A/C.6/53/SR 16; de Aguiar Patriota (Brazil), ibid; Benitez Saenz (Uruguay), ibid; Reza (Indonesia), A/C.6/53/SR 15; O'Hara (Malaysia), ibid; Gray (Australia), A/C.6/52/SR 23; Longva (Norway), A/C.6/53/SR 14; Berman (United Kingdom), ibid; Orrego-Vicuña (Chile), ibid; Fomba (Mali), arguing, however, that the development of human rights should be taken into account A/C.6/53/SR 13; Caflisch (Observer for Switzerland), ibid; Tomka (Slovakia), A/C.6/53/SR 22; Shodeinde (Nigeria), A/C.6/53/SR 17; al-Baharna (Bahrain), A/C.6/53/SR 21.

a full discretion. One delegate stated that States might be influenced by overriding foreign policy concerns in declining the exercise of that right. Moreover, as the individual's claim may be unfounded in international law, the exercise of diplomatic protection should remain within the discretion of the State in order to prevent the individual from putting the State in a 'futile position'.[17] There was also a discussion in the Sixth Committee of the GA of whether diplomatic protection should be considered a human right which could then be construed as giving the individual a right to be protected by his national State and as imposing a corresponding duty on his national State to protect him. One delegate expressed doubts about such a possibility, maintaining that such a view was not supported by existing international law and could not be expected to become part of the legal order in the near future.[18] Another called for the examination of the legal basis (in the views and practice of States) of the right possessed by the individual and pointed to the necessity of considering whether it could be categorized as a human right.[19] The Spanish delegate appeared to support the view that the right to diplomatic protection was a human right, as he contended that the individual had a right to compensation for violations of his rights, as well as for the lack of diplomatic protection.[20] Discussion in the Sixth Committee thus revealed that *some* members of the international legal society do believe in one way or another that the individual should be entitled to diplomatic protection as a matter of right, while *many* do not.

Although limited, some constitutional provisions in a number of States, mainly those belonging to the former communist bloc, recognize the right of the individual to receive diplomatic protection for injuries suffered abroad. These include Albania, Belarus, Bosnia and Herzegovina, Bulgaria, Cambodia, China, Croatia, Estonia, Georgia, Guyana, Hungary, Italy, Kazakhstan, Lao People's Democratic Republic, Latvia, Lithuania, Poland, Portugal, Republic of Korea, Romania, Russian Federation, Spain, the Republic of Macedonia, Turkey, Ukraine, Vietnam, and the Federal Republic of Yugoslavia. Usually the relevant article of the constitution contains formulations such as that the State shall protect the legitimate rights of its nationals abroad or that nationals of the State shall enjoy protection while residing abroad. The Italian, Spanish and Turkish constitutional provisions contain very vague and loose formulations providing for the protection of certain rights of workers abroad or, in the case of Spain, state that the State 'shall try to safeguard the economic and social rights' of its nationals working abroad.[21] The constitution of the Republic of Macedonia is even more limited, stating that the State 'cares for' the well-being of its nationals abroad.

[17] Baker (Israel), A/C.6/53/SR 15. On the first part of the argument, see also Abraham (France), A/C.6/SR 14.

[18] Cede (Austria), A/C.6/53/SR 15.

[19] Gray (Australia), A/C.6/52/SR 23.

[20] Giralda (Spain), A/C.6/53/SR 18.

[21] 1992 Constitution of Spain, Article 42.

At the other end of the spectrum, the constitutions of the Republic of Korea and Guyana establish the 'duty' of those States to protect their nationals abroad. Ukraine 'guarantees' protection, the Polish constitution refers to the right of the individual national to protection abroad, and the Hungarian constitution states that 'Hungarian citizens are entitled to enjoy the protection' of Hungary while residing abroad.[22] It is uncertain whether and to what extent those rights are enforceable under the national law of those States, and whether they go beyond the right of access to consular officials abroad.[23] On the other hand, they suggest that certain States consider diplomatic protection for their nationals abroad to be desirable. Other State practice on this matter in the international field is not copious, although a few constitutions may refer in one way or another to a 'duty' to protect.

Some judicial practice is available. The German Federal Constitutional Court and other German courts have in their decisions confirmed the constitutional obligation on the part of the German authorities to provide diplomatic protection, if certain prerequisites are met.[24] Besides conditions imposed by international law, diplomatic protection must be granted only if it 'does not run counter to truly overriding interests of the Federal Republic'.[25] This condition has been interpreted by the courts to give the political authorities a discretion to determine whether overriding interests of the State and the people as a whole preclude diplomatic protection. Although Israel lacks any formal legal provisions requiring the State to protect Israeli nationals abroad and the exercise of such protection is usually seen to fall within the discretion of the government, the Supreme Court held in 1952 that the State has a duty to protect a national in an enemy country 'insofar as it is able to defend him through the good offices of a friendly Government'.[26] A similar decision was reached by the Haifa District Court in 1954.[27]

In Switzerland, court decisions take the view that the government does not have a duty to exercise diplomatic protection on behalf of its nationals,[28] though certain provisions of the constitution and the 1967 Consular Regulations recognize a limited duty on the part of Swiss consular missions to protect Swiss

[22] 1949 Hungarian Constitution with amendments up to 1997, Article 69.

[23] See the views of Lee, *Consular Law and Practice* (1991) 124 ff.

[24] *Hess-Entscheidung*, 7 July 1975, 90 ILR (1992) 387 (Germany); *Ostverträge*, 16 December 1980, 78 ILR (1988) 177 (Germany). See Klein, 'Anspruch auf diplomatischen Schutz?' in Ress and Stein (eds), *Der diplomatische Schutz im Völker-und Europarecht: Aktuelle Probleme und Entwicklungtendenzen* (1996) 125 and related discussion.

[25] Geck (note 11 above) 1052.

[26] Blum, 'Israel', in Lauterpacht and Collier (eds) (note 15 above) 314, citing *Hakim v Minister of Interior* (1952), 6 Piskei Din 642.

[27] Ibid, referring to *Attorney General v Steiner* (1954), 9 Psakim Mehoziim 489.

[28] This has been established in *Heirs of Oswald v Swiss Government* (1926), Arrêts de Tribunal fédéral 52 II 235 and *Gschwind v Swiss Government* (1932), Arrêts de Tribunal fédéral 58 II 463, *Schoenemann v Swiss Government* (1955), Arrêts de Tribunal fédéral 81 I 159, cited by Caflisch, 'Switzerland', in Lauterpacht and Collier (eds) (note 15 above) 504 ff.

nationals, unless it would prejudice the interest of the Confederation.[29] The UK courts do not recognize the right of individuals to enforce the Crown's duty of diplomatic protection before domestic courts.[30] However, the view has been expressed that it is possible to argue now that British citizens have at least a 'legitimate expectation' that they will be afforded diplomatic protection, if the conditions stated in the rules of the UK applying to international claims (continuous nationality, exhaustion of local remedies, etc) are fulfilled.[31] In France, the right to exercise diplomatic protection is an *acte de gouvernement*—which is not subject to review by administrative bodies or courts.[32] Although there is no general duty on the part of the executive to exercise diplomatic protection on behalf of nationals in the United States of America, it has been held by the judiciary that the so-called Hostage Act requires the president to intervene whenever a United States citizen has been 'unjustly deprived of his liberty by or under the authority of any foreign government.' In such a case the 'president shall use such means not amounting to acts of war and not otherwise prohibited by law, as he may think necessary and proper to obtain or effectuate the release.'[33] In a number of cases brought before other national courts Dutch, Spanish, Austrian, and Belgian claimants have attempted to assert a right, vis-à-vis their national States, to diplomatic protection.[34] The cases were not decided in their favour. All that can be said is that the submission of the claims indicates that the claimants, at any rate, believed that they had such a right vis-à-vis the State.

On the basis on balance of all the above evidence a conclusion has been reached that

> there are signs in recent State practice, constitutions and legal opinion of support for the view that States have not only a right but a legal obligation to protect their nationals

[29] Caflisch, ibid 506 ff.

[30] *Mutasa v Attorney-General* [1976], 3 All ER 257, 261–2; 78 ILR (1988) 490; *R v Secretary of State for Foreign and Commonwealth Affairs: ex p Butt,* unreported judgment of the Court of Appeal of 9 July 1999. See also the response of the UK to the ILC, July 1999, para 3. These last two sources are cited by Dugard (note 10 above) 31 note 150.

[31] See Warbrick (note 15 above) 1009.

[32] Dinh, *Droit International Public* (1999) 777. See also cases cited in Weil, 'France', in Lauterpacht and Collier (eds) (note 15 above) 278–9.

[33] 22 USC 1732 (Supp II 1990). See also Young, 'Torture and Inhumane Punishment of United States Citizens in Saudi Arabia and the United States Government's Failure to Act', 16 Hastings International and Comparative Law Quarterly (1993) 663; Hughes, 'Hostages' Rights: The Unhappy Legal Predicament of an American Held in Foreign Captivity' 26 Columbia Journal of Law and Social Problems (1993) 555. In *Redpath v Kissinger* the Court held that the discretion of the president to enter into diplomatic negotiations to secure the release of an American national was not subject to judicial control: 415 F Supp 566 (WDTex 1976), aff'd, 545 F.2nd 167 (5th Cir).

[34] The *Van Damme Case,* NRC Handelsblad, 5 January 2000; *HMHK v the Netherlands,* 94 ILR (1994) 342; *Commercial FSA v Council of Ministers,* 88 ILR (1992) 691; cases cited in Seidl-Hohenveldern, 'Austria', in Lauterpacht and Collier (eds) (note 15 above) 31; *Mandelier* (1966), 81 Journal des tribunaux 721 (1969) Pasicrisie belge II 246, cited in M. Waelbroeck, 'Belgium', in Lauterpacht and Collier (eds) (note 15 above) 59.

abroad. This approach is in conflict with the traditional view. It cannot, however, be dismissed out of hand as it accords with the principal goal of contemporary international law, - the advancement of the human rights of the individual.'[35]

As a sequel to this conclusion the rapporteur to the ILC, with the intention of 'developing' the law, proposed two articles as follows, which he concluded reflected rules different from what were the traditional rules:

Article 3
The State of nationality has the right to exercise diplomatic protection on behalf of a national unlawfully injured by another State. Subject to article 4, the State of nationality has a discretion in the exercise of this right.[36]

Article 4
(1) Unless the injured person is able to bring a claim for such injury before a competent international court or tribunal, the State of his/her nationality has a legal duty to exercise diplomatic protection on behalf of the injured person upon request, if the injury results from a grave breach of a *jus cogens* norm attributable to another State.
(2) The State of nationality is relieved of this obligation if:
  (a) The exercise of diplomatic protection would seriously endanger the overriding interests of the State and/or its people;
  (b) Another State exercises diplomatic protection on behalf of the injured person;
  (c) The injured person does not have the effective and dominant nationality of the State.
(3) States are obliged to provide in their municipal law for the enforcement of this right before a competent domestic court or other independent national authority.[37]

The question to whom the obligation to protect under Article 4 above was owed was not clearly answered, unless it is to be presumed that the obligation was one owed *erga omnes*.

The ILC, however, was careful in its draft together with a commentary,[38] submitted to the GA after a first reading, to take a view in accord with the traditional view rather than adopt the conclusion of the rapporteur that the law should be 'developed'. Article 1 of the draft pointed out that a State in exercising diplomatic protection adopted 'in its right the cause of its national',[39] thus avoiding any reference to right of the national and emphasizing the rights of the State of nationality. Article 2 then provided:

A State has the right to exercise diplomatic protection in accordance with the present draft articles.[40]

[35] Dugard, (note 10 above) 32. In fact the evidence does not clearly point in the direction noted by Dugard. There is insufficient evidence to postulate a change in the customary law imposing no duty on a national State to protect.
[36] Dugard, ibid 22.
[37] Dugard, ibid 27.
[38] See *Report of the ILC to the GA, 2004* 17 ff.
[39] The commentary cites here the *Interhandel Case,* 1959 ICJ Reports 27, to support this.
[40] *Report of the ILC to the GA, 2004* 18.

The Article did not refer to a duty of the State but rather incorporated the view that the State had a right, in the sense of a liberty, which could not be interfered with by others, to exercise diplomatic protection on behalf of an individual, provided the conditions set forth in the draft Articles were satisfied. The commentary to this Article makes the position clear that diplomatic protection neither imposed a duty on the State affording diplomatic protection nor gave the individual concerned a right recognized by international law to diplomatic protection with a corresponding obligation being imposed by international law on such State.

The commentary[41] pointed out that Article 2 stressed that the right of diplomatic protection belonged to or vested in the State, giving recognition to the Vattelian notion that an injury to a national was an indirect injury to the State, a view which had been formulated more carefully by the PCIJ in the *Mavrommatis Palestine Concessions Case.* There it was said that, 'By taking up the case of one of its subjects and by resorting to diplomatic action or international judicial proceedings on his behalf, a State is in reality asserting its own right—its right to ensure, in the person of its subjects, respect for the rules of international law.'[42] Furthermore, although that view had been frequently criticized as a fiction difficult to reconcile with the realities of diplomatic protection which require continuous nationality for the assertion of a diplomatic claim, the exhaustion of local remedies by the injured national, and the assessment of damages suffered to accord with the loss suffered by the individual, in the view of the ILC, the 'Mavrommatis principle' or the 'Vattelian fiction' (as the notion that an injury to a national is an injury to the State had come to be known) remained the cornerstone of diplomatic protection.

On the next question whether there was a duty imposed on the national State to protect its national, the commentary unequivocally stated that a State had the right to exercise diplomatic protection on behalf of a national, but was not under a duty or obligation to do so, and that, even though the internal law of a State might obligate a State to extend diplomatic protection to a national, international law imposed no such obligation. The statement of the ICJ in the *Barcelona Traction Co Case* was cited:

> ... within the limits prescribed by international law, a State may exercise diplomatic protection by whatever means and to whatever extent it thinks fit, for it is its own right that the State is asserting. Should the natural or legal person on whose behalf it is acting consider that their rights are not adequately protected, they have no remedy in international law. All they can do is resort to municipal law, if means are available, with a view to furthering their cause or obtaining redress... The State must be viewed as the sole judge to decide whether its protection will be granted, to what extent it is granted, and when it will cease. It retains in this respect a discretionary power the exercise of which may be determined by considerations of a political or other nature, unrelated to the particular case.[43]

[41] Ibid. 18 ff.
[42] (1924), PCIJ Series A No. 2, 12.
[43] 1970 ICJ Reports 44.

The commentary also recorded the fact that a proposal that a limited duty of protection be imposed on the State of nationality had been rejected by the ILC as going beyond the permissible limits of progressive development of the law.[44]

The final Draft Articles of 2006 did not change this position.[45] However, the ILC did refer, in the commentary to Article 2, to a later Article 19 which is discussed below.

Thus, for the present and for the foreseeable future, the traditional view that a State has a right, in the sense of a liberty which cannot be interfered with, to protect nationals but no duty to do so has been upheld. Hence, at international law a State has no duty, owed *erga omnes* or otherwise, to protect its nationals. This is so, even though, pursuant to the laws of some States, the State may have a duty, enforceable under national law, to protect its nationals. Those national provisions must be regarded as insufficient to establish a consistent practice with an *opinio iuris* giving rise to a customary rule of international law. It would appear that the duty to protect, recognized in some national laws, is not a duty which States regard as obligatory (observed under an *opinio iuris*) under international law, even if the practice is sufficiently widespread—which it may not be.

It may be noted, nevertheless, that the ILC in its final Draft Articles on Diplomatic Protection submitted to the ILC in 2006 recommended as desirable practices in Article 19 that:

(a) a national State should give due consideration to the possibility of exercising diplomatic, protection, especially when a significant injury had occurred, and
(b) take into account, wherever feasible, the views of injured persons with regard to diplomatic protection and the reparation to be sought.[46]

There is in the wording of this Article a clear understanding, as the commentary indicates,[47] that the practices advocated are not required by international law but are only recommended as desirable. However, the commentary is confusing in that it does imply later that what are said to be recommended practices may already reflect the current law. Thus, the commentary on Article 19 states:

> (1) There are certain practices on the part of States in the field of diplomatic protection which have not yet acquired the status of customary rules and which are not susceptible to transformation into rules of law in the exercise of progressive development of the law....
>
> (2) Subparagraph (a), recommends to States that they should give consideration to the possibility of exercising diplomatic protection of behalf of a national who suffers significant injury. The protection of human beings by means of international law is today one of the principal goals of the international legal order, as was reaffirmed by the 2005 World

[44] *Report of the ILC*, 2004 28.
[45] *Report of the ILC*, 2006 29 ff.
[46] Ibid 94.
[47] Ibid 94–7.

Summit Outcome resolution adopted by the General Assembly on 24 October 2005.[48] This protection may be achieved by many means, including consular protection, resort to international human rights treaties mechanisms, criminal prosecution or action by the Security Council or other international bodies—and diplomatic protection... When the protection of foreign nationals is in issue, diplomatic protection is an obvious remedy to which States should give serious consideration. After all it is the remedy with the longest history and has a proven record of effectiveness...

(3) A State is not under international law obliged to exercise diplomatic protection on behalf of a national who has been injured as a result of an internationally wrongful act attributable to another State. The discretionary nature of State's right to exercise diplomatic protection is affirmed by draft articles and has been asserted by the International Court of Justice[49] and national courts,[50]... Despite this there is growing support for the view that there is some obligation, however imperfect, on States, either under international law or national law, to protect their nationals abroad when they are subjected to significant human rights violations. The Constitutions of many States recognize the right of the individual to receive diplomatic protection for injuries suffered abroad,[51] which must carry with it the corresponding duty of the State to exercise protection. Moreover, a number of national court decisions indicate that although a State has a discretion whether to exercise diplomatic protection or not, there is an obligation on that State, subject to judicial review, to do something to assist its nationals, which may include an obligation to give due consideration to the possibility of exercising diplomatic protection.[52] In *Kaunda and Others v. President of the Republic of South Africa* the South African Constitutional Court stated that:

> There may be a duty on government, consistent with its obligations under international law, to take action to protect one of its citizens against a gross abuse of international human rights norms. A request to government for assistance in such circumstances where the evidence is clear would be difficult, and in extreme cases possibly impossible to refuse. It is unlikely that such a request would ever be refused by government, but if it were, the decision would be justiciable and a court would order the government to take appropriate action.[53]

In these circumstances it is possible to seriously suggest that international law already recognizes the existence of some obligation on the part of a State to consider the possibility of exercising diplomatic protection on behalf of a national who has suffered a siginificant injury abroad. If customary international law has not yet reached this stage of development then draft article 19, subparagraph (a), must be seen as an exercise in progressive development.

(4) Subparagraph (b) provides that a State 'should', in the exercise of diplomatic protection, 'take into account, wherever feasible, the views of injured persons with regard

[48] A/Res/60/I, paras 119–20, 138–40.

[49] *Barcelona Traction Co. Case*, 44.

[50] *R. (Abassi and Juma) v Secretary of State for the Foreign and Commonwealth Office* (2002), 123 ILR 599 (UK); *Kaunda and Others v President of the Republic of South Africa* (2004), 44 ILM 193 (South Africa).

[51] Dugard, 'First Report on Diplomatic Protection', note 10 at 30.

[52] *The Rudolf Hess Case* (1980), 90 ILR 392–296 (FRG); *R. (Abassi and Juma) v Secretary of State for Foreign and Commonwealth Office* (2002), 123 ILR, 599 (UK, England). See, generally, Vermeer-Künzli, 'Restricting Discretion: Judicial Review of Diplomatic Protection' 75 *Nordic Journal of International Law* (2006) 93.

[53] (2004), 44 ILM 186 para 69 (South Africa).

to resort to diplomatic protection and the reparation to be sought'. In practice States exercising diplomatic protection do have regard to the moral and material consequences of an injury to an alien in assessing the damages to be claimed.[54] In order to do this it is obviously necessary to consult with the injured person. So, too, with the decision whether to demand satisfaction, restitution or compensation by way of reparation. This has led some scholars to contend that the admonition contained in draft article 19, subparagraph (b), is already a rule of customary international law.[55] If it is not, draft article 19, subparagraph (b), must also be seen as an exercise in progressive development.[56]

It involves a contradiction to maintain that a practice is law pursuant to a codification, albeit as reflecting a progressive development, when at the same time in that codification it is only a recommended practice. It is presumed, consequently, that Article 19 paragraphs (a) and (b) do no more than make a recommendation and do not lay down rules of international law pursuant to progressive development of the law. Clearly, however, the practices recommended, if adopted generally and accompanied by an *opinion iuris,* could lead to the formation of rules of customary international law in the future. Such rules of law which could emerge are to be recommended as progressive development of international law.[57]

While what is included in Article 19(a) and (b) is to be supported as acceptable progressive development, whether or not subjection of a decision by the national State not to protect its national to judicial review by the court of the national State is required, the imposition of duties upon the national State in regard to the protection of its nationals creates problems. The question arises to whom are the duties owed and who can enforce them at international law. Even if the national

[54] *Chorzow Factory Case (Merits),* PCIJ Series A, No. 17, 28; separate opinion of Judge Morelli in *Barcelona Traction Case,* 1970 ICJ Reports 223.

[55] Bollecker-Stern, *Le Préjudice dans la Théorie de la Responsabilité Internatiionale* (1973) 98; Dubois, 'La distinction entre le droit de l'Etat réclamant et le droit au ressortissant dans la protection diplomatique' *Revue Critique de Droit International Privé* (1978) 615, 624.

[56] *Report of the ILC, 2006* 94–7. The original footnote numbers have been changed but in content the footnotes (present 48–55) have been retained as in the ILC report, with references organized, conformed and corrected.

[57] Orrego Vicuña suggested that the discretion exercised by a government in refusing to espouse a claim on behalf of the individual should be subject to judicial review in the context of the due process: 'The Changing Law of Nationality of Claims' in ILA, *Report of the Sixty-ninth Conference* (2000) 646. The ILA Resolution 5/2006 explains this and states:

> The discretion exercised by a government in refusing to expouse a claim on behalf of the individual should be subject to judicial review in the context of due process and the prevention of arbitrariness, subject to constitutional requirements of the state of nationality.
>
> 2.1 The obligation of the government in undertaking such a review is not necessarily to enforce the taking of diplomatic representations but to ensure that the government of nationality considers the position of the particular individual and the extent to which such action might be taken.
>
> 2.2 Judicial review may consider the question of eventual compensation of the individual by the state refusing to espouse the claim in the light of constitutional or administrative rights. (See <http://www.ila-hq.com>)

Both these sources stop short of ascribing a *duty* to protect a national to the national State. What is referred to is a duty to consider seriously and in good faith the protection of the individual. The resolution includes the exercise of judicial review over a decision not to protect.

may have a right to contest the decision not to protect him in the courts of his national State, this may not be the sole source of effectiveness especially in a case where the courts hold against him in a manifestly unjust decision. If there is no recourse to the national courts available, even then how can the decision to deny protection be contested not only at the national but also at the international level?

The answer to this question seems to lie in postulating that the duties incumbent upon the national State in connection with the protection of the alien are owed at large to the international community of States, ie *erga omnes*. This means that any other State may take up the individual's cause vis-à-vis his national State (but not against the respondent State in a dispute). Without this solution, the obligations upon national States in connection with the protection of their nationals would be toothless and illusory, because there would be no means of contesting the issues at an international level. The international community of States, it could be said, have an interest in intervening in the situation.

All in all, with the suggestion made above as to the rights of States at large corresponding to the duties of the national State, the idea of developing the international law by imposing upon the national State obligations connected with the protection of its national is to be welcomed. This development conflicts with the seminal view that it is solely the right of the national State that is being asserted in diplomatic protection. But the recognition of the interests of the individuals in this development is a truly progressive development. In particular it does not substantially affect the position of the respondent State in a dispute, though it may increase the likelihood of the national State of the alien initiating peaceful action against it on behalf of the alien. It is also to be noted that the development, as conceived, does not create an absolute obligation for national States to protect their nationals. It merely controls the exercise of the national State's discretion to protect its national.

These developments will also help to shift focus from the national State to the alien as concerns the persons or entity in whom the rights violated are vested, although the national State's rights, both primary and remedial, exist. This in turn would be in line with the modern developments, recognizing the individual as the owner of human rights in international law—indeed, as flowing from a *ius cogens*.[58]

[58] Orrego Vicuña suggested, as better reflecting contemporary realities and trends, that

> The *right* of the individual affected by a wrong should be asserted and enforced by means of diplomatic protection as the prevalent interest. A parallel right of the claimant State can also be asserted and enforced in this context but it should not be substituted for the individual's own right. (note 55) 646. Emphasis added.

The ILA in its Resolution No. 5/2006 adopted this position (para 1 of the section on *Nationality of Claims* (<http://www.ila-hq.com>):

The ILA resolution and Orrego Vicuña thus recognize that, when international law is violated in respect of an alien, the rights infringed are both the alien's and his national State's. This is a new development which is recommended. However, it is also recognized that in customary international law the alien must seek to enforce his right remedially through his national State. It must also be acknowledged, then, that the alien may have direct access to an international tribunal to enforce his rights under a convention or treaty which his national State is a party.

10

The Relevance of Nationality

The general rule is that a person, whether natural or juridical, must have the nationality of the State claiming injury at the time at which the injury is inflicted, in order that there may be an actual violation of the substantive rules of international law relating to injuries to aliens. The violation of international law is vis-à-vis that State of nationality, according to the generally accepted current view.

It has also never been contested that the procedural capacity of a State to espouse a person's claim as a rule depends on the latter, whether a natural or juridical person, having the nationality of that State, though in exceptional circumstances that bond may not be required. Both this rule, generally known as the nationality of claims rule, and the exceptions, are referred to in Article 3 of the ILC's Draft Article's of 2006. The rule is applied as a matter of admissibility of the claim.

But the nationality principle has a series of ramifications, depending on what is the situation occurring in practice. The ILC's Draft Articles of 2006 deal with the usual ramifications in Articles 4 to 7 and Articles 9 to 13, proposing at times departures from the customary law as generally understood in the interests of progressive development of the law. The issues to be addressed are discussed hereafter.

By way of introduction, it may be said that the link of nationality cannot be underestimated. A State's right to exercise diplomatic protection is based on the link of nationality between the injured individual and the acting State. Thus, the general rule is that a State may not extend its protection to or espouse claims of non-nationals.[1] In litigation a respondent State may raise the objection to admissibility that the individual concerned does not have the nationality of the claimant State or, where individuals are permitted to bring claims, that the individual

[1] For more judicial authorities on the rule see Van Panhuys, *The Role of Nationality in International Law: An Outline* (1959) 59–73; García Amador, 'Third Report to the ILC'; 2 YBILC (1950) 66; Jessup, *A Modern Law of Nations* (1968 reprint) 99; Ohly, 'A Functional Analysis of Claimant Eligibility', in Lillich (ed), *International Law of State Responsibility for Injuries to Aliens* (1983) 284; C F Amerasinghe, *State Responsibility for Injuries to Aliens* (1967) 61 ff; C F Amerasinghe, *Local Remedies in International Law* (2nd edn, 2004) 43 ff. The nationality of claims in regard to the jurisdiction of the ICJ has been discussed briefly by me in *Jurisdiction of International Tribunals* (2003) 259 ff. In the *Diallo Case (Preliminary Objections)* the ICJ confirmed the relevance of nationality when it noted that Diallo, the claimant State's national, had the nationality of the claimant State: 2007 ICJ Reports, para. 41 (<www.icj-cij.org>), which fact was not disputed.

does not have the nationality of the relevant State party to the agreement instituting the tribunal. On the other hand, while the general rule is as stated above, the fact that an individual has the nationality of the claimant State (or the relevant State) does not always result in the State's having the right to espouse his claim or in the individual's having the right to bring a claim. Thus, correctly stated, the *general* rule has both a negative and positive aspect. A State may not espouse claims of non-nationals (nor may non-nationals bring claims), while also a State may espouse claims of nationals (or nationals may bring claims). The positive side of the rule was referred to by the PCIJ first in the *Panevezys-Saldutiskis Railway Case.*[2] With regard to diplomatic protection the tribunal in the *North American Dredging Co of Texas Case* referred to it as a 'privilege which one State under the rules of international law can extend or withhold *in behalf of its nationals.*[3] The rule that nationality is the appropriate ground for the espousal of claims by States, or for individuals to bring claims before tribunals where they have *locus standi* in cases based on a violation of customary international law, has never been questioned.

Natural Persons: Determination of Nationality

With regard to the determination of nationality the general rule is that 'questions of nationality are in principle within the reserved domain'.[4] While a State's determination on possession of nationality is not lightly to be questioned, its right to determine an individual's nationality is not absolute. This was made clear by PCIJ in the *Nationality Decrees in Tunis and Morocco Opinion* when it stated that the question whether a matter was 'solely within the jurisdiction of a State', including the conferment of nationality, '[i]s essentially a relative question: it depends upon the development of international relations'.[5] Moreover, even if a State in principle has an absolute right to determine nationality, it is arguable that other States may challenge this determination, eg where there is insufficient connection between the State of nationality and the individual or where nationality has been improperly conferred,[6] that is, where the conferment is vitiated for acceptable reasons.

[2] (1939), PCIJ Series A/B No 76, 16.

[3] (1947), 4 UNRIAA 26.

[4] The *Nationality Decrees in Tunis and Morocco Opinion* (1923), PCIJ Series B No 4, 24. This principle was affirmed in Article 1 of the 1930 Hague Convention on Certain Questions Relating to the Conflict of Nationality Laws: 'It is for each State to determine under its own law who are its nationals' (179 LNTS 89). More recently it has been endorsed by the 1997 European Convention on Nationality (ETS No 166, Art 3) and it is difficult to resist the conclusion that it has acquired the status of customary law: see Bar-Yaacov, *Dual Nationality* (1961) 2.

[5] (1923), PCIJ Series B No 4, 24.

[6] Hudson, 'Nationality, Including Statelessness, Report', 2 YBILC (1952), UN Doc A/C 4/50, 10; Verdross and Simma, *Univerzelles Volkerrecht: Theorie und Praxis* 788–9. Article 1 of the 1930 Hague Convention on Certain Questions Relating to the Conflict of Nationality Laws recognized the possibility of limitations by qualifying its affirmation that 'it is for each State to determine

There are now conventions, particularly in the field of human rights, which require States to comply with international standards in the granting of nationality.[7] The IACHR in its *Proposed Amendments to the Naturalization Provisions of the Political Constitution of Costa Rica Opinion* held that it was necessary to reconcile the principle that the conferment of nationality falls within the domestic jurisdiction of a State 'with the further principle that international law imposes certain limits on the State's power, which limits are linked to the demands imposed by the international system for the protection of human rights'.[8]

International custom and general principles of law would appear to accept that there are limits on the conferment of nationality by describing the linkages between State and individual that will result in the nationality conferred by a State being recognized by international law for the purpose of diplomatic protection, in so far as descent, place of birth, and naturalization are specifically the connections generally recognized by international law.[9] Whether in addition to one of these connecting factors, and particularly in the case of naturalization, there must be a genuine or effective link between State and individual is a more difficult question. If this were the case such a link would require adequate definition so as to be identifiable and not too limiting.

That international law does not recognize naturalizations in all circumstances is clear. For example, fraudulently acquired naturalization will not be recognized.[10] Recognition would conceivably be withheld also in the case of forced naturalization, whether or not it reflected a substantial connection between State and individual.[11]

There is, on the other hand, a presumption in favour of good faith on the part of the State conferring nationality. Moreover, as the IACHR said in the *Proposed Amendments to the Naturalization Provisions of the Political Constitution of Costa Rica Opinion,* the State conferring nationality must be given a 'margin of appreciation' in deciding upon the connecting factors that it considers necessary for the

under its own law who are its nationals' with the provision that 'This law shall be recognized by other States in so far as it is consistent with international conventions, international custom and the principles of law generally recognized with regard to nationality' 179 LNTS 89. See also Article 3(2) of the 1997 European Convention on Nationality, ETS No 166, Art 3 ff.

[7] See Article 20 of the American Convention on Human Rights, Article 5(d)(iii) of the International Convention on the Elimination of All Forms of Racial Discrimination, and Article 9 of the Convention on the Elimination of All Forms of Discriminating against Women. See also the ILC Draft Articles on Nationality in Relation to Succession of States, UN Doc A/CN.4/L.581/Add.1.

[8] 79 ILR 296.

[9] For the general law see Bar-Yaacov (note 4 above) 2.

[10] See Brownlie, *Principles of International Law* (2003) 460; Weiss, *Nationality and Statelessness in International Law* (1979) 218–20, 244; Bar-Yaacov (note 4 above) 143; the *Flegenheimer Case* (1958), 25 ILR 98–101; the *Salem Case* (1932) 2 UNRIAA 1184; the *Esphanian Case* (1983), 2 *Iran-US CTR* 166.

[11] Fitzmaurice, 'The General Principles of International Law Considered from the Standpoint of the Rule of Law', 92 Hague Recueil (1957) 196–201; Jones, *British Nationality Law and Practice* (1956) 15.

granting of nationality.[12] However, a general statement made by the ICJ in the *Nottebohm Case (Second Phase)* on the nature of nationality was to the effect that:

According to the practice of States, to arbitral and judicial decisions and to the opinion of writers, nationality is the legal bond having as its basis a social fact of attachment, a genuine connection of existence, interests and sentiments, together with the existence of reciprocal rights and duties. It may be said that it constitutes the juridical expression of the fact that the individual upon whom it is conferred, either directly by the law or as the result of an act of the authorities, is in fact more closely connected with the population of the State conferring nationality than with that of any other State.[13]

This would seem to indicate that there was a general rule requiring an effective link for the conferment of nationality. However, the court, in fact, did not purport to pronounce on the status of Nottebohm's Liechtenstein nationality in the abstract but confined its views to the status of his nationality vis-à-vis Guatemala. The Italian-United States Conciliation Commission in the *Flegenheimer Case* limited the applicability of the 'effective link' principle to cases involving dual nationals, stating that:

When a person is vested with only one nationality, which is attributed to him or her either *jure sanguinis* or *jure soli,* or by a valid naturalization entailing the positive loss of the former nationality, the theory of effective nationality cannot be applied without the risk of causing confusion. It lacks a sufficiently positive basis to be applied to a nationality which finds support in a State law.[14]

The Commission furthermore stated[15] that it was doubtful that the ICJ 'intended to establish a rule of general international law' in the *Nottebohm Case.* That States are unwilling to support such a broad principle requiring always an effective link is evidenced by the failure in practice of the attempt to apply the genuine link principle as such to ships,[16] a field in which social and economic considerations probably justify such a rule. Available State practice also shows little support for such a broad rule.[17]

Legal commentators are divided on this issue. Some do not accept the genuine link requirement as a rule of customary international law.[18] Many of them have pointed out that there is often little connection between the individual upon

[12] 79 ILR 302–3.

[13] 1955 ICJ Reports 23.

[14] (1958), 25 ILR 150.

[15] Ibid 148.

[16] Article 91 of the 1982 United Nations Convention on the Law of the Sea; 1986 Convention on Conditions for the Registration of Ships. See also Article 3(3) of the Agreement to Promote Compliance with International Conservation and Management Measures by Fishing Vessels on the High Seas (1994), 33 ILM 968.

[17] See Warbrick, 'Protection of Nationals Abroad: Current Legal Problems', 37 ICLQ (1988) 1006.

[18] Geck, 'Diplomatic Protection', in 3 EPIL (1992) 1050, Randelzhofer, 'Nationality', in 3 ibid 507; Parry, 'Some Considerations upon the Protection of Individuals in International Law', 90 Hague Recueil (1956) 707; Jones, 'The Nottebohm Case', 5 ICLQ (1956) 239–40, 243–4.

whom nationality has been conferred and *jus soli* or *sanguinis* and that it is difficult to limit the genuine link requirement to cases of naturalization. Others are well disposed towards the genuine link requirement.[19] Support for the general principle of the effective link is to be found also in the ILC where only some members gave it their support in the fifth session debate on nationality, including statelessness.[20] In 1965 the Institut de Droit International adopted the following resolution on the national character of an international claim presented by a State for injury suffered by an individual, which gives some support to the genuine link principle:

An international claim presented by a State for injury suffered by an individual may be rejected by the respondent State or declared inadmissible when, in the particular circumstances of the case, it appears that naturalization has been conferred on that individual in the absence of any link of attachment.[21]

It may be concluded that general international law recognizes that a nationality acquired by fraud, negligence or serious error may not be recognized.[22] It is also the function of an international tribunal, with due regard to the presumption in favour of the validity of a State's conferment of nationality and allowance for a margin of appreciation on the part of the State of nationality, to investigate and, if necessary, set aside a conferment of nationality.[23] This position may be encapsulated as a requirement of good faith. Thus, a conferment of nationality will be recognized (for the purpose of diplomatic protection) provided it is not made in bad faith, the onus of proof being on the respondent State to produce evidence of such bad faith.[24] Beyond that it cannot be said that a general 'effective link' theory has been accepted.

There are two questions which have been addressed. First, discussion has been in terms of whether the conferment of nationality which is a domestic matter has limits imposed by international law which will affect the validity of the

[19] Van Panhuys (note 1 above) 158, 161; Fitzmaurice (note 11 above) 206–7; Ruzié, 'Nationalité, Effectivité et Droit Communitaire', RGDIP (1993) 113; de Castro, 'La Nationalité, la Double et Supra-Nationalité', 102 Hague Recueil (1961) 582.

[20] See 1 YBILC (1953) 180, 186, 239 (Yepes); 181, 218 (Zourek); 184, 237 (Francois); 239 (Amado).

[21] García Amador proposed codification of a similar rule in Article 23(3) of his last report to the ILC in 1961: 'A State may not bring a claim on behalf of an individual if the legal bond of nationality is not based on a genuine connexion between the two' (2 YBILC (1961) 49). See also more recently Orrego Vicuña who has proposed the following rule as one that reflects contemporary 'realities' and 'trends': 'The link of nationality to the claimant State must be genuine and effective', 'The Changing Law of Nationality Claims', in ILA, *Report of the Sixty-ninth Conference* (2000) 646. He does, however, recognize in effect that the rule will have to be applied with 'greater flexibility and adaptation to changing needs' (ibid 638). The ILA in its Resolution 5/2006 endorsed this approach: see <http://www.ila-hq.com>.

[22] The *Flegenheimer Case* (1958), 25 ILR 112, 153; the *Salem Case* (1932), 2 UNRIAA 1185; Bar-Yaacov (note 4 above) 150–52, 158; Brownlie (note 10 above) 422.

[23] The *Flegenheimer Case* (1958), 25 ILR 96–112; the *Flutie Case*, reported in Ralston and Doyle, *Venezuelan Arbitrations of 1903* 34; Van Panhuys (note 1 above) 153–6.

[24] The *Flegenheimer Case* (1958), 25 ILR 99, 107 and 110.

conferment in general and for all purposes. Second, a narrower issue has been the focus of attention: whether the conferment of nationality has limits for the purpose of the nationality of claims rule in diplomatic protection. While the first issue raises fundamental questions the answer to which will affect the enjoyment of nationality for all purposes by a person, whether he or it is a natural person or a juridical person, the second question is more limited. Suffice it to say here that what is relevant for the purpose in hand is the answer to the second question; whatever the answer to the first question, its effects may be broader and more serious than the answer to the more confined second question. Both legal commentators and tribunals have apparently not generally kept the two matters separate in their statements and conclusion. However, it is the better approach to confine what has been said above to the effects of a conferment or acquisition of nationality on the rule of nationality of claims in diplomatic protection.

The 2004 ILC Draft Articles are non-committal both in Article 4 and the commentary on it on the question of the genuine link. But Article 4 does state that acquisition of nationality for the purposes of diplomatic protection must not be inconsistent with international law, after giving a list of non-exclusive methods of acquiring nationality. That article reads:

> For the purposes of diplomatic protection of natural persons, a State whose nationality the individual sought to be protected has acquired by birth, descent, succession of States, naturalization or in any other manner, not inconsistent with international law...

While good faith is the key to answering the question, the commentary also refers to the fact that the benefit of the doubt is to be given to the State of nationality, so that it is for the objector to the nationality of the alien to prove that it is inconsistent with international law.[25]

Natural Persons: Continuous Nationality

The rules relating to continuous nationality up to this time are considerably controversial. The 2006 ILC's Draft Articles in Article 5 take an approach which tries to set to rest the many controversies that have existed. Whether States accept these solutions remains to be seen.

To start with the alleged rules and the disagreements on them need to be examined. Thereafter an attempt may be made to point out the changes recommended in the ILC draft.

[25] For the commentary see 'Report of the ILC to the General Assembly' (2004) 30 ff. (<http://www.un.org>). The views of the rapporteur of the ILC expressed in his 'First Report on Diplomatic Protection' (2000), UN Doc A/CN.4/506, on his proposed Article 5, which is generally similar to the ILC's Draft Article, are not incompatible with the views expressed by me in this section: see Dugard, ibid 34–41. He gives an extensive account of the authorities.

While there is a diversity of views on the rule of continuous nationality, whether it be in judicial decisions or in State practice, among legal commentators or in codification drafts, the rule in its usual form[26] was that from the time of the original factual injury to the alien until the making of the judicial determination the claim must without interruption have belonged to a person or a series of persons having the nationality of the State by which it was espoused. There was sometimes added the proposition that the person or persons referred to must not at any time during this period have the nationality of the respondent State,[27] which is an important consideration. The latter rule is not quite the same as the rules stemming from dual or multiple nationality, when one of the nationalities is that of the respondent State.

Logically, if the injury which is the object of diplomatic protection is to the State of nationality, which has been an assumption made even to this day, then at the time the injury occurred the victim must have the nationality of that State. Also logically, if the injury is to the State of nationality, it should be irrelevant what happens to the victim's nationality after that; the State whose nationality the victim had should have the procedural right to pursue the claim after the violation of its substantive right. But the rule of continuous nationality is a practical procedural rule, rather than being based on rigorous logic. The requirement that the victim should have the nationality of the State instituting the claim (or up to the time of the judicial decision) is the other side of one coin. It flows from a policy which sees diplomatic protection as for the benefit of the victim as well.

On the other hand, it is inadequate that the claimant State should be the national State of the victim only at the time of the filing of the claim (or the giving of the judicial decision). As was stated in the *Administrative Decision No. V* on the basis of political considerations (though, as pointed out above, there are conceptual reasons also for the requirement of nationality at the time of the injury),

> It is no doubt the general practice of nations not to espouse a private claim against another nation unless in point of origin it possesses the nationality of the claimant nation. The reason of the rule is that the nation is injured through injury to its national and it alone may demand reparation as no other nation is injured. As between nations the one inflicting the injury will ordinarily listen to the complaint only of the national injured. A third nation is not injured through the assignment of the claim to one of its nationals or through the claimant becoming its national by naturalization. While naturalization transfers allegiance, it does not carry with it existing State obligations... [A]ny other rule would open wide the door for abuses and might result in converting a strong nation into a claim agency in behalf of those who after suffering injuries should assign their claims to

[26] *Administrative Decision No V,* 1925 AJIL 613–14 *per* Umpire Parker; the *Kren Claim* (1953) 20 ILR 234; Basis of Discussion No 28 of the Preparatory Committee of the 1930 Hague Codification Conference, 2 YBIL (1956) 225; Geck, 'Diplomatic Protection,' EPIL (1992) 1055.

[27] O'Connell, 2 *International Law* (1970) 1037.

its nationals or avail themselves of its naturalization laws for the purpose of procuring its espousal of their claims.[28]

Although the conceptual reason is implicitly referred to in this case, it is not emphasized because what was being addressed was the question why the nationality of the claim at the time of its filing (or of the judicial decision) was not the only relevant consideration. Clearly, by implication, there was no denial that the nationality of the claim at the time of the making of the claim (or of the judicial decision) was equally a requirement. That is the flip side of the coin. That requirement flowed from the understanding that the State bringing the claim must have an interest in protecting one of its nationals, at that time also, even though conceptually its rights had been already violated by the injury being committed at a time when the victim was its national.

The rule was stated in all three of its aspects—time of injury, time of the filing of the claim, and continuity—in the *Kren Case* by the US-Yugoslavia Claims Commission where it was said:

It is a well settled principle of international law that to justify diplomatic espousal, a claim must be national in origin; that it must, in its inception, belong to those to whom the State owes protection and from whom it is owed allegiance (Borchard, *The Diplomatic Protection of Citizens Abroad,* p. 666). Further, although the national character will attach to a claim belonging to a citizen of a State at its inception, the claim ordinarily must continue to be national at the time of its presentation, by the weight of authority (Borchard, *supra,* p. 666), and there is a general agreement that it have a continuity of nationality until it is filed (Feller, *The Mexican Claims Commission,* p. 96).[29]

The rule as explained in this case has been affirmed by the Iran-US Claims Tribunal.[30]

The rule is reflected in the practice of States such as the UK and the USA. The 1985 UK Rules applying to international claims states in Rule 1:

HMG will not take up the claim unless the claimant is a United Kingdom national and was so at the date of the injury.

Comment. International law requires that for a claim to be sustainable, the claimant must be a national of the State which is presenting the claim both at the time when the injury occurred and continuously thereafter up to the date of formal presentation of the claim.

[28] 1925 AJIL at 613–14 *per* Umpire Parker. See also the *Panavezys-Saldutiskis Railway Case* (1939), PCIJ Series A/B No 76, 16–17, for a similar approach.

[29] 20 ILR 234.

[30] See Aldrich, *The Jurisprudence of the Iran-United States Claims Tribunal* (1996) 45–6; Brower and Brueschke, *The Iran-United States Claims Tribunal* (1998) 76–80, and the cases cited there. In the *Diallo Case (Preliminary Objections)* the ICJ accepted the requirement that the claimant State's national must have the nationality of the claimant State continuously from the time of the injury to the time of the presentation of the claim, stating that in the case the parties did not dispute this fact: 2007 ICJ Reports para. 41 (<http://www.icj-cij.org>).

In practice, however, it has hitherto been sufficient to prove nationality at the date of injury and of presentation of the claim.[31]

In 1982 the American Assistant Secretary of State for Congressional Relations wrote a letter to the Chairman of the House Committee on Foreign Affairs stating that:

> under the long-established rule of continuous nationality, no claimant is entitled to diplomatic protection of the State whose assistance is invoked unless such claimant was a national of that State at the time when the claim arose and continuously thereafter until the claim is presented. In effect, a claim must be a national claim not only at the time of its presentation, but also at the time when the injury or loss was sustained.[32]

Conventions setting up mixed claims commissions generally incorporated the rule in one form or another or came to be regarded as incorporating the rule as a result of interpretation of the conventions.[33] The rule has recurred in many treaties, for instance in nearly all of the lump sum agreements concluded after the Second World War.[34] It is to be found in the Declaration of Algiers establishing the Iran-United States Claims Tribunal, which provides that 'claims of nationals of Iran or the United States, as the case may be, means claims owned continuously from the date on which the claim arose to the date on which this agreement enters into force, by nationals of that State . . .'.[35] While it may be argued that the rule is incorporated in these instruments by explicit agreement and is not included because it is a customary rule, there are indications that the States involved did include the rule because it reflected customary international law. The same observation applies to attempts to derive a customary rule from the consistent inclusion of the rule in conventions in general. It may very well be the case that the repetition flowed from the desire to include a customary rule, because there is also evidence of pure custom to support the rule.

Codification drafts have also included the rule or some variations of it.[36] However, it is important to note that in 1932 the Institut de Droit International failed by a small majority to approve the rule of continuous nationality.[37] In 1965 the Institut reaffirmed the requirement of nationality at the time of the injury and the date of presentation of the claim but discarded the need for continuous nationality.[38]

[31] Cited in Warbrick, 'Protection of Nationals Abroad: Current Legal Problems', 37 ICLQ (1988) 1006.

[32] 77 AJIL (1982) 836.

[33] See Sinclair, 'Nationality of Claims: British Practice', 27 BYIL (1950) 127; Dugard (note 25 above), 'Addendum', UN DocA/CN.4/506/Add1 3–4.

[34] See Geck (note 18 above) 1055; Wyler, *La Règle dite de la continuité de la nationalité dans le contentieux international* (1990) 43–8.

[35] (1980), 20 ILM 230.

[36] See Dugard (note 33 above) 6–7.

[37] 37 AIDI (1932) 278.

[38] 51 AIDI (1965-II) 260–2.

As for legal commentators, it is among them that support for the continuity rule as originally conceived is equivocal. The earliest unqualified support for the rule that can be traced was in 1915 by Borchard.[39] But particularly after the Second World War 'opinion ranged from a questioning of the customary status of the rule to criticism of its fairness from the perspective of both the State and the individual'.[40] A comprehensive study published recently in 1990 concludes that few writers are ready to give their unqualified support to the rule.[41]

The case law, earlier State practice, treaty practice, legal commentators, and draft codifications originally supported the rule of continuity of nationality *by and large* rather than opposed it. It is after the Second World War that the rule and its rationale really came to be questioned.

Another matter of concern is that, if such a rule existed, there was little agreement on the actual content of the rule. Apart from the requirement that the claim must have originated in an injury to a national of the dominant State, which is not in dispute, there are some other aspects of the rule on which there was disagreement. What is the date of injury for the purpose of establishing the nationality of the claim has been contested by legal commentators, though the matter was regarded as non-controversial by international tribunals.[42] Issues have been raised as to the definition of national for the requirement of nationality, the contention being that intention to become a national duly declared at the time of the injury was sufficient. But the contention, though examined and sometimes accepted in early jurisprudence, has been rejected by subsequent international claims commissions.[43] The requirement of *continuous* nationality has in practice received little attention in the case law. As Briggs articulated it in 1965,

> If the judicial decisions of international tribunals have thus established the rule that, in order to be admissible, a claim must possess the nationality of the State asserting it not only at the origin but also on the date of its presentation to an international tribunal, is there an additional requirement, namely: that such a claim must have been *continuously* national during the period between these two dates? Tribunals are seldom confronted by such as problem. In most instances where a tribunal has stated *in expressis verbis* that a claim must be "continuously" national, from the origin to its presentation, what the tribunal has actually had to decide was whether or not a claim possessed the nationality of the claimant State on one or both of the two crucial dates. See the *Gleadell* and *Flack* cases, above; and the *Benchiton* case, below. Cases where a tribunal has had to deal with a claim that possessed the required nationality in the period between those two dates have arisen seldom and have been controversial.[44]

[39] Borchard, *The Diplomatic Protection of Citizens Abroad or the Law of International Claims* (1915) 660–7.

[40] Dugard, (note 33 above) 8 and authorities cited in footnotes 24 and 25 therein.

[41] See Wyler (note 34 above) 53.

[42] Borchard (note 39 above) 663.

[43] See Borchard, ibid 662–3; Wyler (note 34 above) 91.

[44] 'La Protection Diplomatique des Individus en Droit International: La Nationalité des Reclamations', AIDI (1965-I) 72–3.

A more palpable dispute relates to the *dies ad quem*, the date until which continuous nationality is required or the second date for the nationality of the claim. Several dates have been suggested and employed: the date on which the government endorses the claim of its national, the date of the initiation of diplomatic negotiation on the claim, the date of filing of the claim, the date of the signature, ratification, or entry into force of the treaty referring the dispute to arbitration, the date of presentation of the claim, the date of conclusion of the oral hearing, the date of judgment, and the date of settlement.[45] First, the date may depend on the terms of the arbitration convention.[46] Second, the date chosen may be of practical significance.[47] In sum, there seems to be no evidence of clear State practice on the basis of which a customary rule pointing to a single date *ad quem* in the absence of agreement can be founded.

It has been pointed out that the objections to the continuous nationality rule are not confined to its uncertain content and to its unfairness but that from a theoretical perspective it is out of line with both the Vattelian thesis that an injury to the alien is an injury to the State itself and the growing tendency to see the individual as a subject of international law.[48] Strict adherence to the logic of the Vattelian thesis has been rejected in the jurisprudence by the adoption of two points of time (if not continuity) for the existence of the nationality connection, however defined. In the *Stevenson Case* the umpire unequivocally stated that there was no precedent permitting the second point of time for the existence of the nationality connection to be ignored, though this was illogical in terms of the Vattelian premise.[49]

It has been suggested that the logical position should be restored, in spite of its weaknesses.[50] Another view is that the policy reason for the continuous nationality rule, which is that it prevents abuse of diplomatic protection by States espousing cases, is outdated.[51] Judge Fitzmaurice in his separate opinion in the *Barcelona Traction Co Case* was of the same view, stating that:

> too rigid and sweeping an application of the continuity rule can lead to a situation in which important interests go unprotected, claimants unsupported and injuries unredressed, not on account of anything relating to their merits, but because purely technical considerations bring it about that no State is entitled to act. This situation is the less defensible at the present date in that what was always regarded as the other main

[45] See discussion of the cases and literature in Briggs, ibid 24 ff; Wyler (note 34 above) 75 ff; Sinclair (note 33 above) 128 ff; Brownlie (note 10 above) 460 ff; García Amador, *The Changing Law of International Claims* (1984) 504.

[46] See *Administrative Decision No V* (1924), 7 UNRIAA 152 ff.

[47] See the *Eschauzier Case*, 5 UNRIAA 209, where the claim was rejected, because the alien lost her British nationality when she married a US national between the presentation of the claim and the award.

[48] Dugard (note 33 above) 12–13.

[49] 9 UNRIAA 506. See also the *Milani Case*, 10 UNRIAA 591.

[50] Wyler (note 34 above) 264.

[51] Dugard (note 33 above) 14.

justification for the continuity rule (and even sometimes thought to be its real *fons et origo*), namely the need to prevent the abuses that would result if claims could be assigned for value to nationals of States whose Governments would compel acceptance of them by the defendant State, has largely lost its validity.[52]

On the ground that the traditional requirement of continuous nationality has outlived its usefulness, it has been proposed that a flexible regime should be established which accords with contemporary international law, and which places emphasis on the individual, but at the same time takes account of the fears of potential abuse which inspired the requirement.[53]

The ILC has acted cautiously. Its Draft has retained the rule of nationality at two points of time, while clarifying how it is stated and is understood. Its formulation does not leave open the requirement of continuity but incorporates a presumption. Article 5 of its 2006 Draft states:

1. A State is entitled to exercise diplomatic protection in respect of a person who was a national of that State continuously from the date of injury to the date of the official presentation of the claim. Continuity is presumed if that nationality existed at both these dates.

2. Notwithstanding paragraph 1, a State may exercise diplomatic protection in respect of a person who is its national at the date of the official presentation of the claim but was not a national at the date of injury, provided that the person had the nationality of a predecessor State or lost his or her previous nationality and acquired, for a reason unrelated to the bringing of the claim, the nationality of the former State in a manner not inconsistent with international law.

3. Diplomatic protection shall not be exercised by the present State of nationality in respect of a person against a former State of nationality of that person for an injury caused when that person was a national of the former State of nationality and not of the present State of nationality.

4. A State is no longer entitled to exercise diplomatic protection in respect of a person who acquires the nationality of the State against which the claim is brought after the date of the official presentation of the claim.

[52] 1970 ICJ Reports 73.

[53] In pursuit of this Dugard proposed to the ILC the following article:

1. Where an injured person has undergone a *bona fide* change of nationality following an injury, the new State of nationality may exercise diplomatic protection on behalf of that person in respect of the injury, provided that the State of original nationality has not exercised or is not exercising diplomatic protection in respect of the injured person at the date on which the change of nationality occurs.

2. This rule applies where the claim has been transferred *bona fide* to a person or persons possessing the nationality of another State.

3. The change of nationality of an injured person or the transfer of the claim to a national of another State does not affect the right of the State of original nationality to bring a claim on its own behalf for injury to its general interests suffered through harm done to the injured person while he or she was still a national of that State.

4. Diplomatic protection may not be exercised by a new State of nationality against any previous State of nationality in respect of an injury suffered by a person when he or she was a national of the previous State of nationality ((note 25 above) 42).

In the commentary it was explained that the continuous nationality rule, which admittedly was well established, might produce great hardship in cases in which an individual changes his or her nationality for reasons unrelated to the bringing of a diplomatic claim, but that suggestions that it be abandoned had been resisted out of fear that this might be abused and lead to 'nationality shopping' for the purpose of diplomatic protection. The ILC was of the view that the continuous nationality rule should be retained but that exceptions should be allowed to accommodate cases in which unfairness might otherwise result. What was being codified was explained further. The commentary proceeded as follows:

Paragraph 1 asserts the traditional principle that a State is entitled to exercise diplomatic protection in respect of a person who was its national both at the time of the injury and at the date of the official presentation of the claim. State practice and doctrine are unclear on whether the national must retain the nationality of the claimant State between these two dates, largely because in practice this issue seldom arises. It is, however, incongruous to require that the same nationality be shown both at the date of injury and at the date of the official presentation of the claim without requiring it to continue between these two dates. Thus, in an exercise in progressive development of the law, the rule was drafted to require that the injured person be a national continuously from the date of the injury to the date of the official presentation of the claim. Given the difficulty of providing evidence of continuity, it is presumed if the same nationality existed at both these dates. This presumption is of course rebuttable.

The first requirement is that the injured national be a national of the claimant State at the date of the injury. The date of the injury need not be a precise date but could extend over a period of time if the injury consists of several acts or a continuing act committed over a period of time.

The second temporal requirement contained in paragraph 1 is the date of the official presentation of the claim. There is some disagreement in judicial opinion over the date until which the continuous nationality of the claim is required. This uncertainty stems largely from the fact that conventions establishing mixed claims commissions have employed different language to identify the date of the claim. The phrase 'presentation of the claim' is that most frequently used in treaties, judicial decisions and doctrine to indicate the outer date or *dies ad quem* required for the exercise of diplomatic protection. The word 'official' is added to this formulation to indicate that the date of the presentation of the claim is that on which the first official or formal demand is made by the State exercising diplomatic protection in contrast to informal diplomatic contacts and enquiries on this subject.

The *dies ad quem* for the exercise of diplomatic protection is the date of the official presentation of the claim. There is, however, support for the view that if the individual should change his nationality between this date and making of an award or a judgment he ceases to be a national for the purposes of diplomatic protection. In 2003 in *Loewn Group Inc v USA* an ICSID arbitral tribunal held that 'there must be continuous material identity from the date of the events giving rise to the claim, which date is known as the *dies a quo*, through to the date of the resolution of the claim, which date is known as the *dies ad quem*'.[54] On the facts, the Loewen case dealt with the situation in which the person sought to be protected changed nationality after the presentation of the claim to that of the respondent State, in which circumstances a claim for diplomatic protection can clearly not be upheld, as is made clear in paragraph 4 of the Draft Article. However, the ILC was not prepared to follow the Loewen tribunal in adopting a blanket rule that nationality must be maintained to the date of resolution of the claim. Such a rule could be contrary to the interests of the individual, as many years may pass between the presentation of the claim and its final resolution and it could be unfair to penalize the individual for changing nationality, through marriage or naturalization, during this period. Instead, preference is given to the date of the official presentation of the claim as the *dies ad quem*. This date is significant as it is the date on which the State of nationality shows its clear intention to exercise diplomatic protection—a fact that was hitherto uncertain. Moreover, it is the date on which the admissibility of the claim must be judged. This determination could not be left to the later date of the resolution of the claim, the making of the award.

While the ILC decided that it was necessary to retain the continuous nationality rule, it agreed that there was a need for exceptions to this rule. Paragraph 2 accordingly provides that a State may exercise diplomatic protection in respect of a person who was a national at the date of the official presentation of the claim but not at the time of the injury provided that three conditions are met: first, the person seeking diplomatic protection had the nationality of a predecessor State or has lost his or her previous nationality; secondly, that person has acquired the nationality of another State for a reason unrelated to the bringing of the claim; and thirdly, the acquisition of the new nationality has taken place in a manner not inconsistent with international law. The paragraph is concerned with cases in which the injured person has lost his or her previous nationality, either voluntarily or involuntarily. In the case of the succession of States, and, possibly, adoption and marriage when a change of nationality is compulsory, nationality will be lost involuntarily. In the case of other changes of nationality the element of will is not so clear. For reasons of this kind, the paragraph does not require the loss of nationality to be involuntary.

Fear that a person may deliberately change his or her nationality in order to acquire a State of nationality more willing and able to bring a diplomatic claim on his or her behalf is the basis for the rule of continuous nationality. The second condition contained in paragraph 2 addresses this fear by providing that the

[54] 7 ICSID Reports (2005) 485. See also the *Eschauzier Claim* (1931, GB v Mexico), 5 UNRIAA 207, and authorities cited in Jennings and Watts (eds), 1 *Oppenheim's International Law* (1992) 512.

person in respect of whom diplomatic protection is exercised must have acquired his or her new nationality for a reason unrelated to the bringing of the claim. This condition is designed to limit exceptions to the continuous nationality rule mainly to cases involving compulsory imposition of nationality, such as those in which the person has acquired a new nationality as a necessary consequence of factors such as marriage, adoption, or the succession of States. The exception in paragraph 2 will not apply where the person has acquired a new nationality for commercial reasons connected with the bringing of the claim.

The third condition that must be met for the rule of continuous nationality not to apply is that the new nationality has been acquired in a manner not inconsistent with international law which was a general condition connected with the determination of nationality in the first place.

Paragraph 3 adds another safeguard against abuse of the lifting of the continuous nationality rule. Diplomatic protection may not be exercised by the new State of nationality against a former State of nationality of the injured person in respect of an injury incurred when that person was a national of the former State of nationality and not the present State of nationality.

Paragraph 4 provides that if a person in respect of whom a claim is brought becomes national of the respondent State after the presentation of the claim, the applicant State loses its right to proceed with the claim as in such a case the respondent State would in effect be required to pay compensation to its own national. This was the situation in *Loewen group Inc v. USA* and a number of other cases[55] in which a change in nationality after presentation of the claim was held to preclude its continuation. In practice, in most cases of this kind, the applicant State will withdraw its claim, despite the fact that in terms of the fiction proclaimed in the *Mavrommatis Case* the claim is that of the State and the purpose of the claim is to seek reparation for injury caused to itself through the person of its national. The applicant State may likewise decide to withdraw its claim when the injured person becomes a national of a third State after the presentation of the claim. If the injured person has in bad faith retained the nationality of the claimant State until the date of presentation and thereafter acquired the nationality of a third State, equity would require that the claim be terminated, but the burden of proof will be upon the respondent State.

Draft Article 5 leaves open the question whether the heirs of an injured national, who dies as a consequences of the injury or thereafter, but before the official presentation of the claim, may be protected by the State of nationality of the injured person if he or she has the nationality of another State. Judicial decisions on this subject, while inconclusive, as most deal with the interpretation of particular treaties, tend to support the position that no claim may be brought

[55] The *Ebenezer Barston Case* in Hackworth, 5 *Digest of International Law* (1943) 805; the *Executors of F Lederer Case* in 3 Recueil Decisions des Tribunaux Arbitraux Mixtes 763; the *Hawaiian Claims* in Nielson, *America and British Claims Arbitration* (1926) 30.

by the State of nationality of the deceased person if the heir has the nationality of a third State.[56] Where the heir has the nationality of the respondent State it is clear that no such claim may be brought.[57] There is some support for the view that where the injured national dies before the official presentation of the claim, the claim may be continued because it has assumed a national character.[58] But in some cases, in spite of considerations of equity, the view has been repudiated.[59]

Natural Persons: Dual and Multiple Nationality

Dual Nationality Including the Respondent State

With regard to dual nationality, on the assumption that the nationalities concerned are recognizable for the purposes of diplomatic protection, an issue that has risen is whether one national State may exercise diplomatic protection against another national State of the same person in the application of the nationality of claims rule. That a person may have two or more recognizable nationalities is acknowledged.[60]

There is no settled opinion in the sources in support of the view that the State of dominant nationality, however defined, may espouse a claim against another State of nationality, nor is there support for the converse principle that a claim may never be brought against a State of nationality. The 1929 Harvard Draft Convention on Responsibility of States for Damage Done in Their Territory to the Person or Property of Foreigners provides in Article 16(a) that, 'A State is not responsible if the person injured or the person on behalf of whom the claim is made was or is its own national.' This principle was endorsed by the 1930 Hague Convention on Certain Questions relating to the Conflict of Nationality Laws, which provided in Article 4 that, 'A State may not afford diplomatic protection to one of its nationals against a State whose nationality such person also possesses.' That the concept of dominant or effective nationality was to be considered in the treatment of dual nationals who did not have the nationality of the respondent was made clear by Article 5 of the same Convention, which provided that:

[56] The *Eschauzier Claim* (1931, GB v Mexico), 5 UNRIAA 207; the *Gleadell Claim* (1929, GB v Mexico), 5 ibid 44; the *Kren Claim* (1951–1954), US International Claims Commission, 20 ILR 234; but contra the *Straub Claim* (1951–1954), US International Claims Commission, 20 ILR 228.

[57] The *Stevenson Claim* (1903, GB v Venezuela), 9 UNRIAA 494; the *Bogovic Claim* (1951–1954), US International Claims Commission, 20 ILR 156.

[58] The *Straub Claim* (1951–1954), US International Claims Commission, 20 ILR 228.

[59] The *Eschauzier Claim* (1931, GB v Mexico), 5 UNRIAA 207. It must be noted that the claims cited in footnotes 55 to 58, which were decided by the US International Claims Commission, were decided by a national claims commission and not by an international tribunal. The exact date of each decision is uncertain but was between 1951 and 1954.

[60] See Article 3 of the 1930 Hague Convention on Certain Questions Relating to the Conflict of Nationality Laws: 179 LNTS 89.

Within a third State, a person having more than one nationality shall be treated as if he had only one. Without prejudice to the application of its law in matters of personal status and of any conventions in force, a third State shall, of the nationalities which any such person possesses, recognize exclusively in its territory either the nationality of the country in which he is habitually and principally resident, or the nationality of the country with which in the circumstances he appears to be in fact most closely connected.

The treaty came into force in 1937.[61]

There were many early arbitrations in which the principle of dominant nationality had been applied vis-à-vis another national State, though in most of them the result was that the claimant State's nationality was found not to be the dominant of the two nationalities.[62] There were several such arbitrations in which the principle was rejected as such and not applied, the claimant thus losing the case on admissibility.[63]

In two cases in which the facts did not call for the consideration of an application of the principle as such the ICJ seems to have implied or indicated conflicting preferences. In the *Reparation Case* the court referred to the practice of States not to protect their nationals against another State of nationality as the ordinary practice,[64] while in the *Nottebohm Case (Second Phase)* the Court stated that:

International arbitrators have decided in the same way numerous cases of dual nationality, where the question arose with regard to the exercise of diplomatic protection. They have given their preference to the real and effective nationality, that which accorded with the facts, that based on stronger factual ties between the person concerned and one of the States whose nationality is involved.[65]

[61] Only twenty States are parties to this treaty (referred to herein as the 1930 Hague Convention). The 1960 Harvard Draft Convention on the International Responsibility of States for Injuries to Aliens, (referred to herein as the 1960 Harvard Draft) does not clearly permit or deny the right of the State of nationality. However, it leans against such a claim by providing in Article 23(5) that; 'A State is entitled to present a claim of its national arising out of the death of another person only if the person was not a national of the State alleged to be responsible': see Sohn and Baxter 'Responsibility of States for Injuries to the Economic Interest of Aliens', 55 AJIL (1961) 548. A further attempt to formulate a rule on this subject was made by the Institut de droit international in 1965. Article 4(a) of a resolution adopted provided that, 'An international claim presented by a State for injury suffered by an individual who possesses at the same time the nationalities of both claimant and respondent States may be rejected by the latter and is inadmissible before the court (jurisdiction) seized of the claim', *Resolutions de l'Institut de Droit international, 1957–1991,* (1992) 56. I was of the view in 1967 that the law as it stood was that the claim was inadmissible, if the person had the nationality of the respondent State, irrespective of dominance or effectiveness of the other nationality: C F Amerasinghe (note 1 above) (*State Responsibility*) 63.

[62] See the account in Dugard (note 25 above) paras 128–136. Of the 11 cases there mentioned only in three was the dominant nationality found to be that of the claimant State: the *Hein Case* (1921), AD 1919–22, No 148; the *Blumenthal Case* (1923), Recueil des Decisions des Tribunaux Mixtes 616; the *Barthez de Monfort Case* (1925), AD 1925–26, No 206.

[63] See Dugard (note 25 above) paras 138–140. It is not known what the result would have been had the principle been applied. The tribunals simply decided not to apply the principle.

[64] 1949 ICJ Reports 186.

[65] 1955 ICJ Reports 22.

Neither of these cases applied either the principle of dominant nationality or its reverse, because the cases did not involve the claimant's national having the nationality of the respondent State.

There are some arbitrations, decided after the *Nottebohm Case,* in which the principle of dominant or effective nationality has been applied in cases of dual nationality where the person involved has had the nationalities of both States involved in the litigation, sometimes to exclude the claim as inadmissible, sometimes with the reverse effect. These were decided by the Italian-United States Conciliation Commission (1955) and the Iran-US Claims Tribunal (1981 to present).[66]

While two rapporteurs of the ILC[67] take the view that the rule of the dominant or effective nationality with its effect favouring claimants, where otherwise their claims would clearly be inadmissible, should be applied in the case of dual nationality, legal commentators have not shown such a consensus.[68] The little State practice that there is on the exercise of diplomatic protection is also equivocal, though it may demonstrate a move away from the restrictive principle of non-recognition of the dominant nationality to its recognition as an answer to inadmissibility. Both the UK and the USA have demonstrated this trend.[69] On the other hand, in the past the Chilean government

[66] The key cases were the *Mergé Case* in the Conciliation Commission (1955), 16 UNRIAA 247 (para V.5), and the *Esphanian Case* and *Case No A/18* in the second chamber of the Iran-US Claims Tribunal (1983), 2 Iran-US CTR at 166 ff and (1984), 5 ibid 251. The above commission was a *conciliation* commission where the nationality of claims rule was applicable but, nevertheless, it was not an arbitral body in every respect. In the Iran-US Tribunal in the *Esphanian Case* the tribunal of three arbitrators described the tribunal as not being the 'typical exercise of diplomatic protection' because the State did not espouse claims: (1983), 2 ibid 165. This, however, is a distinction without a difference. Most of the tribunals in which the nationality of claims rule has been applied to admissibility were similar to the Iran-US tribunal. The rule has been regarded as applicable without a difference or distinction whether the claimant was the State itself or whether persons had *locus standi* before the tribunal, subject to express provisions to the contrary or modifying the rule, in the constitution of the tribunal. The Iran-US Tribunal clearly had to apply the same rule applicable to adjudications in which States were parties before the tribunal. It is significant that in *Case No A/18* the full tribunal of nine (with three dissenting) made no reference to the distinction made earlier by the tribunal of three. The rule applied by the tribunal purported to be the same rule applicable to cases of diplomatic protection in which States were the direct parties, and the correctness of the rule applied must stand or fall by the same criteria applicable to those cases. It has never been denied that the Iran-US Claims Tribunal, in so far as it covered claims by persons against either of the States involved, was adjudicating cases of diplomatic protection to which the nationality of claims rule was applicable subject to the express or implied provisions of the constitutive instruments. The fact that persons were claimants as opposed to their national States, as in the case of the 19th and 20th century claims commissions, made no material difference. However, there were conceivably some other special circumstances connected with the settlement of the disputes brought to the tribunal and which were reflected in the constitutive instruments of the tribunal.

[67] Garcia Amador, (note 1 above) 61, and Dugard, (note 25 above) 42–54. The view is supported by Orrego Vicuña, (note 21 above) 646, as rapporteur for the ILA. The ILA in Resolution 5/2006 *Nationality of Claims* followed the rapporteur's recommendation (<http://www.ila-hq.com>).

[68] See the writers referred to in Dugard (note 25 above) 49, 52.

[69] See Bar-Yaacov (note 4 above) 64–72, 147–55; Brownlie (note 10 above) 404; Warbrick (note 17 above) 1007.

seems impliedly to have taken the position that it cannot refuse diplomatic protection against another State of nationality.[70] At the same time, the FRG was not opposed to the informal exercise of such protection,[71] whereas Switzerland, although considering non-responsibility to be the general rule, did not deny the possibility of protection against another State of nationality in exceptional cases.[72]

It is also to be noted that, as already pointed out, in 1949 the ICJ in the *Reparation Case* took the view that claims could not be brought against the State of nationality. The trend is unclear but there seems to be some evidence that in the case of the person with dual nationality having the nationality of the respondent State the principle of the dominant or effective nationality is favoured to some extent in determining admissibility of the claim. In the event that this is the applicable principle, what the ICJ said about the determination of the dominant nationality becomes relevant:

> Different factors are taken into consideration, and their importance will vary from one case to the next; the habitual residence of the individual concerned is an important factor, but there are other factors such as the center of his interests, his family ties, his participation in public life, attachment shown by him for a given country and inculcated in his children, etc.[73]

Because the rule applied in the recent cases had earlier been rejected or was in doubt, it was only after the *Mergé* series of cases,[74] decided by a conciliation commission (and not solely an arbitral body), that the rule applied came to be respected. Also since many important authorities were against the rule as applied, the claim of the rule to be established may be questioned. It will also be noted that the six arbitrators in the majority in *Case No A/18*[75] in the Iran-US Claims Tribunal were the three US arbitrators and the three European non-party arbitrators.[76] Moreover, it may be observed that dissenting arbitrator Shafeiei's

[70] Orrego Vicuña, 'Chile', in Lauterpacht and Collier, *Individual Rights and the State in Foreign Affairs* (1977) 141. The implication arises from a Note of the Chilean Consular Department in connection with the protection of Chilean Jews in Germany in 1938. It is not clear, however, whether such persons necessarily had German nationality: see reference in Orrego Vicuña, ibid 181 note 71.

[71] Seidl-Hohenveldern, 'Federal Republic of Germany', in Lauterpacht and Collier (eds), *Individual Rights and the State in Foreign Affairs: An International Compendium* (1977) 247.

[72] Caflisch, 'Switzerland', in ibid 499.

[73] The *Nottebohm Case (Second Phase),* 1955 ICJ Reports 22.

[74] (1955), 16 UNRIAA 247 (para V.5).

[75] (1984), 5 Iran-US CTR 251.

[76] They were Lagergren, Mangard, Riphagen and from the US, Aldrich, Holtzmann, Mosk. It is questionable whether the opinion of these six arbitrators, admittedly a majority but no more, could establish a good precedent for customary international law in general. First, the context of the Iran-US Claims Tribunal was special in terms of the treatment of nationality in relation to claims. Secondly, the opinion took a position which was contradictory to the real earlier trends and to what was regarded as the better and more authoritative view—and that without a particularly well-reasoned argument of policy in favour of its position.

opinions both in the *Esphanian Case* and in *Case No A/18* were far more thorough than the opinions of the six in the majority.[77]

In the circumstances it is necessary to consider the basic principles involved, particularly because the absence of clear agreement on the principle applied raises some questions about the soundness of the rule as applied recently. As pointed out by the present author in 1967 and above in Chapter 7, diplomatic protection is in reality postulated on the reconciliation of conflicting interests.[78] The rule supported by more cogent authority at the time and not clearly rejected later, that the injured person must *not* have the nationality of the respondent State was, perhaps, the most important rule in the law of diplomatic protection which clearly recognized the interests of the respondent State. The reason for this was that diplomatic protection was conceived as a concession to foreign States and foreign nationals in circumstances in which there was no

[77] The dissent of the three Iranian arbitrators is to be found in *Case No A/18* (1984), 5 Iran-US CTR 257–337. The original dissent of arbitrator Shafeiei is in the *Esphanian Case,* (1983), 2 ibid 178.

[78] These are principally the interests of the injured national State, of the injured alien, and of the defendant State. Each of these interests has been given prominence in the choice of the different relevant rules, as pointed out by me. Indeed, it cannot be said that the interests of a national State and of the injured alien are necessarily given preference always to the detriment of the defendant State. See for a discussion of these matters, C F Amerasinghe (note 1 above) *(State Responsibility)* 63 ff. As was said there:

> It is evident that the rules relating to the diplomatic protection have not been developed by reference to the single principle that the right or interest violated is that of the national State, so that this principle can be called the sole basis of diplomatic protection, in spite of the emphasis given to it in international jurisprudence. The notion that the alien's interest is injured has also played a significant role in the formation of certain rules. Also at times the interest of the defendant State or other national States are given preference to the rights of some national State,... These conflicting interests have been resolved in practice in relation to specific rules by choices in favour of one or the other without any apparent order or scheme referable to a hierarchy of social policy values. Thus, it is not possible to assert with any conclusiveness that one or the other of these interests is necessarily superior to any of the others. (pp 64–5)

See also C F Amerasinghe (note 1 above) (*Local Remedies*) 43–56 and above. The point is that it is not the protection of the injured person or an injured national State that is always paramount. The systems for the *protection* of human rights are not in issue. They are generally based on conventions and create obligations owed to all the parties to the specific convention. This is apart from any recognition there may be by general principles of law or customary international law of substantive human rights as such. Earlier it was recognized that the rule that the injured alien must not be a national of the respondent State for any other State to exercise diplomatic protection was fully recognized, as was pointed out by me (note 1 above) (*State Responsibility*) 63). Any qualification to the rule as thus stated negatively was a weak minority view. Thus, the change that has taken place must be approximately justified by altered circumstances in international society. As far as I know, no such circumstances relating to diplomatic protection can be identified. The fact that a *conciliation* commission and a group of six judges all from capital exporting countries (the Iran-US Claims Tribunal) that could have a vested interest in asserting the law in the manner it was stated formulated a new rule raises questions about the rule. The fact that such judges purported to assert with firmness a rule that, to say the least, had been in grave doubt, and was supported by less cogent authority than the reverse of the rule, makes it undeniably suspect. Accepting the new rule requires a rejection of the view that the interests of the defendant State were important at all, because the reverse of the rule applied was the only circumstance in fact in which those interests were given a clearly affirmative recognition.

general reason not to recognize the prerogatives of domestic jurisdiction. The fundamental underpinning is still valid. Thus, the interests of the international community and the interests of the respondent (host) State would require that at present the person concerned should, negatively, not have the nationality of the respondent State, it being irrelevant that he had or did not have another nationality.

As an exception, however, the possession of another nationality in addition to that of the host State could only be given value if there are cogent reasons for not recognizing that the possession of the respondent State's nationality rules out any opportunity for diplomatic protection by other States. The possession of a dominant (or effective) nationality is clearly not the only reason, for it has nothing to do with the respondent State or its conduct. Circumstances in which the negative rule could be qualified would only be, if the context requires, that in addition to the possession of a second, dominant nationality by the person concerned which gives the other State of nationality some claim to protect, the right of the respondent State to treat the person as one of its nationals for the purpose of the rule has in some respect been forfeited. This would occur, for example, if the conduct of the respondent State is so heinous or uncivilized that the person merits to be protected by the other national State.

The term 'uncivilized' is used intentionally, though the connotation is more fundamental than was envisaged in the 18th and early 19th century when civilization was equated with the value systems of a limited group of countries which paradoxically included the approval of such conduct as inhuman and oppressive colonial exploitation and the like, and different standards from those applied to those countries themselves were used in judging whether civilization existed or not. Clearly such conduct as denying freedom of religious conscience, use of mutilation or torture, degrading and inhuman treatment such as stoning for adultery, and failure to grant adequate protection for the right to life would now qualify as heinous and uncivilized. On the other hand, the mere taking of property would not, although here again the deprivation of a total livelihood may do so. The conclusion suggested is that a dominant nationality, properly proved, is one (but not the only) consideration to be taken into account in modifying the rule that a person must not have the nationality of the respondent State. The other factors connected with the conduct of the respondent State are also relevant.[79]

All this having been said, it is fitting to point out that the ILC in Article 7 of its Draft Articles opted for the solution of the dominant nationality provided it is

[79] The 'First Report to the ILC' (2000) by its rapporteur (note 25 above) 42, supports the rule as enunciated in the *Mergé Case* and the Iran-US Claims Tribunal Cases. While that report also suggests that on the merits for good reason an award may be denied if the lack of nationality of the respondent has been abused (pp 53–4), this is not a matter for admissibility and does not need to be considered. There are modern authors who support the view taken in that report: see Aldrich (note 30 above) 76–9, Brower and Brueschke (note 30 above) 296–322.

dominant both at the time of the injury and at the date of the official presentation of the claim.[80]

Dual or Multiple Nationality—Not Including the Respondent State

Dual or multiple nationality, where the nationalities involved do not include the respondent's nationality, also raises problems. The issue is whether the respondent State can object that the dominant nationality is that of a third State and not that of the claimant State or the State connected with the claim, as an obstacle to the admissibility of the claim.

In such cases the dominant nationality theory has been applied by tribunals to identify which national State has the right of claim.[81] The 1930 Hague Convention[82] and several draft codification proposals[83] also incorporate the principle. On the other hand, there is some authority for the rule that there is no need to show dominant nationality, it being sufficient that the person injured had the nationality of the claimant State, irrespective of other nationalities than that of the respondent State.[84] A compromise rule has been offered by the Iran-US Claims Tribunal, namely that in the case of dual or multiple nationality, dominance need not be proved, provided there is a bona fide link between the injured person and the claimant State.[85]

In this case of such dual or multiple nationality it is true that the interests of the respondent State are not particularly prejudiced, unless it is subjected to more than one claim for the same injury. Therefore, the rule that any State of nationality may bring a claim—which is in effect a new rule that has been supported recently—may be recognized provided it is also made a condition that the filing of a claim by one national State bars the filing of a claim by any other national State. This proviso is important and is a defence to admissibility whether the original claim has been successful, withdrawn, or otherwise dealt with after it was filed. The filing of a joint claim by two or more national States may also be permitted with the above proviso. As a proviso, and in addition, the application of a genuine link theory, as a general principle (apart from the rule in the *Nottebohm Case)*,

[80] See explanation and discussion in Report of the ILC (2006), UN doc A/61/10, 43 ff and cases there cited both for and against this choice. Such cases were decided both before and after the *Mergé Case.*

[81] See the *de Born Case,* (1926) AD 1925–1926, No 205; the *Uiterwyk Corporation Case* (1988), 19 Iran-US *CTR* 118; the *Asghar Case* (1990), 24 ibid 242–3, among cases decided by the Iran-United States Claims Tribunal.

[82] Article 5, 179 LNTS 89.

[83] See Article 4(b) of the 1965 resolution of the Institut de droit international (note 54 above) 56, Article 23(3) of the 1960 Harvard Draft (note 54 above) 548. See also C F Amerasinghe (note 1 above) (*State Responsibility*) 63; (note 1 above) (*Local Remedies)* 50, where the same view is reflected.

[84] The *Salem Case* (1932), 2 UNRIAA 1188; the *Flegenheimer Case* (1958), 25 ILR 149; the *Stanovic Case* (1963), 40 ILR 155; the *Mergé Case* (1955), 16 UNRIAA 247.

[85] The *Dallal Case,* (1983), 3 Iran-US CTR 10. See Bederman, 'Nationality of Individual Claimants before the Iran-United States Claims Tribunal', 42 ICLQ (1993) 123–4.

may be useful. Thus, the interests of the respondent State will be given added recognition in circumstances where it is really the interests of the injured person that are given special recognition.[86]

The ILC Draft Articles of 2006 in Article 6 adopted a solution favouring multiple claims in the case discussed above without the provisos referred to above, thus, completely favouring the alien as against the respondent State.

Multiple Nationality Including That of the Respondent State

A problem arises, for example, where the person has the nationality of the respondent State and also two or more other nationalities. The question is whether the theory of the dominant nationality is to be applied as between the two other nationalities if it is recognized that in certain circumstances a claim may be brought against a national State. If the rule is that a claim may never be brought against a national State, *cadit quaestio.*

There is no reason why in the circumstances postulated the theory of the dominant nationality as between the two other nationalities should not be applied in the circumstances where a national State other than the respondent State may bring a claim against the latter. Vis-à-vis the respondent State this would mean that only the State of the truly dominant nationality could bring a claim. The matter has not been discussed either in decided cases or by legal commentators nor have relevant situations appeared in State practice. However, the application of a dominant (or more dominant) nationality theory would protect both the respondent State and the person injured. Clearly, if the view expressed with regard to multiple nationalities of injured persons is adopted, in addition to the claimant being the State of dominant nationality or the person claiming having the dominant nationality as between two other nationalities, the respondent State (of nationality) would have to be guilty of some 'heinous' conduct, which results in its forfeiting the right to treat that person as its national in the context of diplomatic protection.

Natural Persons: the Effective Link Theory

Where the respondent State is not a State of nationality what has come to be called the rule in the *Nottebohm Case*[87] permits a defence to admissibility, even if the claimant is a State of nationality or the person claiming has the relevant nationality. There has been some difficulty in identifying exactly what is the rule.

[86] The 'First Report on Diplomatic Protection' to the ILC (Dugard) in Article 7 adopts the principles stated above without the proviso which is significantly important: (note 25 above) 54.

[87] 1955 ICJ Reports 4 (*Second Phase*).

The case, which involved Liechtenstein and Guatemala, concerned the former's claim to restitution and compensation on behalf of Nottebohm for actions of Guatemala alleged to be in violation of international law. Nottebohm was a German national when in 1939 he applied for and was granted naturalization in Liechtenstein. He was at all material times a permanent resident of Guatemala. His only connection with Liechtenstein was the residence of his brother in Vaduz. He paid certain sums of money and taxes to Liechtenstein and took an oath of allegiance to the reigning prince. He returned to Guatemala on a Liechtenstein passport after a visit to Vaduz to complete the formalities. He had lost German nationality.[88] The issue was whether Liechtenstein could espouse his claim before the court in the exercise of diplomatic protection. This involved the question whether the nationality conferred on him by Liechtenstein could be successfully invoked against the respondent State, whose nationality also he did not have.

The court explained in broad terms that:

> According to the practice of States, to arbitral and judicial decisions and to the opinions of writers, nationality is a legal bond having as its basis a social fact of attachment, a genuine connection of existence, interests and sentiments, together with the existence of reciprocal rights and duties. It may be said to constitute the juridical expression of the fact that the individual upon whom it is conferred, either directly by the law or as the result of an act of the authorities, is in fact more closely connected with the population of the State conferring nationality than with that of any other State. Conferred by a State, it constitutes a translation into juridical terms of the individual's connection with the State which has made him its national.[89]

The court pointed out that Nottebohm had connections with his family members in Germany, and had business connections with Germany. It was said that:

> He had been settled in Guatemala for 34 years. He had carried on his activities there. It was the main seat of his interests. He returned there shortly after his naturalization, and it remained the center of his interests and of his business activities. He stayed there until his removal as a result of war measures in 1943. He subsequently attempted to return there, and he now complains of Guatemala's refusal to admit him. There, too, were several members of his family who sought to safeguard his interests.
>
> In contrast, his actual connections with Liechtenstein were extremely tenuous. No settled abode, no prolonged residence in that country at the time of his application for naturalization, the application indicates that he was paying a visit there and confirms the transient character of this visit by its request that the naturalization proceedings should be initiated and concluded without delay. No intention of settling there was shown at that time or realized in the ensuing weeks, months or years—on the contrary, he returned to Guatemala very shortly after his naturalization and showed every intention of remaining there. If Nottebohm went to Liechtenstein in 1946, this was because of the refusal of Guatemala to admit him. No indication is given of the grounds warranting

[88] See Judge Read's dissenting opinion, ibid 42. There is no reason to question Judge Read's statement of this fact.

[89] Ibid 23.

the waiver of the condition of residence, required by the 1934 Nationality Law, which waiver was implicitly granted to him. There is no allegation of any economic interest or any activities exercised or to be exercised in Liechtenstein, and no manifestation of any intention whatsoever to transfer all or some of his interests and his business activities to Liechtenstein. It is unnecessary in this connection to attribute much importance to the promise to pay the taxes levied at the time of his naturalization. The only links to be discovered between the Principality and Nottebohm are the short sojourns already referred to and the presence in Vaduz of one of his brothers: but his brother's presence is referred to in his application for naturalization only as a reference to his good conduct. Furthermore, other members of his family have asserted Nottebohm's desire to spend his old age in Guatemala.[90]

On the basis of these facts the court concluded that, 'Liechtenstein…is not entitled to extend its protection to Nottebohm vis-à-vis Guatemala and its claim must, for this reason, be held to be inadmissible',[91] explaining further that:

These facts clearly establish, on the one hand, the absence of any bond of attachment between Nottebohm and Liechtenstein and, on the other hand, the existence of a long-standing and close connection between him and Guatemala, a link which his naturalization in no way weakened. That naturalization was not based on any real prior connection with Liechtenstein, nor did it any way alter the manner of life of the person upon whom its was conferred in exceptional circumstances of speed and accommodation. In both respects, it was lacking in the genuineness requisite to an act of such importance, if it is to be entitled to be respected by a State in the position of Guatemala. It was granted without regard to the concept of nationality adopted in international relations.

Naturalization was asked for not so much for the purpose of obtaining a legal recognition of Nottebohm's membership in fact in the population of Liechtenstein, as it was to enable him to substitute for his status as a national of a belligerent State that of a national of a neutral State, with the sole aim of thus coming within the protection of Liechtenstein but not becoming wedded to its traditions, its interests, its way of life or of assuming the obligations—other than fiscal obligations—and exercising the rights pertaining to the status thus acquired.[92]

There has been considerable writing, and different views expressed, on the case,[93] but it is difficult to conclude that the case is authority for the proposition that the nationality of a person who has the claimant State's nationality must always be an effective one based on a 'genuine link', as described by the court. In the *Nottebohm Case* Nottebohm (a) had already had the nationality of another State

[90] Ibid 25–6.

[91] Ibid 26.

[92] Ibid.

[93] Jones, 'The Nottebohm Case', 5 ICLQ (1956) 230; Makarov, 'Das Urteil des Internationalen Gerichtshofes im Fall Nottebohm', 16 ZAORV (1956) 407; Maury, 'L'arrêt Nottebohm et la Condition de la nationalité effective', 23 *Zeitschrift für auslandisches und internationales Privatrecht* (1958) 515; de Visscher, 'L'affaire Nottebohm', 60 RGDIP (1956) 238; Van Panhuys (note 1 above) *passim*.

which he had lost, and (b) the action by the State of his current acquired nationality, Liechtenstein, was against a third State with which he had for some time had, and at the current time did actually have, a closer connection than with Liechtenstein or any other State. These two special features may restrict the scope of any general principle of 'genuine link'. Had Nottebohm retained German nationality, for instance, it does not follow from the ICJ's decision that Germany would not have had the right, as the national State, to make a claim against Guatemala in the circumstances.

The 'effective or genuine link' principle as enunciated in the *Nottebohm Case* is at least limited to situations where, firstly, the person concerned has no genuine or effective connection with the claimant State and, secondly, where his connection with the respondent State is clearly genuine and more effective even though he may not have the nationality of that State. Not only is the second requirement a necessary feature of the rule but it is clear that relevance of a genuine link becomes one based on a comparison between the person's relationship with the respondent State and the claimant State.[94] There is also some problem with how much value should be given to the fact that a person has lost the nationality of a third State which he previously had, perhaps by acquiring the nationality of the claimant State, while he had continuing connections with that third State. In short, the *Nottebohm Case* seems to be a very special case and the rule extracted from it may have a broad extension or a very narrow application based on the detailed facts of the case, depending on the approach taken to diplomatic protection. It would seem, however, that there is no good reason to construe the rule as being as broad as to require a genuine or effective link in the abstract between the person and the State of nationality making the claim. At the least, the relationship between the respondent State and the person must be taken into account on a comparative basis, as well as the fact that the current national State's nationality was an acquired one. The reason for not recognizing a broad rule is that it has the effect of curtailing the protection granted to injured persons through the institution of diplomatic protection, while also limiting the right of a national State to protect. The interests of respondent States which are protected by the rule do not need so much protection at the expense of national States and injured persons as to warrant a broad extension of the rule.

The ILC in its 2006 Draft Articles has omitted mention in any form of the rule discussed above. The rule of the 'effective link' as framed herein in a narrow manner is a useful one and account should be taken of it, even though it results in less protection for the alien. It is also backed by the authority of the ICJ.

[94] The same point was made by me in C F Amerasinghe, 'The Jurisdiction of the International Centre for the Settlement of Investment Disputes', 19 IJIL (1979) 202–3 and (note 1 above) (*Jurisdiction*) 646–7.

Natural Persons: Stateless Persons and Refugees

In customary international law diplomatic protection did not extend to stateless persons. As was stated in the *Dickson Car Wheel Company Case,*

> A State . . . does not commit an international delinquency in inflicting an injury upon an individual lacking nationality, and consequently, no State is empowered to intervene or complain on his behalf either before or after the injury.[95]

It was also understood that refugees also would not be protected by States in customary international law. At the 1930 Hague Codification Conference the Netherlands proposed that the right of the receiving State to protect refugees be recognized. The proposal failed to be adopted.[96] There was no controversy about the absence of protection apart from treaty law specifically giving such protection for stateless persons and refugees.

The ILC's 2006 Draft Articles make a breakthrough on this front. Article 8 fearlessly and positively removes the barrier to protection and, consequently, discards for this purpose the thesis that an injury to an alien is an injury to his State of *nationality* as the subject with rights in international law. The Article states:

1. A State may exercise diplomatic protection in respect of a stateless person who, at the time of the injury and at the date of the official presentation of the claim, is lawfully and habitually resident in that State.
2. A State may exercise diplomatic protection in respect of a person who is recognized as a refugee by that State, in accordance with internationally accepted standards when that person, at the time of injury and at the date of the official presentation of the claim, is lawfully and habitually resident in that State.
3. Paragraph 2 does not apply in respect of an injury caused by an internationally wrongful act of the State of nationality of the refugee.

The change in the law, as the commentary to the Article states, is necessitated by the current concern for the status of both stateless persons and refugees, a concern evidenced by such conventions as the Convention on the Reduction of Statelessness of 1961[97] and the Convention on the Status of Refugees of 1951.[98] The provision does not touch on the status of such persons by changing in this particular case the connecting factor of nationality. This was done in the interests of giving certain aliens—who otherwise would not have had it—access to international protection.

Article 8(1) deals with stateless persons. The commentary states that it gives no definition of stateless person; that such a definition is to be found in the

[95] 4 UNRIAA 678.
[96] See Van Panhuys (note 1 above) 72.
[97] 989 UNTS 175.
[98] 189 UNTS 150.

Convention Relating to the Status of Stateless Persons of 1954 which defines a stateless person as a person who is not considered as a national by any State under the operation of its law;[99] that this definition can no doubt be considered as having acquired a customary status; and that a State may exercise diplomatic protection in respect of such a person, regardless of how he became stateless, provided that he was *lawfully* and *habitually* resident in that State both at the time of injury and at the date of the official presentation of the claim. The requirement of both lawful residence and habitual residence sets a high threshold. While it is possible that this threshold could lead to a situation of lack of effective protection for the individuals involved, the combination of lawful residence and habitual residence is justified in the case of an exceptional measure introduced *de lege ferenda*. There are two temporal requirements as in the case of nationality. The stateless person must be a lawful and habitual resident of the claimant State both at the time of the injury and at the date of the official presentation of the claim. This ensures that non-nationals are subject to the same rules as nationals in respect of the temporal requirements for the bringing of a claim.

Article 8(2) deals with the diplomatic protection of refugees by their State of residence. Diplomatic protection by the State of residence is particularly important in the case of refugees, because they are unable or unwilling to avail themselves of the protection of the States of nationality[100] and, if they do so, run the risk of losing refugee status in the State of residence. While the requirements in Article 8(2) are the same as for stateless persons there are also important differences between refugees and stateless persons. The ILC decided to insist on lawful residence and habitual residence as preconditions for the exercise of diplomatic protection of refugees, as with stateless persons, despite the fact that Article 28 of the Convention Relating to the Status of Refugees sets the lower threshold of lawfully 'staying' rather than residing[101] for contracting States in the issuing of travel documents to refugees. Two factors account for this. The first was that the issue of travel documents, in terms of the convention, did not in any way entitle the holder to diplomatic protection.[102] The second was that there was a need to set a high threshold when introducing an exception to a traditional rule, *de lege ferenda*. In addition, the term 'refugee' in Article 8(2) is not limited to refugees as defined in the 1951 Convention Relating to the Status of Refugees and its 1967 Protocol but is intended to cover, in addition, persons who do not strictly conform to this definition. The ILC preferred to set no limit to the term in order to allow a State to extend diplomatic protection to any person that it considered and treated as a refugee. This would be of particular importance for refugees in States not party to the existing international

[99] Article 1, 360 UNTS 117.

[100] Article 1(A)(2) of the Convention Relating to the Status of Refugees.

[101] The *travaux préparatoires* of this convention make it clear that 'stay' indicates less than durable residence.

[102] See para 16 of the Schedule to the convention.

or regional instruments. The two temporal requirements for the bringing of the claim are the same as for nationality. The refugee must be a lawful and habitual resident of the claimant State both at the time of the injury and at the date of the official presentation of the claim.

Article 8(3) provides that the State of refuge may not exercise diplomatic protection in respect of a refugee against the State of nationality of the refugee. To have permitted this would have contradicted the basic approach of the present ILC articles, according to which nationality is the predominant basis for the exercise of diplomatic protection. The paragraph is also justified on policy grounds. Most refugees have serious complaints about their treatment at the hands of their State of nationality, from which they have fled to avoid persecution. To allow diplomatic protection in such cases would be to open the floodgates for international litigation. Moreover, the fear of demands for such action by refugees might deter States from accepting refugees.

In the case of both stateless persons and refugees the State concerned has a discretion to exercise diplomatic protection. A State has a discretion under international law whether to exercise diplomatic protection in respect of a national. A fortiori it has a discretion whether to extend such protection to a stateless person or refugee.

The commentary also makes it clear, it should be noted, that Article 8 is concerned only with the diplomatic protection of stateless persons and refugees and not with the conferment of nationality upon such persons. The exercise of diplomatic protection in respect of a stateless person or refugee cannot and should not be seen as giving rise to a legitimate expectation of the conferment of nationality. Article 28 of the 1951 Convention Relating to the Status of Refugees, read with paragraph 15 of its Schedule, makes it clear that the issue of a travel document to a refugee does not affect the nationality of the holder. A fortiori the exercise of diplomatic protection in respect of a refugee, or a stateless person, should in no way be construed as affecting the nationality of the protected person.

Finally, Article 8 may be construed as creating a new category of rights enjoyed by States in addition to the right they have in respect of nationals, namely the right not to have stateless persons and refugees residing in their territory injured contrary to international law. This construction is warranted, particularly if aliens are regarded by international law as enjoying international rights.

Natural Persons: Crews of Ships

The 2006 ILC's Draft Article 18 affirms the right of the State or States of nationality of a ship's crew to exercise diplomatic protection on their behalf, while at the same time acknowledging that the State of nationality of the ship also has a right to seek redress on their behalf, irrespective of their nationality, when they have been injured in the course of an injury to the vessel resulting from an internationally wrongful act. The right of the State of nationality to exercise diplomatic protection on behalf of the members of a ship's crew has not been taken away or replaced by that of the State of nationality of the ship. As in the case of dual nationality, the two rights coexist, although the right of the flag State cannot be characterized as diplomatic protection in the absence of the bond of nationality between the flag State and the members of a ship's crew. There is, however, a close resemblance between this type of protection and diplomatic protection.

There is clear support in the practice of States and in judicial decisions for the position that the State of nationality of a ship (the flag State) may seek redress for members of the crew of the ship who do not have its nationality.[103] State practice emanates mainly from the US. Under US law foreign seamen have traditionally been entitled to the protection of the US, while they serve on US ships. The US view was that once a seaman enlisted on a ship, the only relevant nationality was that of the flag State.[104] This status of foreigners serving on US vessels has been reaffirmed in diplomatic communications and consular regulations of the US.[105] Doubts have, however, been raised by the US itself as to whether this practice provides evidence of a customary rule.[106]

International case law favours rather than opposes the right of a State to extend protection to non-national seamen. In *McCready (US)* v *Mexico* umpire Thornton held that 'seamen serving in the naval or mercantile marine under a flag not their own are entitled, for the duration of that service, to the protection of the flag under which they serve'.[107] In the *'I'm Alone' Case*, which arose from the sinking of a Canadian vessel by a US coastguard ship, the Canadian government successfully claimed compensation on behalf of three non-national crew members, on the basis that, where a claim was on behalf of a vessel, members of the crew were to be deemed, for the purposes of the claim, to be of the same nationality as the vessel.[108] In the *Reparation Case* two judges of the ICJ, in their separate

[103] Legal commentators also support this position: Myers, *The Nationality of Ships* (1967), 90–108; Dolzer, 'Diplomatic Protection of Foreign Nationals' in 1 EPIL (1992) 1068. These authors refer to the practice of States and judicial precedents. See also on State practice, Borchard (note 39 above) 475; O'Connell (note 27 above) 1050.

The right of the flag State of a ship as the national State of the ship to claim in respect of damage to the ship or of any unlawful act in regard to the ship is assumed to remain intact, though this matter is not dealt with in the 2004 ILC Draft Articles. The issue of the rights of the national States of the owners of the ship is also not dealt with in the Articles. The law is presumed to remain as it was before, ie that both groups of States have the right of protection.

[104] This view goes back to *Ross* v *McIntyre* (1891), 140 US 453. For the UK approach which was similar to that of the US see *R* v *Carr* (1882), 10 QBD 85; *R* v *Anderson* (1868), 1CCR 165–7; McNair, 2 *International Law Opinions* (1956) 172.

[105] See Hackworth, 3 *Digest of International Law* (1942) 418, and 4 ibid 883–4.

[106] This communication is on file with the Codification Division of the Office of Legal Affairs of the UN: see Dugard, 'Fifth Report on Diplomatic Protection' to the ILC, UN Doc A/CN.4/538, 22.

[107] Moore, 3 *International Arbitrations* 2536.

[108] 29 AJIL (1935) 326. The US in this case argued against the rule.

opinions, affirmed the right of a State to exercise protection on behalf of alien crew members.[109]

More recently the ITLOS in the *M/V 'Saiga' (No. 2) Case*[110] in effect gave its support to recognizing the right of the flag State to seek redress for non-national crew members. In this case the M/V 'Saiga' was arrested and detained by Guinea, while it was supplying oil to fishing vessels off the coast of Guinea. The ship was registered in St Vincent and the Grenadines and its master and crew were Ukrainian nationals. There were also three Senegalese workers on board at the time of the arrest. Following the arrest of the ship, Guinea detained the ship and crew. Before the ITLOS Guinea objected to the admissibility of the claim of the State in which the ship was registered, inter alia, on the ground that the injured crew members were not nationals of that State. The tribunal dismissed these challenges to the admissibility of the claim and held that Guinea had violated the rights of the ship's flag State by arresting and detaining the ship and its crew. It ordered Guinea to pay compensation to the flag State both for the damages to the M/V 'Saiga' and for injury to the crew.

Although the tribunal perhaps treated the dispute mainly as one relating to a direct injury to the flag State,[111] the tribunal's reasoning indicates that it saw the case also as a case involving something akin to diplomatic protection. Guinea clearly objected to the admissibility of the claim in respect of the crew on the ground that it constituted a claim for diplomatic protection in respect of non-nationals of the flag State.[112] The claimant State clearly insisted that it had the right to protect the crew of a ship flying its flag 'irrespective of their nationality'.[113] In dismissing Guinea's objection the tribunal cited several provisions of the UN Convention on the Law of the Sea, including Article 292, pointing out that they drew no distinction between nationals and non-nationals of the flag State.[114] It stated that:

> the ship, everything on it, and every person involved or interested in its operations are treated as an entity linked to the flag State. The nationalities of these persons are not relevant.[115]

Apart from the authorities there are good policy reasons for allowing the flag State to seek redress for the ship's crew. This was recognized by the ITLOS

[109] 1949 ICJ Reports 202–3 and 206–7. There are some international cases which are equivocal. In two involving Germany and Chile as defendants in claims brought by aliens serving on US vessels before Claims Commissions, the claims were rejected because the *compromis* restricted claims to those of US citizens; see also *Richelieu* v *Spain*. These and other cases are cited and discussed in Dugard (note 106 above) 23–4.

[110] (1999), ITLOS Reports (1999) 10 (also <http://www.itlos.org>).

[111] Ibid para 98.

[112] Ibid para 103.

[113] Ibid para 104.

[114] Ibid para 105.

[115] Ibid para 106.

in the above case, when it called attention to 'the transient and multinational composition of ships' crews' and stated that large ships:

> could have a crew comprising persons of several nationalities. If each person sustaining damage were obliged to look for protection from the State of which such a person is a national, undue hardship would ensue.[116]

As a practical consideration, it is much easier and more efficient for one State to seek redress on behalf of all crew members than to require the States of nationality of each crew member to bring separate claims on behalf of their nationals. The claims on behalf of the crew members are in addition to the flag State's claims in respect of the injury to the vessel. There have been no problems with recognizing the right of the flag State as the national State of the ship and of the owners of the ship to bring claims.

While the flag State's right in respect of crew members is akin to but not really that of diplomatic protection, it exists together with the right of diplomatic protection by the State of nationality. Further, neither has priority. Ships' crews are often exposed to hardships emanating both from the flag State, in the form of poor working conditions, and from third States, in the event of the ship being arrested. In these circumstances they should receive the maximum protection that international law can offer. Their national States may clearly espouse their claims against the flag State. Clearly, on the other hand, in an appropriate situation the duplication of claims on behalf of the crew cannot be permitted.[117]

Legal or Juridical Persons

Corporations

In regard to the nationality of corporations, while in principle what has been said above in regard to natural persons would apply, one of the matters with which there has been some difficulty is determining their nationality in certain circumstances.[118] The clearest rule is that a corporation does not necessarily have the nationality of the majority of its shareholders. It will ordinarily have the nationality of the State in which it is incorporated and has its seat of

[116] Ibid para 107. See the extensive discussion of this case in Dugard (note 106 above) 25–8. See also the *Grand Prince Case* (*Belize v France*, 2001), <http://www.itlos.org>.

[117] On this section see the 2006 ILC Draft Article 18 and commentary thereon. Dugard, (note 106 above) 29–31, discusses the position of passengers on ships, passengers and crew on aircraft and the crew of spacecraft in terms of whether they should be given the same treatment as ships' crew. In general there is no State practice in this area and he points out that the position of those persons is different from that of a ship's crew, there being an exception for the crew of spacecraft. But he concluded that the law in this area was not ripe for progressive development. The ILC omitted any reference to these situations in its 2006 Draft Articles.

[118] See the discussion in the *Barcelona Traction Co Case*, ICJ Pleadings (1970) passim.

management.[119] In the *Barcelona Traction Co Case*, decided by the ICJ, the court applied this principle to find that the nationality of the corporation was Canadian so that only Canada could espouse a claim in respect of the corporation, while Belgium, the State of nationality of the shareholders, had no standing to do so.

The issue which raises problems relates to the right of the national State of the shareholders or a majority of them to espouse a claim in respect of an injury to the corporation. The *Barcelona Traction Co Case*[120] repays close examination in this connection.

The Barcelona Traction Co was a company incorporated in 1911 in Toronto, Canada, where it had its head office. It was carrying on business in Spain. In the period after 1918 the company's share capital came to be held largely by Belgian nationals, whether natural or legal persons. At the relevant time it was estimated that 88 per cent of the shares were held by Belgian nationals. As a result of a number of measures taken by the Spanish authorities the company was rendered economically defunct. Belgium, the State of nationality of the majority shareholding, and not Canada, the State of nationality of the corporation, then instituted proceedings against Spain for reparation. One of the preliminary objections raised by Spain concerned the right of Belgium to exercise diplomatic protection on behalf of its shareholders in a company incorporated in Canada. The objection was upheld by the Court on the ground that it was Canada and not Belgium which was the national State with the right to bring a claim.[121] The court made some significant statements and rulings in coming to this conclusion.

The court said that it was concerned only with the question of the diplomatic protection of shareholders in a limited liability company whose capital was represented by shares. Such companies were characterized by a clear distinction between company and shareholders. Whenever a shareholder's interests were harmed by an injury to the company, it was to the company that the shareholder must look to take action, for, although two separate entities may have suffered from the same wrong, it was only one entity whose rights had been infringed.[122] Only where the act complained of was aimed directly at the rights of the shareholders did the national State of the shareholders have an independent right of action.[123] Such principles governing the distinction between company

[119] See the *Barcelona Traction Co Case*, 1970 ICJ Reports 42–3, where it was said that international law 'attributes the right of the diplomatic protection of a corporate entity to the State under the laws of which it is incorporated and in whose territory it has its registered office'. See now also the *Diallo Case (Preliminary Objections)*, 2007 ICJ Reports, para 61 ff (<http://www.icj-cij.org>). What happens when the State of incorporation and the seat of corporate management are not the same was not settled by the *Barcelona Traction Co Case* judgment.

[120] 1970 ICJ Reports 3.

[121] Belgium's claim was rejected by fifteen votes to one.

[122] Ibid 35.

[123] Ibid 36. See also the *Diallo Case (Preliminary Objections)*, where the right of the national State of shareholders to protect shareholders was recognized where their 'direct rights' were infringed. The ICJ also pointed out that what these rights were depended on the internal law of the State of nationality of the corporation: 2007 ICJ Reports, paras 68 ff (<http://www.icj-cij.org>).

and shareholders were derived from national law and not international law, the corporation being a creature of national law.

Consequently, the court affirmed the rule that the right of diplomatic protection in respect of an injury to a corporation belonged to the State under the laws of which the corporation was incorporated and in whose territory it had its registered office, and not to the national State or States of the shareholders of the corporation. In so finding the court declined to follow as precedents for the case in hand both judicial decisions dealing with the characterization of enemy corporations in time of war[124] and State practice in respect of lump sum agreements,[125] which had been cited as authority for a rule in favour of lifting the corporate veil in order to allow the State or States of nationality of shareholders to exercise diplomatic protection on their behalf. Although the court acknowledged that bilateral or multilateral investment treaties could and did confer direct protection on shareholders and that there was a body of general arbitral jurisprudence arising from the interpretation of such treaties which recognized shareholders' claims, this was not regarded as providing evidence of a rule of customary international law in favour of the right of the State or States of nationality of shareholders to exercise diplomatic protection on their behalf. All these practices and decisions based on treaties were rightly considered *lex specialis*.

The court also specifically said that the State or States of nationality of shareholders might exercise diplomatic protection on their behalf in two situations: first, where the company had ceased to exist as a legal person in its place of incorporation[126] (which was not the case with the Barcelona Traction Co), and secondly, where the State of incorporation was itself responsible for inflicting injury on the company and the foreign shareholders' sole means of protection on the international level was through their State or States of nationality,[127] which was not the case either with the Barcelona Traction Co. The court did not, however, as such endorse this latter exception.[128] The argument that the protection might be allowed on the grounds that the protection of shareholders might be allowed on grounds of equity was dismissed by the court in the circumstances of the case before it,[129] although it did not deny as such that in the appropriate case

[124] 1970 ICJ Reports 39.

[125] Ibid 40.

[126] Ibid 40–1.

[127] Ibid 48. This position has been affirmed as a rule in case law: see eg, the *Mexican Eagle Company Case* (1938), Cmd. 5758. See also Wortley, 'The Mexican Oil Dispute 1938–46', 1957 TGS 15 and cases discussed there.

[128] 1970 ICJ Reports 48.

[129] Ibid 48, 50. For a number of reasons, including the absence of treaty between Canada and Spain conferring jurisdiction on the International Court of Justice, Canada declined to institute proceedings on behalf of the Barcelona Traction Co: see, ibid 45. In the *Diallo Case (Preliminary Objections)* as in the *Barcelona Traction Co Case*, reference was made to the possibility of the protection of shareholders on the grounds of equity *infra legem*, but, while the courts did not commit itself to the view that this was possible, it found that there was no reason to apply equity in the case before it; 2007 ICJ Reports, paras 82 ff (<http://www.icj-cij.org>).

shareholders may be protected (eg by substitution) where equity—*infra legem*—demanded it. The court also declined to recognize the existence of a secondary right of diplomatic protection attaching to the State or States of nationality of shareholders where, as in the case of the Barcelona Traction Co, the State of incorporation declined to exercise diplomatic protection on behalf of the company, by instituting proceedings before the court, inter alia, because there was no valid jurisdictional instrument.[130] The argument that the decision of the International Court in the *Nottebohm* Case,[131] which it was said required the existence of a genuine link between an injured individual and the State of nationality seeking to protect him, might be applied to corporations (with the consequence that Belgium, with which Barcelona Traction was most genuinely linked by virtue of its nationals holding 88 per cent of the shares in the company, was the appropriate State to exercise diplomatic protection) was not accepted. On the other hand, the court pointed out that in the case before it there was 'a close and permanent' link between Barcelona Traction Co and Canada, as it had its registered office there and had held its board meetings there for many years,[132] thus, not clearly rejecting the relevance of the genuine link to the diplomatic protection of corporations.

In reaching its decision that the State of incorporation of a company and not the State or States of nationality of the shareholders in the company is the appropriate State to exercise diplomatic protection in the event of injury to a company, the court referred to several policy considerations. First, when shareholders invest in a corporation doing business abroad they undertake risks, including the risk that the corporation may in the exercise of its discretion decline to exercise diplomatic protection on their behalf.[133] Secondly, if the State of nationality of shareholders is permitted to exercise diplomatic protection, this might lead to a multiplicity of claims by different States, as frequently large corporations comprise shareholders of many nationalities.[134] In this connection the court said that, if the shareholder's State of nationality was empowered to act on his behalf there was no reason why every individual shareholder's national State should not enjoy such a right.[135] Thirdly, the court was reluctant to apply by way of analogy rules relating to dual nationality to corporations and shareholders and to allow the States of nationality of both to exercise diplomatic protection.[136]

Some food for thought is provided by four separate opinions in which support was given to the view that the State or States of nationality of the shareholders may exercise diplomatic protection. Judge Tanaka found that, though there was

130 1970 ICJ Reports 45, 49.

131 *(Second Phase)* 1955 ICJ Reports, 4.

132 1970 ICJ Reports 42. The Court recognized on the facts, in addition to incorporation, a 'genuine link', although not requiring it as a matter of law.

133 Ibid 35, 46, 50.

134 Ibid 48–9.

135 Ibid 48.

136 Ibid 38, 50.

no rule of international law which allowed two kinds of diplomatic protection to a company and its shareholders respectively, there was no rule of international law which prohibited double protection.[137] Judges Fitzmaurice, Jessup and Gros did not go as far as Judge Tanaka, but held that *in certain circumstances*, particularly where the State of nationality of the corporation was the wrongdoing State, the State of nationality of the shareholders had the right to exercise diplomatic protection.[138] Judge Gros, moreover, felt that the foundation of a rule of economic international law must abide by economic realities and that, where the company's link of bare nationality did not reflect any substantial economic bond, as between the two possibilities the one on the test of which the law and the facts coincide must be chosen which meant that the State whose national economy is in fact adversely affected possesses the right to take legal action.[139]

Judges Morelli, Padilla Nervo and Ammoun, on the other hand, in separate opinions supported the reasoning of the court and, further, rejected any suggestion that the State of nationality of the shareholders might take action where the State of nationality of the corporation was the wrongdoing State.[140] Judge Padilla Nervo was of the view that it is the poorer or weaker States, where the investments take place, that need to be protected against unwarranted diplomatic pressure from governments who appear to be always ready to back at any rate their national shareholders.[141]

While the court ostensibly did not require a 'genuine link' in addition to incorporation for the company to be protected by its national State, four judges in the majority did make that a requirement.[142]

The court also acknowledged that the shareholders' national State might extend diplomatic protection to it in three situations: first, where the direct rights of the shareholders are infringed;[143] secondly, where the company ceases to exist;[144] and thirdly, possibly, where the State of nationality of the corporation is the wrongdoing State.[145]

Thus, the court in that case did accept that the State or States of nationality of shareholders *might* exercise diplomatic protection on their behalf in three

[137] Ibid 131.

[138] Judge Fitzmaurice, ibid 72–5, Judge Jessup, ibid 191–4, Judge Gros, ibid 279.

[139] Ibid.

[140] Judge Morelli, ibid 240–1, Judge Padilla Nervo, ibid 257, Judge Ammoun, ibid 318.

[141] Ibid 258.

[142] Judge Fitzmaurice, ibid 80, Judge Jessup, ibid 186, Judge Padilla Nervo, ibid 254, Judge Gros, ibid 281.

[143] Ibid 36.

[144] Ibid 40–1.

[145] Ibid 48. Another exception may be where the national State of the corporation lacks the capacity to take up its case, as where the State ceases to exist or has no effective government: see *Republic of Somalia* v *Woodhouse* (1993) QB 54. The reasoning and conclusions of the court in this case have been criticized: see the writers cited in Dugard 'Fourth Report on Diplomatic Protection' to the ILC, UN Doc A/CN.4/530 6–9, and Dugard's views therein. On this section above dealing with the *Barcelona Traction Co Case* see particularly Dugard, ibid 2–5.

situations two of which were: (i) where the company had ceased to exist in its place of incorporation; (ii) where the State of incorporation was itself responsible for inflicting injury on the company and the foreign shareholders' sole means of protection on the international level was through their State or States of nationality. As the shareholders in a company may be nationals of different States, several States of nationality may be able to exercise diplomatic protection in terms of these exceptions. As to the first of these two exceptions the court set a high threshold for determining the demise of a company. The 'paralysis' or 'precarious financial situation' of a company was dismissed as inadequate; the test of 'practically defunct' was likewise rejected as one 'which lacks all legal precision'; the 'company's status in law' alone was considered relevant; only in the event of the legal demise of the company were the shareholders deprived of the possibility of a remedy available through the company and it was only if they had been deprived of all such possibility that an independent right of action for them and their State could have arisen.[146] Subsequent support has been given to this test by the European Court of Human Rights.[147] The ICJ did not expressly state that the company must have ceased to exist in *the place of incorporation* as a precondition to shareholders' intervention. Nevertheless, it seems clear in the context of the proceedings before it that the court intended that the company should have ceased to exist in the State of incorporation and not in the State in which the company was injured. A company is 'born' in the State of incorporation when it is formed or incorporated there. Conversely, it 'dies' when it is wound up in its State of incorporation, the State which gave it its existence. It therefore seems logical that the question whether a company has ceased to exist and is no longer able to function as a corporate entity must be determined by the law of the State in which it is incorporated.

There is some evidence in State practice and arbitral awards which supports the second exception referred to in the previous paragraph.[148] However, the strongest support for the right of the State of nationality of the shareholders to exercise diplomatic protection is to be found in three cases in which the injured corporation had been compelled to incorporate in the wrongdoing State: the *Delagoa Bay Railway Case*, the *Mexican Eagle Case*, and the *El Triunfo Case*. While it is in

[146] 1970 ICJ Reports 40–1. See also the separate opinions of Judges Nervo, ibid 256, and Ammoun, ibid 319–20. A less stringent test had been used in cases decided before the *Barcelona Traction Co Case*: see the *Delagoa Bay Railway Co Case*, Moore, 6 *Digest of International Law* (1906) 648; the *El Triunfo Case* (1902), 15 UNRIAA 466; the *Baasch & Romer Case* (1903), 10 UNRIAA 723.

[147] The *Agrotexim Case*, ECHR, Series A, No 330-A 25.

[148] See the *Delagoa Bay Railway Co Case*, Moore, 6 *Digest of International Law* (1906) 648; the *Mexican Eagle Case*, Whiteman, 8 *Digest of International Law* 1272–4; the *Romano-Americano Case*, Hackworth, 5 *Digest of International Law* 841; the *El Triunfo Case* (1902), 15 UNRIAA 467; the *Deutsche Amerikanische Petroleum Gesellschaft Oil Tankers Case* (1926), 2 UNRIAA 790. Caflisch, *La protection des sociétés commerciales et des interest en droit international public* (1969); Jones, 'Claims on Behalf of Nationals who are Shareholders in Foreign Companies', 26 BYIL (1949) 225, and Jiménez de Aréchaga 'International Responsibility', in Max Sørensen (ed), *Manual of International Law* (1968), 580–1, have examined the authorities and offered conclusions.

the circumstances of these cases that the protection is most needed, the decisions do not expressly limit protection to these circumstances.

In the *Barcelona Traction Co Case*, the respondent State, Spain, was not the State of nationality of the injured company. Nevertheless, the court did refer *obiter* to this exception, stating that:

> It is quite true that it has been maintained that, for reasons of equity, a State should be able, in certain cases, to take up the protection of its nationals, shareholders in a company which has been the victim of a violation of international law. Thus a theory has been developed to the effect that the State of the shareholders has a right of diplomatic protection when the State whose responsibility is invoked is the national State of the company. Whatever the validity of this theory may be, it is certainly not applicable to the present case, since Spain is not the national State of *Barcelona Traction*.[149]

After the *Barcelona Traction Co Case* was decided in 1970 the exception has been considered mainly in the context of treaties which, it is arguable, are a *lex specialis*. As such they support the right of the national State of the shareholders to intervene against the State of incorporation of the company, when it has been responsible for causing injury to the company.[150] In the *ELSI Case*[151] a chamber of the ICJ allowed the USA to bring a claim against Italy in respect of damages suffered by an Italian company whose shares were wholly owned by two US companies. The court avoided pronouncing on the proposed exception, even though Italy objected that the company whose rights were alleged to have been violated was incorporated in Italy and that the USA sought to protect the rights of shareholders in that company. This is probably because the court was not concerned with customary international law but with the interpretation of a bilateral Treaty of Friendship, Commerce and Navigation which in general provided for the protection of US shareholders abroad. However, the court did not oppose the exception in favour of the right of the national State of shareholders in a corporation to intervene against the State of incorporation where it is responsible for causing injury to the corporation.[152] The case was decided on the merits against

[149] 1970 ICJ Reports 48. Judges Fitzmaurice (ibid 72–5), Tanaka (ibid 134) and Jessup (ibid 191–3) supported the right of the State of nationality to grant protection when the corporation was injured by the State of incorporation. Judges Fitzmaurice and Jessup did not limit that right to circumstances where incorporation in the respondent State was required as a precondition for doing business in that State. Judges Padilla Nervo (ibid 257–9), Morelli (ibid 240–1) and Ammoun (ibid 318) were opposed to any form of exception.

[150] See the *SEDCO Inc Case* (1985), 84 ILR 496 (interpreting Article VII of the Algiers Claims Settlement Declaration); the *LETCO Case* (1987), 26 ILM 652–4 (interpreting Article 25 of the ICSID Convention).

[151] 1989 ICJ Reports 15.

[152] See for this view, Dinstein, 'Diplomatic Protection of Companies under International Law', in Wellens (ed), *International Law: Theory and Practice* (1988) 512. On the avoidance of application of the customary law see the comments of Gill, 'ELSI Case', 84 AJIL (1990) 257–8, also Mann, 'Foreign Investment in the International Court of Justice', 86 AJIL (1992) 92. On the *ELSI Case* see generally Stern, 'La protection diplomatique des investissements internationaux', JDI (1990) 897.

the USA, the claimant and the State of nationality of the shareholders, the decision being based on the interpretation of the treaty.

In any event this case possibly involved the infringement of the direct rights of the shareholders—an exception recognized in the *Barcelona Traction Co Case*.[153] Moreover, it is possible that this was a case in which the company had ceased to exist because it had gone into liquidation—another exception to the general rule recognized in the *Barcelona Traction Co Case*. Further, in this case, it may be contended, the court gave an affirmative answer to the question left open in the *Barcelona Traction Co Case*, whether the shareholders' national State might protect them when the company was injured by the State of incorporation. It cannot, thus, be concluded that there was a change from the position taken in the earlier case.[154] There are also many distinguishing factors.

It is to be noted that bilateral investment treaties and lump sum settlements as such do not reflect customary international law. They were rightly rejected as practice in the *Barcelona Traction Co Case*. Clearly, such agreements and treaties may be taken to reflect rather the desire of States to make certain that specific rules are applied under them which may be contrary to the customary law.

It must be acknowledged that the *Barcelona Traction Co Case* is today widely viewed not only as an accurate statement of the law on the diplomatic protection of corporations, particularly in the matter of the second exception, but as a true reflection of customary international law. Also, the practice of States in the diplomatic protection of corporations is today guided by that case.[155] This was, inter alia, clearly demonstrated by the response of delegates in the Sixth Committee to the question whether the rule in *Barcelona Traction* should be reconsidered.[156]

[153] See further on this, Lowe, 'Shareholders' Rights to Control and Manage: From Barcelona Traction to ELSI', in Ando et al (eds), *Liber Amicorum Judge Shigeru Oda* (2002) 269; also Dinstein (note 151 above).

[154] *Contra* Murphy, 'The ELSI Case: an Investment Dispute at the International Court of Justice', 16 YJIL 420.

[155] See the rules issued by the British government in 1987, published in 37 ICLQ (1988) 1006. Rule IV, in providing that the United Kingdom may take up the claim of a company incorporated in the United Kingdom, expressly states, in the commentary thereto, that it is founded on the *Barcelona Traction Co Case*.

[156] The following questions were put to States on this subject:

In the Barcelona Traction case, the International Court of Justice held that the State in which a company is incorporated and where the registered office is located is entitled to exercise diplomatic protection on behalf of the company. The State of nationality of the shareholders is not entitled to exercise diplomatic protection, except, possibly, where:

(a) The shareholders' own rights have been directly injured;
(b) The company has ceased to exist in its place of incorporation;
(c) The State of incorporation is the State responsible for the commission of an internationally wrongful act in respect of the company.

Should the State of nationality of the shareholders be entitled to exercise diplomatic protection in other circumstances? For instance, should the State of nationality of the majority of the shareholders have such a right? Or should the State of nationality of the majority of the shareholders in a company have a secondary right to exercise diplomatic protection?

Of the 15 delegates who spoke on this subject, only one[157] suggested that the case should be reconsidered. All but one of the delegates who spoke on this subject represented developed States, which is an important fact, as it is unlikely that developing States would show much support for rules which accord more protection to shareholders of foreign companies to replace those in the *Barcelona Traction Co Case*. The writings of publicists do treat the case as the seminal decision on the diplomatic protection of corporations and the starting point of any discussion on the subject,[158] even though there is criticism of those rules.

To sum up, before the *Barcelona Traction Co Case* there was some support for the exception as formulated broadly, though there was some disagreement among legal commentators in interpreting the precedents in judicial decisions and State practice, especially on the extent of the exception. The *obiter dicta* in the judgment in the case and in the separate opinions of Judges Fitzmaurice, Jessup and Tanaka have undoubtedly added to the weight of authority in favour of the broad exception. Subsequent developments, albeit in the context of judicial treaty interpretation, may have confirmed this trend.[159]

On the assumption that the law of shareholder protection was being seriously evaluated, the ILC was presented by its rapporteur with the following options[160] in codifying and progressively developing the law:

(i) The State of incorporation has the sole right of protection subject to the exceptions envisaged in the *Barcelona Traction Co Case* for the protection of shareholders.
(ii) The State of incorporation and with which the corporation has a genuine connection, usually in the form of economic control, has the right of protection subject to the same exceptions as in (i).

Official Records of the General Assembly, Fifty-seventh session, Supplement No. 10, UN Doc A/57/10, para 28.

157 Germany described the decision in the *Barcelona Traction Co Case* as 'unsatisfactory' and urged the grant of a subsidiary right of protection to shareholders (UN Doc A/C.6/57/SR.20, paras 25–6). The USA, while supporting the decision, stated that it takes the nationality of shareholders into account in deciding whether to exercise diplomatic protection, and urged that shareholders be protected where the State of nationality is itself responsible for injury to the company (UN Doc A/C.6/57/SR.23, para 52).

158 Daillier and Pellet (eds), *Nguyen Quoc Dinh's Droit International Public* (1999) 773; Shaw, *International Law* (1997) 566; Brownlie, *Principles of Public International Law* (1998) 491–5; Kooijmans, *Internationaal Publiekrecht in Vogelvlucht* (2002) 116; Shearer (ed), *Starke's International Law* (1994) 286–7; Caflisch, 'The Protection of Corporate Investments Abroad in the Light of the *Barcelona Traction Case*', 31 ZAORV (1971) 196.

159 According to the United Kingdom's 1985 Rules Applying to International Claims, 'where a United Kingdom national has an interest, as a shareholder or otherwise, in a company incorporated in another State and of which it is therefore a national, and that State injures the company, Her Majesty's Government may intervene to protect the interests of the United Kingdom national' (Rule VI), reprinted in 37 ICLQ (1998) 1007.

160 See Dugard (note 145 above) 12 ff for these options and for the explanation and discussion thereof, with references to authorities.

(iii) The State of the *siege social* or domicile has the right of protection.[161]
(iv) The State in which the economic control of the company is located has the right of protection.[162]
(v) Both the State of incorporation and the State of economic control have the right of protection. This would permit a form of dual protection similar to that which applies in the case of dual nationality of natural persons.[163]
(vi) The State of incorporation in the first instance has the right of protection, with the State of economic control enjoying a secondary right of protection in the event of failure on the part of the State of incorporation to exercise protection.[164]
(vii) The State or States of nationality of all shareholders have the right of protection.[165]

After discussion and consideration, inter alia, of these alternatives, the ILC drafted the following articles regarding diplomatic protection and corporations, which not only clarify the rules as understood but modify and develop

[161] Principally, see O'Connell (note 27 above) 1041–2; Levy, *La Nationalité des sociétés* (1984) 183–96; Harris, 'The Protection of Companies in International Law in the Light of the Nottebohm Case', 18 ICLQ (1969) 295–301. Decisions of arbitral tribunals show that there is a close correlation between *siege social* or domicile and incorporation: see Schwarzenberger, 1 *International Law* (1957), 393–7, after an examination of the *Canevaro Case*; Scott, 2 Hague Court Reports 284; *La Suédoise Grammont* v *Roller*, 3 TAM, 570; the *Mexico Plantagen GmbH Case*, AD 1932–32, Case No. 135; *Flack (GB)* v *United Mexican States* (1929), 5 UNRIAA 61; the *Madera Company Case* (1929), ibid 156; the *Interoceanic Railway of Mexico Case* (1931), ibid 178.

[162] This view relies heavily on the test of 'effective control' for determining the enemy character of corporations. Principally, see Seidl-Hohenveldern, *Corporations in and under International Law* (1987), 27–9; *Daimler Co v Continental Tyre and Rubber Co* [1916], 2 AC 307. A similar test has also been employed by the UN in respect of its resolution imposing economic sanctions against Libya: Security Council Rs 883 (1993) of 11 November 1993. See further the discussion of this resolution by the special rapporteur of the ILC in the 'Fourth Report on Nationality in Relation to the Succession of States', 2 YBILC (1998) UN Doc A/CN.4/489, paras 15–17. The test was rejected by the ICJ in the *Barcelona Traction Co Case*, 1970 ICJ Reports 39, and has been criticized as a valueless analogue: O'Connell (note 27 above) 1042. However, it may be a viable test for the diplomatic protection of corporations.

[163] This alternative is supported, inter alia, by Judges Tanaka and Jessup in the *Barcelona Traction Co Case*, 1970 ICJ Reports 130–3 and 199–202 respectively.

[164] See, inter alia, Judge Fitzmaurice in the *Barcelona Traction Co Case*, 1970 ICJ Reports 76, Procedures of the UNCC, Decision 7 of the Governing Council, UN Doc S/AC.26/1991/7/Rev. 1 (17/3/1992) para 26.

[165] The alternative was rejected by the ICJ in the *Barcelona Traction Co Case*, 1970 ICJ Reports 49, and by Judge Padilla Nervo, ibid 264. However, the position was supported by Judges Tanaka and Fitzmaurice, ibid 128–31 and 79 respectively. The argument that a multiplicity of proceedings would result was countered by both these judges: ibid 133–9 and 77 respectively. Support for their view is to be found in Higgins, 'Case concerning the Barcelona Traction Light and Power Company Ltd', 11 VJIL (1971) 339, and 'Panel:—Nationality of Claims—Individuals, Corporations, Stockholders', 63 ASIL Proceedings (1969) 30.

them, I believe, in an acceptable manner, considering particularly that the rules emerging from the *Barcelona Traction Co Case* enjoyed general respect:

CHAPTER III
LEGAL PERSONS

Article 10
Continuous nationality of a corporation

1. A State is entitled to exercise diplomatic protection in respect of a corporation that was a national of that State, or its predecessor State, continuously from the date of injury to the date of the official presentation of the claim. Continuity is presumed if that nationality existed at both these dates.

2. A State is no longer entitled to exercise diplomatic protection in respect of a corporation that acquires the nationality of the State against which the claim is brought after the presentation of the claim.

3. Notwithstanding paragraph 1, a State continues to be entitled to exercise diplomatic protection in respect of a corporation which was its national at the date of injury and which, as the result of the injury, has ceased to exist according to the law of the State of incorporation.

Article 11
Protection of shareholders

A State of nationality of shareholders in a corporation shall not be entitled to exercise diplomatic protection in respect of such shareholders in the case of an injury to the corporation unless:

(*a*) The corporation has ceased to exist according to the law of the State of incorporation for a reson unrelated to the injury; or
(*b*) The corporation had, at the date of injury, the nationality of the State alleged to be responsible for causing the injury, and incorporation in that State was required by it as a precondition for doing business there.

Article 12
Direct injury to shareholders

To the extent that an internationally wrongful act of a State causes direct injury to the rights of shareholders as such, as distinct from those of the corporation itself, the State of nationality of any such shareholders is entitled to exercise diplomatic protection in respect of its nationals.

In the Commentary to these Articles and Article 9 certain important points were made. These relate to the clarification and development of the law. They will be addressed here:

(i) Article 9

The Article recognizes that diplomatic protection may be extended to corporations. The provision makes it clear that in order to qualify as the state of nationality for the purpose of diplomatic protection of a corporation certain conditions must be met, as is the case with the diplomatic protection of natural persons.

State practice is largely concerned with the diplomatic protection of corporations, that is profit-making enterprises with limited liability whose capital is generally represented by shares, and not other legal persons. Thus, this Article and Articles 10 to 12 are concerned with the diplomatic protection of corporations and shareholders in corporations.

As with natural persons, the granting of nationality to a corporation is 'within the reserved domain' of a State.[166] Again, as the ICJ stated in the *Barcelona Traction Case*:

> ... international law has to recognize the corporate entity as an institution created by States in a domain essentially within their domestic jurisdiction. This in turn requires that, whenever legal issues arise concerning the rights of States with regard to the treatment of companies and shareholders, as to which rights international law has not established its own rules, it has to refer to the relevant rules of municipal law.[167]

Although international law has no rules of its own for the creation, management, and dissolution of a corporation or for the rights of shareholders and their relationship with the corporation, and must consequently turn to national law for guidance on this subject, it is for international law to determine the circumstances in which a State may exercise diplomatic protection on behalf of a corporation or its shareholders. This matter was addressed by the also ICJ in the *Barcelona Traction Case* when it stated that international law 'attributes the right of diplomatic protection of a corporate entity to the State under the laws of which it is incorporated and in whose territory it has its registered office'.[168] Here the court set two conditions for the acquisition of nationality by a corporation for the purposes of diplomatic protection: incorporation and the presence of the registered office of the company in the State of incorporation. As the laws of most States require a company incorporated under its laws to maintain a registered office in its territory, even if this is a mere fiction, incorporation is the most important criterion for the purposes of diplomatic protection. The court in the *Barcelona Traction Case* was not, however, satisfied with incorporation as the sole criterion for the exercise of diplomatic protection. Although it did not reiterate the requirement of a 'genuine connection' as applied in the *Nottebohm Case*,[169] and acknowledged that 'in the particular field of the diplomatic protection of corporate entitled, no absolute test of the "genuine connection" has found general acceptance',[170] it suggested that in addition to incorporation and a registered office, there was a need for some 'permanent and close connection' between the State exercising diplomatic protection and the corporation.[171] On the

[166] *Nationality Decrees in Tunis and Morocco Opinion* (1923), PCIJ Series B No 4. See also the *Diallo Case (Preliminary Objections)*, 2007 ICJ Reports, para 61 ff (<http://www.icj-cij.org>).

[167] *Barcelona Traction Co Case*, 1970 ICJ Reports 33–4. See also the *Diallo Case* (*Preliminary Objections*), 2007 ICJ Reports, para 61 ff (<http://www.icj-cij.org>).

[168] *Barcelona Traction Co Case*, 1970 ICJ Reports 42.

[169] Ibid. See the *Nottebohm Case* (*Second Phase*), 1955 ICJ Reports 22.

[170] 1970 ICJ Reports 42.

[171] Ibid.

facts of this case the court found such a connection in the incorporation of the company in Canada for over fifty years, the maintenance of its registered office, accounts and share register there, the holding of board meetings there for many years, its listing in the records of the Canadian tax authorities and the general recognition by other States of the Canadian nationality of the company.[172] All of this meant, that 'Barcelona traction's links with Canada are thus manifold'.[173] In the *Barcelona Traction Case* the court was not confronted with a situation in which a company was incorporated in one State but had a 'close and permanent connection' with another State. The court did not indicate what it might have decided in such a situation. Article 9 does, however, provide for such cases.

Article 9 accepts the basic premise of the *Barcelona Traction Case* that it is incorporation that confers nationality on a corporation for the purposes of diplomatic protection. However, it provides an exception in a particular situation where there is no other significant link or connection between the State of incorporation and the corporation itself, and where certain significant connections exist with another State, in which case that other State is to be regarded as the State of nationality for the purpose of diplomatic protection. Policy and fairness dictate such a solution. It is wrong to place the sole and exclusive right to exercise diplomatic protection in a State with which the corporation has the most tenuous connection as in practice such a State will seldom be prepared to protect such a corporation.

Article 9, thus, provides that in the first instance the State in which a corporation is incorporated is the State of nationality entitled to exercise diplomatic protection. When, howeve, the circumstances indicate that the corporation has a closer connection with another State, a State in which the seat of management and financial control are situated, that state is to be regarded as the State of nationality with the right to exercise diplomatic protection. Certain conditions must, however, be fulfilled before this occurs. First, the corporation must be controlled by nationals of another State. Secondly, it must have no substantial business activities in the State of incorporation. Thirdly, both the seat of management and the financial control of the corporation must be located in another State. Only where these conditions are cumulatively fulfilled does the State in which the corporation has its seat of management and in which it is financially controlled quality as the State of nationality for the purposes of diplomatic protection.

In the *Barcelona Traction Case* the ICJ warned that the granting of the right of diplomatic protection to the States of nationality of shareholders might result in a multiplicity of actions which 'could create an atmosphere of confusion and insecurity in international economic relations'.[174] The same confusion might result from the granting of the right to exercise diplomatic protection to several States with which a corporation enjoys a link or connection. Article 9 does not

[172] Ibid 42–3. [173] Ibid.
[174] Ibid 49.

allow such multiple actions. the State of nationality with the right to exercise diplomatic protection is *either* the State of incorporation *or*, if the required conditions are met, the State of the seat of management and financial control of the corporation. If the seat of management and the place of financial control are located in different States, the State of incorporation remains the State entitled to exercise diplomatic protection.

(ii) Article 10

The general principles relating to the requirement of continuous nationality have been addressed in connection with the protection of natural persons. In practice problems of continuous nationality arise less in the case of corporations than with natural persons. Whereas natural persons change nationality easily as a result of naturalization, marriage or adoption, and State succession, corporations generally change nationality only by being re-formed or reincorporated in another State, in which case the corporation assumes a new personality, thereby breaking the continuity of nationality of the corporation.[175] The most frequent instance in which a corporation may change nationality without changing legal personality is in the case of State succession.

Paragraph 1 of Article 10 asserts the traditional principle that a State is entitled to exercise diplomatic protection in respect of a corporation that was its national both at the time of the injury and at the date of the official presentation of the claim. It also requires continuity of nationality between the date of the injury and the date of the official presentation of the claim. These requirements have been discussed in connection with natural persons. Those requirements are relevant here as well. The date of the official presentation of the claim, as explained earlier, is preferred to that of the date of the award. An exception is, however, made in paragraph 22 Article 10 to cover cases in which the corporation acquires the nationality of the State against which the claim is brought after the presentation of the claim.

The requirement of continuity of nationality is met where a corporation undergoes a change of nationality as a result of the succession of States.[176] In effect, this is an exception to the continuity of nationality rule. This matter is covered by the reference to 'predecessor State' in Article 10(i).

[175] See Mixed Claims Commission, United States-Venezuela, constituted under the Protocol of 17 February 1903, the *Orinoco Steamship Company Case* (1903) 9 UNRIAA 180. Here a company incorporated in the United Kingdom transferred its claim against the Venezuelen Government to a successor company incorporated in the United States. As the treaty establishing the Commission permitted the United States to bring a claim on behalf of its national in such circumstances, the claim was allowed. However, Umpire Barge made it clear that, but for the treaty, the claim would not have been allowed: ibid 192. See also now *Loewen Group Inc. v. U.S.A.* (2005) 7 ICSID Reports 484.

[176] See further on this subject the *Panevezys–Saldutiskis Railway Case* (1939), PCIJ Series A/B No. 76, 18. See also 'Fourth Report on Nationality in Relation to the Succession of States', UN Doc. A/CN.4/489, which highlights the difficulties surrounding the nationality of legal persons in relation to the succession of States.

In terms of Article 10, paragraph 2, a State is not entitled to exercise diplomatic protection in respect of a corporation that acquires the nationality of the State against which the claim is brought after the presentation of the claim. This paragraph is designed to cater for the type of situation that arose in the *Loewen* case[177] in which a corporation ceased to exist in the state in which the claim was initiated (Canada) and was reorganized in the respondent State (the USA). This matter of the change of nationality was also considered in connection with natural persons.

Difficulties arise in respect of the exercise of diplomatic protection of a corporation that has ceased to exist according to the law of the State in which it was incorporated and of which it was a national. If one takes the position that the State of nationality of such a corporation may not bring a claim as the corporation no longer exists at the time of presentation of the claim, then no State may exercise diplomatic protection in respect of an injury to the corporation. A State could not avail itself of the nationality of the shareholders in order to bring such a claim as it could not show that it had the necessary interest at the time the injury occurred to the corporation. This matter troubled several judges in the *Barcelona Traction Case*[178] and it has troubled certain courts and arbitral tribunals[179] and scholars.[180] Paragraph 3 of Article 10 adopts a pragmatic approach and allows the State of nationality of a corporation to exercise diplomatic protection in respect of an injury suffered by the corporation when it was its national and has ceased to exist—and therefore ceased to be its national—as a result of the injury. In order to qualify, the claimant State must prove that it was because of the injury in respect of which the claim is brought that the corporation has ceased to exist. This paragraph is to be read in conjunction with Article 11, paragraph (a), explained below, which makes it clear that the State of nationality of shareholders will not be entitled to exercise diolomatic protection in respect of an injury to a corporation that led to its demise.

(iii) Article 11

The most fundamental principle of the diplomatic protection of corporations is that a corporation is to be protected by the State of nationality of the corporation and not by the State or States of nationality of the shareholders in a corporation.

177 (2005) 7 ICSID Reports (para. 220).

178 Judges Jessup, 1970 ICJ Reports 193, Gros ibid 277, and Fitzmaurice, ibid 101–2, and Judge ad hoc Riphagen, ibid 345.

179 See the *Kunhardt and Co. Case* (1903, USA v. Venezuela), 12 UNRIAA 171 and particularly the dissenting opinion of the Venezuelan Commissioner, ibid 180; *F.W. Flack, on behalf of the Estate of the Late D.L. Flack (Great Britain) v. United Mexican States*, Decision No. 10 (1929), 5 UNRIAA 63.

180 Caflisch, *La protection des sociétés commerciales et des intérèst indirects en droit international public* (1969) 206–7; Beckett, 'Diplomatic Claims in Respect of Injuries to Companies' 17 *Transactions of the Grotus Society* (1932) 191; Wyler, *La Regle Dite de la Continuite de la Nationalité dans le Contentieux International* (1990) 197–202.

This principle was strongly reaffirmed by the ICJ in the *Barcelona Traction Co Case*.[181] The shareholders had to look to the corporation to take action. It was only where the act complained of was aimed at the direct rights of the shareholders that a shareholder's national State had an independent right of action.[182]

Article 11(a) and (b) deal with two exceptions to the rule that it is only the national State of the corporation that has the right of protection and not that or those of the shareholders. Article 11(a) requires that the corporation shall have ceased to exist in the place of incorporation before the State or States of nationality of the shareholders may intervene on their behalf. This is in keeping with the ruling in the *Barcelona Traction Co Case* where, though the relevance solely of the State of incorporation was not expressly mentioned, it was implied.

Article 11(b) gives effect to the exception allowing the State or States of nationality of the shareholders in a corporation to exercise diplomatic protection on their behalf where the State of incorporation is itself responsible for inflicting injury on the corporation. The exception, however, is formulated in a restrictive manner so as to limit it to cases where incorporation was required by the State inflicting injury on the corporation as a precondition for doing business there. There is here a change from what could have been the position taken earlier in State practice, judicial decisions, and textual authority. It would seem that the restriction is reasonable in the circumstances, largely protecting, as it does, respondent States.

In the *Diallo Case* (*Preliminary Objections*), the ICJ, while referring to the exception referred to in Article 11(b), left open the question whether it reflected good *lex lata*. The court found that on the facts, it had not been established that the incorporation of the companies in the DRC had been required of their founders, in order to enable the companies to function in the economic sector concerned, so that the question of protection by 'substitution' of the companies did not have to be answered.[183]

(iv) Article 12

This Article retains a right of diplomatic protection accorded to the national State or States of shareholders which has always been recognized and was affirmed in the *Barcelona Traction Co Case*.[184] The court did so, even though the claimant State, Belgium, made it clear that it did not base its claim on a direct infringement of the rights of the shareholders.

The issue of the protection of the direct rights of shareholders was before the ICJ in the *ELSI Case*.[185] However, in that case, the rights in question, such as the

[181] 1970 ICJ Reports 34–7. The relevant law has been discussed earlier in this chapter.

[182] Ibid 36.

[183] 2007 ICJ Reports, paras 92–3 (<http://www.icj-cij.org>).

[184] 1970 ICJ Reports 36. See also the *Agrotexim Case*, ECHR, Series A No. 330-A. Both cases affirmed this right, though the issue was not the subject of either case.

[185] 1989 ICJ Reports 15. See now the *Diallo Case (Preliminary Objections)*, 2007 ICJ Reports paras 49 ff (<http://www.icj-cij.org>). In this case it was pointed out that the right of protection

rights of the shareholders to organize, control, and manage the company, were to be found in the Treaty of Friendship, Commerce and Navigation that the court was called upon to interpret and the court did not expound the rules of customary international law on this subject.

Article 12 makes no attempt to provide an exhaustive list of the rights of shareholders as distinct from those of the corporation itself. In the *Barcelona Traction Co Case* the ICJ mentioned the most obvious rights of shareholders—the right to a declared dividend, the right to attend and vote at general meetings, and the right to share in the residual assets of the company on liquidation—but made it clear that this list was not exhaustive. This means that it is left to courts to determine, on the facts of individual cases, the limits of such rights. It will be necessary to draw clear lines between shareholders' rights and corporate rights, particularly in respect of the right to participate in the management of corporations. That Article 12 is to be interpreted restrictively is emphasized by the phrases 'the rights of the shareholders as such' and rights 'as distinct from those of the corporation itself'.

Article 12 does not specify the legal order that must determine which rights belong to the shareholder as distinct from the corporation. In most cases this is a matter to be decided by the national law of the State of incorporation. Where the company is incorporated in the wrongdoing State, however, there may be a case for the invocation of general principles of company law in order to ensure that the rights of foreign shareholders are not subjected to discriminatory treatment.[186]

Other Legal (or Juridical) Persons

A legal (or juridical) person is any object, association or institution which the law endows with the capacity of acquiring rights and incurring obligations and is not a natural being. Legal personality is not a natural phenomenon but a creation of law.[187] A legal system may confer legal personality on whatever object, association or institution it pleases. There is no consistency or uniformity among legal systems in the conferment of such legal personality. What is common to legal systems is that a legal person must have recognition by law, ie by a national legal system, to claim legal personality. Both the ICJ and the ECJ have accepted and stressed this truth. This is the practical reality though there is much scholarly

of direct rights of shareholders was no more than the right to protect nationals as such, not being derived from the right to protect the corporation.

[186] In his separate opinion in the *ELSI Case* Judge Oda wrote of the 'general principles of law concerning companies' in the context of shareholders' rights: 1989 ICJ Reports 87–8. See on shareholders' rights, Vaughan Lowe, 'Shareholders' Rights to Control and Manage: From Barcelona Traction to ELSI' in *Liber Amicorum Shigeru Oda* (2002) 269–84.

[187] Beale, 2 *Conflict of Laws* (1935) para 120.2.

discussion about, and many theories explaining, the legal nature of juristic personality[188] and in particular, about the manner in which a legal person comes into being. In the *Barcelona Traction Co Case* the ICJ said:

In this field international law is called upon to recognize institutions of municipal law that have an important and extensive role in the international field. This does not necessarily imply drawing any analogy between its own institutions and those of municipal law, nor does it amount to making rules of international law dependent upon categories of municipal law. All it means is that international law has had to recognize the corporate entity as an institution created by States in a domain essentially within their domestic jurisdiction. This in turn requires that, whenever legal issues arise concerning the rights of States with regard to the treatment of companies and shareholders, as to which rights international law has not established its own rules, it has to refer to the relevant rules of municipal law. Consequently, in view of the relevance to the present case of the rights of the corporate entity and its shareholders under municipal law, the Court must devote attention to the nature and interrelation of those rights.[189]

On freedom of establishment the ECJ stated, 'It should be borne in mind that, unlike natural persons, companies are creatures of the law... They exist only by virtue of the varying national legislation which determines their incorporation and functioning.'[190]

Regardless of origin and history[191] there are today a wide range of legal persons with differing characteristics, including corporations, public enterprises, universities, schools, foundations, churches, municipalities, non-profit-making associations, non-governmental organizations, and in some States even partnerships. It is impossible to find common, uniform features in all these legal persons.[192] However, the corporation, with a firm distinction between it and its shareholders, with limited liability attaching to the latter and with commerce and profit-making as its purpose, unlike public enterprise, the university, the municipality, the foundation, and other such legal persons, engages in foreign trade and investment. Moreover, its activities promote international economic life and oil the machinery of international dispute settlement. Thus, diplomatic protection in respect of legal persons has come to be mainly about the protection of foreign

[188] See for the theories Wolff, 'On the Nature of Legal Persons' 54 LQR (938) 496 ff.

[189] 1970 ICJ Reports 34–5.

[190] Case 81/87, *The Queen v Treasury and Commissioners of Inland Revenue, ex parte Daily Mail and General Trust*, 1988 ECR para 19.

[191] On history dating back to Roman Law, see Hahlo and Kahn, *The South African Legal System and its Background* (1968) 104–5.

[192] Dugard, 'Fourth Report on Diplomatic Protection' to the ILC, *Addendum*, UN Doc/A/CN.4/530/Add/1, 5 ff, comments that it is for this reason that writers on both public and private international law largely confine their consideration of legal persons in the context of international law to the corporation—the commercial, profit-making enterprise whose capital is represented by shares, in respect of which there is a firm distinction between the separate entity of the corporation and the shareholders, with limited liability attaching to the latter.

investment. This is why the corporation is the legal person upon which there is focus in the field of diplomatic protection.[193]

Be that as it may, the corporation is not the only legal person that may merit diplomatic protection. Regard must be had to other legal persons in the context of diplomatic protection. As has been observed,[194] the case law of the PCIJ:

> shows that a commune[195] (municipality) or university[196] may in certain circumstances qualify as nationals of a State and as legal persons. There is no reason why such legal persons should not qualify for diplomatic protection if injured abroad, provided that they are autonomous entities not forming part of the apparatus of the protecting State...
>
> Non-profit-making foundations, comprising assets set aside by a donor or testator for a charitable purpose, constitute legal persons without members. Today many foundations fund projects abroad to promote health, welfare, women's rights, human rights and the environment in developing countries. Should such a legal person be subjected to an internationally wrongful act by the host State, it is probable that it would be granted diplomatic protection by the State under whose laws it has been created. Non-governmental organizations[197] engaged in worthy cases abroad would appear to fall into the same category as foundations.

Legal persons may take a variety of forms. For example, partnerships in most legal systems are not legal persons and it is the interests of the individual partners which would be subject to diplomatic protection in international law, but in some legal systems the partnership enjoys legal personality,[198] in which case it is possible that the individual partners be treated in the same manner as shareholders. A different situation arises, for instance, with the European Economic Interest Grouping (EEIG), created by European Community law.[199] According to Article 1(2) of the regulations creating that entity, 'A grouping so formed shall, from the date of its registration as provided for in Article 6, have the capacity, in its own name, to have rights and obligations of all kinds, to make contracts or accomplish

[193] There is a vast literature on the law governing the protection of foreign investment. The ICSID was created for the settlement of foreign investment disputes. On foreign investment and its protection see, recently, eg Sornarajah, *The International Law of Foreign Investment* (2004).

[194] Dugard (note 192 above) 6–7, and 'Report of the ILC 2004' 66–7, <http://www.un.org>.

[195] In the *German Interests in Polish Upper Silesia (Merits) Case* (1926), PCIJ Series A, No 7, 73–5, the PCIJ held that the commune of Ratibor fell within the category of 'German national' within the meaning of the German-Polish Convention concerning Upper Silesia of 1922.

[196] In the *Appeal from a Judgment of the Czechoslovak-Hungarian Mixed Tribunal (Peter Pázmány University* v *Czechoslovakia) Case* (1932), PCIJ Series A/B, No 61 208, 227–32, the Permanent Court held that the Peter Pázmány University was a Hungarian national in terms of Article 250 of the Treaty of Trianon and therefore entitled to the restitution of property belonging to it.

[197] There are conflicting views on non-governmental organizations and the possibility of diplomatic protection for them, as legal persons with a nationality: see for a contrary view to Dugard's, Doehring, 'Diplomatic Protection of Non-Governmental Organizations' in *El derecho internacional en un mundo en transformación: liber Amicorum: en homenaje al professor Eduardo Jiménez de Aréchaga* (1994) 571–80.

[198] Dorresteijn, Kuiper and Morse, *European Corporate Law* (1994) 13.

[199] Council Regulation (EEC) No. 2137/85 of 25 July 1985 on the European Economic Interest Grouping, OJ No. L 199, 31/07/1985, 1.

other legal acts, and to sue and be sued.' Article 1(3) then stipulates: 'The member States shall determine whether or not groupings registered at their registries, pursuant to article 6, have legal personality.' The same types of entities, endowed with equal legal capacities by a uniform statute, may therefore be granted legal personality in one European Union Member State and left without it in another. Although the common law treats companies and partnerships as entirely separate creatures, some legal systems recognize hybrid forms.[200]

In view of the diversity of species of legal persons, the ILC has taken the course of drafting a provision that extends the principles of diplomatic protection adopted for corporations to other legal persons—subject to necessary changes to take account of the different features of each legal person. Draft Article 13 of the ILC provides that the principles governing the State of nationality of corporations and the application of the principle of continuous nationality to corporations, contained in Draft Articles 9 and 10 respectively apply 'as appropriate', to the diplomatic protection of legal persons other than corporations. There is a lack of precedent, whether in State practice or in international judicial decisions. Thus, the proposed draft Article, without being revolutionary, supplies a filling for a defined gap. Clearly, also whether legal persons such as those being discussed have the nationality of a State for the purposes of diplomatic protection will be determined primarily by the law of that State.[201]

[200] See Dorresteijn, Kuiper and Morse (note 198 above) 25–6, where the German Kommanditgesellschaft auf Aktien is referred to and discussed.

[201] On the issue of the national state's rights in connection with shareholders of a corporation and of partners, the ILA in Resolution No. 5/2006 decided that:

12. Shareholders of a foreign company may be protected by the state of their nationality if their rights have been directly infringed, as well as in other special circumstances where they would otherwise be deprived of protection.
13. Shareholders of a foreign company may also be protected by the state of their nationality for wrongs affecting such company if the state of nationality of the company is unable or unwilling to exercise such protection or is the defendant state.
14. Control of a foreign company by shareholders of a different nationality, may entitle the state of nationality of such shareholders to exercise diplomatic protection on their behalf or otherwise to consider the company as having its nationality.
15. If a company or partnership is prevented from claiming because of its nationality, shareholders or partners not so affected may claim in proportion to their interest in such company, including indirect or minority interest, or otherwise be entitled to diplomatic protection by the state of their nationality, particularly if incorporation in the host state has been required by that state as a condition of conducting business there. (<http://www.ila-hq.com>)

These conclusions were based on the examination of the matter by Orrego Vicuña (note 21 above) 642 ff, and on the conclusions reached by him, ibid 646–7. The conclusions go beyond what was recommended by the ILC in its 2006 Draft Articles. The ILC's approach is acceptable.

11

Exhausting Local Remedies

The rule that, where there has been a violation of international law in the treatment of an alien by a State, local remedies must be exhausted by the alien before his claim may be espoused by his national State has in some respects had a distinguished history.[1] It can hardly be said that in the context of modern international law it is defunct or has ceased to be relevant, although a tendency may have arisen to try sometimes to circumvent it by various techniques.[2] As had been pointed out by the ILC in its draft articles on State responsibility, the non-observance of the rule is an objection to admissibility of an international claim.[3] The rule is firmly established. Moreover, its raison d'être is still to be deemed unchanged and viable.

The rule sprang up primarily as an instrument designed to ensure respect for the sovereignty of host States in this particular area of international dispute settlement. Basically, this is the principal reason for its survival today. In the modern law of diplomatic protection the raison d'être of the rule is the recognition given by members of the international community to the interest of the host State, flowing from its sovereignty, in settling international disputes of a certain kind by its own means before international mechanisms are invoked. The utility of this policy value underlying the rule cannot be denied. Even though the disputes concerned, involving individuals as they do, are international disputes, the same reasons that led to the formation of the rule through the years have really survived the development of more sophisticated systems of international dispute settlement. Functionally, to date, the accelerated interaction between aliens and foreign States because of the ease of international travel, the growing sense of community in the world, and the demands of economic development, in both developed and developing nations, means that the rule could be important in

[1] See C F Amerasinghe, *Local Remedies in International Law* (2004) 22 ff and authorities there cited. The rule of exhaustion of local remedies has been considered and discussed in detail in the above work.

[2] C F Amerasinghe, ibid 247 ff 425; C F Amerasinghe, 'Whither the Local Remedies Rule?' 5 ICSID Review (1990) 293 ff. For an assessment of the usefulness of the rule and its future see ibid 309–10; C F Amerasinghe (note 1 above) 425 ff.

[3] Article 44(b): Crawford, *The International Law Commission's Articles on State Responsibility* (2002) 70, 264–5. Now see also Article 2006 14(1) of the ILC's Draft Articles on Diplomatic Protection: *Report of the ILC (2006)* 20, 71.

the settlement of international disputes that may arise from the exercise of, or in the context of situations which may lead to, diplomatic protection. The respect, shown by reference to the rule, for the sovereignty of the respondent State in conflict situations involving diplomatic protection in general international law has not waned. The ICJ has recognized the viability of the rule in several cases.[4]

Although the value attached to respect for the sovereignty of the host or respondent State is at the heart of the implementation of the rule, there is evidence in the evolution of the rule that international law attaches importance, in the rule's application, to values other than the interests of the host or respondent State. Such interests as those of the alien or individual, of the national State of the alien, and of the international community have been taken into consideration. In different situations, the conflict between or among the various interests has been resolved in favour of one or other of the interests besides those of the host or respondent State, while sometimes the roll of the dice has favoured the latter. Generally, it may be concluded that there has been a judicious weighing of conflicting interests, particularly by judicial or quasi-judicial organs of the international community, before a solution has been reached.

It is apparent that local remedies operate as a step or steps in the orderly procedure of settling international disputes. The rule is no more and no less than a method of ascribing to sovereign States a dispute settlement function in international disputes to which they are parties. While States are surely capable of responsibly and constructively discharging the trust placed in them by the international community in conferring on them a role which flows from respect for their sovereignty, it is reasonable to expect that the rule should operate essentially as a means of securing economically and efficiently the settlement of international disputes in the areas relating to the protection of aliens. Thus, while on the one hand a sovereign State is given every opportunity of settling such disputes equitably through its own organs, and it is in the interest of all concerned that such disputes should be settled at the earliest possible opportunity at a local level, on the other hand it is logical that some recognition should also be given to the countervailing interests of all parties concerned in efficient justice without, inter alia, financial waste.

Scope of the Rule

An issue which is crucial to the operation of the rule in practice concerns the extent to which local remedies must be exhausted. As already pointed out, the interplay between the two principal sets of conflicting interests, those of the host

[4] See the statement of the ICJ in the *ELSI Case*, 1989 ICJ Reports 42; particularly also the *Interhandel Case*, 1959 ICJ Reports 27; the *Diallo Case* (*Preliminary Objections*), 2007 ICJ Reports, para 42, <http://www.icj-cij.org.>.

or respondent State arising from its sovereignty and those of the alien in securing a fair and equitable solution to his complaint without being put to undue expense or hardship, is significant here, although there tends to be a greater emphasis on those of the host or respondent State in having an opportunity to settle the dispute by its own means. The question is how extensive must be the resort to local remedies in order to enable the host or respondent State to have a proper opportunity of settling the dispute.[5] The development of the rule, particularly through judicial decisions, demonstrates that, while great respect is shown for the sovereignty of the host or respondent State, there has been some concern for the interests of the alien, so as not to make the extent of resort required unreasonable.

There has in the past been some discussion of the question of what remedies must be exhausted in order that the requirements of the rule be satisfied, particularly with respect to extraordinary remedies. The theory of the matter has not been paid much attention in discussions in the past. However, it is reasonably clear that in the past practice relating to diplomatic protection the rule has been applied generally to remedies of a judicial nature.[6] Indeed, in 1864 Phillimore, in an opinion to the British Crown, specifically defined the term local redress which he used as being redress 'through courts of law'.[7]

It was usual to include remedies available through special courts, provided they were legally constituted, in the concept of 'judicial remedies'.[8] Remedies which could lead to reparation according to rules of law are included among those to be exhausted.[9] In principle courts have certainly been included in the concept of local remedies, even in the decisions of international tribunals. Thus, in the *Croft Case*,[10] a special court which had jurisdiction over the cancellation of patent rights was held to be a local remedy to which the aggrieved alien should have had resort. Remedies available through a special system of administrative courts are also to be characterized as exhaustible remedies.[11] The fact that resort

[5] See on this particularly C F Amerasinghe (note 1 above) 182 ff.

[6] For decisions see eg *Mavrommatis Palestine Concessions Case,* PCIJ Series A No 5 (1925); the *German Interests in Upper Silesia Case,* PCIJ Series A No 6 (1925); the *Chorzów Factory Case,* PCIJ Series A No 9 (1927); the *Phosphates in Morocco Case,* PCIJ Series A/B No 74 (1938); the *Panavezys-Saldutiskis Railway Case,* PCIJ Series A/B No 76 (1939); the *Electricity Co of Sofia Case,* PCIJ Series A/B No 77 (1939); the *Norwegian Loans Case,* 1957 ICJ Reports 14; the *Interhandel Case,* 1959 ICJ Reports 11; the *ELSI Case*, 1989 ICJ Reports 15; the *Arrest Warrant of 11 April 2000 Case*, <http://www.icj-cij.org>; the *Finnish Ships Arbitration* (Finland v Great Britain), 3 UNRIAA p. 1479 (1934); the *Ambatielos Claim* (Greece v UK), 12 UNRIAA 83 (1956); other cases cited in de La Pradelle-Politis, *RAI*, vol 1, 24, 48, 131, 138, 161, 460, 474, 476, 582 and 592; vol 2, 103, 112, 121, 275, 291, 294, 486, 487, 594, 673, 674 and 710; and vol 3, 116, 121 and 123. There are also some cases in Moore, 6 *International Arbitrations* (1898) and the UNRIAA series. For some diplomatic practice, see eg Moore, *International Law* (1906) 656 ff; Hackworth, 5 *Digest* (1943) 501 ff; and McNair, 2 *International Law Opinions* (1956) 312 ff.

[7] McNair, 2 ibid 312.

[8] C F Amerasinghe (note 1 above) 183.

[9] See C F Amerasinghe, ibid 183–4.

[10] (Great Britain v Portugal, 1856), 59 BFSP (1859–60) 1288.

[11] See the *Phosphates in Morocco Case*, PCIJ Series A/B No 74, 17 (1938); the French pleadings in PCIJ Series C No 84, 209 ff.; and the Italian pleadings in PCIJ Series C No 84, 439 ff.

has already been had to the same courts before would not seem to matter, even if the legal means available are in reality extraordinary ones, provided a legal remedy may be available.[12] In the *Ambatielos Claim*, the tribunal put the matter succinctly by characterizing the remedies to be exhausted as 'legal' when it said: 'It is the whole system of legal protection, as provided by municipal law, which must have been put to the test.'[13]

Legal commentators generally discuss the rule on the assumption that it is limited to remedies of a judicial or legal nature.[14] Codification drafts of an official nature clearly make the same assumption in general.[15] García Amador's draft is an exception in that it refers to 'all the remedies and proceedings established by municipal law'.[16]

Private bodies have not been so specific or limited in their formulations.[17] Some support is given for these formulations by a statement made by the PCIJ in the *Phosphates in Morocco Case* to the effect that a failure of local remedies might result 'either from a lacuna in the judicial organization or from the refusal of administrative or extraordinary methods of redress designed to supplement its deficiencies'.[18] Nowhere, in that case, however, did the parties refer to any remedies except judicial remedies, which were available through administrative courts. Hence, the statement could consistently be interpreted to cover only

[12] See the *Interhandel Case*, 1959 ICJ Reports 27.

[13] Greece v UK, 12 UNRIAA 120 (1956).

[14] Anzilotti, 'La Responsabilité internationale des étâts à raison des dommages soufferts par des étrangers', 13 RGDIP (1906) 8; Borchard, *The Diplomatic Protection of Citizens Abroad* (1916) 381; Ralston, *The Law and Procedure of International Tribunals* (1926) 95; Eagleton, *The Responsibility of States in International Law* (1929) 95; Eagleton, 'Une théorie au sujet du commencement de la responsabilité de l'état', 11 RDILC (1930) 643; Hoijer, *La Responsabilité internationale des étâts* (1930) 374; Borchard, in 38 AIDI (1931-I) 424; Dunn, *The Protection of Nationals* (1932) 156; Witenberg, 'La Recevabilité des réclamations devant les juridictions internationales', 41 Hague Recueil (1932) 50; H Friedmann, 'Épuisement des voies de recours internes', 14 RDILC (1933) 318; Ténékidès, 'L'épuisement des voies de recours internes comme condition préalable de l'instance internationale', 14 RDILC (1933) 514; Fachiri, 'The Local Remedies Rule in the Light of the Finnish Ships Arbitration', 17 BYIL (1936) 19; Ago, 'La Regola del Previo Esaurimento dei Ricorsi Interni in Tema di Responsabilità Internazionale', 3 ArchivDP (1938) 181; Freeman, *The International Responsibility of States for Denial of Justice* (1937) 407 and 422; Fawcett, 'The Exhaustion of Local Remedies: Substance or Procedure?', 31 BYIL (1954) 452; Verzijl, in 45 AIDI (1954-I) 5, 84 and in 46 AIDI (1956) 13 ff; C de Visscher, 'Le Déni de justice en droit international', 52 Hague Recueil (1935) 421 ff; Shea, *The Calvo Clause* (1955); Bagge, 'Intervention on the Ground of Damage Caused to Nationals, with Particular Reference to Exhaustion of Local Remedies and the Rights of Shareholders', 34 BYIL (1958) 162; Law, *The Local Remedies Rule in International Law* (1961); Mummery, 'The Content of the Duty to Exhaust Local Judicial Remedies', 58 AJIL (1964) 389; Gaja, *L'Esaurimento dei Ricorsi Interni nel Diritto Internazionale* (1967); Haesler, *The Exhaustion of Local Remedies in the Case Law of International Courts and Tribunals* (1968) 28 ff; Chappez, *La Régle de l'épuisement des voies de recours internes* (1972); and Cançado Trindade, *The Application of the Rule of Exhaustion of Local Remedies in International Law* (1983) 58. I have also considered this aspect of scope in *Local Remedies in International Law* (2004) 182 ff.

[15] YBILC (1956), vol 2 221 ff.

[16] Article 18, YBILC (1961), vol 2 48.

[17] See for examples C F Amerasinghe (note 1 above) 185.

[18] PCIJ Series A/B No 74, 28 (1938).

'administrative or extraordinary methods of redress' of an essentially judicial nature.[19] That an act of grace does not come under the concept of remedies to be exhausted seems to have been accepted later. Thus, remedies which would result in a non-binding recommendation given by the deciding body to an executive organ of the host or respondent State seem to be excluded from those which must be exhausted.[20]

Later in the arguments in the *Barcelona Traction Co Case* some views on either side were expressed by the contending States on the issue of ordinary and extraordinary remedies. The Spanish government in its preliminary objections stressed that it was the whole system of legal protection afforded by the respondent State that had to be tested.[21] In the case there were certain remedies arguably involved which may be described as extraordinary. One was the action which could be brought against a corrupt judge in the event that he was fraudulent in giving a decision. The second was contentious administrative proceedings in respect of administrative decisions taken by an executive organ, beginning with a hierarchical appeal to the Minister and followed by recourse to the administrative courts. The Spanish argument was emphatic that the first remedy should have been exhausted because it fell within the category of exhaustible remedies.[22] As regards the contentious administrative proceedings, the Spanish government was of the view that these were certainly included as the kind of remedies to be exhausted, although they were extraordinary.[23]

The Belgian government did not dispute the principle enunciated in the Spanish government's argument relating to contentious administrative proceedings.[24] Thus, there seems to have been agreement on the principle that the extraordinary remedy of contentious administrative proceedings including a hierarchical appeal was not excluded per se from those remedies that had to be exhausted by virtue of its character. With regard to the extraordinary remedy by way of action against a corrupt judge, on the other hand, the Belgian government objected that this was not a normal case of remedies, although it could have resulted in the overturning of the decision of the judge in question.[25]

The Belgian argument concerning the action against a corrupt judge seems to be based on the idea that exceptional recourse is not as such included in the

[19] There is an early British precedent relating to reprisals which contradicts this view: see McNair, 2 *International Law Opinions* (1956) 312. But not only is this an old precedent but it refers to the use of force.

[20] See the *Neptune's Case* (1977), where an opinion given by the House of Lords to the British Government would not have been binding: Moore, 3 *International Arbitrations* (1898) 3043.

[21] ICJ Pleadings (1962–9), vol 4, 592–3.

[22] 'Exceptions preliminaries présentées par le Gouvernernent espagnol' ICJ Pleadings (1962–9), vol 1, 242. The Spanish government also referred to the remedy by way of revision of the bankruptcy judgment, which, it argued, although extraordinary, should have been exhausted: ICJ Pleadings (1962–9), vol 9, 923.

[23] ICJ Pleadings (1962–9), vol 1, 242.

[24] 'Observations et conclusions du Gouvernement Belge', ICJ Pleadings (1962–9), vol 1, 267–8.

[25] Ibid 221.

concept of the remedies to be exhausted, rather than that it was not to be expected that the remedy would be invoked because it was not reasonable to demand this of the aggrieved aliens. There was an element of disagreement on the character of the remedy that must be exhausted.

Generally, except for a few broad statements, particularly in some codification drafts, the tendency has been to accept some limitations on the nature of the remedy to which resort must be had. The question then relates to the extent of the limitations. There are references to, for example, 'normal usage' and the exclusion of exceptional recourse. But in fact most descriptions refer to the exhaustion of legal or judicial remedies as being required. The better view is that only those remedies which are of a judicial or quasi-judicial character must be exhausted, although they may not be confined to those provided by the regular courts of law. The 2006 ILC Draft Article 14(2) is not sufficiently specific. It refers merely to ordinary or special remedies, whether provided by judicial or administrative courts or bodies.[26]

[26] The Commentary to Article 14 expresses views which reflect what has been said above: Report of the ILC (2006) 71–2. Now in the *Diallo Case* (*Preliminary Objections*) the ICJ had something to say on what kinds of remedies must be exhausted. The Court explained that, while extraordinary, administrative remedies must be exhausted, remedies involving acts of grace need not be exhausted:

> 47 The Court further observes that, even if this was a case of expulsion and not refusal of entry, as the DRC maintains, the DRC has also failed to show that means of redress against expulsion decisions are available under its domestic law. The DRC did, it is true, cite the possibility of requesting reconsideration by the competent administrative authority (see paragraph 36 above). The Court nevertheless recalls that, while the local remedies that must be exhausted include all remedies of a legal nature, judicial redress as well as redress before administrative bodies, administrative remedies can only be taken into consideration for purposes of the local remedies rule if they are aimed at vindicating a right and not at obtaining a favour, unless they constitute an essential prerequisite for the admissibility of subsequent contentious proceedings. Thus, the possibility open to Mr. Diallo of submitting a request for reconsideration of the expulsion decision to the administrative authority having taken it — that is to say the Prime Minister — in the hope that he would retract his decision as a matter of grace cannot be deemed a local remedy to be exhausted. (2007 *ICT Reports*, para 47—<http://www.icj-cij.org>)

With regard to both the claims made by the claimant State, Guinea, in respect of (i) the alleged wrongful expulsion of its national and (ii) the alleged direct injury to him as a shareholder of two companies incorporated in the Democratic Republic of Congo (DRC), the respondent, the court held that there were no effective remedies to exhaust. In respect of the first claim the court pointed out, as seen above, that there were no 'legal' remedies available, let alone effective ones. The court then stated that

> 48. Having established that the DRC has not proved the existence in its domestic legal system of available and effective remedies allowing Mr. Diallo to challenge his expulsion, the Court concludes that the DRC's objection to admissibility based on the failure to exhaust local remedies cannot be upheld in respect of that expulsion. (Ibid, para 48)

With regard to the second claim the court in effect found that the respondent had not established that there are any effective internal remedies to which resort could have been had by Mr. Diallo in seeking redress for the alleged violation of his direct rights as a shareholder of the two companies—the remedies available being no different from those relating to the claim based on his alleged expulsion. The court said:

> 74. The Court notes that the alleged violation of Mr. Diallo's direct rights as *associé* was dealt with by Guinea as direct consequence of his expulsion given the circumstances in which that

In principle the policies behind the rule of local remedies would not warrant an unlimited extension of the concept of remedies to all types of remedies. Although the respondent State is given an opportunity of redressing a wrong, it is also relevant that for social ends the alien is being prevented from obtaining what may be less expensive justice by a direct recourse to an international tribunal. It would be proper, then, that he should be compelled to use only those means by which he has an opportunity to obtain justice according to law. What international law is interested in is the determination according to law, in an impartial manner, of the alien's rights. Hence, the emphasis on the judicial or quasi-judicial nature of remedies cannot be out of place. It would be improper to insist on his seeking remedies from sources which do not operate impartially and have no obligation to decide according to legal principles. Thus, to expect him to approach the administration or the legislature in the hope of having his problem solved as a result of the beneficence of either would be unreasonable. It would seem, therefore, that it is only where remedies enjoy a character which ensures impartial determination of disputes, according to law and not purely by uncontrolled discretion, that the alien must resort to them. This is the test that must be applied to determine the exhaustibility of remedies outside the normal judicial sphere. Hence, administrative tribunals and the like may fall within the category of exhaustible remedies, if they share the required character.

A distinction must, of course, be made between the method of deciding the dispute and the procedure for implementing the decision. It is only the former that is of relevance here. The fact that the implementation of a decision is at the discretion of the respondent State would not affect the position, since this lies within the sovereign powers of the State and a truly judicial determination may in any case be disregarded. The respondent State has a right to determine the alien's right in the proper way, and whatever the subsequent attitude it may adopt towards fulfilling its secondary obligation of reparation, this fact should not affect the classification of a remedy in such a way that it is incumbent upon the alien to resort to it. The distinction which is viable is between those remedies which are legal or judicial and quasi-judicial and those that are not.

> expulsion occurred. The Court has already found above (see paragraph 48), that the DRC has not proved that there were effective remedies, under Congolese law, against the expulsion Order against Mr. Diallo. The Court further observes that at no time has the DRC argued that remedies distinct from those in respect of Mr. Diallo's expulsion existed in the Congolese legal system against the alleged violations of his direct rights as *associé* and that he should have exhausted them. The Parties have indeed devoted discussion to the question of the effectiveness of local remedies in the DRC but have confined themselves in it to examining remedies open to Africom-Zaire and Africontainers-Zaire, without considering any which may have been open to Mr. Diallo as *associé* in the companies. Inasmuch as it has not been argued that there were remedies that Mr. Diallo should have exhausted in respect of his direct rights as *associé*, the question of the effectiveness of those remedies does not in any case arise.
>
> 75. The Court concludes from the foregoing that the objection as to inadmissibility raised by the DRC on the ground of the failure to exhaust the local remedies against the alleged violations of Mr. Diallo's direct rights as *associé* of the two companies Africom-Zaire and Africontainers-Zaire cannot be upheld. (ibid, paras 74 and 75)

Both natural and juridical persons must exhaust local remedies, while a foreign company financed partly or mainly by public capital is also required to exhaust local remedies when it engages in *acta jure gestionis*, and aliens who are non-nationals of a State which may exercise protection in exceptional circumstances must exhaust remedies.[27]

As was stated in the *ELSI Case*, the essence of the claim should be brought before the local judicial bodies and all available and accessible remedies must be 'exhausted' in that they have been pursued as far as is permitted or required by local law so that a final decision is given.[28] This also means that the alien must use the procedures, evidentiary ones especially, which are available to him to support his claim in the process of exhausting remedies and that he fails to exhaust remedies, if the preparation or presentation of his claim at the local level is faulty and results in a wholly or partially unsuccessful resort to remedies.[29]

It is to be noted that the ILC's 2006 Draft Articles, also in Article 15(a), in addition make it clear that only reasonably available local remedies which provide effective redress need be exhausted.

Exceptions to or Limitations on the Rule

Respect for the sovereignty of the respondent or host State constitutes the foundation of the rule that local remedies must be exhausted. Recognition of other interests, such as those of the alien claimant in avoiding undue hardship and excessive expense in pursuing local remedies, has resulted in limitations being placed on or exceptions being made to the operation of the rule. In its positive form, the rule was not absolute and had certain parameters in so far as exhaustion was initially limited to remedies which were, for example, of a legal nature, available, and effective. In a sense, the negative requirements are the other side of the coin. The limitations, thus directly resulting, and such others as may have been placed on the rule flow primarily out of consideration for the interests of the alien claimant, but also because of the need to have justice dispensed efficiently and economically, which is an interest of the international community. The limitation that those remedies which are ineffective or inadequate need not be exhausted, raises some issues of definition which have been addressed in the various sources of the law.

[27] Ibid 69. See also C F Amerasinghe (note 1 above) 197–8.

[28] 1989 ICJ Reports 45–6. See also C F Amerasinghe (note 1 above) 195 ff; Commentary on Article 14 of the ILC Draft: Report of the ILC (2006) 73; the *Finnish Ships Arbitration* (1938), 3 UNRIAA 1502, where slightly different language was used in describing what aspects of the claim must be presented to the local institutions.

[29] See C F Amerasinghe (note 1 above) 195–6, 216 ff; commentary on Article 14 of the ILC Draft Articles: Report of the ILC (2006) 73 ff.

The interests of the alien claimant are an important consideration in deciding how the rule of local remedies is to be applied. These interests were noted in the *Finnish Ships Arbitration*,[30] particularly in regard to the setting of limits upon the rule. It was also pointed out by the arbitral commission in the *Ambatielos Claim* that the rule could not be strained too far, even though respect for the sovereignty of the respondent or host State required that the whole system of legal protection be tested and exhausted,[31] thus implicitly giving particular value to the interests of the alien claimant. However, identifying the limitations on the rule requires more than mere regard for such interests. The process demands reconciliation of the conflict between the interests of the respondent or host State in having an opportunity of doing justice, and other interests, including those of the alien as claimant in avoiding undue hardship and in a quick and efficient dispute the settlement procedure. In jurisprudence and practice some categories of limitation have been clearly established. Theoretically, however, there is room for expansion of these categories when new situations arise which may be eligible for consideration. While the outcome of such consideration may not always be foreseeable, it is clear that in each case a careful weighing of the conflicting interests must take place. In this exercise, because of the history of the rule and of the manner in which it has evolved, the important place held by respect for the sovereignty of the host or respondent State, which requires that it be given a fair opportunity of doing the justice through its own system, cannot be ignored. Consequently, it is only where the interests of the alien claimant or other interests clearly dominate and require recognition that a limitation is to be accepted. Where limitations have been imposed it is because a reasonable case has been made for such limitations. Similarly, where future limitations are canvassed the same principle would apply.

The first systematic attempt to deal with the problem of exceptions to or limitations on the application of the rule of local remedies was, perhaps, in the *Finnish Ships Arbitration*.

The limitations on the rule of local remedies seem to have been described in its early history as being based on the absence of exhaustible justice but this may not be the sole raison d'être of all the limitations. In a broad sense, the absence of exhaustible justice may be a highly important consideration, particularly as the inapplicability of the rule is viewed from the point of view primarily of the host or respondent State in so far as the limitations on the rule are related to the inability of that State to do justice. But, as was implied in the *Finnish Ships Arbitration*, it was really consideration also of the alien's interest in not being put to undue hardship that gave rise to the limitation which was found to exist in that case. The tribunal concluded that it was 'hard' (or unjust or unfair) to expect the alien

[30] Finland v Great Britain, 3 UNRIAA 1497 (1934).

[31] Greece v UK, 12 UNRIAA 120 (1956). See also p 125 (Alfaro) and p 128 (Spiropoulos) for comparable ideas.

to pursue remedies any further in the circumstances which prevailed in the case. Thus, at the heart of the problem of limitations is the question of justice or fairness, which in turn is inextricably involved with a balancing of the conflicting interests in reality associated with the rule.

There may be remedies which, although available, are not in the circumstances applicable to the particular injury of which the alien complains. International courts or organs have then tended to regard the remedy as not available. Apart from the cases discussed earlier in which the remedy was held not to be available in this sense, there have been cases which came before the UN Human Rights Committee in which the remedy was held not to be exhaustible because it was not available according to law.[32] Thus, it is not the theoretical existence of a remedy under the law of the host or respondent State which makes it exhaustible, but rather whether according to that law it is applicable to the claimant's case. By the same token it would follow that it must be quite clear according to the law of the host or respondent State that the remedy in question is inapplicable to the claimant's case.

(a) Ineffective Remedies

The limitation arising from the positive requirement that the remedy be effective or adequate for the object of the claim implies that ineffective remedies need not be exhausted. In the application of the rule to the problem of appeals from one court to another within the same national system in the *Finnish Ships Arbitration* it was held that a claimant was not under an obligation to resort to an appeal which was obviously futile. It was insufficient that the remedy merely appeared to be futile for the alien to be exempt from making the appeal. On the other hand, the alien was not absolutely compelled to take his case through to the highest court, whatever the circumstances might be:

> As regards finally the third question, whether the local remedy shall be considered as not effective only where it is obviously futile on the merits of the case which are to be taken into account, to have recourse to the municipal remedy, or whether, as the Finnish Government suggests, it is sufficient that such a step only appears to be futile, a certain strictness in construing this rule appears justified by the opinion expressed by Borchard when mentioning the rule applied in the prize cases. Borchard says (a.a. § 383): 'In a few prize cases it has been held that in the face of a uniform course of decisions in the highest court a reversal of the condemnation being hopeless, an appeal was excused; but this rule was most strictly construed, and if substantial right of appeal existed, failure to prosecute an appeal operated as a bar to relief.'[33]

[32] Some early cases: Communication No 8/1977, HRC *Selected Decisions* 48; Communication No 28/1978, HRC *Selected Decisions* 58–9; and Communication No 44/1979, HRC *Selected Decisions* 77 and 79.

[33] Finland v Great Britain, 3 UNRIAA 1504 (1934). The term 'effective remedy' was used at p. 1495.

Accordingly, it was held that, where the finding of fact by a board under an Indemnity Act was final and the success of the claimant's case depended on a different finding of fact, an appeal to a higher court[34] or a reference to a different court or body[35] was 'obviously futile'. Furthermore, it was held that in any case there was no effective remedy by way of petition of right to the king of the respondent State, the UK, since such a remedy lay only in contract cases and there was no contract in that case.[36]

The resulting principle excused the alien from exhausting remedies in certain circumstances as opposed, on the one hand, to laying upon him the absolute obligation to appeal to all available sources of justice, and, on the other, to excusing him from such appeal in any circumstances in which he chose, whether on a bona fide estimate of the effectiveness of the remedies available or not.[37] Where it is clear that the resort to an appeal or reference to another court or tribunal would not be a source of adequate redress, the alien is excused from spending his money and time. Also, in this situation nothing has been lost by the respondent State, as far as its interest in doing justice by its own means is concerned.

This rule which evolved in the *Finnish Ships Arbitration* was applied more recently by Judge Lauterpacht in the *Norwegian Loans Case,* where the issue of non-exhaustion of local remedies was raised but not decided by the court. The plaintiff State, France, argued that there were no remedies to exhaust, but Judge Lauterpacht in a separate opinion held that the Norwegian objection was good because it was not clear that resort to the Norwegian courts would have been absolutely futile.[38] In the *Interhandel Case,* the Court similarly held that there was still a possibility of success in the US courts for the Swiss Interhandel Company so that it could not be said that there were no remedies available, and therefore the Swiss aliens should have exhausted local remedies before having their case taken up before an international tribunal.[39]

In the law of diplomatic protection the principle that local remedies need not be exhausted where they are 'obviously futile' seems to be established. The *Finnish Ships Arbitration* made it clear that the test is obvious futility or manifest ineffectiveness, not the absence of a mere reasonable prospect of success or the improbability of success, which are less strict tests. The absence of a reasonable prospect of success as a test seems to have found its way into the law relating to the protection of human rights. The test of obvious futility clearly requires more than the probability of failure or the improbability of success, but perhaps less than the absolute certainty of failure. The test may be said to require

[34] Ibid 1543.

[35] Ibid 1545.

[36] Ibid 1550.

[37] Fachiri criticized this particular solution: 'The Local Remedies Rule in the Light of the Finnish Ships Arbitration', 17 BYIL (1936) 36.

[38] 1957 ICJ Reports 39 ff.

[39] 1959 ICJ Reports 26 ff.

evidence from which it could reasonably be concluded that the remedy would be ineffective.[40]

The application of the test of obvious futility has resulted in the dismissal of the objection that local remedies had not been exhausted in several kinds of cases. First, it has been held that, where resort to the courts will result in the repetition of a uniform line of decisions adverse to the alien, the remedy is obviously futile.[41] What this means is that the mere likelihood of an adverse decision is insufficient, something more than probability of defeat but less than certainty being required. It seems readily to be accepted that a *jurisprudence constante* or *bien établie,* or the existence of a series of decisions which shows that resort to remedies will not end in success, exempts the alien or claimant from exhausting local or internal remedies. This point was either explicitly or implicitly conceded in the written pleadings and oral arguments in the *Barcelona Traction Co Case*.[42]

Second, as in the *Finnish Ships Arbitration,* there is no need to resort to a court or body which has no jurisdiction over the issue raised by the alien. This is so whether it is a case of resort to a court of first instance or a court of appeal. However, in such a case this point must be strictly proved, as it was in the *Finnish Ships Arbitration*. In the *Panavezys-Saldutiskis Railway Case,* the argument was raised that it would have been useless to take the matter to the Lithuanian courts because they would not take jurisdiction over an 'act of state', an act *jure imperii,* since this was an act in performance of the government's public function and not a matter 'concerning a civil right' within the meaning of the Lithuanian Code of Civil Procedure. The PCIJ held that it was not satisfied that this was the

[40] Mummery requires that the absence of a proper remedy be 'reasonably clear': 'The Content of the Duty to Exhaust Local Judicial Remedies', 58 AJIL (1964) 401. In the *ELSI Case*, a chamber of the ICJ held that what was important was whether it could be concluded from all the circumstances that the possibility of success of a remedy was remote: 1989 ICJ Reports 47–8. In that case it was found that the remedy identified as not having been exhausted could not have been regarded as possibly relevant to the success of the alien's claim.

[41] *Finnish Ships Arbitration* (Finland v Great Britain), 3 UNRIAA 1495 (1934), endorsed this principle. In the *ELSI Case,* 1989 ICJ Reports 47–8, the ICJ found that it was clear that the alien company could not have succeeded in the local courts, because the established law worked definitely against its contentions: see on this point in the case Adler, 'The Exhaustion of Local Remedies Rule after the International Court of Justice's Decision in ELSI', 39 ICLQ (1990) 651. A similar conclusion exempting the alien from exhausting local remedies was reached for the same basic reason as in the *ELSI Case,* in the *Interpretation of the Treaty of Finance and Compensation Arbitration* (Austria v FRG, 1972), 32 ZAORV 49. See also the *Johnson Case* (United States v Peru, 1878); de La Pradelle-Politis, 2 RAI 593 ff; and Freeman (note 14 above) 421.

[42] See ICJ Pleadings (1962–9), vol 1, 256; ICJ Pleadings (1962–9), vol 3, 814; ICJ Pleadings (1962–9), vol 9, 593 and 609 (the Spanish view); and ICJ Pleadings (1962–9), vol 8, 577–8 (the Belgian view). See also the *Panavezys-Saldutiskis Railway Case,* PCIJ Series A/B, 1939, No 76, 4 and 18; *'S.S. Lisman'* (1937) 3 UNRIAA, 1773; *'S.S. Seguranca'* (1939), 3 UNRIAA 1868. Human rights cases under the European Convention on Human Rights have followed suit: see eg *X* v *Federal Republic of Germany,* 1 *Yearbook of the European Convention on Human Rights* (1956), 138; *X* v *Federal Republic of Germany,* 2 ibid (1958–1959) 344; *X* v *Austria,* 3 ibid (1960) 202.

case in the absence of a Lithuanian court decision on the point.[43] The difference between the two cases is that in the *Finnish Ships Arbitration* the law consisting of statute and common law was clear, while in the *Panavezys-Saldutiskis Railway Case* the law, as it stood, was not so clear and therefore the court refused even to examine it. In the *Norwegian Loans Case,* Judge Lauterpacht's view was similar, namely that the position was not clearly what the French government made it out to be.[44] In the *Interhandel Case,* the ICJ took basically the same stand.[45] The fact that in the *Panavezys-Saldutiskis Railway Case* the court refused to examine the issue must be explained by the fact that it was not clear on the face of it that the Estonian argument was a good one. In the *Finnish Ships Arbitration* the converse was the case and, therefore, the tribunal examined the law to find that the Finnish argument was a good one. Thus, it may further be asserted that unless it appears that there is a clear case that no tribunal has jurisdiction in the case in hand, an international tribunal will not even examine the national law.

Third, where it is clear that a national law justifying the acts of which the alien complains would have to be applied by the local organs or courts, thus rendering recourse to them obviously futile, local remedies need not be exhausted. In the *Forests of Central Rhodope Case,*[46] the international wrong was the confiscation of certain forests under a national law permitting such confiscation. Since all State organs would have had to apply that law, it was obvious that recourse to local remedies would have been futile. Hence, the arbitral tribunal held that they did not have to be exhausted.

Fourth, absence of independence of the courts has been held to exempt the alien or claimant from resorting to the courts. In the *Robert E Brown Case,*[47] an alien was excused from exhausting local remedies because the courts were at the time completely under the control of the executive. The obvious futility of recourse to the State judicial organs in these circumstances is based on the absence of justice in the true sense.

Fifth, where the remedies available clearly will not satisfy the object sought by the claimant, they need not be resorted to because they are ineffective or obviously futile. There are several decided cases on this point concerning

[43] PCIJ Series A/B, 1939, No 76, 18. See also the *Arbitration under Article 181 of the Treaty of Neuilly*, reported in 28 AJIL (1934) 789; *Claims of R Gelbtrunk and Salvador Commercial Co et al*, 15 UNRIAA, 476–477; *'The Lottie May' Incident* (1899, Honduras v UK), 15 UNRIAA, 31.

[44] 1957 ICJ Reports 39 ff.

[45] 1959 ICJ Reports 26 ff. Where the applicant's appeal is on the facts and a higher court has no jurisdiction except in appeals on matters of law, there is no need to appeal to the higher court: see Communication No 27/1978, HRC *Selected Decisions* 14, which is a case on human rights protection.

[46] Greece v Bulgaria, 3 UNRIAA 1405 (1933). See also *Arbitration under Article 181 of the Treaty of Neuilly*, 28 AJIL (1934), 789; *Ambatielos Claim*, 12 UNRIAA 119; *Interhandel Case* 1959, *ICJ Reports* 28.

[47] (1923, USA v GB), 6 UNRIAA 120. See also on the similar position in human rights protection, eg Communication No 63/1979, HRC Selected Decisions 102; the *Vélasquez Rodríguez Case* (1989), 28 ILM 304 ff.

the protection of human rights under the European Convention on Human Rights.[48] For this same reason, where it is obvious that the reparation available under the national remedy would not be adequate in terms of what the alien is entitled to in international law, the remedy would be 'obviously futile' and resort need not be had to it. In the *Finnish Ships Arbitration,* Finland argued that the remedy of the shipowners with the Admiralty Board was ineffective because the rates by which the Board was bound in assessing compensation did not represent fair market rates. The arbitrator rejected the argument because he found that the redress which would be given under the Indemnity Act was adequate redress.[49] It is evident that for the exception to operate on the ground that reparation is not adequate for the purpose of satisfying the international claim, the inadequacy of the remedy for the specific object must be proven beyond reasonable doubt.

Sixth, apart from the inaccessibility of remedies, which is a reason for not exhausting them, the absence of due process of law in the legal system of the host or respondent State is clearly a good excuse for not exhausting remedies.[50]

In the *Ambatielos Claim,* it was stated that, where the futility of a remedy otherwise available is the result of the alien's fault, there is no exemption from the application of the rule.[51]

The ILC has taken a strange course. While examples which in any case satisfy the test of 'obvious futility' (many of which have been referred to above and which have been interpreted to do so) and Judge Lauterpacht's separate opinion in the *Norwegian Loans Case* were cited, the ILC opted for the test of absence of a

[48] *Becker* v *Denmark*, Application No 7011/75, Decisions and Reports, ECHR, vol 4, 227–8 and 232–3. See also *X* v *Denmark,* Application No 7465/76, Decisions and Reports, ECHR, vol 7, 154; *X* v *Austria*, Application No 6701/74, Decisions and Reports, ECHR, vol 5, 78–9; and *Zamir* v *UK,* Application No 9174/80, Report of the Commission; *Kornmann* v *Federal Republic of Germany,* Application No 2686/65, 22 *Collection* 10.

[49] Finland v Great Britain, 3 UNRIAA 1496 (1934). See also the *Vélasquez Rodríguez Case* (1989), 28 ILM 304–9; *Yağci and Sargin* v *Turkey*, Judgment of 8 June 1995, European Court of Human Rights, Reports and Decisions, No 319, 17, para 42; *Hornsby* v *Greece*, Judgment of 19 March 1997, 1997-II European Court of Human Rights, Reports and Decisions, No 33, 509, para 37.

[50] The ground has been supported by the Institut de Droit International: see 36(I) AIDI (1935) 435; and 45 AIDI (1954) 28 ff. See also HLS, 'Research in International Law II. Responsibility of States' (1929) 23 AJIL (1929), Supplement, 134. This ground is specifically referred to in Article 46(2)(a) of the ACHR. Although not all forms of denial of justice may have the result of exempting the alien or claimant from exhausting remedies, certainly this one would seem to have the effect of rendering remedies obviously futile in so far as proper justice and fairness cannot be expected to prevail. The exception would be relevant even in the absence of specific provisions for it in a conventional instrument. The exception was found to be applicable by the IACHR in Resolution No 1a/88, where it held that the irregularities pertaining to legal process inherent in Chilean military justice were reflected in the abusive recourse to secrecy in the conduct of the proceedings, with the result that it was initially impossible to gain access to basic elements of the trial and the military authorities were allowed to control the evidence submitted. Therefore, the Commission held that due process of law was non-existent and local remedies did not have to be pursued: see Resolution No 1a/88, Case 9755, *Ann Rep IAComHR 1987–88*, 137.

[51] Greece v UK, 12 UNRIAA 122 (1956).

'reasonable possibility' of effective redress,[52] rejecting the 'obvious futility' test as being different and not generous enough to injured aliens. It referred to three tests for determining whether remedies were ineffective and need not be exhausted: (i) obvious futility, (ii) absence of a reasonable prospect of success, and (iii) absence of a reasonable possibility of effective redress. While a difference between (i) and (ii) is apparent in that under (ii) it is easier than under (i) to establish whether remedies need not be exhausted, it is difficult to see a material difference between (i) and (iii). If there is no reasonable *possibility* of redress, exhausting remedies would be obviously futile. The intention of the ILC was, however, to interpret the current law as requiring a lower threshold for the absence of a need to exhaust remedies. That a lower threshold reflects the law is questionable. The ILC's formulation, if it does lower the threshold, can only be accepted as an attempt at development of the law. The ILC's test is based on a statement by Judge Lauterpacht in his separate opinion in the *Norwegian Loans Case*. What he did say in reference to the situation prevailing in the case was that:

> The legal position on the subject cannot be regarded as so abundantly clear as to rule out as a matter of reasonable possibility an effective remedy before Norwegian courts.[53]

A close reading of this statement, particularly taking into account the requirement of abundant clarity of the legal position, the reference to possibility rather than certainty, and the absence of an explicit rejection of, or even reference to, the prevailing 'obvious futility' test of which the judge must be deemed to have been aware, leads to the conclusion that Judge Lauterpacht was merely redefining the 'obvious futility' test. It is too much to assume that he was replacing the accepted test with another test without even a reference to or dismissal of the former. Moreover, the formulation he put forward is clearly no more than a definition of the 'obvious futility' test, because that test does not require *certainty* of failure which means that it is based on absence of even a *possibility* of success. The addition of the epithet 'reasonable' to describe the possibility does not do much to dilute the meaning given to obvious futility.

On the other hand, a requirement that there must be no 'reasonable prospect of success' which is the test used in most human rights cases, particularly under the European Convention of Human Rights,[54] may be more generous to the claimant in that what is meant is that only an absence of *probability* of success results in the remedies being ineffective. The commentary to the ILC Draft Articles excludes this test as applicable in cases of diplomatic protection, clearly on this assumption.

[52] See Report of the ILC (2006) 77–9 (the Commentary) and Article 16(a) of the Draft Articles.

[53] 1957 ICJ Reports 39.

[54] See the Commentary to Article 15(a) of the ILC Draft Articles: Report of the ILC (2006) 78 and cases therein referred to in footnote 202.

Whatever the test, the question whether remedies are effective or ineffective must be determined with regard to the local law and circumstances at the time at which they are to be used and the decision on this matter must be made on the assumption that the claim is meritorious.[55]

(b) Undue Delay

Undue delay in the administration of justice has been held to be a good reason for not exhausting local remedies. This exception may be closely related to the general exception based on obvious futility but it is better considered separately, as delay may not always signify that there is a clear indication that the alien or claimant will not succeed after a lapse of time. However, undue delay in the administration of justice is regarded as a denial of justice in itself and is certainly one which does not require any further exhaustion of remedies. In the *El Oro Mining and Railway Co Case*,[56] it was held that a court's delay in taking action for nine years was sufficient to make it an ineffective remedy.

The delay necessary to make a remedy ineffective in each case will, of course, vary, it being impossible to lay down a specific time limit for all cases, since several circumstances including the volume of work involved in a thorough examination of the case are relevant.[57] In the *Interhandel Case*, although ten years had already passed since the institution of the action, the court did not hold that there had been undue delay in the provision of a remedy.[58] Dissenting Judge Armand-Ugon was of the view that, because a further unknown period would have to elapse before remedies were exhausted, ten years already having passed, such

[55] See the *Finnish Ships Arbitration* (1934), 3 UNRIAA 1504; the *Ambatielos Claim* (1956), 12 UNRIAA 119–20. The ILC's 2006 Draft Article 15(a) states that local remedies need not be exhausted where 'there are no reasonably available local remedies to provide effective redress, or the local remedies provide no reasonable possibility of such redress', *Report of the ILC (2006)* at 20. The Commentary explains the Article, ibid at 77–9, as receiving a lower threshold than that referred to in the cases and the text above.

The ICJ has explained the matter of burden of proof in connection with effective and ineffective remedies. Most recently in the *Diallo Case (Preliminary Objections)* it pointed out that the respondent state, the DRC, had 'not proved the existence in its domestic legal system of available and effective remedies allowing Mr. Diallo to challenge his expulsion...' (2007 ICJ Reports, para 48, <http://www.icj-cij.org>) stating that:

44. In matters of diplomatic protection, it is incumbent on the applicant to prove that local remedies were indeed exhausted or to establish that exceptional circumstances relieved the allegedly injured person whom the applicant seeks to protect of the obligation to exhaust available local remedies (see the *ELSI Case,* 1989 ICJ Reports, 43–44, para. 53). It is for the respondent to convince the Court that there were effective remedies in its domestic legal system that were not exhausted (see ibid., p. 46, para. 59). Thus, in the present case, Guinea must establish that Mr Diallo exhausted any available local remedies or, if not, must show that exceptional circumstances justified the fact that he did not do so; it is, on the other hand, for the DRC to prove that there were available and effective remedies in its domestic legal system against the decision to remove Mr Diallo from the territory and that he did not exhaust them. (ibid para 44)

[56] (1931, GB v Mexico), 5 UNRIAA 191.

[57] Ibid 198.

[58] 1957 ICJ Reports 6.

remedies were too slow and could not be called adequate or effective and could be dispensed with.[59] There was clearly a difference of opinion on whether there had been undue delay in the case. However, although the court did not reject the view that delay can operate in the alien's favour, it is clear that it did not consider the lapse of time as sufficiently long and important to influence its decision.

While the principle that undue delay would operate in customary international law to exempt the claimant or applicant from exhausting remedies is undisputed (the reason behind it being that justice is being in some way denied the claimant or applicant, even though resort to remedies in the circumstances may not be obviously futile), a more difficult question is how undue delay is to be further defined. It is impossible to lay down a definite length of time that would constitute undue delay for all cases, and it would be imprudent to attempt to do so. The circumstances of each case would certainly be a determining factor. Much would depend on the judicial assessment of the situation in each case. As has been seen, in the *Interhandel Case* Judge Armand-Ugon differed from the court on the question of whether in the circumstances the time that had elapsed since remedies had initially been invoked was sufficient to constitute undue delay. Clearly, such matters as the nature of the wrong would be relevant, it being easier, for instance, to prescribe specific shorter time limits for violations of personal and civil rights than for injuries to property. The nature of the claimant may also be a pertinent factor, injuries to large corporations, which may give rise to more complicated issues than injuries to individuals, being subject to longer limits than injuries to individuals. In the ultimate analysis, such considerations can only provide guidelines, there being no hard and fast rules defining undue delays.[60]

Article 15(c) of 2006 the ILC's Draft Articles refers to undue delay as a ground for not requiring the alien to exhaust local remedies. The commentary concludes also that what is undue delay depends on the circumstances of each case.[61]

(c) *Repetition of Injury or Likelihood of Further Damage*

It has been suggested that a remedy need not be resorted to, that is, a final decision of the last instance does not need to be waited for, if for some reason or other

[59] Ibid 89.

[60] See also Dugard, 'Third Report on Diplomatic Protection' (ILC), UN Doc. A/CN.4/523, 35–7, Article 14(e) of his draft, and the legal commentators referred to therein. The principle of undue delay has been applied and elaborated upon in the law of human rights protection: see C F Amerasinghe (note 1 above), Chapter 13. There have been some text writers who have considered the question of defining undue delay in the context of human rights protections: see eg Wiebringhaus, 'La Règle de l'épuisement prealable des voies de recours interne dans la jurisprudence de la Commission européenne des droits de l'homme', 5 AFDI (1959) 685; Schaffer and Weissbrodt, 'Exhausting Remedies in the Context of the Racial Discrimination Convention', 2 HRJ (1969) 639 ff. See also the other cases referred to above in this section.

[61] Report of the ILC (2006) 80.

further damages are expected or the same injury will be repeated.[62] Some support for this is to be found in a ruling in the *De Sabla Claim*:

There is great force in the contention of the claimant as to the hardship imposed on her by forcing her to resort to opposition on each application [for grants of the land by others]. The facts of the case show that one opposition, even when successful, accomplished no more than to kill the particular application opposed, and did not even prevent subsequent grants to the identical persons who had previously been successfully opposed... The Commission therefore find that the machinery of opposition, as actually administered, did not constitute an adequate remedy.[63]

The situation envisaged may not necessarily compel the conclusion that remedies would be obviously futile, if exhausted, in so far as in each case it is possible to have a final decision given. While the tribunal in the *De Sabla Claim* stressed the inadequacy of remedies in the circumstances, the inadequacy seems to have rested directly and specifically on the hardship caused to the alien claimant. The exception seems to have been derived from a balancing of the interests of the alien claimant and those of the respondent State. Here the scales tipped in favour of the alien claimant.

The 2006 ILC Draft Articles omits any reference to the exception referred to above.

(d) Circumstances Not Limiting the Operation of the Rule

In the development of the rule of local remedies, in practice and through judicial decision, certain circumstances have been identified as not giving rise to limitations on or exceptions to the rule. In a negative sense, therefore, these circumstances cannot have an effect on the operation of the rule. Such circumstances have been adverted to in the law of diplomatic protection and in the area of human rights protection, but particularly in the latter. While it has sometimes been said both by judicial and arbitral authorities[64] and by legal commentators[65] that the rule is flexible and is to be applied in accordance with the circumstances, it cannot be said that there is scope for broad equitable considerations in the formulation of exceptions. The strength of the value attached to the sovereign rights of the respondent State in doing justice in its own way is so pervasive that, as has been seen, it is only when the interests of the alien claimant or individual clearly outweigh those of the respondent State that an exception may be allowed. Consequently, there are many situations in which the argument that the local remedies rule was not applicable has been raised but rejected.

[62] See Freeman (note 14 above) 418; and Law (note 14 above) 70.

[63] (1933, USA v Panama), 26 AJIL (1934) 607.

[64] See eg the *Norwegian Loans Case*, 1957 ICJ Reports 39 *per* Judge Lauterpacht in a separate opinion; the *Salem Case* (United States v Egypt), 2 UNRIAA 1189 (1932); the *Panavezys-Saldutiskis Railway Case*, PCIJ Series A/B No 77 138 (1939) *per* Judge de Visscher in a dissenting opinion.

[65] Law (note 14 above) 147; and Jenks, *The Prospects of International Adjudication* (1964) 536. See also Schwarzenberger, 1 *International Law* (1957) 604.

It has been confirmed on more than one occasion that lack of pecuniary means on the part of the alien claimant or individual does not constitute a valid reason for not pursuing local remedies. In the *David Adams Case*,[66] the arbitral tribunal was faced with the argument that the owner of a ship confiscated in Canada did not pursue a right of appeal partly because of the absence of pecuniary means. The excuse was not recognized in law as being a reason for not exhausting local remedies.[67]

The better view seems to be that statements by government officials or even in a judgment that in effect there were no further effective remedies available do not of themselves excuse the alien claimant from exhausting remedies.[68] However, as will be seen later, there may be considerations of estoppel or waiver that may operate in some situations, but then the release from the requirement that local remedies must be exhausted is not to be treated as an exception but as being based on good faith or consent.

Particularly in the area of human rights protection, many invalid excuses have been considered.[69] There is no good reason why these circumstances, which have been found inadequate to provide an excuse for not exhausting local remedies in the area of human rights protection, should not have the same effect in the law of diplomatic protection. In general, the definition of their inadequacy seems reasonably conceived and appropriate, particularly because as such they bear no relationship to the effectiveness, adequacy or availability of local remedies.

(e) Circumstances Rendering the Requirement of Exhaustion of Remedies Unreasonable

The exception to or limitation on the rule of local remedies based on a broad test of 'unreasonableness' was introduced in the 2004 Draft Articles of the ILC. In Article 16(c) was found the statement that local remedies need not be exhausted where 'the circumstances of the case otherwise make the exhaustion of local remedies unreasonable'. Thus, where local remedies cannot be described as ineffective or offer a reasonable possibility of effective redress, it may, nevertheless, be unreasonable or cause unjustifiable hardship to the injured alien to require him to exhaust local remedies. In these circumstances an exception would be recognized exempting the alien from exhausting local remedies. The ILC has elaborated on this exception in the commentary to its 2004 Draft Articles as follows:

[66] (1921, USA v GB), 6 UNRIAA 85 (1921).

[67] See also the *Napier Case* (USA v UK) (1921), de La Pradelle-Politis, 3 RAI 121. As emerges from the discussion in the next section, this rule may be subject to change.

[68] See the *Interhandel Case*, 1959 ICJ Reports 27; the *Norwegian Loans Case*, 1957 ICJ Reports 41 *per* Judge Lauterpacht in a separate opinion; and the *Salem Case* (United States v Egypt), 2 UNRIAA 1189 (1932). Judge Read in his dissenting opinion in the *Norwegian Loans Case* cast some doubt on this view: 1957 ICJ Reports 98.

[69] See C F Amerasinghe (note 1 above) Chapter 13.

The second part of paragraph (c) is designed to give a tribunal the power to dispense with the need for the exhaustion of local remedies where, in all the circumstances of the case, it would be unreasonable to expect compliance with this rule. Each case will obviously have to be considered on its own merits in making such a determination and it would be unwise to attempt to provide a comprehensive list of factors that might qualify for this exception. It is, however, suggested that the exception might be exercised where a State prevents an injured alien from gaining factual access to its tribunals by, for instance, denying him entry to its territory or by exposing him to dangers that make it unsafe for him to seek entry to its territory; or where criminal conspiracies in the host State obstruct the bringing of proceedings before local courts; or where the cost of exhausting local remedies is prohibitive.[70]

The test of unreasonableness, covering as it does undue hardship to the alien, is very broad and to some extent it may be considered vacuous. There is a danger that it might be misapplied. However, it is a useful safety valve, provided its applicability is not abused. In addition to applying the exception to the situations envisaged by the ILC, an opportunity may be provided, for example, for reconsidering the relevance of indigence of the alien in certain circumstances (not caused by his own unreasonable actions) to determining whether the rule of local remedies is applicable in a given situation.[71] The test clearly, of course, will need to be applied judiciously by decision-makers and judges to avoid undue extension of the exceptions to the rule and depriving the host State of a genuine opportunity of settling a dispute through means of local redress.

In the 2006 Draft Articles of the ILC this exception has been omitted. There is only a reference in Article 15(d) to an exception on the ground that the alien has been manifestly precluded from pursuing local remedies. The formulation of the exception in the 2004 Draft Articles is to be preferred.

Waiver of Rule

The principles of consent and good faith are relevant to the law relating to the rule of local remedies in so far as the rule may be excluded by the operation of either of them. The application of the principle of consent results in the exclusion of the rule on the basis that it has been waived, either expressly or impliedly, by the host or respondent State[72] while the principle of good faith has the effect of excluding

[70] Report of the ILC (2004) 20, 82.

[71] See section (d) above. In the human rights area indigence of the injured applicant has caused much difficulty to international courts confronted with the issue of applying the local remedies rule: see C F Amerasinghe (note 1 above) Chapter 13.

[72] Waiver has generally been accepted in principle both in judicial decisions and by legal commentators and in codification draft: see eg the *ELSI Case*, 1989 ICJ Reports 42; *De Wilde, Ooms and Versyp*, ECHR, 50 ILR 670 (1971); *Government of Costa Rica Case*, IACHR, 67 ILR 587; C F Amerasinghe, 'The Local Remedies Rule in an Appropriate Perspective', 36 ZAORV (1976) 752; Garcia Amador, 'Third Report on State Responsibility', YBILC (1958), vol 2, 93; Borchard,

the application of the rule in circumstances such as where the doctrine of estoppel or its equivalent would operate.

(a) Express Waiver

Express waiver takes place where the host or respondent State expressly agrees that the rule of local remedies will not apply to a particular dispute or particular disputes. In the law of diplomatic protection, this may take place either before or after the dispute has arisen and may even be by a unilateral act by the host or respondent State. Such waivers have been given in both multilateral treaties and bilateral treaties and do not raise any real problems. Examples of such waivers in bilateral treaties are to be found in those that set up the Mixed Arbitral Tribunals and Mixed Claims Commissions between the two World Wars. Particular reference may be made to Article V of the Convention of 1923 establishing the US-Mexican General Claims Commission.[73] A more recent example is the treaty between Canada and the US setting up to *Gut Dam Arbitration* in 1965.[74] The Convention for the Settlement of Disputes between States and Nationals of Other States is an example of a multilateral treaty which excludes the operation prima facie of the rule. By virtue of Article 26 of that Convention,[75] where a host State and an alien whose national State is a party to the Convention agree to submit to international arbitration under the auspices of ICSID, established under the Convention, there is no need for the alien to exhaust local remedies before seeking arbitration unless specific provision is otherwise made for such recourse. This is also a case where the waiver has been given before the dispute arises, unlike in respect of most bilateral treaties.[76]

The Diplomatic Protection of Citizens Abroad (1915) 819 and 825; Borchard, 'Theoretical Aspects of the International Responsibility of States', 1 ZAORV (1929) 240; Witenburg, 'La Recevabilité des reclamations devant les juridictions internationales', 41 Hague Recueil (1932) 55; Ipsen, *Völkerrecht* (1990) 313; Kokott, 'Interim Report on Exhaustion of Local Remedies', in ILA, *Report of the Sixty-ninth Conference* (2000) at p. 613; Dugard, 'Third Report on Diplomatic Protection' (ILC), UN Doc A/CN.4/523 (2002) 17 ff and the authorities there cited; Article 15(e) of the ILC's 2006 Draft Articles and Commentary thereto: Report of the ILC (2006) at 83 ff. The latter Article refers to waiver as a circumstance which exempts the alien from exhausting local remedies; the commentary then explains waiver. The impact of investment treaties on waiver of the rule of local remedies is discussed in chapter 15.

[73] See Feller, *The Mexican Claims Commissions 1923–1934* (1935) 34; Nielsen, *International Law Applied to Reclamations* (1933) 70; and Eagleton, 'L'épuisement des recours internes et le déni de justice, d'après certaines decisions récentes', 16 RDILC (1935) 518–19 and 525–6. On the reasons for waiver, see C F Amerasinghe, *State Responsibility for Injuries to Aliens* (1967) 207. The validity of express waiver has been confirmed by text writers: see the writers referred to in note 72 above and eg Doehring, 'Exhaustion of Local Remedies', in Bernhardt et al (eds), 3 EPIL (1977) 240; Briggs, 'The Local Remedies Rule: A Drafting Suggestion', 50 AJIL (1956) 925; and C F Amerasinghe 1990 (note 2 above) 293–4.

[74] See Erades, 'The Gut Dam Arbitration', 16 NILR (1969) 161. García Amador recognized an express waiver by agreement in 1958 in Article 17 of his draft to the ILC: see García Amador (note 72 above) 55, 57–8 and 72.

[75] See 55 UNTS 159.

[76] It may be noted that, in the area of adjustment or settlement of environmental disputes, there is a marked tendency towards waiver of the rule. For a discussion of this, see eg Hoffman, 'State

Where the express waiver is given in a bilateral or multilateral treaty and after or before the dispute arises, it is normally irrevocable[77] although it may be revoked by the agreement of the parties or with the consent of the State of the alien affected. In the case of the ICSID Convention, for example, the express terms of the waiver in the Convention permit revocation by unilateral act of the respondent or host State at any time before it consents to arbitration under the Convention, which consent must be given by a separate act in writing, the other party being required also to give its consent. Thus, while agreement to arbitrate raises a presumption that there has been an express waiver of the rule of local remedies, that presumption is rebuttable by a unilateral act by the host or respondent State, or by agreement between the alien and the State party to the dispute, provided the revocation is done before or at the time that the consent to arbitration is given by the host or respondent State.[78]

Where there is a bilateral or multilateral agreement between States to submit to arbitration or international judicial settlement disputes between their nationals and host States, there is generally no understanding that the rule of local remedies is waived by the very fact of such submission to arbitration or judicial settlement, as is evidenced by the numerous decided cases in which disputes were submitted to such arbitration or judicial settlement under such agreements. No reference was made to the specific inclusion of the rule in the treaties or agreements and the rule was held to be prima facie applicable.[79]

This issue is discussed further later in this Chapter in regard to implied waiver. Difficulties arise in connection with express agreements made between host States and aliens excluding the rule or express renunciations of the rule. In the case of the above express agreements or renunciations, the question is whether such agreements or renunciations may be unilaterally revoked. Clearly, if the agreement or renunciation is governed by a law other than that of the host State, no revocation according to the law of the host State can take place. But what if, for instance, the agreement appears in a contract governed by the law of the

Responsibility in International Law and Transboundary Pollution Injuries', 25 ICLQ (1976) 513 ff; Poulantzas, 'The Rule of Exhaustion of Local Remedies and Liability for Space Vehicle Accidents', 17 RHDI (1964) 103–4; Jenks, 'Liability for Ultra-Hazardous Activities in International Law', 117 Hague Recueil (1966) 191 ff. There are express waivers in bilateral investment treaties: see C F Amerasinghe (note 1 above) 267 ff. The extent of the waiver depends on the interpretation of the particular treaty.

[77] Clearly, there is a presumption which may be rebutted by evidence to the contrary. On irrevocability as such, see C F Amerasinghe (1967) (note 73 above) 294–5; C F Amerasinghe (note 72 above) 737; and the UK pleadings in the *Anglo-Iranian Oil Co Case,* ICJ Pleadings (1951) 118–19. In the same case, Iran argued against irrevocability: ibid 501. The grounds on which this argument was made are not clear.

[78] The provisions of Article 26 apply only to arbitration and not to conciliation under the Convention. Whether the rule of local remedies applies to conciliation proceedings per se is a different question. If it did, the rule would not have been waived under the Convention. The incidence of the rule of local remedies and to what exactly the express waiver applied are not clearly addressed in the ICSID Convention although the implications of Article 26 can be deciphered.

[79] The *Interhandel Case*, 1959 ICJ Reports 6.

host State which was legally terminated according to the law of the host State? Can the alien or his national State then rely on the express waiver of the rule by the host State? The answer would seem to hinge on whether parts of a contract could be governed by a different law from that which governs other parts. In the case of arbitration clauses in State contracts with aliens, it seems possible to take the view that cancellation of the contract does not result in the cancellation of the arbitration clause, probably on the basis that the arbitration clause stands on its own and is not subject to the total law of the host State. While it may be interpreted in accordance with that law, it cannot be unilaterally and arbitrarily terminated under that law, although there may be refinements of this rule. A similar principle may be applicable to a waiver of the rule of local remedies in a State contract with an alien or a simple renunciation of the rule by a unilateral act in respect of an alien.[80]

(b) Implied Waiver

Reference was made earlier to the fact that, where a dispute involving an alien is submitted to international arbitration or adjudication by the States parties thereto, in the context of diplomatic protection, there is no presumption generally that the rule of local remedies does not apply, unless it is expressly invoked or reserved. There is, indeed, considerable evidence to support this view.[81] But, while this is the better view, it has apparently not gone uncontested.[82] In any

[80] It may be noted that the 1956 resolution of the Institut de Droit International clearly stated: 'La régle ne s'applique pas:...b) au cause où son application a été ecartée par l'acccord des Etas intéressés' 46 AIDI (1956) 358. But in fact what is really required is the consent of the host or respondent State, given in any form either generally or to the alien or to his national State. Such consent constitutes an express waiver. On the issue of conciliation and the rule of local remedies there are conflicting views: see eg the *Interhandel Case* 1959 ICJ Reports 29, 45 *per* Judge Córdova in a separate opinion, 84 *per* Judge Winiarski dissenting, 121 *per* Judge Lauterpacht dissenting, ICJ Pleadings (1959) 573 (Swiss oral argument); Gaja, (note 14 above) 157–60; and Cot, *La Conciliation internationale* (1968) 23–5. See further below in this Chapter.

[81] The *Ziat and Ben Kiran Case* (Great Britain v Spain), 2 UNRIAA 731 ff (1924); *Canadian Hay Importers Case* (Great Britain v US) 6 UNRIAA 142 ff (1925); the *A.G. Studer Case* (US v Great Britain), 6 UNRIAA 149 ff (1925); the *R.T. Roy Case* (US v Great Britain), 6 UNRIAA 147 ff (1925); the *Mexican Union Ltd. Railway Case*, 5 UNRIAA 9 and 123 (1926); the *George Pinson Case* (France v Mexico), 5 UNRIAA 351 (1928); the *Panavezys-Saldutiskis Railway Case*, PCIJ Series A/B No 76 (1939); the *Electricity Co of Sofia Case*, PCIJ Series A/B No 77 104 (1939) *per* Judge Urrutia in a dissenting opinion; and *Switzerland v Federal Republic of Germany*, 25 ILR 42 ff (1958). For legal commentators, see eg Freeman, *The International Responsibility of States for Denial of Justice* (1938) 414 ff; Guggenheim, 2 *Traité droit international public* (1954) 22; Schwarzenberger, *International Law* (1957) 610 ff; Witenberg (note 72 above) 52; García Amador (note 72 above) 60; and Verzijl, 'Rapport supplémentaire sur la règle de l'épuisement des recours internes', 46 AIDI (1956) 3 ff. On implied waiver now, see also in general Dugard (note 72 above) 20 ff and the authorities there cited. While the circumstances of the case matter, it must be emphasized that a clear intention to waive the application of the rule must be established: see the *ELSI Case*, 1989 ICJ Reports 42.

[82] The *R L Trumbull Case* (US v Chile) (1889); Moore, *International Arbitration* (1898) 3369; the *Selwyn Case* (GB v Venezuela), 9 UNRIAA 380 (1903); the *Forests of Central Rhodope Case* (Greece v Bulgaria), 3 UNRIAA 1419 (1933); the *German Interests in Polish Upper Silesia Case*, PCIJ Series A No 6, 13–14 (1925); the *Panavezys-Saldutiskis Railway Case*, PCIJ Series A/B No 76, 35 ff

event, as is evidenced by recent cases which have come before the ICJ, such as the *Norwegian Loans Case* and the *Interhandel Case*,[83] neither State practice nor judicial opinion warrants the opposite view. Thus, though the matter may be regarded as unsettled, it may be concluded that the better view referred to above should prevail in modern international law. This view is also supported by the fact that in most cases of waiver, whether express or implicit, it is waiver of the rule not explicitly invoked in bilateral or multilateral agreements between States, or in agreements between States and aliens, that is usually discussed. Further, most of the cases and practice supporting the other view may be explained on the basis that the rule had been for one reason or another implicitly waived in the circumstances of each case.

The question which really arises is whether and when a waiver can be implied. This question obviously raises problems of interpretation, and as a rule each situation should be looked at individually to determine whether there has been a waiver.[84] Clearly, to the extent that there has been a waiver, there can generally be no room for unilateral determination of the waiver. The view taken above of express waivers would support this opinion. Further, while the existence of a waiver will usually have to be determined on the merits of each case, there has been some practice on the question.

(i) The optional clause

In connection with signatures of the optional clause under Article 36 of the Statute of the ICJ, the PCIJ in the *Panavezys-Saldutiskis Railway Case* took the view that such a signature of the corresponding clause under its Statute did not involve an implied waiver of the rule of local remedies by the signatory.[85] In the same case, Judge van Eysinga disagreed with this view in a dissenting opinion.[86] The issue was not raised as such by the applicant State in the *Norwegian*

(1939) *per* Judge Van Eysinga in a dissenting opinion; the *Lighthouses Arbitration* (France v Greece), 23 ILR 639 (1936); and the British memorial in the *Anglo-Iranian Oil Co Case*, ICJ Pleadings (1952) 122 ff. For legal commentators, see eg Borchard (1916) (note 14 above) 819; Gaja (note 14 above) 156 ff; Ténékidès, 'L'épuisement des voies de recours internes comme condition préalable de l'instance internationale', 14 RDILC (1933) 519 ff; and Schwebel and Wetter, 'Arbitration and the Exhaustion of Local Remedies', 60 AJIL (1966) 484. Many legal commentators do not make a distinction between diplomatic protection and arbitration between States and private individuals who may be legal or natural persons. In the relevant cases it is not clear that the doctrine of the implied waiver was not being used to explain the position.

[83] *Norwegian Loans Case*, 1957 ICJ Reports 9. Neither State argued that the rule had been waived by submission to the ICJ. The Court did not decide the preliminary objection based on the local remedies rule, but none of the judges who dealt with this objection took the view that such submission amounted to a waiver. *Interhandel Case*, 1959 ICJ Reports 6. Neither the court nor the parties took the view that there had been a waiver of the rule of local remedies by submission to an international jurisdiction.

[84] See the argument of the French government in the *Norwegian Loans Case* which related to the existence of an implied waiver of the rule: ICJ Pleadings (1957), vol 1, 407 ff.

[85] PCIJ Series A/B No 76 (1939).

[86] Ibid 35 ff.

Loans Case[87] or in the *Interhandel Case*[88] where the ICJ was confronted with the question of local remedies, although signatories of the optional clause under Article 36 of the Statute of the Court were involved. In the latter case the ICJ applied the local remedies rule as a preliminary objection. Since the acceptance of the compulsory jurisdiction of the ICJ does not basically militate against the preservation of the jurisdiction of national courts, the view may be taken that the opinion of the PCIJ has validity.[89]

(ii) Submission by States to international adjudication or arbitration

Submissions to international adjudication or arbitration by agreements between States entered into before the dispute has arisen evidently stand on the same footing as acceptance of the optional clause of Article 36 of the Statute of the ICJ. In the *ELSI Case* a Chamber of the ICJ held that an agreement in a treaty to submit to adjudication by the ICJ, entered into before the dispute arose, did not by itself imply a waiver of the rule of local remedies.[90] The ICJ made it quite clear that implying a waiver in these circumstances was not an easy matter in the absence of a clear intention to do so. On the other hand, the situation is not quite the same in regard to treaties signed after disputes have arisen. In fact, it would seem that the PCIJ and the ICJ have not had to address this situation. However, in so far as the two Courts have enunciated an undifferentiated general principle which supports the view of the majority taken in other decisions, there is added support for that view. This majority view is that, whether such treaties are signed before or after disputes arise, no implied waiver of the rule of local remedies may be generally assumed to exist. The presumption, rebuttable though it is, is that there is no waiver.[91] The ILC in the commentary to its Draft Article 16(d), however, suggests that there is initially an implied waiver where the treaty to arbitrate or adjudicate comes into force after the dispute arises.[92] This has been the minority view.

(iii) The issue of arbitrability

An implied waiver may be construed to take effect as a result of the circumstances surrounding an agreement between States where the issue to be decided by an

[87] 1957 ICJ Reports 9.

[88] 1959 ICJ Reports 6.

[89] Now see the *ELSI Case,* 1989 ICJ Reports 31, where the importance of the local remedies rule for the law of diplomatic protection was asserted and confirmed.

[90] 1989 ICJ Reports 42.

[91] See *Steiner and Gross v Polish State*, AD (1927–8) 472ff. Dugard (note 72 above) 21–3, distinguishes between general arbitration agreements entered into before disputes arise and ad hoc arbitration agreements entered into after disputes arise, stating that it is easier to imply waiver in the latter cases than in the former. See also the authorities there cited at notes 100–102. But the distinction is neither of an absolute nature nor is it really useful. In every case it is a question of interpretation. There is no need for additional presumptions. The presumption logically should be against implied waiver as such. See also C F Amerasinghe (note 1 above) 253ff for a further discussion of this.

[92] See Report of the ILC (2006) 85.

international tribunal concerns the arbitrability of the dispute. In this situation the ICJ has held that the rule of local remedies is not applicable.[93] On the other hand, a conflicting decision seems to have been pronounced by the same court. In the *Interhandel Case* the Court refused to determine the question of arbitrability because local remedies had not been exhausted.[94] However, in this case there were some strong dissenting opinions[95] which took the view adopted in the earlier *Ambatielos Case* that the local remedies rule was not applicable to the issue of arbitrability. It would seem that the better view is that the question of arbitrability may be decided without local remedies having been exhausted, in particular since the issue does not relate to material compensation or restitution.[96] Also, it is important in this connection that, even if a pronouncement is made on the issue of arbitrability, this does not pre-empt the arbitral tribunal from making a determination on the question whether local remedies had been exhausted.[97] In this situation, however, it must be noted that it may be expressly agreed that local remedies should be exhausted before an international tribunal decided the issue of arbitrability.

(iv) Non-inter-State arbitration agreements between States and private parties

The questions of whether and to what extent there has been an implied waiver of the rule of local remedies may arise in connection with arbitration clauses which are included in State contracts with aliens and which are not also covered in some way by an inter-State agreement between the States concerned. Such contracts would not be on a par with treaties,[98] nor strictly would they be contracts within the international legal system, nor between international persons, although they might be governed by transnational law.[99] A preliminary question that must be answered is whether arbitration clauses included in such contracts would become ineffective, if the contracts themselves are terminated or cease to have effect for some reason. The question is of some importance, because, if arbitration clauses could become ineffective in this way, the question of whether there has been an implied waiver of the rule of local remedies may often become moot. The problem becomes particularly significant where, for example, the contract is governed by the national law of the State party to the contract and the contract is terminated under that law, perhaps by legislation.

93 The *Ambatielos Case*, 1953 ICJ Reports 16. See also the *Chemin de Fer Zeltweg Case* (Austria v Yugoslavia), 3 UNRIAA 1803 (1934).

94 1959 ICJ Reports 29.

95 See 1959 ICJ Reports 32 *per* Judge Carry, 82 *per* Judge Klaested, 84 *per* Judge Winiarski and 120 ff *per* Judge Lauterpacht.

96 See Judge Lauterpacht in the *Interhandel Case*, 1959 ICJ Reports 93.

97 See the *Ambatielos Case*, 1953 ICJ Reports 16.

98 See the *Anglo-Iranian Oil Co Case*, 1952 ICJ Reports 93.

99 See eg the discussion in C F Amerasinghe (1967) (note 73 above) 108 ff and the authorities there cited, and (note 1 above), Chapter 5.

It seems to be the better view that such arbitration clauses survive contracts between States and aliens.[100] Hence, the substantive issues of whether and to what extent a waiver of the rule of local remedies can be implied where such an arbitration occurs assumes importance. There appear to be many cases in which arbitration has been resorted to under a State contract with an alien and in which the argument has not been raised by the respondent State that the alien has not exhausted local remedies before seeking arbitration.[101] In a few cases concerning this kind of arbitration which came before the PCIJ and the ICJ, the issue was raised by the respondent State, and the plaintiff State argued for a waiver of the rule, but in none of these cases was the issue decided.[102] The fact that the issue of local remedies has not been contested in the majority of cases may lend some support to the view that an arbitration clause of this kind does imply a waiver of the rule of local remedies, at least in regard to the merits of the dispute, although it may not be conclusive. The absence of an international decision to the contrary would also not militate against this position. Indeed, it would be reasonable to conclude from the fact that arbitration has been chosen as the means of settling disputes that it was intended as such in the absence of contrary indications to withdraw the merits of the dispute from the jurisdiction of the local courts and institutions at least until the arbitral award had been given. This is the better view supported by authority. It would be difficult to find acceptable arguments for the opposite view.[103] The ILC does not deal specifically with this issue.

(v) Failure to raise preliminary objection

The right to object to the jurisdiction of an international court or tribunal may be waived because of the failure on the part of the respondent State to raise the objections based on the rule of local remedies at the proper time in the international proceedings. This is an implied waiver of the application of the rule on the basis of a procedural position taken by the respondent State and takes place during the international proceedings. Once the waiver has taken place it is irrevocable. The forfeiture of the right to rely on the rule of local remedies is grounded in a general principle that applies to the raising of preliminary objections in general.[104]

[100] See discussion in C F Amerasinghe, ibid 257.

[101] Schwebel and Wetter (note 82 above) 486 ff.

[102] The *Affaire Losinger and Co*, PCIJ Series A/B No 67 (1936), and Pleadings, Oral Statements and Documents (1936), PCIJ Series C No 78; the *Anglo-Iranian Oil Co Case*, 1952 ICJ Reports 93, ICJ Pleadings (1951); the *Electricité de Beyrouth Co Case*, 1954 ICJ Reports 107, ICJ Pleadings (1954); and the *Compagnie du Port, des Quais et des Entrepôts de Beyrouth and the Société Radio-Orient Case*, ICJ Pleadings (1960).

[103] The better view is that there is an implied waiver in this situation: see the discussion in C F Amerasinghe (note 1 above) 258 ff.

[104] This general principle is mentioned by, inter alios, Rosenne, *Law and Practice of the International Court, 1920–1966* (1997), vol 2, 684–5. See now C F Amerasinghe, *Jurisdiction of International Tribunals* (2003) 303. In the human rights context the principle is often referred to as an 'estoppel': see C F Amerasinghe (note 1 above) Chapter 13. The conduct of the respondent

(vi) Request for a declaratory judgment

As a consequence of two judgments of the PCIJ on jurisdiction it has been concluded that a request for a declaratory judgment precludes the raising of the objection by the respondent State that local remedies have not been exhausted. In the *German Interests in Polish Upper Silesia Case* the PCIJ held that the rule did not apply where the plaintiff State requested only an 'interpretation of certain clauses of the Geneva Convention'.[105] The decision was explained in the subsequent *Chorzów Factory Case*, where the Court said that the application in the first case 'only asked the Court for a declaratory judgment between states, which only the Court could give, whereas the present application seeks an indemnity'.[106] The distinction, thus, lies between cases in which a judgment merely declaring a violation of international law is sought and that in which a remedial right is asserted.[107]

Among legal commentators the matter is not regarded as settled,[108] while in its oral argument in the *Interhandel Case* the US government apparently did not categorically take the view that the waiver was unqualified.[109] The ILC, on the other hand, appears earlier to have supported the view that the rule of local remedies does not apply where a declaratory judgment alone is sought.[110] Now the ILC has taken the opposite view in Article 14(3) of its 2006 Draft Articles, on the ground that seeking a declaratory judgment may be a means to avoid the exhaustion of local remedies.[111]

(c) *The Principles of Estoppel and Good Faith*

The principles of estoppel and good faith may operate to exclude the application of the rule of local remedies. The doctrine of estoppel in broad terms prevents one party from taking advantage of another when the former by his actions has led the latter to act in a certain manner detrimental to the latter's own interests. The principle of good faith is at the root of this doctrine. The exact scope of the

State during proceedings is covered by Article 15(e) of the 2006 ILC Draft Articles on waiver: see Commentary, *Report of the ILC (2006)* at 86.

105 PCIJ Series A No 6, 20 (1925).

106 PCIJ Series A No 9, 26–7 (1925).

107 Beckett, 'Les Questions d'intérêt général au point de vue juridique dans la jurisprudence de la Cour permanente de justice internationale', 39 Hague Recueil (1932) 164; de Visscher, 'Le Déni de justice en droit international', 52 Hague Recueil (1935) 425; and Kaufmann, 'Règles générales de droit de la paix', 54 Hague Recueil (1935) 456. See the explanation and the discussion in C F Amerasinghe (note 1 above), 266.

108 See the discussion at the Institut de Droit International: 46 AIDI (1956) 302 ff. See also the *Air Services Agreement Case* (1978, USA v France) 18 UNRIAA 415; the *UN Headquarters Agreement Opinion*, 1988 ICJ Reports 29, para 41.

109 ICJ Pleadings (1959) 501 ff.

110 Report of the ILC (1977): 2 YBILC (1977) Part II, 50. The EComHR has taken the opposite view that declaratory relief, even by way of interpretation, may not be given unless local remedies have been exhausted: *Donnelly and Others v UK*, Applications Nos 5577-83/72, COE Doc 43, 662–06.2, 83, and see C F Amerasinghe (note 1 above), Chapter 13.

111 See Report of the ILC (2006) 20 and 76.

doctrine in international law is not fully defined. For the purpose of the application of the rule of local remedies, the statement in the *Chorzów Factory Case*, which purported to advert to an aspect of this doctrine, may be a good starting point. The PCIJ said:

> It is, moreover, a principle generally accepted in the jurisprudence of international arbitration, as well as by municipal courts, that one party cannot avail himself of the fact that the other has not fulfilled some obligation or has not had recourse to some means of redress, if the former party has, by some illegal act, prevented the latter from fulfilling the obligation in question, or from having recourse to the tribunal which would have been open to him.[112]

The court pointed to an illegal act in particular. However, the principles of good faith and estoppel have a broader coverage than that. In fact, any conduct on the part of one party which is intended to lead and induces the other party to act in a manner which is detrimental to his interests could qualify, there being no special requirement that the conduct be illegal.

While the principles of estoppel and good faith may have a general application to the exclusion of the rule of local remedies in appropriate circumstances, the manner in which they are applicable seems to have a strict definition. There must be cogent evidence that the conduct was not only intended to lead the alien or individual to believe that local remedies need not be further exhausted, for whatever reason, but also that the latter could reasonably be expected to rely on that conduct, did rely on it, and for that reason did not resort to the local remedies which were available. Thus, in the *Interhandel Case*, the ICJ did not consider that the conduct of the US government was of this nature when it said:

> The Court does not consider it necessary to dwell upon the assertion of the Swiss Government that 'the United States itself has admitted that Interhandel had exhausted the remedies available in the United States courts'. It is true that the representatives of the Government of the United States expressed this opinion on several occasions, in particular in the memorandum annexed to the Note of the Secretary of State of January 11th, 1957. This opinion was based upon a view which has proved unfounded. In fact, the proceedings which Interhandel had instituted before the courts of the United States were then in progress.[113]

It would appear that in the circumstances of the case the court considered that it was not reasonable to expect that the alien would rely on the opinion of the US government, which was a party to the dispute and had no control on the US courts, and whose opinion on the existence of remedies was not necessarily an expert one. What is required for the principle of good faith and estoppel to operate is not merely that the host or respondent State express a general view about the existence of remedies, but that it conduct itself in such a way that a

[112] (1927), PCIJ Series A No 9, 31.
[113] 1959 ICJ Reports 27.

reasonable opponent would conclude that he was relieved of the duty to exhaust local remedies or that the rule would not be invoked.

In the *ELSI Case*, a chamber of the ICJ dealt with the argument that the rule of local remedies had been excluded by estoppel. While not denying that estoppel could have been relevant to the matter in hand, the court held that estoppel did not operate to exclude the rule on the facts of the case. It explained the doctrine of estoppel and its application to the facts as follows:

53. There was a further argument of the Applicant, based on estoppel in relation to the application of the local remedies rule, which should be examined. In the 'Memorandum of Law' elaborating the United States claim on the diplomatic plane, transmitted to the Italian Government by Note Verbale of 7 February 1974, one finds that the whole of Part VI (pp. 133 *et seq.*) deals generally and to some length with the 'Exhaustion of Local Remedies'. There were also annexed the opinions of the lawyers advising the Applicant, which dealt directly with the position of Raytheon and Machlett in relation to the local remedies rule. The Memorandum concluded that Raytheon and Machlett had indeed exhausted 'every meaningful legal remedy available to them in Italy'... In view of this evidence that the United States was very much aware that it must satisfy the local remedies rule, that it evidently believed that the rule had been satisfied, and that it had been advised that the shareholders of ELSI had no direct action against the Italian Government under Italian law, it was argued by the Applicant that Italy, if it was indeed at that time of the opinion that the local remedies had not been exhausted, should have apprised the United States of its opinion. According to the United States, however, at no time until the filing of the Respondent's Counter-Memorial in the present proceedings did Italy suggest that Raytheon and Machlett should sue in the Italian courts on the basis of the Treaty. The written aide-mémoire of 13 June 1978, by which Italy rejected the 1974 Claim, had contained no suggestion that the local remedies had not been exhausted, nor indeed any mention of the matter.

54. It was argued by the Applicant that this absence of riposte from Italy amounts to an estoppel. There are however difficulties about drawing any such conclusion from the exchanges of correspondence when the matter was still being pursued on the diplomatic level. In the *Interhandel* case, when Switzerland argued that the United States had at one time actually 'admitted that Interhandel had exhausted the remedies available in the United States courts', the Court, far from seeing in this admission an estoppel, dismissed the argument by merely observing that 'this opinion was based upon a view which has proved unfounded' *(Interhandel,* Judgment, ICJ Reports 1959, p. 27). Furthermore, although it cannot be excluded that an estoppel could in certain circumstances arise from a silence when something ought to have been said, there are obvious difficulties in constructing an estoppel from a mere failure to mention a matter at a particular point in somewhat desultory diplomatic exchanges.[114]

[114] 1989 ICJ Reports 43–4. On silence, see also the *Heathrow Airport User Charges Arbitration*, 102 ILR 285 (1996). The distinction between implied waiver and estoppel may be fine. It is suggested that estoppel, as distinguished from implied waiver, be defined as above in this section in order to make the differentiation useful. The fact that the term 'estoppel' may often be used broadly to include true situations of implied waiver, particularly in the context of human rights protection, does not materially affect the reality.: see C F Amerasinghe (note 1 above), Chapter 13. The most

Inapplicability of the Rule

Questions relating to the incidence of the rule of local remedies in connection with the category of claims have been raised mainly out of concern that the rule may be applied to situations for which it was not in principle intended. There is considerable diplomatic practice in this area while there is also judicial precedent on the subject. What has been in issue in the situations which have arisen is whether, in cases where an alien is involved in asserting his rights or having some protection exercised by a protecting State, there are circumstances in which the rule will not be applicable, or whether the rule is applicable in all situations where an alien is involved. The history of the rule in international law has shown that major concerns have in practice been articulated about the over-extension of the rule, rather than about the possibility that it may not be implemented when it should. Although the discussion reflects the clash of interests involved, it has taken the form of invoking such considerations as the intrinsic nature of the rule as an instrument in the settling of disputes essentially concerned with the protection of rights belonging to aliens, rather than of emphasizing the prerogatives of State sovereignty, which could have the effect of highlighting exclusively the interests of respondent States. As a result, the views expressed on these questions have taken into account the historical antecedents and development of the rule and its relevance in inter-State relationships, while there has been some expression of the need to see that the rule does not necessarily obstruct the protection of what are essentially rights or interests of aliens. The tendency has certainly not been to conclude that the rule is automatically applicable to any context in which an alien's rights or interests are involved or affected by the acts or omissions of a sovereign State.

(a) The Direct Injury

The situation in which the incidence of the rule has been questioned relates to the so-called 'direct injury'. What is implied in this concept is that the injury directly affects the litigating State, even though an alien may be involved, so that, while the latter is concerned indirectly in the legal proceeding, the State is really protecting its own interests, apart from those centering around the right of diplomatic protection, rather than those of the alien. There are very few judicially decided cases on this issue, while there has been some exchange of arguments on the subject before the ICJ and there have been views impliedly expressed in separate and dissenting opinions in the ICJ.

In both the *Norwegian Loans Case* and the *Interhandel Case*, the applicant governments argued that there had been a direct injury to the State which resulted

recent work on waiver and estoppel is to be found in Dugard (note 72 above) 17 ff. The conclusions reached on the subject are identical with mine.

in the irrelevance of the rule of local remedies. In the former case, the French government referred in its observations to '*le caractère international du différend qui s'est élevé directement entre les deux Etats*',[115] and stated that '*une telle réclamation, d'Etat à Etat, ... n'a pas été soumise a des recours internes*'.[116] The Norwegian government did not deny that there could be situations in which the rule of local remedies was inapplicable because of the nature of the dispute, but contested the contention that the situation confronting the court involved a direct injury and not a dispute concerning essentially the obligations of Norway relative to the service of its debts owed to French bondholders which basically activated the rule of local remedies.[117]

In the *Interhandel Case*, the Swiss government, while accepting that in principle the rule of local remedies was applicable when an alien was injured, submitted that the rule was not applicable in the case before the court, because the injury '*constitue une violation directe du droit international et lése immédiatement l'Etat demandeur*'.[118] It further emphasized that in the instant case '*le dommage a été causé directement à l'Etat lésé.*'[119] The US government seems to have ignored the issue in its entirety, concentrating its arguments on the fulfilment of the requirements of the rule, because it took the view that the rule was applicable in the case and that there was no possibility that it could be excluded in the circumstances.[120]

In the *Aerial Incident Case,* the government of Israel observed that the rule of local remedies was inapplicable because the respondent State had violated a right directly vested in the applicant State,[121] thus raising the argument based on the direct injury. The Bulgarian government did not deny the principle that the rule could be excluded where there was a proper direct injury but implicitly took the view that the situation in the case was not one in which the rule could be avoided.[122]

In the *Arrest Warrant of 11 April 2000 Case*, the ICJ held that, where there is a direct injury to the State, even though an alien has been harmed, the rule of local remedies does not apply. The court held as follows:

The Court notes that the Congo has never sought to invoke before it Mr. Yerodia's personal rights. It considers that, despite the change in professional situation of Mr. Yerodia, the character of the dispute submitted to the Court by means of the Application has not changed: the dispute still concerns the lawfulness of the arrest warrant issued on 11 April 2000 against a person who was at the time Minister for Foreign Affairs of the Congo,

115 1 ICJ Pleadings (1957) 182.
116 Ibid.
117 Ibid 277 ff.
118 ICJ Pleadings (1959) 402.
119 Ibid. See also the oral argument of the Swiss government: ibid 547.
120 Ibid 315 ff (written pleadings) and 612 ff (oral argument).
121 ICJ Pleadings (1959) 158. See also the oral argument of the Israeli government, ibid 530 ff and 590.
122 Ibid 570 ff (oral argument).

and the question whether the rights of the Congo have or have not been violated by that warrant. As the Congo is not acting in the context of protection of one of its nationals, Belgium cannot rely upon the rules relating to the exhaustion of local remedies.[123]

It may be concluded from the evidence presented above that there are judicial precedents and State practice which generally support the proposition that a direct injury to the injured State could affect the incidence of the rule where the rights of aliens are concerned by making it inapplicable, however direct injury is defined.

To add to the supporting evidence, there may be mentioned the opinions of legal commentators who either expressly or impliedly take the view that the direct injury is a valid reason for excluding the application of the rule of local remedies, even though an alien may have been injured.[124]

Thus, there is no reason to question the validity of the position which postulates that the rule of local remedies does not become relevant where there is a direct injury to a State, even though there may also be an infringement of the rights of one of its nationals.

The ICJ has also given indication of what is a direct injury which would result in the rule of local remedies not being applicable to a situation involving an alien. The court has, further, given a negative indication of what the direct injury is not. On the other hand, individual judges have expressed positive views on what could constitute a direct injury, although their views either conflict with those of the court and are therefore unacceptable, or stand by themselves in circumstances in which the court has not expressed a view on the matter, so that they need to be evaluated in terms of principle.

As emerges from the *Arrest Warrant of 11 April 2000 Case*, where the issue is whether the rights of a State have been violated in a situation in which the State is not acting in the context of the *protection of one of its nationals*, the rules relating to the exhaustion of local remedies cannot be relied on by the

[123] 2002 ICJ Reports: see <http://www.cij-icj.org>, para 40. See also the *Air Services Agreement Arbitration* (France v USA), 18 UNRIAA 432 (1978), where the tribunal referred to the international agreement as containing 'a right granted by one *government* to the other *government*' which is a reference to a right the violation of which results in a direct injury. Earlier, the tribunal referred to an obligation of 'result' (presumably in contrast to an obligation of 'conduct') and for all practical purposes regarded the characterization as an unnecessary fifth wheel (ibid). The distinction invoked is misplaced for the purposes of the local remedies rule, is not universal or general in national laws and was imported by Ago, 'Sixth Report on State Responsibility', YBILC (1977), vol 2, Part II, 22 ff, as it appears, indiscriminately from the Italian law. Neither is it at all possible to see its relevance to the rule of local remedies nor is it or was it supported by any kind of authority or reasoning in relation to the rule.

[124] See Freeman (note 14 above) 404; Eagleton (1929) (note 14 above) 51 and 103; Hyde, *International Law Chiefly as Interpreted and Applied by the United States* (1947), vol 2, 888; Jessup, *A Modern Law of Nations* (1956) 118 ff. See also Meron, 'The Incidence of the Rule of Exhaustion of Local Remedies', 35 BYIL (1959) 84 ff. There are several other authorities, including those who have expressed views at the Institut de Droit International and the 1956 Granada resolution of the Institut. See particularly C F Amerasinghe (1967) (note 73 above) 174 ff. Cançado Trindade (note 14 above) 173–4, also has some remarks on the subject.

respondent State.[125] This is a positive statement of what is at the heart of the exception of the direct injury.

In the *Interhandel Case* one issue was whether the US objection that local remedies had not been exhausted in relation to the taking of the property of Interhandel, a national of the applicant Swiss government, should be upheld. The arguments raised by the Swiss government included one based on the direct injury exclusion. The court said that for the reason adduced by the Swiss government the dispute referred to was not deprived:

> of the character of a dispute in which the Swiss Government appears as having adopted the cause of its national, Interhandel, for the purpose of securing the restitution to that company of assets vested by the Government of the United States. This is one of the many cases which give rise to the application of the rule of exhaustion of local remedies.[126]

The Swiss government had argued that the case involved non-execution of an international judgment given under an international agreement, which in its view was a direct injury.

It is clear that what the court did was to reject the contention that, where an injury to an alien is caused in the course of violating an international judgment given under an international agreement between the respondent and applicant States, the injury caused in that way per se resulted in a direct injury which would obviate the need to exhaust local remedies. Thus, there was here a negative pronouncement on what would not constitute a direct injury. It must now be taken as settled that the violation of an international judgment or an international agreement, binding upon both the host State and the alien's national State, does not per se cause the act which injures an alien to become a direct injury to the alien's national State.

A chamber of the ICJ held in the *ELSI Case* that the violation of a treaty does not necessarily exclude the application of the rule of local remedies on the basis that the injury caused is direct.[127] In that case it was found that there was no other injury which was distinct from and independent of that which arose from the violation of the treaty in regard to the entities in respect of which diplomatic protection was being exercised.

The view of the ICJ, in addition to its negative descriptions of the direct injury, is that the intervention of the injured State must be 'in the context of the protection of one of its nationals', if the local remedies rule is to be applicable.

Apart from the pleadings in the two cases discussed above, there is one other case in which the issue of the direct injury was raised but not decided either by

[125] 2002 ICJ Reports: see <http://www.icj-cij.org>, para. 40.

[126] 1959 ICJ Reports 28–9.

[127] 1989 ICJ Reports 42–3. In *Swiss Confederation v Federal Republic of Germany (No. 1)*, 25 ILR 42 (1958), the arbitral tribunal stated in effect that the mere fact that the dispute related to the interpretation of a treaty did not convert the injury caused into a direct injury. The arbitration was between two States.

the court or in separate or dissenting opinions, because the case was dismissed on the basis of another preliminary objection and because neither the court nor the judges giving separate or dissenting opinions touched on the objection based on the rule of local remedies. The pleadings in this case may be considered. The *Aerial Incident Case* arose out of the shooting down by Bulgaria of an Israeli civilian plane that had penetrated into Bulgarian airspace without authorization. In answering the Bulgarian objection based on the local remedies rule, the Israeli government stated in its observations:

The contention fails to appreciate the nature of the present case. From the fact that 4X-AKC was registered in Israel . . . and was wearing the Israel colours it *is the State of Israel which is directly and primarily injured* by the improper actions of the military forces of the Bulgarian State acting *jure imperii*. Local remedies are therefore irrelevant, and the particulars of claims contained in Annexes 40, 41 and 42 of the Memorial are also not relevant except in connection with the calculation of pecuniary damages the duty to pay which is one of the consequences of the breach of international law on the part of Bulgaria.[128]

The basis of the contention of the Israeli government was explained more fully in the oral argument:

the character of this case as a whole is that the Bulgarian act of which complaint is made affects Israel in its quality of a State. It is the international personality of Israel which has been injured—and sorely injured—by this breach of international law. The action of the Bulgarian authorities has violated rights which are the intrinsic attribute of Israel as a State, the right that an Israel aircraft going about its lawful business should not be improperly obstructed or otherwise interfered with, and certainly not destroyed, in the course of its voyage, and its innocent occupants exposed to the gravest terror and danger . . . This is not a case in which the injuries to the individual preceded the injury to the State and in which the injury to the individual forms the substance, in fact and in law, of the injury to the State.[129]

The Israeli argument was based on the theory that the alleged injury was primarily to the sovereignty of Israel made manifest in the nationality colours and markings on the plane which was shot down, and not to the Israeli nationals; the injury to Israel preceded the injury to the aliens and, therefore, this was not a case of diplomatic protection; the claims on behalf of the airline company and the affected individuals were subsidiary to the main claim which related to the violation of the rights of the State of Israel. In principle, the argument that there must be a primary injury to the State rather than to the alien in order that a direct injury be committed is a reasonable one. The next question, however, is whether in the circumstances of the case there was such a primary injury to the State of Israel. Both the principal idea and the latter question will be considered after a look is taken at the legal commentators on the subject.

[128] ICJ Pleadings (1959) 158–9.
[129] Ibid 530–1.

One such commentator who discussed the matter with State responsibility in general in mind, and not particularly in the context of the rule of local remedies, has stated:

> Nevertheless, various situations in the history of international claims reveal that in addition to the rights of its nationals a state has, in its relations with other states, certain rights which appertain to it in its collective or corporate capacity. The typical cases are those in which injury is done to an official of the state, particularly a consular or diplomatic official. The recognition accorded their special status in traditional international law is extended because of their representative character and not because of their status as individuals, although a supplementary claim may lie for the injury to the individual as such... International tribunals have frequently distinguished between a general injury to a state and specific damage.[130]

The writer gives many examples of injuries to consular or diplomatic officials but also mentions other injuries, such as damage caused to State-owned ships, which could be considered direct injuries.

A list of direct injuries might be useful, but it would be very difficult to compile one. Further, a list cannot be exclusive, as room must be left for the inclusion of situations which may not be foreseeable at the time the catalogue is made. What is more important is that some general legal principle be evolved which would govern the situation.

The question has been examined by a legal commentator who has expressed the general view that:

> The principal reason for the non-applicability of the rule of exhaustion of local remedies to cases of direct injury is that in such cases the injured State represents principally its own interests rather than the interests of its nationals and is the real claimant...
>
> An attempt to formulate a general theoretical distinction between cases of direct injury and cases of diplomatic protection is bound to be difficult. In the first place it should be observed that there is an extremely close connexion between all the facts of a given case and the classification of that case as one belonging to either of these two categories... most instances of direct injury contain, in a certain degree, also elements of diplomatic protection... It is suggested that the classification of a case as one of direct injury or as one of diplomatic protection depends on the element or elements which are preponderant. It is further suggested that once a case has been classified in this way, the international claim, including all its elements, must generally be regarded as a unity and may not be split into its constituent elements, such as those of direct injury and those of diplomatic protection.[131]

As general considerations these are relevant and basically do not create problems. The writer then suggests that regard must be had to two main factors, namely, the

[130] Jessup (note 124 above) 118–20. The 1956 Granada resolution of the Institut de Droit International also refers to some direct injuries to which the rule of exhaustion of local remedies does not apply. Injuries to heads of state and diplomats are mentioned.

[131] Meron (note 124 above).

subject of the dispute or the action impugned in the proceedings and the nature of the claim.[132]

This approach poses certain problems. For example, in determining whether the subject of the dispute falls into the category of a direct injury, the writer suggests that violations of treaties generally fall into this category. But this is prima facie not the case, as is shown by the *Interhandel Case*. Further, the alternative request of the Swiss government in that case was for a declaration that there was an obligation to settle the dispute by arbitration or conciliation.[133] The claim clearly concerned the right of the Swiss government to an arbitration or a conciliation procedure and did not in substance concern the right of the Swiss government to proper treatment for its nationals. A very real object of the Swiss government was the securing of its right to arbitration or conciliation, although it may be said that the ultimate object was the protection of its right to the proper treatment of its nationals. On one interpretation of the 'real object or interest' of this claim it was possible to find that the alternative request was to secure a different international right from the mere protection of nationals to which the State was entitled.[134] The court, however, did advert to the object of the claim and stated that:

> One interest and one alone, that of Interhandel, which has led the latter to institute and to resume proceedings before the United States courts, has induced the Swiss Government to institute international proceedings. This interest is the basis for the present claim and should determine the scope of the action brought before the Court by the Swiss Government in its alternative form as well as in its principal form. On the other hand, the grounds on which the rule of the exhaustion of local remedies is based are the same, whether in the case of an international court, arbitral or conciliation commission. In these circumstances the Court considers that any distinction so far as the rule of exhaustion of local remedies is concerned between the various claims or between the various tribunals is unfounded.[135]

Although 'objects and interests' were referred to, it would seem that the court ultimately took the simple view that the rule of exhaustion of local remedies

[132] Ibid 86–7. He then explains these elements. He cites also the present Article 38(1) and (2) of the Rules of Court of the ICJ in this connection, on the ground that those provisions, which deal with the contents of an application instituting proceedings, refer to these two concepts, but points out that the concept of the direct injury concerns substantive factors rather than procedural features. Cançado Trindade (note 14 above) supports the relevance of the nature of the claim.

[133] 1959 ICJ Reports 19.

[134] As was held by Judge Lauterpacht, dissenting, ibid 120, and Judge Winiarski, dissenting, ibid 83.

[135] Ibid 29. Four dissenting judges differed on this point: see Judge Carry, ibid 32; Judge Klaestad, ibid 82; Judge Winiarski, ibid 84; and Judge Lauterpacht, ibid 120. The view taken by the dissenting judges is supported by Law, (note 14 above) 95 ff. The decision in the *Ambatielos Case,* in which it was stated that the Court could not consider whether local remedies had been exhausted in deciding the question whether there was an obligation upon the respondent State to submit to arbitration under treaty provisions: 1953 ICJ Reports 22 ff, also runs counter to the holding in the *Interhandel Case,* even though it does not expressly contradict that case.

would have prevented an action being taken for the determination of the main question before an arbitral or conciliation commission just as much as before an international court. However, at least *obiter* the court did refer to 'objects and interests' as being relevant to the determination of the question whether the rule of exhaustion is applicable. Judge Basdevant, on the other hand, in a declaration laid emphasis on the 'subject of the dispute' as the criterion of the validity of the objections put forward.[136]

While there is some conflict of opinion on the proper criterion, it would seem that the concept of the 'subject of the dispute' is not entirely adequate, if it refers to categories of acts. On the other hand, the 'nature of the claim', defined as being determined by the 'real objects and interests' of a State, would seem to come closer to a satisfactory solution of the problem. The important point is to avoid giving the claimant's formulation of the claim too much weight so as to blur the true nature of the claim. Thus, a possible refinement of this approach may be suggested. While 'objects and interests' of a State in bringing a particular claim may be relevant, it would seem that the real question concerns not so much the 'nature of the claim' as the 'nature of the injury or right violated' on which the claim is based. In so far as the former, as determined by the real objects and interests of the State, depends on the latter it becomes of relevance. It is the 'real objects and interests', which are the essence of the injury committed or the right violated, that govern the answer to the question whether local remedies should have been exhausted. This is so, because ultimately the claim, whatever it may be, depends on the right violated. The rule of exhaustion relates to the right violated or the injury committed and not to the claim based on it as such, which reflects a secondary or remedial right. It is also the essence of the substantive right violated, as determined by the objects and interests promoted therein, that is of importance.

That an international right belonging to a State has been violated, as has been seen, does not necessarily result in the exclusion of the rule. Indeed, an injury to an alien which violates international law is also a violation of his State's right. What is required is a further inquiry into the essence of the State's right. If the State's right in its essence has for its object the protection of its nationals as such, and if this is the main interest sought from it, it may be concluded that the rule of exhaustion applies to it. Hence, a claim based on its violation, whatever the *form* of that claim, cannot be espoused until local remedies have been exhausted. The claim may be for an apology or for an indemnity for damage caused to an alien, or merely damages for the insult to the alien's State, but this would not make a difference if the essence of the substantive right violated is the right to the protection of the alien. Conversely, if the essence of the right violated is different, then the rule of local remedies would not apply to a claim based on that wrong. Thus, where a diplomat is injured by a State, the diplomat's State can assert that

[136] 1959 ICJ Reports 30.

a right has been violated which has for its object the carrying on of functions of State and not merely the protection of nationals. In such a case, no local remedies need be exhausted in respect of any claim based on that violation of international law, although it may be that a claim might be made which purports to recover damages for the personal loss suffered by the diplomat, an alien. Further, it may be that in certain circumstances it is necessary for an international court to weigh conflicting interests and objects behind a substantive right so as to determine whether the predominant interest is that of protecting a national.[137] It is certain that the fact that the protective right is embodied in a treaty does not make it any less a protective right, as was seen above.

This approach is compatible with Judge Basdevant's theory which stresses the subject of a dispute, for the substantive right is, indeed, the subject of the dispute. However, it goes a little further in attaching importance to the objects and interests which form the essence of that right (not of the claim, as such). Also, it is compatible with the theory of 'objects and interests' propounded *obiter* in the *Interhandel Case*, which may in fact seem to support it. Thus, it is the objects and interests underlying a right that really matter, although the claim may in the way it is formulated not be relevant.

That this view of the position is tenable is supported by the fact that, in cases of injury to aliens where local remedies are exhausted and adequate redress is obtained by the injured alien, the delinquent State's responsibility is completely discharged and all claims arising from the injury are extinguished. There is no room for a claim of damages for the international injury to the alien's State or for an apology based on the fact that the alien's State also suffered injury. This shows that, where local remedies must be exhausted, it is the aspect of the State's right that involves protection of the alien which is given emphasis. The protective interest which is inherent in the substantive right that an alien should not be injured is, thus, rightly used as the determining factor in the incidence of the rule of local remedies.

The above approach is best supported by the view expressed rather succinctly by the ICJ in the *Arrest Warrant of 11 April 2000 Case*, where it was stated that:

> As the Congo is not acting in the context of the *protection of one of its nationals*, Belgium cannot rely upon the rules relating to the exhaustion of local remedies.[138]

[137] An analogous operation is performed by some, mainly national, courts in determining whether an ordinary offence is a political offence for the purposes of the law of extradition: see C F Amerasinghe, *Studies in International Law* (1969) 164ff; and Gutteridge, 'The Notion of Political Offences and the Law of Extradition', 31 BYIL (1954) 430ff; Evans, 'Reflections upon the Political Offense in International Practice', 57 AJIL (1963) 11ff.

[138] Emphasis added: <http://www.icj-cij.org>, para 40. In the *Air Services Agreement Arbitration* (France v US), 18 UNRIAA 431 (1978), the tribunal referred to the core of the rights and duties which are the subject of the dispute, stating that:

> the rule of international law relating to the requirement of exhaustion of local remedies, when making a distinction between the State-to-State claims in which the requirement applies, and claims which are not subject to such a requirement, must necessarily base this distinction on

It is quite clear that this statement emphasizes the 'essence' of the right violated, which is substantially what matters, as is pointed out above, insofar as it points to the 'context of the protection of one of its nationals' as being what is relevant to the incidence of the rule of local remedies.[139] The statement also supports the further conclusion arrived at above that other considerations such as the 'subject of the dispute' without more and the 'nature of the claim', as formulated, are not as such relevant. On the other hand, the 'real objects and interests' of the State, adequately defined, may be synonymous with the 'essence of the right' infringed.

The ILC 2006 Draft Article 14(3) refers to the claim being brought 'preponderantly on the basis of an injury to a national...'[140] for the rule of local remedies to be applicable. This is an adequate and positive general characterization of the basis for the incidence of the rule and implies that the converse is true, namely that, where the claim is based preponderantly on an injury to the State and not to a national, the rule of local remedies is not applicable.[141] The explanation of the 'direct' injury to the State in the commentary[142] correctly refers to the possibility of 'mixed' claims and to the preponderance of the 'direct' element, in order that the rule be applicable. It additionally refers as a test of an indirect claim to 'whether the claim would not have been brought but for the injury to the national'. But all this having been said, it is really the nature of the 'right' violated as being preponderantly one relating to an alien or his property that needs to be considered in determining the indirectness of the injury.

(b) Jurisdictional Connection

Another question that has been raised is whether, in cases where a State is obviously protecting its national, ie genuine cases of diplomatic protection, there could arise situations in which the application of the rule of local remedies is excluded. Clearly, there can be little doubt that, where, for instance, State A improperly

> the *juridical* character of the *legal relationship* between States which is invoked in support of the claim. Consequently, with respect to the applicability of the local remedies rule, a distinction is made between 'cases of diplomatic protection' and cases of direct injury.

This statement clearly supports the views expressed in the text above which refer to the nature of the real interests or right protected as the basis of the distinction between what is a direct injury and what is not. See also the statement which is somewhat relevant and was made by the arbitral tribunal in *Swiss Confederation v Federal Republic of Germany* (*No. 1*), 25 ILR 42–3 (1958), that there must be a claim based on impairment of the rights of a national of the claimant State in violation of international law, in order to trigger the rule of local remedies.

[139] It is to be noted that Dugard, 'Second Report on Diplomatic Protection' (ILC), UN Doc. A/CN.4/514 (2001) 10–15, in draft Article 11, concedes that protection of a national, 'as a preponderant element', is what is important but, first, does not recognize that it is really the 'essence' of the right violated which is the right to protect a national that matters, and, secondly, in the discussion of the subject confuses the issues and elements involved.

[140] See Report of the ILC (2006) 20. See also now the *Avena Case*, 2004 ICJ Reports 12, para 40.

[141] The drafting could have emphasized rather the latter aspect than the former.

[142] Report of the ILC (2006) 74–6. The commentary on this point lacks clarity.

imprisons a national of State B who is resident in State A, the rule applies, but there may be situations where the applicability of the rule may be questioned where there is doubt as to whether there is an adequate 'jurisdictional connection'. Examples that may be given are (i) where naval officers of State A improperly treat nationals of State B on a ship belonging to State C on the high seas, or (ii) where diplomatic officers of State A in State B treat a national of State C in a manner which violates a treaty between State A and State B. In all cases, especially of this kind, the issue raised is one concerned with jurisdictional connection which would require, in the above examples, the nationals of State B to exhaust local remedies in State A before State B may exercise diplomatic protection over its nationals. On the other hand, the commoner examples of cases where the jurisdictional connection may be assumed to have been established, apart from the case where the alien takes up residence either temporarily or permanently in the territory of the host or respondent State, are those where an alien engages in business in, owns property in,[143] or enters into contractual relations with[144] the government of the host or respondent State.

It would appear that in almost all decided cases that have been reported where the rule has been applied the question never arose as to whether there was an adequate jurisdictional connection, because apparently one did exist. In general, most of these cases concerned situations in which the alien was temporarily or permanently resident in, or was physically present in, or had some kind of contractual connection with the host State. The history of the diplomatic practice related to the rule also shows that the circumstances in which the rule was invoked were those in which the alien had some physical connection with the host State. Hence, it is not surprising that a legal commentator in 1915 expressed the idea that the rule was applicable because the 'alien is deemed to tacitly submit and to be subject to the local law of the state of residence'[145] thus consecrating the requirement of residence. But, as cases like the *Ambatielos Claim* show,[146] the rule has been regarded as being applicable in cases where the alien is not resident or even physically present in the host State but where he has some connection, such as a contractual one, with the host State.

The authorities, whether judicial or other, have not generally faced the problem of the jurisdictional connection in any systematic way, although there has been some discussion of the problem. In the cases and arguments before the ICJ there have been a few broad statements of the circumstances in which the rule that local remedies must be exhausted is applicable, without any apparent qualification.[147]

[143] See, eg, the facts in the *Panavezys-Saldutiskis Railway Case,* PCIJ Series A/B No 76 (1939), and the facts in the *Interhandel Case,* 1959 ICJ Reports 6, where the rule was applied.

[144] See, eg, the type of situation involved in the *Ambatielos Claim* (Greece v UK), 12 UNRIAA 83 (1956), where the rule was applied, and in the *Norwegian Loans Case,* 1957 ICJ Reports 9.

[145] Borchard (1916) (note 14 above) 817. See HLS (note 50 above) 152–3.

[146] Greece v UK, 12 UNRIAA 83 (1956).

[147] See, eg, Judge Cordova in the *Interhandel Case,* 1959 ICJ Reports 46. Some support for a broad view of the circumstances in which the rule of local remedies is applicable is to be found

On the other hand, there have been more limited statements in the cases and argument before the ICJ such as the one made in the *Interhandel Case*:

the rule has been generally observed in cases in which a State has adopted the cause of its national where rights are claimed to have been disregarded in another State in violation of international law. Before resort may be had to an international court in such a situation, it has been considered necessary that the State where the violation occurred should have an opportunity to redress it by its own means.[148]

This explanation attaches importance to the place where the violation of international law took place. France in the *Norwegian Loans Case* emphasized residence in the delinquent State as a criterion of limitation.[149] Judge Read in a dissenting opinion in the same case said that the rule was not limited to circumstances in which the injured alien was resident in the delinquent State, but did not refer to the limitations on the incidence of the rule.[150] In the *Salem Case*, an arbitral tribunal stated, in terms similar to the French argument, that:

as a rule, a foreigner must acknowledge as applicable to himself the kind of justice instituted in the country in which he did choose his residence.[151]

In the *Aerial Incident Case*, Israel argued for a limitation based on some notion of a voluntary link.[152] Bulgaria opposed Israel's argument on the ground that the voluntary link was not part of international law, although it did not indicate, in turn, whether there were any limitations on the incidence of the rule of local remedies.[153] It may also be mentioned that in early British practice it was asserted that, where an alien suffered injury on the high seas, by seizure or capture of a vessel, local remedies had to be exhausted in the seizing or capturing State with no reference to a voluntary link or other connection.[154] It is doubtful, one may comment, whether the practice would be recognized today.

among text writers: see, eg, Reuter, 'La responsabilité internationale', *Droit International Public (Cours)* (1955–6) 161 ff; McNair, *International Law Opinions* (1956), vol 2, 219; Gaja (note 14 above) 91. See also the Norwegian argument in the *Norwegian Loans Case*: 2 ICJ Pleadings (1957) 156.

148 1959 ICJ Reports 27. There are authors who base the incidence of the rule on (i) the residence of the alien in the territory of the respondent State: eg Mummery, 'The Content of the Duty to Exhaust Local Judicial Remedies', 58 AJIL (1964) 390 ff; O'Connell, 2 *International Law* (1970) 950 ff, or (ii) the presence of the alien or his property in the territory of the respondent State: see, eg, Parry, 'Some Considerations upon the Protection of Individuals in International Law', 90 (note 14 above) 688; Law, note 14 above, 104; and Head, 'A Fresh Look at the Local Remedies Rule', 5 CYIL (1967) 153.

149 1 ICJ Pleadings (1957) 409.

150 1957 ICJ Reports 97.

151 (1932, USA v Egypt), 2 UNRIAA 1202.

152 ICJ Pleadings (1959) 531–2.

153 ICJ Pleadings (1959) 565. For a similar view see Secretary of State McLane in 1834: Moore (1898) (note 6 above) 658; see also Secretary of State Seward in 1866: Moore, ibid 660.

154 See McNair (note 6 above) 302.

Legal commentators who have remarked on the problem also assert in one way or another that there are some limitations on the incidence of the rule.[155] Largely on the basis of the Israeli argument in the *Aerial Incident Case*, the view has been expressed that there must be a genuine link between the alien and the respondent State in order that the rule of local remedies be applicable. This view ultimately relied on a voluntary link.[156]

While no international court or tribunal has up to now had to decide the specific issue raised here, it appears that the rule has actually been applied in a strictly circumscribed sphere. Simply because no case has decided that the rule does not apply in every situation in which an alien is injured by a foreign State, it would not be in keeping with the policies behind the rule that it should apply in every such circumstance. Hence, the broad unqualified statements referred to above cannot be regarded as properly reflecting the law.

At the other extreme, to insist on the residence or presence of the alien in the delinquent State at the time of the injury would not be compatible with the application of the rule in some of the decided cases. Judge Read was, therefore, correct in rejecting this formulation of the rule by France in the *Norwegian Loans Case.*

It would seem, then, that the solution lies somewhere in between these two extremes. In terms of the policies behind the rule of local remedies, it is apparent that it is only where the delinquent State can be said to be entitled to jurisdiction over the issue that the rule may be applied. As is generally known, international law does not for a general purpose define the circumstances in which a State will be entitled to jurisdiction over any particular issue, so that resort to other fields of international law may not be very helpful. In this sense the analogy of the 'voluntary or genuine link' which may have some relationship to the rules of the nationality of claims may not be so apt, since policy may demand a different approach. On the other hand, such concepts mentioned as 'location of the wrong', 'voluntary subjection to jurisdiction by entering into the sphere of operation' (understood in a general sense), 'tacit subjection to jurisdiction' and 'free and voluntary submission to jurisdiction' are more relevant to the problem in hand. These concepts are divisible into two groups, representing respectively the idea of 'the location of the wrong' and the notion of 'free and voluntary submission to the jurisdiction'.

In view of the fact that the ICJ in the *Interhandel Case* distinctly and clearly expressed its agreement with the view that 'the State *where* the *violation occurred* should have an opportunity to redress it by its own means',[157] the proper starting point for a consideration of the limitations on the incidence of the rule of

[155] Borchard, 'L'épuisement des recours internes et le déni de justice', 16 RDILC (1935) 523; Law (note 14 above) 104.

[156] Meron (note 124 above) 95–6. Other legal commentators who apparently support the theory of the voluntary link are Head (note 148 above), 153; Jiménez de Aréchaga, 'International Responsibility' in Sørensen (ed), *Manual of Public International Law* (1968) 583; and Chappez (note 14 above) 48 ff.

[157] 1959 ICJ Reports 27 (emphasis added).

local remedies is the 'location of the wrong'. If the wrong must be located in the territory of the delinquent State, whatever the difficulties of determining the locus of the wrong,[158] then it would generally mean that the person or property must also be located in the delinquent State. Inter alia, if a subjective approach to the problem of the locus of the wrong were taken, it may be possible to say that the locus of the person or property injured may be outside the delinquent State, while the locus of the wrong remained within. That would happen where the act constituting the wrong is begun within the delinquent state but terminates on a person or property outside the delinquent State. This anomaly can be overcome by adopting a test for the locus which embodies the objective approach and fixes on the place where the last event necessary to make an actor liable for an alleged wrong takes place.[159]

There is certainly one circumstance in which the theory of the locus of the wrong may have to be modified, and that is, where the determination that the locus of the wrong is in the delinquent state is dependent on the presence of the alien's person or property in the delinquent State and that presence of person or property is the result of a seizure made in violation of international law, attributable to the delinquent State. Here the principle *ex iniuria non oritur ius* is applicable.[160] It is to be noted that this exception is not co-extensive with the absence of voluntariness or consent freely given. Although in the incidence of the exception there will be found to be absence of voluntariness or consent, it does not follow that in every case in which there is absence of voluntariness or consent the exception will apply. For instance, the facts of the *Aerial Incident Case* would have shown that the exception did not apply, because the presence of the aircraft in Bulgarian airspace was not attributable to an illegal seizure by Bulgaria, regardless of the question of whether or not it was there voluntarily. On the other hand, the old British view that a seizure on the high seas requires exhaustion of local remedies in the delinquent State cannot be supported in modern law where this exception applies. It is clear also that the principle *ex iniuria non oritur ius* as applied in this context refers only to an *iniuria* attributable to the respondent State.

The application of the theory of the locus of the wrong to a breach of contract, *where such breach is internationally wrongful,* may give rise to apparent difficulties, because such a breach of contract will often be an omission. A solution may be found in regarding a breach of contract in such circumstances as an interference with the alien's rights in the contract, ie his right to performance. Since this is in the nature of a *chose in action,* the *situs* of the *chose in action* will determine

158 The same problem arises in connection with criminal jurisdiction: see the *Lotus Case,* PCIJ Series A No 10 (1927), which deals with the objective test of the locus of a crime. The locus of a tort has to be determined for the purpose of the conflict of laws (private international law): see, eg, Collins (ed), 2 *Dicey and Morris on the Conflict of Laws* (2000) 1507 ff.

159 *Restatement of the Law of Conflict of Laws* (1934), section 377.

160 This principle is applicable to questions of jurisdiction when seizures are made contrary to international law: see Morgenstern, 'Jurisdiction in Seizures Effected in Violation of International Law', 29 BYIL (1952) 265 ff, especially at 279.

the locus of the wrong. The determination of *situs* will depend on general principles of law as found in the conflict of laws (private international law).[161]

The theory of the locus of the wrong, with the exception outlined above, not only has the virtue of recognizing the view of the ICJ and the policies behind the rule of local remedies and of adequately balancing two principal interests involved, but is also compatible with all the decided cases that can be explained by reference to it.

It is quite clear that the broad generic view of 'free and voluntary submission to jurisdiction' as such finds no general support in the decided cases or State practice, with the exception of the Israeli argument in the *Aerial Incident Case*.[162] An example will illustrate the point. If bandits in State A seize an alien (in relation to State B) and bring him across the border to State B, where a delictual violation of international law in respect of the alien in relation to the alien's national State is subsequently committed, there is no reason why there should be no jurisdictional connection for the exercise of jurisdiction on the basis that there had been no free and voluntary submission by the alien to the jurisdiction of State B, where the wrong has occurred. The principle, *ex iniuria non oritur ius*, does not apply because under this principle the *iniuria* must be committed by State B (in this example). There is clearly no reason why an exception should be made to State B's entitlement to have local remedies exhausted in its territory. Here, State B's interests are clearly paramount.

The conclusion to be drawn on a policy basis is that a broad absence of 'free and voluntary submission' exception may not be as such the sole relevant factor for determining whether the rule of local remedies does not apply. The *ex iniuria non oritur* principle by itself—a general principle of law—is certainly one exception legitimately to protect the two principal interests. Conversely, the 'free and voluntary submission to jurisdiction' principle does not have support as such as a general principle of law.

A recent rapporteur of the ILC incorporated in Article 14 of his draft the 'free and voluntary link' principle as such.[163] The discussion and analysis which follows this Draft Article[164] is not merely inconclusive as to the acceptance of the principle in State practice and in judicial decisions or by legal commentators but rather supports its non-acceptance, because the evidence shows that (i) where such a principle or some variation of it has been recognized as an exception, there has been an explicit or implicit waiver, on the basis of the principle, of the rule of local remedies in the circumstances; (ii) the reference to treaties as establishing the exception does not reveal that such treaties give rise to customary international law, because of a lack of a clear *opinio iuris* in any case, apart from the absence of cogent practice; (iii) existing judicial decisions of relevance as such do

[161] See Collins (note 158 above) 924 ff. A breach of contract per se by a State is usually not a violation of international law. There must be a denial of justice in such contract cases before violation of international law in the treatment of an alien occurs.

[162] ICJ Pleadings (1959) 31–2.

[163] Dugard (note 139 above) 26.

[164] Ibid 26–35.

not come anywhere near to supporting the principle as an exception; and (iv) legal commentators are not in agreement at all that the exception as such is applicable but rather ignore it. What is eminently clear is that there are judicial decisions, inter alia, which categorically support the view that the basic principle of jurisdiction is that of the 'location of the wrong', there being little or no discussion of the exception based on 'absence of voluntary submission'. The only reference to this principle is in the Israeli argument in the *Aerial Incident Case,* a reference which is not based on any kind of precedent, authority, or a general principle of law—nor apparently substantiated by policy reasons except the idea that an alien must by choice assume the risk of local remedies being applicable for the rule to apply. That may be a cogent policy value but must be weighed against the sovereign rights of a State to exercise jurisdiction over violations of law in its territory.

While the *ex iniuria non oritur ius* principle itself may not have been applied hitherto, inter alia, in any international judicial decisions on the rule of local remedies, there are international judicial decisions which have recognized it in other areas[165] and it is clearly an accepted general principle of law. Thus, there is no difficulty in applying it as a general principle of both international and national law in the context of the rule of local remedies.

Article 15(c) of the 2006 ILC Draft Articles states that local remedies do not need to be exhausted where there is no relevant connection between the injured person and the respondent or host State. In the commentary to this section of Article 15 the voluntary link principle for the incidence of the rule of local remedies is referred to but not canvassed, while the idea that there must be an 'assumption of risk' by the injured alien is supported.[166] However, it may be going too far to deprive the host or respondent State of the opportunity of redressing the injury to the alien even where there is no voluntary link between the alien and such State, provided the maxim *ex iniuria non oritur ius* is not applicable to the situation. Absence of free and voluntary submission to jurisdiction by itself as the criterion for inapplicability of the rule of local remedies may be too broad a characterization.

Perspectives

The importance of respect for the sovereignty of the host or respondent State has been attested to in many areas of the law relating to the rule of local remedies

[165] That the principle is a general principle of both international law and national law needs no support of authority. In any case, see note 160 above and such cases decided by the PCIJ and the ICJ as the *Jurisdiction of the Courts of Danzig Opinion*, PCIJ Series B No 15, 26 (1928); the *Legal Status of Eastern Greenland Case,* PCIJ Series A/B No 53, 75 and 95 (1933); and the *Namibia Opinion*, 1977 ICJ Reports 46–7. In the last mentioned opinion, for instance, the ICJ said specifically that a State which does not fulfil its own obligations flowing from an international relationship cannot be recognized as having the rights which it claims to derive from that relationship, thus stating a principle which reflects the broader principle *ex iniuria non oritur ius*.

[166] Report of the ILC (2006) 82–3. The commentary refers to a subjective element connected with the alien rather than an objective one, which is what is proposed in the text above, on the basis of particularly the judicial authorities.

and it is right that this should be so. Particular mention may be made of the approach to the scope of the rule. The law relating to extraordinary remedies, to the raising of substantive issues, and to the persons who should exhaust remedies for instance, has resulted in a substantial role being assigned to the local or domestic system of dispute settlement, as has the conclusion that in the usual case what is required is a normal use of remedies—but not in the sense that what reasonable counsel might have done was necessarily adequate. In certain respects the stringency with which waivers are implied from agreements by the host or respondent State, and the rather strict manner in which the doctrines of estoppel and good faith have recently been applied, particularly in the *ELSI Case*, also flow from regard for the sovereignty of the host or respondent State.

On the other hand, consideration for other concerned interests has led to limitations on the incidence of the rule by reference to the concepts of direct injury and jurisdictional connection. While these limitations do not in reality inappropriately detract from the sovereignty of the host or respondent State, they have clearly arisen from the policy objective of containing the application of the rule and confining it to situations which the host or respondent State may justifiably claim to be subject to its system of dispute settlement. Other limitations, such as the requirement that only remedies of a legal nature need to be exercised, also flow from a rational approach to the balancing of the conflicting interests involved, which recognizes and gives effect to interests other than those of the host or respondent State. The recent application, by the ICJ, inter alia, of the law relating to the availability of remedies in the *ELSI Case* also reveals some concern that the rule should not be applied in such a manner as to rob it of its balanced effectiveness by over-protecting the interests of the host or respondent State.

The principle of avoiding undue hardship to the alien or individual, which has been clearly recognized in international jurisprudence and practice, and was explicitly acknowledged in the *Finnish Ships Arbitration,* has, it appears, especially been applied to impose limitations upon the operation of the rule. To the extent that the quality of the remedies offered is controlled, the principle has been effective. On the other hand, in so far as the general limitation relating to the quality of remedies propounded in the *Finnish Ships Arbitration* has been strictly construed, there has been a tendency to lean towards the sovereignty of the host or respondent State. The rejection of some excuses which clearly favour the interests of the alien or individual, confirms the respect accorded the sovereignty of the host or respondent State. It is understood that the principle of avoiding undue hardship to the alien or individual has a specific and important relevance and is tempered by the basic principle of respect for the sovereignty of the host or respondent State. However, it cannot be said that the interests of the alien or individual have necessarily been prejudiced. There is, nevertheless, a tendency which has been observed to avoid the application of the rule by express or implied waiver, more recently through the instrument of the BIT. Jurisprudence and practice have been found to have considerably developed the implication of waivers. While explicit waivers tend to be strictly construed, as already pointed out, the implication of waivers has been more liberal in connection with certain specific situations, just as the doctrines of estoppel and good faith have also to a large degree worked in favour of excluding the application of the rule. Perhaps these trends indicate a certain impatience with the rule, particularly on the part of protecting States. The approach to implication of waivers and estoppel or good faith, however, has not been overly protective of the interests of aliens or individuals and of protecting States, although such interests have clearly been considered. Generally, waivers have been implied and estoppel or good faith has been effective only where the circumstances justify a conclusion which requires a modification of the recognition of the sovereign interests of the host or respondent State. While waivers of the rule may sometimes be given after the injury has been committed, the numerous cases involving the rule in the field of diplomatic protection which have come before the PCIJ, the ICJ, and other tribunals, such as the *Interhandel Case,* the *Norwegian Loans Case*, and the *ELSI Case*, prove that waivers are not automatic and that the doctrines of estoppel, in the narrow sense, and good faith do not often operate to exclude the application of the rule.[167]

The rule may, thus, still be regarded as an important instrument of dispute settlement in the international system. Nor has the point been reached at which it may be concluded that the rule is not a useful mechanism for defusing international disputes before they reach an international level, provided there is always a judicious balancing of the interests involved.

Finally, the question of whether the rule has been applied too strictly in the law of diplomatic protection may be broached. As already pointed out, the primary purpose of the rule is to give the host or respondent State an opportunity of rectifying a situation which is alleged to be in violation of the law. Consequently, it would defeat that purpose, if the rule were implemented in such a manner, or if such an approach were taken, as to make it too easy for aliens to have direct access to international fora, particularly judicial, by avoiding recourse to local remedies without giving the host or respondent State a fair chance of doing justice. What is required is that the rule be applied in such a way that justice is not travestied by too much regard for the interests of host or respondent States and too little consideration of the other interests involved, particularly of the alien. There is no evidence that decision-makers in the international system of dispute settlement have not hitherto tended to respect the demands of justice in the implementation of the rule. It is principally in the area of limitations on the rule, particularly by reference to the principle of avoiding undue hardship to the alien and in the application of the principle of consent to the non-application of the rule, that the

[167] Indeed, in 2002, as a result of the NAFTA, there has been agitation and discontent both among US investors and other interest groups, and concern in the US Government, that the exclusion of the local remedies rule under the NAFTA and other BITs in general has back fired. Thus, there is now a move to retain in investment agreements some control by local law and courts, or, at any rate, its effect: *Financial Times*, 2 October 2002, 7. The reasoning behind the new position does not appear clearly from this report but the short point is that the US is unhappy with the position that foreign investors are not subject to US law, believed to be compatible with the international law and applied by the US courts, in relation to the treatment of investment.

legitimate parameters of the rule need to be kept in mind. The development of the rule has shown that these parameters have generally been judiciously and sagaciously established and may be maintained in the future by prudent interpretation. There is no reason to believe that, when decision-makers are confronted with the application of the rule to new situations, they cannot duly apply the rule, having considered all the relevant interests, in such a way as not to overemphasize or ignore certain interests in relation to others. It is really a matter of balancing interests and finding a result which would ensure justice, which after all may be a question of common sense and reason.[168]

[168] Attention is also drawn to the work of the ILA on the rule of local remedies. In Resolution N0 5/2006 adopted at the 2006 ILA Conferance it was stated:

1. Under general principles of international law the exhaustion of local remedies is a procedural precondition for the exercise of diplomatic protection.
2. Local remedies means the remedies which are open to natural or juridical persons under the internal law of the state against which diplomatic protection is sought.
   2.1. The term local refers to the internal legal order of the host state,
   2.2. The term remedy normally encompasses both administrative and judicial procedures, as well as other adequate and effective procedural devices.
3. Exhaustion presupposes that the alleged victim:
   3.1. pursues the claim through the instances which the domestic legal order of the host state provides,
   3.2. presents the claim at least in substance before those instances, and
   3.3. resorts to those means of procedure which in the same court are essential to establish the claim.
4. As a general rule, the claimant is exempt from exhaustion of local remedies if under general principles governing the observance of the rule of law the process does not meet the necessary conditions to ensure this requirement in the wrongdoing state, in particular where:
   4.1. for whatever reason, there is no effective remedy capable of redressing the violation available to him,
   4.2. the claimant is factually prevented from access to existing remedies,
   4.3. a firmly established jurisprudence offers ex ante no chance of a change in the matter concerned,
   4.4. the respondent Government waived the exhaustion of local remedies,
   4.5. the respondent Government forfeited its right to the exhaustion of local remedies.
5. The exhaustion of local remedies rule can be waived expressly or tacitly. Tacit waiver requires a clear demonstration of intent.
6. The host state is stopped from invoking the non-exhaustion of local remedies, if:
   6.1. a time-limit set for invoking the plea has passed without the plea having been made,
   6.2. in the light of the words and conduct or for any other reason the raising of the plea does not meet essential requirements of good faith.
7. In respect of the burden of proof:
   7.1. The claimant has the burden of proving that local remedies were exhausted, or that he was exempted from so doing.
   7.2. The host state has to prove that further remedies existed which were not exhausted. <http://www.ila-hq.org>.

These conclusion are in accord with what emerged from the consideration of the rule of local remedies by me in *Local Remedies in International Law* (1990), chapters 6 to 13 (see now the second edition of book—(2004), chapter 6–12 and 15).

The conclusions of the ILA in the 2006 resolution were reflected in the Final Report of its Committee on Diplomatic Protection of Persons and Property (2006)—<http://www.ila-hq.org>—and were based on Kokott, Interim Report on 'The Exhaustion of Local Remedies', in ILA *Report of the Sixty-ninth Conference* (2000) 606–30.

12

The Effect of a Calvo Clause

Origin and Forms of the Calvo Clause

Civil wars, international disturbances, and revolutions were frequent in Latin America in the late nineteenth century and early twentieth century. Nationals of States in Europe and of the USA affected by these civil disruptions often suffered injury to person and property. When the host State refused to assume responsibility for such injuries, aliens frequently sought the intervention of their national States, requesting them to claim compensation for the alleged wrong at an international level. That there was abuse of this liberty cannot be denied. Thus, the observation has been made that:

> Nationals often felt entitled to complete security of their persons and property, and appealed to their governments on rather flimsy evidence and without any real effort to obtain local redress. The petitioned government, acting on limited, one-sided evidence, and often under domestic political pressure, sponsored claims that frequently were not based upon strict justice. Utilization of armed force to compel the weaker nations to honor these dubious claims was not infrequent, and it sometimes happened that the severity of the measures adopted in seeking compensation for the alleged injuries was far out of proportion to the extent of the initial damages suffered.[1]

Moreover, the international tribunals (commissions) established to settle the disputes which arose were regarded by Latin American States as prejudiced in favour of the protecting States.

It was this scenario that led Latin American States to try to weaken, to the extent of eliminating, diplomatic protection by formulating theories which in reality challenged its very foundation. The Drago Doctrine, later codified in the Porter Convention of 1907, declared in the early twentieth century that intervention by the use of force principally to collect public debts was illegal. This doctrine was occasioned by the German, British, and Italian intervention in Venezuela in 1902. Earlier the Calvo Doctrine sought to outlaw all forms of diplomatic protection by invoking two principles: first, the sovereign equality of all States, which prohibited foreign intervention, and second, the equality of nationals and

[1] Shea, *The Calvo Clause: A Problem of Inter-American and International Law and Diplomacy* (1955) 12.

aliens, which deprived aliens of their claim to privileged treatment.[2] On the second principle, Calvo stated that

> It is certain that aliens who establish themselves in a country have the same right to protection as nationals, but they ought not to lay claim to a protection more extended...
>
> The responsibility of Governments toward foreigners cannot be greater than that which these Governments have towards their own citizens.[3]

On the one hand, attempts to enforce the Calvo Doctrine by treaty were largely unsuccessful. On the other, the Calvo Clause, a clause which came to be inserted in a contract between an alien and the host State in which the alien agreed to forego his right to request diplomatic protection in any dispute arising out of the contract, purported to embody and implement the Calvo Doctrine.

With the object of excluding international claims by other States arising from the breach of contracts entered into with alien contractors, there was inserted in the contractual documents a Calvo Clause, by which basically in effect all but national law remedies of the host State were renounced. The immediate occasion of the earliest formulation of the clause by Calvo in 1868 was the intervention of France and Great Britain in Argentina, Uruguay, and Mexico, and its purpose was to deprive the US and European States of the right to meddle in Latin American politics, on the pretext, genuine or not, of protecting their national creditors.[4] The contractor had the option of entering into the contract on the condition that international intervention and even international law were excluded or of not entering into it at all. The clause generally had two parts: the first provided that all disputes concerning the terms of the contract, its interpretation, or facts relating to its performance or non-performance, should be decided in the courts of the contracting State, whose law was to be the proper law; the second provided for a complete or partial surrender of rights under international law by the contractor and most importantly a waiver of protection by the contractor's own State.[5] That is, the contractor in effect contracted away the right to exercise diplomatic protection of his national State. The fundamental question arises: what powers does an alien have in respect of his national State's right to exercise diplomatic protection?

[2] Hersley, 'The Calvo and Drago Doctrines', 1 AJIL (1907) 26.

[3] 6 *Le Droit International: Théorique et Pratique* (1896) 231. Translation to be found in Shea (note 1 above), 18–19.

[4] See Calvo (note 3 above) 322 ff.

[5] See particularly on the Calvo clause Shea (note 1 above); Lipstein, 'The Place of the Calvo Clause in International Law', 22 BYIL (1945) 130; Ténékidès, 'Considerations sur le Clause Calvo', 43 RGDIP (1936) 270; O'Connell, 2 *International Law* (1970) 1059 ff, and other works cited therein 1060 footnote 26; and now Dugard, 'Third Report to the ILC on Diplomatic Protection, Addendum' (2002), UN Doc A/CN.4/523/Add.1.

The Calvo Clause could take several forms.[6] As one author has stated,

> Sometimes, it merely consists of a stipulation that the foreign individual concerned will be satisfied with the action of the local courts. In other cases, the Clause embodies a more direct and broader waiver of diplomatic protection, as when it provides that disputes which may arise shall in no circumstances lead to an international claim, or else that the foreign individuals or corporate bodies are to be deemed to be nationals of the country for the purposes of the contract or concession.[7]

In principle, however, the Calvo Clause seems to relate to the contractual relationship between alien and host State and could be applicable to disputes concerning the interpretation, application, or performance of the contract.[8] Whether it can go beyond this is in dispute. Particularly, it is unclear whether any exclusion can apply to a denial of justice that may occur in proceedings relating to the contract before a national court.[9]

In principle the objects of the clause in its usual form were to confine the alien to local remedies like anyone who was a national of the host State *and* to exclude the exercise of diplomatic protection by the national State of the alien. The questions remain whether these objectives could be achieved in international law and, if only less could be achieved, what exactly was the effect of a clause with these objectives.

State Practice

A comprehensive study on the Calvo Clause, published in 1955, permits the conclusion that at that time the Calvo Clause was recognized in the practice, laws, or constitutions of most Latin American States, so much so that it would be regarded as a Latin American regional custom.[10] State practice outside Latin America was very different. The US has long claimed that the clause did not and could not waive the right of the State of nationality to provide diplomatic protection and that, in any case, the individual's waiver did not cover cases of denial of justice.[11] Other States were divided on the issue. According to their replies to a questionnaire on

[6] See O'Connell (note 5 above) 1059–60; Eagleton, *The Responsibility of States in International Law* (1928) 168; Geck, 'Diplomatic Protection', 1 EPIL (1992) 1058; Dunn, *The Protection of Nationals: A Study in the Application of International Law* (1932) 169; Lipstein (note 5 above) 131–4. The clause may be included in the host State's legislation: see O'Connell (note 5 above) 1064.

[7] García-Amador, 'State Responsibility. Some New Problems', 94 Hague Receuil (1958-II) 455–6 (hereafter referred to as 'State Responsibility'); García-Amador, 'International Responsibility, Third Report', 2 YBILC (1958) 58, Document A/CN.4/111 (hereafter referred to as 'Third Report').

[8] García-Amador, 'State Responsibility' 456.

[9] See the conflicting views of García Amador, 'State Responsibility' 458 and Dugard (note 5 above) 15.

[10] Shea (note 1 above) 269–79.

[11] Ibid 37–45.

the subject circulated to States prior to the 1930 Hague Codification Conference, South Africa, Australia, and Austria considered such clauses as having no effect; Finland, the Netherlands, and Germany recognized the validity of the clause, whereas several States, namely, Belgium, Denmark, Great Britain, Hungary, India, Japan, Norway, New Zealand, Poland, Switzerland, and Czechoslovakia, did so only as far as the rights of the individual were concerned but not in respect of the waiver of the right of the State to diplomatic interposition in cases of violations of international law. Canada took the position that the clause was valid, if the State of nationality of the injured individual permitted the individual to enter into such a contract.[12] The reply of Great Britain fully supported its interpretation of the decision in the *North American Dredging Co Case,*[13] which is referred to below, upholding the limited validity of the Calvo Clause.[14]

Legal Commentators

Subsequent to the 1926 decision in the *Dredging Co Case* particularly, there has been a plethora of writing on the Calvo Clause. The discussion in the literature has been not about whether the Calvo Clause is contrary to international law but rather about its purpose and scope, largely in the context of the *Dredging Co Case.* There is on the whole, however, little consensus among writers about the scope of the Calvo Clause or on how it is to be interpreted so as to be consistent with international law. There are several ideas which emerge from the literature. The first is that the Calvo Clause is of limited validity only, in the sense that it does not constitute a complete bar to diplomatic intervention. It applies only to disputes relating to the contract between alien and host State containing the clause and not to breaches of international law. This interpretation would seem to run counter to the real purpose of the Calvo Clause, which is to exclude diplomatic protection in all cases. It has been criticized by Latin American writers on this ground.[15] This interpretation, however, which is the one espoused in the *Dredging Co Case,* is accepted in State practice, as has been seen, and is widely supported by juristic opinion.[16]

A second opinion is that the Calvo Clause confirms the importance of the exhaustion of local remedies rule. Although some writers[17] have suggested that

[12] 3 *Bases of discussion* (Doc C.75.M.69.1929.V): 'Responsibility of States for Damages Caused in their Territory to the Person or Property of Foreigners', Question XI (d), 133–5.

[13] (1926, USA v. Mexico), 4 UNRIAA 26. Hereafter referred to as the *Dredging Co Case.*

[14] Note 12 above 134. On State practice see also Dugard (note 5 above) 8.

[15] Gomez Robledo, *La Cláusa Calvo ante el derecho international* (1939) 176; Sépúlveda Gutiérrez, *La responsbilidad internacional del estado y la validez de la Cláusula Calvo* (1944) 69–71.

[16] Shea (note 1 above) 217–18; Freeman, *The International Responsibility of States for Denial of Justice* (1938) 489–90; Brownlie, *Principles of Public International Law* (1998), 548–9; Jennings and Watts (eds), 1 *Oppenheim's International Law* (1992) 931.

[17] Lipstein (note 5 above) 145; Freeman (note 16 above) 489–90; Quoc Dinh, *Droit International Public* (Daillier and Pellet (eds)) (1999) 778 (para 492); Feller, *The Mexican Claims Commission 1923–1934. A Study in the Law and Procedure of International Tribunals* (1935) 192.

the limited validity accorded to the clause in the *Dredging Co Case* makes it nothing more than a reaffirmation of the local remedies rule, and thus a superfluous restatement of the obvious, most writers see it as going beyond such a reaffirmation. Opinions differ, however, as to what this extra dimension is. One explanation is probably to be found in the ruling in the *Dredging Co Case* that the Calvo Clause may trump a provision in a compromise waiving the requirement that local remedies should be exhausted.[18]

A third explanation is that it reflects the right of an alien to waive by contract his own power or right to request his national State to exercise diplomatic protection on his behalf, which right international law does not preclude.[19]

A fourth assessment is that an alien cannot by means of a Calvo Clause waive rights which in international law belong to his State because diplomatic protection is premised on the concept that an injury to a national arising from a breach of international law is an injury to the national State itself. An alien cannot waive this right as it is not in his power to do so.[20]

A fifth view is that the waiver in a Calvo Clause extends only to disputes arising out of the contract, which are not, in any event, concerned with breaches of international law.[21] It does not extend to violations of international law, and, in particular, it does not extend to a denial of justice. While there is widespread support for this proposition,[22] there is some uncertainty about denial of justice associated with or arising from the contract containing the Calvo Clause, primarily because of the variety of meanings given to denial of justice.[23]

[18] Shea states:

> This much effectiveness cannot be denied, for the six recent arbitral rulings can be cited in support of it. Perhaps this is the full effectiveness of the Clause... Consequently, if future conventions conform to what would appear to be the recent trend in international arbitration [of waiving the local remedies rule in the *compromis*] then the Calvo Clause, even if restricted in effectiveness to overcoming a general waiver of the local remedies rule contained in the *compromis,* will continue to have a determinative effect on the admissibility of international claims. ((note 1 above) 260)

See also ibid 215, 217, 257.

[19] Jimenez de Aréchaga, 'International Responsibility', in Sørensen (ed), *Manual of Public International Law* (1968) 591; García Amador, 'State Responsibility', 459–60; Jessup, *A Modern Law of Nations* (1968) 11, 117; Shea (note 1 above) 261–3.

[20] Eagleton (note 6 above) 170; Borchard, *The Diplomatic Protection of Citizens Abroad* (1915) 809; Quoc Dinh (note 17 above) 778; García Amador, 'State Responsibility', 460.

[21] Brownlie (note 16 above) 549.

[22] Jimenez de Aréchaga (note 19 above) 591–2; Freeman (note 16 above) 489–90; O'Connell (note 5 above) 1064; Shea (note 1 above) 217–18.

[23] Thus, see García Amador, who, on the one hand, acknowledges that

> whatever form it may take, the 'Calvo Clause' invariably relates to a contractual relationship, and only operates with regard to disputes concerning the interpretation, application or performance of the contract or concession ('State Responsibility' 456)

but states, on the other hand, that:

> in principle, the 'Clause' is valid as a bar to the exercise of diplomatic protection even in cases of 'denial of justice'. It is not to be overlooked that it operates only with regard to disputes concerning the interpretation, application of performance of contracts or concessions. In this sense, only a specific case of denial of justice would be involved, not all the cases where some other rights

A sixth attempt to explain the effect of the rule submitted that:

> The clause is binding on the individual so as to preclude him from having resort to the municipal law remedies of his own country, but does not prevent his government from making a claim in respect of a breach of international law. Where his own law has a doctrine of absolute sovereign immunity resort to it against the contracting State would be unavailing. Therefore the significance of the rule is limited to cases where under the private contractor's law the contracting State may be sued.[24]

Attempts at Codification

Attempts to codify the Calvo Clause among Latin American States have been largely successful, while the USA has reserved its position on more than one occasion.[25] Codification of the Calvo Clause at the more general international level outside the Americas has been attempted but without success. In 1930 the Conference for the Codification of International Law (The Hague) had before it the 1926 Guerrero Report,[26] the 1929 Harvard Law School Draft,[27] and the 1929 Bases of Discussion drawn up by the Preparatory Committee of the

> of the alien or interests of another kind could be affected. At first sight, this exception to the principle which governs international responsibility for acts and omission of this nature might appear unjustified. In reality, however, it is not unjustified. Contractual interests and rights are not, so to speak, in the same class as the other rights enjoyed by the alien in international law. Not only are they of an exclusively monetary character, but the alien acquires them by virtue of a contract or concession, the acceptance of which depends solely on his own volition. With this reasoning one does not seek to minimize the importance of this category of rights and interests, but to stress that, by their very nature, they can form the subject of an infinite variety of operations and transactions which can be effected merely by the consent of the contracting parties. In brief, these are rights and interests in respect of which the alien may waive diplomatic protection in whatever terms he considers most conducive to the acquisition of the benefits which he expects to derive from the contract or concession. (ibid 458)

On the different meanings of denial of justice see C F Amerasinghe, *Local Remedies in International Law* (2004) 84ff. García Amador submits, drawing on the opinion of Shea (note 1 above) 265, that the Calvo clause requires proof of an *aggravated* form of denial of justice before an international claim may be brought. He finds support for his view, he argues, in the cases: 'State Responsibility' 459. This conclusion is, however, suspect. While a denial of justice may be required, there is no reason for it to be aggravated.

[24] O'Connell (note 5 above) 1065.

[25] For these attempts at codification and the US's position see the account of the 1902 (2nd), 1933 (7th) and 1948 (9th) International Conferences of American States in Dugard, loc. cit. (note 5 above) 4–5.

[26] 'Responsibility of States for Damage done in their Territories to the Person or Property of Foreigners': see 20 AJIL (1926) 182–5 (Special Supplement).

[27] Draft Convention on Responsibility of States for Damage Done in their Territory to the Person or Property of Foreigners. Article 17 of the Draft provided:

> A State is not relieved of responsibility as a consequence of any provision in its own law or in an agreement with an alien which attempts to exclude responsibility by making the decisions of its own courts final; nor is it relieved of responsibility by any waiver by the alien of the protection of the State of which he is a national. (see 23 *AJIL* (1929) 202–3 (Special Supplement))

Conference,[28] all of which contained proposals on the Calvo Clause. The clause was not, however, considered at the Conference, for several reasons, one of which was the issue of denial of justice. The Conference adjourned without agreeing on a Convention.

In 1961 the Harvard Law School formulated another Draft Convention on the International Responsibility of States for Injuries to Aliens which provided as follows, in Article 22:

(4) No claim may be presented by a claimant if, after the injury and without duress, the claimant himself or the person through whom he derived his claim waived, compromised, or settled the claim.

(5) No claim under this Convention may be presented by a claimant with respect to any injury listed in subparagraph 2 (e), 2 (f), 2 (g), or 2 (h) of article 14[29]

(a) if prior to his acquisition of property rights or of a right to exercise a profession or occupation in the territory of the State responsible for the injury, or as a condition of obtaining rights under a contract with or a concession granted by that State, the alien to whom such rights were accorded agreed to waive such claims as might arise out of a violation by the respondent State of any of the rights thus acquired.

(b) if the respondent State has not altered the agreement unilaterally through a legislative act or in any other manner, and has otherwise complied with the terms and conditions specified in the agreement; and

(c) if the injury arose out of the violation by the State of the rights thus acquired by the alien.

[28] See García Amador, 'First Report on State Responsibility': (ILC), 2 YBILC (1956) 223–5. The relevant bases for discussion are Nos 26, 27, 5 and 6, which provide:

26. An undertaking by a party to contract that he will not have recourse to the diplomatic remedy does not bind the State whose national he is and does not release the State with which the contract is made from its international responsibility. If in a contract a foreigner makes a valid agreement that the local courts shall alone have jurisdiction, this provision is binding upon any international tribunal to which a claim under the contract is submitted; the State can then only be responsible for damage suffered by the foreigner in the cases contemplated in bases of discussion Nos. 5 and 6.

27. Where the foreigner has a legal remedy open to him in the courts of the State (which term includes administrative courts), the State may require that any question of international responsibility shall remain in suspense until its courts have given their final decision. This rule does not exclude application of the provision set out in cases of discussion Nos. 5 and 6.

5. A State is responsible for damage suffered by a foreigner as the result of the fact that: (1) he is refused access to the courts to defend his rights; (2) a judicial decision which is final and without appeal is incompatible with the treaty obligation or other international obligations of the State; (3) there has been unconscionable delay on the part of the courts; (4) the substance of judicial decision has manifestly been prompted by ill-will towards foreigners as such or as subjects of a particular State.

6. A State is responsible for damage suffered by a foreigner as the result of the courts following a procedure and rendering a judgment vitiated by faults so gross as to indicate that they did not offer the guarantees indispensable for the proper administration of justice.

[29] The references are to destruction of, damage to, or loss of property; deprivation of use or enjoyment of property; deprivation of means of livelihood; and loss or deprivation of enjoyment of rights under a contract or concession.

(6) No claim may be presented by a claimant with respect to any of the injuries listed in paragraph 2 of article 14, if as a condition of being allowed to engage in activities involving an extremely high degree of risk, which privilege would otherwise be denied to him by the State, the alien has agreed to waive any claim with respect to such injuries and if the claim arises out of an act or omission attributable to the State which had a reasonably close relationship to such activities. Such a waiver is effective, however, only as to injuries resulting from a negligent act or omission or from a failure to exercise due diligence to afford protection to the alien in question and not as to injuries caused by a wilful act or omission attributable to the State.[30]

Article 24 (1) furthermore provided:

A State is not entitled to present a claim if the claimant or a person through whom he derives his claim has waived, compromised, or settled the claim under paragraph 4, 5, or 6 of article 22.

Between 1956 and 1961, the Special Rapporteur on State Responsibility in the ILC presented a number of reports which touched on the Calvo Clause. In his first report of 1956, he suggested the following basis for discussion:

Renunciation of diplomatic protection, either by State or by foreign private individuals. Renunciation of diplomatic protection by a private person constitutes an exonerating circumstance in so far as the *Calvo clause* does not refer to rights which, by their nature, are not capable of being renounced, or to questions in which the private person is not the only interested party.[31]

In 1961, in his sixth and final report, he proposed:

(2)... in the case of the non-performance of obligations stipulated in a contract or concession, the international claim shall not be admissible if the alien concerned has waived the diplomatic protection of the State of his nationality and the circumstances are in conformity with the terms of the waiver...

(4) The waiver of diplomatic protection... shall not deprive the State of nationality of the right to bring an international claim in the circumstances and for the purposes [of preventing the repetition of the injurious act].[32]

The matter was not considered by the ILC at that stage and was virtually dropped from the agenda till much later.

[30] See 55 AJIL (1961) 578–9. According to Article 22 (1), the word 'claimant' refers to the injured alien.

[31] Basis of discussion No V (2) (b): see García Amador (note 28 above) 220. Emphasis in original.

[32] 'Responsibility of the State for Injuries Caused in its Territory to the Person or Property of Aliens: Revised Draft', Article 19: 2 YBILC (1961) 48, UN Doc A/CN.4/134 and Addendum. See further on the history of this subject before the ILC, Graham, 'The Calvo Clause: Its Current Status as a Contractual Renunciation of Diplomatic Protection', 6 *Texas International Law Forum* 297–300.

More recently the subject of the Calvo Clause was considered by the ILC. The Special Rapporteur on Diplomatic Protection proposed the following Article on the Calvo Clause:

Article 16

(1) A contractual stipulation between an alien and the State in which he carries on business to the effect that:
  (a) the alien will be satisfied with local remedies; or
  (b) no dispute arising out of the contract will be settled by means of an international claim; or
  (c) the alien will be treated as a national of the contracting State for the purposes of the contract,

  shall be construed under international law as a valid waiver of the right of the alien to request diplomatic protection in respect of matters pertaining to the contract. Such a contractual stipulation shall not, however, affect the right of the State of nationality of the alien to exercise diplomatic protection on behalf of such a person when he or she is injured by an internationally wrongful act attributable to the contracting State or when the injury to the alien is of direct concern to the State of nationality of the alien.

(2) A contractual stipulation referred to in paragraph 1 shall be construed as a presumption in favour of the need to exhaust local remedies before recourse to international judicial settlement.[33]

The Special Rapporteur, further, pointed out that:

the Calvo doctrine, already reflected in General Assembly resolution 1803 (XVII) of 14 December 1962, on permanent sovereignty over natural resources, appeared again in the Charter of Economic Rights and Duties of States, contained in General Assembly resolution 3281 (XXIX) of 12 December 1974, which proclaimed that disputes over compensation arising from the expropriation of foreign property have to be settled under the domestic law of the nationalizing State. The influence of the Calvo doctrine was also to be seen in decision 24 of the Andean Pact. On the other hand, the North American Free Trade Agreement (NAFTA), which permitted foreign investors to resort to international arbitration without first exhausting local remedies, was seen by some as representing a departure from the Calvo doctrine.

Two options were open to the Commission: either to decline to draft any provision on the subject on the ground that to do so would be superfluous if one took the view that the Calvo clause simply reaffirmed the exhaustion of local remedies rule; or to draft a provision limiting the validity of the Calvo clause to disputes arising out of the contract containing the clause, without precluding the right of the State of nationality of the alien to exercise its diplomatic protection on behalf of that individual where he or she had been injured as a result of an internationally wrongful act attributable to the contracting State. Paragraph 2 provided that such a clause constituted a presumption in favour of the need to exhaust local remedies before recourse to international judicial settlement, where there was a *compromis* providing for an exception to the exhaustion of local remedies rule.[34]

33 Dugard (note 5 above) 2.

34 See the *Report of the ILC (2002)* 162.

What took place in the debate in the ILC may be summarized as follows.[35] The view was expressed by some that, subject to a few drafting improvements, article 16 should be retained. As a codified rule, it would clarify the limits of contractual relationships between a State and an alien, particularly by guaranteeing the rights of the State of nationality under international law. Some members also expressed the view that the proposed article did not deal with the Calvo Clause in its classical sense, but with a mere obligation of exhaustion of local remedies in particular circumstances. It was suggested that the provision placed useful emphasis on the exhaustion of local remedies rule. Indeed, the view was expressed that the codification of the exhaustion of local remedies rule would be incomplete without a recognition of the Calvo Clause.

Another view expressed was that the Calvo Clause's value was not merely historical and symbolic, but that it remained an important issue in the modern world with international implications far exceeding those of contractual stipulations under domestic law. Moreover, though resort to the Calvo Clause had been largely confined to Latin America, the problems it had sought to address had a global, not merely regional, dimension. As such, by including the provision, the Commission would be codifying a regional customary rule, which could legitimately be elevated to the rank of a universal rule.

The view was further expressed that the Calvo Clause was not contrary to international law, on account of two important principles, namely, the sovereign equality of States, which entailed a duty of non-intervention, and the equal treatment of nationals and aliens. It was also noted that Article 16 did not set out to codify the Calvo Clause as such, but instead laid down limits to its application in international relations. It also clarified the relationship between the rights of the individual and of the State in that area, which was that a foreign individual or company had the right to seek, and a State the right to exercise, diplomatic protection.

Others spoke against the inclusion of the provision in the draft articles on diplomatic protection, and preferred its deletion. The view was expressed that article 16 was beyond the scope of the Commission's Statute: it was not a rule of law and, therefore, did not lend itself to codification. The Calvo Clause was said to be a mere contractual drafting device.

Some pointed out that the national of the State could not replace the State, since it was not his own rights that were involved, but those of the State. An alien could not waive a right that was not his. As such, the legal significance of the waiver in paragraph 1 was uncertain since the alien's request was not a precondition for the exercise of diplomatic protection. The alien could, however, undertake, first, to rely only on the laws of the host country and, secondly, not to seek the diplomatic protection of his State of origin. What could not be done was to guarantee that the State of nationality would not intervene to ensure respect for

[35] Ibid 162–4.

its right to see international law respected in the person of its national. Hence, the question was not whether the Calvo Clause was valid or not under international law. It was neither prohibited under international law nor regarded as lawful. There would be a breach of contract, but no breach of an obligation under international law, either by the alien or by the State of nationality, if the alien requested diplomatic protection from that State.

It was also noted by some that while the Calvo Clause was of historical importance, in practice, it was used less and less. Furthermore, the international context differed from that in which the Calvo Clause has been formulated a century before. The concerns underlying the Calvo doctrine had to a large extent been addressed by developments in the latter half of the twentieth century, including the adoption of several important international texts referred to in the Special Rapporteur's report. Likewise, the conduct of States in the modern-day world was strongly influenced, if not conditioned, by common standards imposed by international human rights law. Furthermore, the importance that governments attached, and the recognition they accorded, to private entrepreneurship made it possible for foreign private investments to enjoy a secure legal environment. For example, it was more common for States to conclude investment agreements making provision for direct recourse to international arbitration in the event of a dispute.

Disagreement was further expressed with the inclusion of paragraph 2. It was thought to contradict the exhaustion of local remedies rule. The existence of a Calvo Clause was not necessary to create a presumption in favour of the exhaustion of local remedies. That presumption existed independently of any contractual clause.

Because of the multiplicity of views and the widespread disagreement within the ILC, the ILC decided not to refer Article 16 to its Drafting Committee[36] which meant that the provision on the Calvo Clause was dropped from the ILC's draft articles on diplomatic protection.

The Case Law

The right of an alien contractor to exclude international law by surrendering the right of his State to protect him has generally not been recognized. While the possible negative effect of this part of the Calvo Clause has been contested, it cannot be said that a Calvo Clause is of no import. It has been the subject of several arbitrations and varying effect has been given to it.

The earlier arbitrations in which the Calvo Clause was dealt with focused on the terms of the contract.[37] In later arbitrations, however, the compatibility of

[36] Ibid 164.

[37] The *Day & Garrison Case* (1885, USA v Venezuela); Moore, *International Arbitrations* 3548; the *Woodruff Case* (1903, USA v Venezuela), 9 UNRIAA 213; the *Turnbull Case* (1904,

such a clause with international law has been considered. In the *Dredging Co Case*, already referred to above, which is the leading authority on the question, the tribunal defined the issue so as to place the burden on the claimant State of establishing that a positive rule of international law opposed the Calvo Clause, rather than on the respondent State of establishing that the clause was universally accepted or universally recognized.[38] It has also been held, however, that each Calvo Clause must be treated on its merits.[39] Further, the clause may be construed to be either compatible or incompatible with international law, and this matter cannot be decided by imposing on the one or other party a burden of proving that international law does or does not condemn the clause, or does or does not permit it. The real question is whether international law recognizes the right of an alien contractor to surrender all rights, particularly his State's, in international law and waive all protection of his national State. To this question arbitral tribunals which have examined it have given a negative answer.[40] As a result a Calvo Clause, to have any validity, needs to be construed as compatible with rules of international law.

The accepted view, as it emerges from the cases, is that the portion of the Calvo Clause which seeks to exclude the protection of the national State is of no effect, while the clause may have limited effect and is not rendered altogether invalid.[41] As an example of this approach in State practice may be cited the reply of Great Britain to a Questionnaire of the Preparatory Committee of the League of Nations Conference on Responsibility of States in 1930, which stated:

No rule of international law prevents the inclusion of a stipulation in a contract between a Government and an alien that in all matters pertaining to the contract the jurisdiction of the local tribunals shall be complete and exclusive, nor does it prevent such a stipulation being obligatory, in the absence of any special agreement to the contrary, between the two Governments concerned, upon any international tribunal to which may be submitted a claim arising out of the contract in which the stipulation was inserted.[42]

The implication is that entering into a contract containing a Calvo Clause does mean that there is a contractual submission by the alien to the local courts and the

USA v Venezuela), 9 ibid 305; the *Orinoco Steamship Co Case* (1903, USA v Venezuela), 9 ibid 193 ff; the *Martini Case* (1903, Italy v Venezuela), 10 ibid 644.

[38] The *Dredging Co Case* (1926, USA v Mexico), 4 UNRIAA 25. This case was reargued in 1947 when the validity of the Calvo Clause was rejected in the context. See also Nielsen (dissenting) in the *International Fisheries Co Case* (1931, USA v Mexico), 4 ibid 703 ff. However, the original ruling of law in the *Dredging Co Case* (1926) has been subsequently respected and accepted.

[39] Each Calvo Clause is to be treated on its merits in order to determine its validity and effect: the *Mexican Union Ltd Railway Case* (1930, GB v Mexico), 5 ibid 125.

[40] This is implied in the cases: see, eg, the *Martini Case* (1903, Italy v Venezuela), 10 ibid 644; the *Woodruff Case* (1903, USA v Venezuela), 9 ibid 213; the *International Fisheries Co Case* (1931, USA v Mexico), 4 ibid 691.

[41] *The Dredging Co Case* (1926, USA v Mexico), 4 ibid 29. The reason for this is based on the concept that when an alien is injured by a violation of international law, the injury is a violation of the national State's rights.

[42] 3 *Bases of Discussion* (note 12 above) 134.

local law. These courts must in the first instance determine the rights and duties of the parties. If the clause is no more than an inclusion, both of the requirement that there must be a denial of justice by the local courts for a violation of international law to occur and of the law concerning exhaustion of local remedies thereafter, it becomes superfluous except, perhaps, for the purpose of determining the initial question of the proper law and for defining the initial jurisdiction to deal with the questions arising under the contract.

The next question is whether the clause can effect a modification of this position which is the usual position of the respective parties.[43] The answer to this question could depend upon whether, before the contractor's rights under the national law can be established so as to found an international law right, an affirmative judgment must have been obtained. Under the local remedies rule an ultimate affirmative judgment is not required, provided every avenue of recourse which is not 'obviously futile' has been explored. If the Calvo Clause requires an affirmative judgment, the 'obvious futility' of litigating the issue in a national court would not found jurisdiction in an international tribunal. This approach to the local remedies rule and the effect on it of a Calvo Clause is not really acceptable.

There is only one judicial authority in favour of the proposition that in the case of a Calvo Clause an affirmative decision on the alien contractor's rights is a precondition for an international claim.[44] Other tribunals have consistently construed the contract as requiring no more than the ultimate exhaustion of local remedies, and not as requiring an affirmative judgment. This construction would appear to be necessary to sustain the compatibility of the clause with the rule that an individual cannot contract out of international law remedies from which he benefits but are not his in theory. If he could contract out in this way, the failure of the respondent's national court either to give a proper interpretation or to enter a proper judgment would not found an international claim, and this would defeat the rule that the Calvo Clause must be compatible with international law.[45]

However, there is something more in a Calvo Clause. This relates to international arbitration or adjudication. An international arbitral tribunal derives its existence from consent based ultimately on a treaty or *compromis,* and hence its jurisdiction is circumscribed by the intentions of the States parties, as indicated in the treaty or *compromis.* These intentions may be inferred by reference to the intentions of the parties to a private contract. If it is the intention of the treaty not to disturb the agreement in the private contract, international jurisdiction may not be conferred on the particular tribunal. Then, the provision in the Calvo Clause trumps any exclusion of the local remedies rule in the *compromis.* It is this form of

[43] See the *Orinoco Steamship Co Case* (1903, USA v Venezuela), 9 UNRIAA 200; and, by implication, the *Turnbull Case* (1904, USA v Venezuela), 9 ibid 261.

[44] The *Turnbull Case* (1904, USA v Venezuela), 9 ibid 304.

[45] Lipstein takes the view that the Calvo Clause does no more than incorporate the local remedies rule: (note 5 above) 130 ff.

argument rather than arguments based on compatibility with international law that has been raised in arbitrations involving the Calvo Clause.[46]

In the *Dredging Co Case* the tribunal first analysed the intentions of the parties to the contract, and then in the light of those intentions, discussed whether it was the intention of the treaty of arbitration that this claim should be subject to its jurisdiction. So far as the intention of the contract was concerned, it said that the purpose of the Calvo Clause 'was to bind the claimant to be governed by the laws of Mexico and to use the remedies existing under such laws'.[47] The question which arose, then, was whether it was the intention of the treaty to ratify or disturb this contractual provision. The treaty had provided that 'no claim shall be disallowed or rejected by the Commission by the application of the general principle of international law that the legal remedies must be exhausted as a condition precedent to the validity or allowance of any claim'. The international law rule requiring exhaustion of local remedies was abrogated by this provision. But the next question had to be asked whether this abrogation covered the express and specific contractual provision to resort to local remedies which was contained in the Calvo Clause. The tribunal held in effect that such an extended intention must clearly emerge from the context. The effect of the Calvo Clause, then, was to require exhaustion of local remedies before submission to arbitration, whereas other claimants not bound by a Calvo Clause were not so required. The presence of the Calvo Clause in a contract was known to the parties to the *compromis* and, thus, there was a clear intention not to renounce the applicability of the local remedies rule in such a situation. This is the best explanation of the tribunal's conclusion.

One proposition that emerges is that, it is only where it is the intention of the treaty to confer jurisdiction on a tribunal in cases in which local remedies have not been resorted to in pursuance of a Calvo Clause, that the respondent State may not set up the Calvo Clause as a bar to the claim.[48] Where a tribunal is empowered to decide questions on an equitable basis, the ordinary rules of international law governing responsibility are superseded by the law of the *compromis,* and hence the Calvo Clause exception may not be raised in this regard.[49] But a tribunal may refuse to allow the contractor under a Calvo clause to take the short cut of by-passing local remedies on the ground that this 'infects the claim with a *vitium proprium*'.[50] If it did not do this, the tribunal would not only sanction a deviation from the contract but it would also unilaterally sanction it so as to place one party to the contract in an advantageous jurisdictional position.

[46] The *Martini Case* (1903, Italy v Venezuela), 10 UNRIAA 644; the *Selwyn Case* (1903, GB v Venezuela), 9 ibid 380; the *American Electric & Manufacturing Co Case* (1904, USA v Venezuela), 9 ibid 145.

[47] (1926, USA v Mexico), 4 ibid 30.

[48] The *Martini Case* (1903, Italy v Venezuela), 10 ibid 644.

[49] The *Georges Pinson Case* (1928, France v Mexico), 5 ibid 327.

[50] The *Rudloff Case* (1903, USA v Venezuela), 9 ibid 244.

The role of the Calvo Clause, limited as it may be, depends on the contract and its performance. The alien contractor is held not to have contracted out of such rights as he may have possessed in respect of acts and events extraneous to the contract, though reflecting upon its performance. Hence damage to property or other tortious actions is not generally contemplated by the Calvo Clause. A difficulty arises, however, when the Calvo Clause is drafted so widely as to include a possible waiver of rights in the matter of 'all interests connected with the contract'. The issue is whether this extends the contractual area to situations of fact not strictly associated with the contract. Two rules have been formulated by the tribunals that have dealt with the question. The first is that a Calvo Clause must be strictly construed against the general presumption that an alien contractor does not intend to contract out of his rights, and the second is that, to be given effect to at all, the renunciation of rights and the submission to a tribunal's jurisdiction must be precisely framed so as to admit of no doubts concerning the parties' intentions. Both rules were utilised in one case by the tribunal to exclude altogether the application of a Calvo Clause of this extended sort.[51]

Further, a legislative enactment, which provides that all alien residents or contractors shall have no more rights than nationals possess, can likewise have no effect in international law, so far as the right of a foreign government to protect its nationals is concerned.

Attempts have been made to state the essence of the rule relating to the Calvo Clause in terms of the compatibility of the clause with the international law and its effect in the international law. For example, in the *Dredging Co Case* it was said:

> Under the rules of international law may an alien lawfully make such a promise? The Commission holds that he may, but at the same time holds that he cannot deprive the government of his nation of its undoubted right of applying international remedies to violations of international law committed to his damage.[52]

In explanation of this position it has been said that 'the commission held that the clause was binding on the individual in that it precluded him from presenting to his government any claim connected with the contract, but not binding on his state in that it would not prevent his government from espousing a claim based on the violation of international law'.[53] But the heart of the problem is whether the rule is wider than a mere restatement of the rule relating to resort to and the exhaustion of local remedies. What is the significance of the proposition that the individual is 'precluded from' presenting a claim to his State, while the latter is not precluded from making one, when generally a State does not make a claim, unless the alien has first complained to it? In any case, if the alien contractor does invoke his national State's protection and thereby breaches the contract, this has,

[51] The *McNeill Case* (1931, GB v Mexico), 5 ibid 135.
[52] (1926, USA v Mexico), 4 ibid 29.
[53] Shea (note 1 above) 217.

as it has been held, no relevance to the validity and jurisdictional propriety of the claim which the State then takes up. The State's claim cannot be precluded, because the State exercises a right belonging to it.

What is of prime importance is that, where there has been an alleged violation of international law in respect of the alien's contract, whether before or after resort to local remedies, an international claim brought by the alien's national State would not be precluded. In this case the Calvo Clause is no more than a restatement of rules relating to resort to and exhaustion of local remedies. The international legal right of the alien's national State to protect the alien cannot be interfered with by an agreement to which only the alien and not his national State is a party. That is the national State's right and survives any such agreement.[54] This is basic, whatever other ramifications a particular Calvo clause as drafted may have, which it clearly and possibly may have.

The Impact of Recent Developments

As the Special Rapporteur to the ILC on Diplomatic Protection has stated:

> The Calvo Clause was born out of the fear on the part of Latin American States of intervention in their domestic affairs by European States and the United States of America under the guise of diplomatic protection. Resistance to the Calvo Clause, on the other hand, stemmed from the fear on the part of the European States and the United States of America that their nationals would not receive fair treatment in countries whose judicial standards fell below the international minimum standard created by the latter States in their own image. Today the situation has changed. European States and the United States of America respect the sovereign equality of Latin American States and have confidence in their judicial systems, which, as in Europe, are subject to both regional and international monitoring.[55] Consequently the aggressive assertions of diplomatic protection that once characterized relations between Europe and the United States, on the one hand, and Latin America, on the other, have come to an end. This does not mean that the debate over the Calvo Clause has lost its relevance. While international legal opinion in Europe and the United States likes to see the Calvo Clause as a relic of a past era of inequality in international relations,[56] Latin American States still cling to the Clause as an important feature

[54] See by implication Lipstein (note 5 above) 134; O'Connell (note 5 above) 1066.

[55] By bodies established under the American Convention on Human Rights and the International Covenant on Civil and Political Rights. This is a footnote in the text cited.

[56] According to Rudolf Dolzer, 'International practice confirming the Calvo Doctrine is nowhere visible, and the legal opinions of the Western capital-exporting nations definitely refute the argument that all major groups affected have consented to a change in customary law over the Calvo Doctrine', in 'New Foundation of the Law of Expropriation of Alien Property', 75 AJIL (1981) 571. That the Calvo Clause has not been repudiated by legal opinion in the United States is illustrated by *Reavis v Exxon Corporation,* United States, New York Supreme Court, Special Term, New York County (Gellinoff J), decision of 28 July 1977, reported in 66 ILR (1984) 314,

of their regional approach to international law. While they have demonstrated some flexibility in their attitude to new institutions creating dispute settlement procedures for foreign investors, there is no doubt that many of these institutions are still judged by their adherence to the Calvo Clause.[57]

Since 1945 the UN has taken a specific approach on the resort to local remedies. In the Charter of Economic Rights and Duties of States, contained in General Assembly Resolution 3281 (XXIX) of 12 December 1974, it is stated that disputes over compensation arising from the expropriation of foreign property, 'shall be settled under the domestic law of the nationalizing State and by its tribunals, unless it is freely and mutually agreed by all States concerned that other peaceful means be sought on the basis of the sovereign equality of States and in accordance with the principle of free choice of means.'[58] The resolution on *Permanent Sovereignty over Natural Resources* of 14 December 1962, which preceded the Charter, had already stated that in the case of a dispute over compensation for expropriated property the national jurisdiction of the State taking such measures shall be exhausted.[59]

In Latin America the Andean Pact, establishing a common market between Bolivia, Colombia, Ecuador, Peru, and Venezuela, by agreement among sovereign States in principle incorporated the idea that States should not exercise diplomatic protection. Decision 24 provides:

> In no instrument relating to investments or the transfer of technology shall there be clauses that remove possible conflicts or controversies from the national jurisdiction and competence of the recipient country or allow the subrogation by States to the rights and actions of their national investors.[60]

Decision 220, less drastically provides that

> For the settlement of disputes or conflicts deriving from direct foreign investments or from the transfer of foreign technology, Member Countries shall apply the provisions established in their local legislation.[61]

In 1991 while the Andean Pact countries revised and liberalized their foreign investment code in decision 291, the element relating to the national legal system was left unchanged.[62]

in which the court seriously considered, but did not apply, the Calvo Clause. This is in a footnote in the cited text.

[57] Dugard (note 5 above) 15.

[58] Chap II, Article 2, para 2 (c).

[59] General Assembly Resolution 1803 (XVII), para 4.

[60] *Decision No 24 on the Common Regime of Treatment of Foreign Capital and of Trademarks, Patents, Licenses and Royalties*, 30 November 1976, Article 51: 16 ILM (1976) 153.

[61] *Decision No 220 on the Andean Code on the Treatment of Foreign Capital and on Trademarks, Patents, Licenses and Royalties*, 11 May 1987, Article 34: 27 ILM (1987) 986.

[62] *Decision No 291 on the Common Code for the Treatment of Foreign Capital and on Trademarks, Patents, Licenses and Royalties*, 21 March 1991, Article 10: 30 ILM (1991) 1291.

Now Article 27 of the ICSID Convention which regulates foreign investment disputes and is a multilateral convention provides:

> No contracting State shall give diplomatic protection, or bring an international claim, in respect of a dispute which one of its nationals and another Contracting State shall have consented to submit or shall have submitted to arbitration under this Convention, unless such other Contracting Party shall have failed to abide by and comply with the award rendered in such dispute.[63]

Most Latin American States have become parties to this convention. The Multilateral Investment Guarantee Agency (MIGA) Convention which facilitates investment in developing countries by making political risk insurance available to investors wishing to do business in developing countries has provisions permitting arbitration only in cases in which the dispute cannot be resolved through negotiation or conciliation.[64] Today most Latin American States are parties to MIGA, also.

While it is clear that both the above instruments permit international arbitration to settle disputes, and up to a point avoid the exercise of diplomatic protection, their provisions are double-edged and do not concede what the Calvo Clause purported to proscribe. While diplomatic protection is relegated, exhaustion of local remedies by the investor is also excluded as a rule.[65] This is contrary to the expectations of the Calvo Clause and the Calvo Doctrine. The fact that Latin American countries have subscribed to such instruments is thus an indication that there is less insistence on the Calvo Doctrine, where in effect an international arbitral process is substituted for local remedies under a multilateral convention to which they are parties.

It may also be mentioned that the North American Free Trade Agreement (NAFTA) of 1992 between the United States, Canada, and Mexico permits a foreign investor in certain circumstances to resort to international arbitration, rather than exhaust local remedies, among other things.[66] Here again, international arbitration is in effect substituted for the exhaustion of local remedies in the case of their nationals by agreement among the three contracting parties. While diplomatic protection is not contemplated, the expectation is that local remedies will not need to be exhausted. This is also a departure from the Calvo Doctrine and the underlying premise of the Calvo Clause.

These and other recent developments, including often the provisions of bilateral investment treaties, have led to the substitution in many cases of some kind of international arbitration under international conventions or treaties to which the relevant States are parties for the exhaustion of local remedies. This is clearly a departure from the Calvo Doctrine and conflicts with the intentions of the Calvo

[63] (1965), 575 UNTS 164.
[64] 25 ILM (1985) 1598.
[65] Eg, Article 26 of the ICSID Convention, (1965), 575 UNTS 164.
[66] 32 ILM (1993) 605.

Clause. That Latin American States are parties to such instruments is an indication that they are willing and prepared to accept some kind of international arbitration in the agreed circumstances in lieu of the exhaustion of local remedies by the foreigner. What is clear also is that, in the case of the ICSID Convention particularly, the pressure inherent in the exercise of diplomatic protection by the national State of the foreigner is not to be applied,[67] as stated in Article 27, until the host State has failed to implement an arbitral award against it.

The ILC, as already pointed out, dropped any reference in its 2006 Draft Articles to the Calvo Clause. However, in the Commentary (to Article 14) it made a passing reference to it, merely taking note of the disagreement over it.[68]

Conclusion

Some of the material on the Calvo Clause, including the case law, is rather confusing. However, a few conclusions may be drawn and suggested.

An important principle is that the right of the national State of an alien to exercise diplomatic protection, in the appropriate circumstances, where the alien has by agreement promised not to seek the protection of his national State, remains unaffected. On the basis that at international law the right violated when one State injures a national of another State is that of the national State of the alien, the right of the national State to protect the alien remains vested in the national State and cannot be taken away by an act of the alien. Thus, the Calvo Clause does not affect the rights of the national State of the alien. While this result, according to some, is produced by reliance on a legal fiction, the fact of the matter is that this is the manner in which international law regards the situation and the result must be recognized.

It is no answer to argue that the alien has breached a binding promise he has made not to seek the protection of his national State if he has, as is usually the case, approached his national State for protection, and that, therefore, the national State of the alien may not exercise protection. It is recognized that the alien's breach of promise does not affect the right of his national State.

Another way of approaching the problem is to ask whether in breaking a promise the alien has created a situation as a result of which his national State does not come with clean hands (*mains propres*) to exercise diplomatic protection. Clearly, international law, as it stands now, either does not interpret the breach of promise as infecting the hands of the national State or may not regard the doctrine of 'clean hands' as relevant to diplomatic protection, where it is applied to the condition of the alien being protected.[69]

[67] For this kind of practice and its implications for the local remedies rule see C F Amerasinghe (note 23 above) 267 ff.

[68] See *Report of the ILC (2006)* 73–4.

[69] On the 'clean hands' doctrine and its relevance to diplomatic protection see below Chapter 13.

To regard the alien's promise not to seek diplomatic protection as effectively taking away the right of his national State to exercise diplomatic protection would require a complete change in the law. In any case there remains the delicate question whether the right of the national State to exercise diplomatic protection may be taken away by a promise made by the alien, where he does not actively seek the protection of his national State and cannot be proved to have done so. The accepted position in international law is that, regardless of whether the alien sought protection, the right of the alien's national State to exercise diplomatic protection remains unaffected. The premise underlying the law of diplomatic protection that it is the State's right that is violated when one of its nationals is injured by another State in his person or in his property holds good for this purpose, although it is not the only premise of the law.

What the Calvo Clause does do is to have an effect at the national level of remedies. It preserves the right of the host State to have the alien exhaust local remedies in its territory. This would seem to be superfluous, because the duty to exhaust remedies exists anyway, unless it is waived. Nevertheless, this is the clause's effect. On the other hand, the presence of a Calvo Clause is an indication that the rule of local remedies has not been waived.

Another effect in respect of local remedies in the host State is that, where a *compromis* for the settlement of disputes between the national State and the host State excludes only generally the local remedies rule, the interpretation of the *compromis* may lead in the context to the situation that the requirement in the Calvo Clause is superior to that exclusion and trumps it. Local remedies must in such a case have been exhausted by the alien pursuant to the Calvo Clause before an international forum can take up his case consequent upon the exercise of diplomatic protection, on the basis that the parties intended this, even though the *compromis* may *appear* to provide differently. This view taken in the cases could seem to be illogical, because the view may be taken that the host State has knowingly renounced its rights under the local remedies rule in the *compromis*—this being so whether the *compromis* was entered into after or before the provisions of a Calvo Clause became effective. Moreover, the *compromis* is an international instrument and, when the host State's rights are knowingly renounced in it, the provisions of the instrument should prevail over the Calvo Clause in a contract. The international cases have, however, taken a different direction by constructively interpreting the *compromis* in the context. This leaves room for a different interpretation in an appropriate situation.[70]

[70] Logic may not always produce a desirable solution. Interpretative justice, on the other hand, may support an acceptable policy value which gives the host State more protection. However, there is no hard and fast rule that a Calvo Clause inherently and incontrovertibly trumps a provision relating to local remedies in the *compromis*. The conclusion reached on the matter depends on the circumstances of each case. A *compromis* could contain a provision drafted in such a manner as to render Calvo Clauses ineffective in regard to the requirement that local remedies should be exhausted.

Further, the alien is precluded by submitting to the insertion of a Calvo Clause in his contract from resorting to remedies in other national internal courts than those of the host State. Thus, while there may be restraints imposed by the operation of the rules of sovereign immunity, even in the absence of these, the alien may not resort to other national courts for satisfaction.

It may also be noted that the Calvo Clause does not generally apply to injuries other than those caused by breach of the contract in which it appears, such as tortious injuries. However, it is possible that the clause may be formulated in such a way that it is intended to have the widest coverage. In whatever way it is framed, for the exercise of diplomatic protection, the requirement would be: (i) a denial of justice after resort to local remedies in contractual claims against the host State's agencies followed by exhaustion of local remedies, and (ii) in the case of non-contractual injuries by the host State the exhaustion of local remedies by the alien in respect of those injuries.

The clause does not require the alien to have secured an affirmative award before his State may exercise diplomatic protection. To require an affirmative award after exhaustion of local remedies would make nonsense of the concept of diplomatic protection. It is precisely because the alien has not received due satisfaction that diplomatic protection is exercised. All that is required is that the alien not be granted satisfaction after he has exhausted local remedies, whether there is an affirmative or negative award.

The manner in which the international law surrounding the Calvo Clause has developed emphasizes to a large extent the rights of the national State of the alien as the injured party—but this only in order that the alien may not be deprived of protection. Though the Calvo Clause relates to the exhaustion of local remedies, the rules relating to which pay attention to the alien as the person whose rights have been violated, international law has not developed in such a way as to permit the alien to exclude effectively his national State from exercising its protection based on the premise that it is its rights that have been violated. Nor has international law given precedence to the interests of the host State in avoiding the exercise of diplomatic protection by the national State, while it does emphasize those interests by confirming the exhaustion of local remedies rule. It is by particular recognition of the rights of the national State of the alien that international law has been able to afford the alien an overriding protection. This is so even though, to satisfy the interests of the host State, it has been held that in principle a Calvo Clause in a contract trumps and nullifies a general waiver of the local remedies rule in the *compromis* for international judicial settlement and, as has been suggested, in any case prevents that alien from seeking redress in any other national forum than that of the host State.

13

The 'Clean Hands' Doctrine

The 'clean hands' (*mains propres*) doctrine is applied in many national systems of law, is based on good faith and may even be considered a general principle of law. Its effect is basically to prevent at some stage in the proceedings an action being brought where such action arises from or is involved with the wilful wrongdoing of the complainant. But depending on circumstances it is possible that it may have a lesser effect. The doctrine is reflected in such maxims as '*ex dolo malo non oritur actio*', '*ex iniuria non oritur ius*' and 'he who comes to equity for relief must come with clean hands'.[1] As applied to inter-State relations the following explanation has been given:

> a State which is guilty of illegal conduct may be deprived of the necessary *locus standi in judicio* for complaining of corresponding illegalities on the part of other States, especially if these were consequential on or were embarked upon in order to counter its own illegality—in short were provoked by it.[2]

As applied to diplomatic protection the underlying principle is intended to preclude a State from exercising diplomatic protection, if the national it seeks to protect has suffered an injury in consequence of his or her own wrongful conduct. It could also apply to prevent a national State from protecting an alien, where that State has been guilty of wrongdoing against the host State in connection with the injury suffered by the alien, but it is in the former sense that the importance of the principle has been emphasized.

Thus, in general international law there are potentially three situations in which the doctrine of 'clean hands' may be applied, if it is found to be relevant:

(i) in direct inter-State relations;
(ii) in diplomatic protection, where the national State of the alien is guilty of wrongdoing vis-à-vis the host State in connection with the alleged injury to the alien. This instance is similar to (i) above, except that it is solely concerned with the protection of a national; and

[1] Other maxims expressing the same idea are '*nemo ex suo delicto meliorem conditionem facere potest*' and '*nullus commodum capere potest de sua proprio iniuria*'.

[2] Fitzmaurice, 'The General Principles of International Law Considered from the Standpoint of the Rule of Law', 92 Hague Recueil (1957) 119.

(iii) in diplomatic protection, where the protected alien is himself guilty of wrongdoing.

Direct Inter-State Relations

As to the first situation, in practice the doctrine has most frequently been raised in the context of inter-State relations where States (or dissenting judges) have sought to have a claim declared inadmissible or dismissed for the reason, apparently, if not explicitly, that the applicant State's hands are unclean.

Most recently Israel in the advisory proceedings before the ICJ in the *Construction of a Wall Case* raised the argument that

> Palestine, given its responsibility for acts of violence against Israel and its population which the wall is aimed at addressing, cannot seek from the court a remedy for a situation resulting from its own wrongdoing. In this context, Israel has invoked the maxim *nullus commodum capere potest de sua iniuria proprio*, which it considers to be relevant in advisory proceedings as it is in contentious cases.[3]

Israel concluded that good faith and the principle of 'clean hands' provided a compelling reason for the court to refuse the General Assembly's request for an advisory opinion. The court did not consider this argument to be pertinent on the ground that the opinion was to be given to the General Assembly and not to a specific State or entity. On the other hand, the court did not reject the relevance of the argument to inter-State disputes in contentious proceedings.

In the *Oil Platforms Case* the US raised an issue of a preliminary character. It requested the court to dismiss the claims of Iran because of the latter's own unlawful conduct. Iran characterized the objection as being based on a 'clean hands' theory which was, so it claimed, irrelevant in direct State-to-State claims as a ground for inadmissibility of a claim, although it may be relevant in claims for diplomatic protection. Iran, however, acknowledged that the principle might be relevant at the merits stage. The ICJ rejected the argument that the claim of the US was one of inadmissibility but found that it was unnecessary to deal with the request to dismiss the claim of Iran on the basis of conduct attributed to the latter.[4] The Court left open the question whether the 'clean hands' principle was a ground for inadmissibility of a claim only in the context of diplomatic protection, omitting to deal with it.

In the *La Grand Case* the US objected to Germany's claim on grounds which appeared to relate to the 'clean hands' theory. The US argued that Germany's submissions were inadmissible on the ground that Germany sought to have a standard applied to the US which was different from that of its own practice.

[3] See the pleadings in Doc A/ES-10/273 and Corr 1.
[4] 2003 ICJ Reports paras 27–30.

The US maintained that it would be contrary to basic principles of administration of justice and equality of the parties to apply against the US alleged rules that Germany appeared not to apply to itself. Germany denied that it was seeking adherence to standards with which Germany itself did not comply. The ICJ found that it did not need to decide whether the objection of the US, if proven, would result in the inadmissibility of Germany's submissions because the evidence adduced by the US did not support the conclusion that Germany's own practice failed to conform to the standards it demanded of the US.[5]

In the *Avena Case* the US raised an argument similar to the one it raised in the *La Grand Case* without describing it as a 'clean hands' argument. The objection was presented in terms of the interpretation of Article 36 of the Vienna Convention on Consular Relations of 1963. The interpretation given by the US was based on the rule that a treaty may not be interpreted so as to impose a significantly greater burden on any one party than the other. The ICJ dismissed the argument. The court relied on an approach to the interpretation of the Vienna Convention which did not permit it to accept the argument of the US. It then said:

> Even if it were shown, therefore, that Mexico's practice as regards the application of article 36 was not beyond reproach, this would not constitute a ground of objection to the admissibility of Mexico's claim.[6]

The ICJ did not deny the possibility that in an appropriate case the 'clean hands' principle could apply, limiting itself to an interpretation of the convention before it. The ICJ in the *Gabčíkovo-Nagymaros Project Case* declined to apply the 'clean hands' doctrine. It stated:

> The Court, however, cannot disregard the fact that the Treaty has not been fully implemented by either party for years, and indeed that their acts of commission and omission have contributed to creating the factual situation that now exists. Nor can it overlook that factual situation—or the practical possibilities and impossibilities to which it gives rise—when deciding on the legal requirements for the future conduct of the Parties.
>
> This does not mean that facts—in this case facts which flow from wrongful conduct—determine the law.[7]

There was an *in specie* rejection of the argument based on the 'clean hands' doctrine, again based on the need to give the treaty a reasonable application. In the *Arrest Warrant Case* the Belgian judge ad hoc, Judge van den Wyngaert, dissenting, held that:

> The Congo did not come to the Court with clean hands. In blaming Belgium for investigating and prosecuting allegations of international crimes that it was obliged to investigate and prosecute itself, the Congo acts in bad faith.[8]

[5] 2001 ICJ Reports paras 61–63.
[6] 2004 ICJ Reports para 47.
[7] 1997 ICJ Reports 76, para 133.
[8] 2002 ICJ Reports para 35 of Judge van den Wyngaert's dissenting opinion.

The ICJ did not deal with the 'clean hands' principle when it decided against the respondent. Because Judge van den Wyngaert held that the application of the doctrine resulted in dismissal of the case, it would seem that impliedly the court was of the opinion that the doctrine did not apply, at least in the case in hand (or that the claimant's conduct did not violate the principle).

In the *Nicaragua Case*, Judge Schwebel, dissenting, held that the clean hands doctrine should be applied against Nicaragua, in a situation in which the court held in favour of the complainant, Nicaragua. He said:

> Nicaragua has not come to Court with clean hands. On the contrary, as the aggressor, indirectly responsible—but ultimately responsible—for large numbers of deaths and widespread destruction in El Salvador apparently much exceeding that which Nicaragua has sustained, Nicaragua's hands are odiously unclean. Nicaragua has compounded its sins by misrepresenting them to the Court. Thus both on the grounds of its unlawful armed intervention in El Salvador, and its deliberately seeking to mislead the Court about the facts of that intervention through false testimony of its Ministers, Nicaragua's claims against the United States should fail.[9]

There do not seem to be any arbitral awards involving direct inter-State relations in which the principle being discussed has been applied.

The cases before the ICJ which have been examined are somewhat equivocal. While there is no explicit rejection by the court of the principle, there is no case in which the decision went against the claimant State as a result of the application of the principle. There are cases such as the *Arrest Warrant Case*, on the other hand, in which the principle was without explanation ignored or implicitly regarded as irrelevant. There are also cases in which the court has found that in any case the principle had not been violated in that the claimant's hands were not unclean. It is difficult to conclude in the circumstances that the ICJ is of the view that the principle is inapplicable to direct inter-State cases. It is very likely that the court could recognize it as applicable in an appropriate case as a general principle of law.[10]

[9] 1986 ICJ Reports 392, para 268. Judge Schwebel examined in his opinion several cases decided by the PCIJ, none of which are exactly in point in regard to the principle here discussed but did illustrate the general maxim that 'he who seeks equity must do equity': ibid 392 ff, paras 269 and 270. The court itself was of the view, it appears, that on the facts Nicaragua was not guilty of wrongdoing. In the oral argument on the issues of provisional measures and jurisdiction in the *Legality of the Use of Force Case* (ICJ) between Yugoslavia as claimant and members of NATO as respondents several respondents made the point that Yugoslavia did not come to the court with clean hands: see Dugard, 'Sixth Report on Diplomatic Protection' (2005), UN Doc A/CN 4/546, 5.

[10] There was a veiled reference by the ICJ to the doctrine of 'clean hands' in terms of 'good faith' behaviour in the *Nauru Phosphate Lands Case*, 1992 ICJ Reports 255.

The court said:

> 37. Australia's fifth objection is that 'Nauru has failed to act consistently and in good faith in relation to rehabilitation' and that therefore 'the Court in exercise of its discretion, and in order to uphold judicial propriety should... decline to hear the Nauruan claims'.

Diplomatic Protection by a State with Unclean Hands

The situation may arise where State A attempts to exercise diplomatic protection in favour of one of its nationals and against a defendant State in circumstances in which State A has been guilty of, eg, inciting violence in the defendant State's territory without the particular involvement of the alien being protected and the alien being protected has not acted in violation of the law in any way. The question is whether the defendant State may successfully argue that State A has unclean hands and, therefore, cannot protect its national.

If the theory introduced by Vattel, proclaimed by the PCIJ in the *Mavrommatis Case* and still believed to be fundamental to the law of diplomatic protection, namely that it is the international legal right of the national State that is violated when another State injures one of its nationals, is respected, the answer to the question posed should be that the 'clean hands' doctrine disqualifies the national State of the alien from exercising diplomatic protection against the delinquent State. However, there is no priority about the underlying principles of the law of diplomatic protection. As has been seen, there are circumstances in which the alien must act and, for example, exhaust local remedies before seeking his national State's protection, which means that regard for the rights of the national State is diluted and qualified. Some rules, among others, relating to nationality of the alien also disregard the Vattelian principle.

In the absence of authority on the matter, the solution to the problem is a pragmatic one, depending in reality on whether the interests of the alien in being protected or those of the defendant State in having the national State of the alien come with clean hands and therefore not being placed in the position of respondent are to be recognized as more important in determining the rule of law applicable. Given that in areas of international law involving individuals (eg human rights law), there is a tendency in favour of giving individuals substantial protection, it is suggested that the 'clean hands' doctrine not be applied in the circumstances to deprive the alien of protection. There is an element of choice in the determination of the rule between truly conflicting interests and the choice should in this instance aim at a policy of giving protection to the alien. This is so, particularly, because there is no treaty, State practice or case law on the matter, and even though purists may argue that based on the Vattelian principle

> 38. The Court considers that the Application by Nauru has been properly submitted in the framework of the remedies open to it. At the present stage, the Court is not called upon to weigh the possible consequences of the conduct of Nauru with respect to the merits of the case. It need merely note that such conduct does not amount to an abuse of process. Australia's objection on this point must also be rejected.

In the *Legality of the Use of Force Case* (see <http://www.icj-cij.org>) some respondents argued that the claimant, Serbia, did not come to court with clean hands. The cases were discussed at the jurisdiction stage and the ICJ did not rule on the 'clean hands' issue.

the national State is disqualified from exercising diplomatic protection in respect of its injured national.

Diplomatic Protection of an Alien with 'Unclean Hands'

An important question which has been discussed is whether in the law of diplomatic protection the defence that the alien whom his national State seeks to protect must himself have 'clean hands', ie not have done anything wrongful vis-à-vis the defendant State. Apart from any difficulty there may be in determining whether on the facts the alien may be said not to have 'clean hands' or the meaning of 'clean hands' in this context, answering the question whether the 'clean hands' principle applies to the acts of an alien being protected is, indeed, a difficult one to answer, particularly on the basis of policy.

The ICJ has not faced the problem. There are many arbitrations, however, in which the 'clean hands' doctrine was addressed, often without specific mention of it. The earliest case in which the problem was faced was the *Brig 'Lawrence'* where the presiding arbitrator in dealing with a claim based on the allegedly unlawful condemnation of a ship stated:

> the African slave trade at the time of this condemnation, being prohibited by all civilized nations, was contrary to the law of nations, and being prohibited by the laws of the United States, the owners of the *Lawrence* could not claim the protection of their own government, and, therefore, in my judgment, can have no claim before this commission.[11]

In the *'Good Return'* and *'Media'* claims the presiding arbitrator in disqualifying the US from bringing the claims on behalf of its national referred to and applied the maxim '*nemo ex suo delicto meliorem suam conditionem facit*'.[12] In the *Frierdich and Co Case*[13] the tribunal, in discussing the case, referred to and applied the maxim: 'He who comes into equity must come with clean hands.' The tribunal pointed to the misconduct of the alien as having caused the impeached conduct of the host State in his regard. There were some other cases decided in the latter half of the nineteenth century and in the early twentieth century in which the arbitrating commissioners have ostensibly, if not explicitly, applied the principle, sometimes finding that the principle was not violated.[14]

[11] (1855, USA v UK), Moore, 3 *History and Digest of the International Arbitrations to which the United States Has Been a Party* (1898) 2825.

[12] (1865, USA v Ecuador), Moore, 3 ibid. at 2738–9.

[13] (1905, France v Venezuela), 10 UNRIAA 50.

[14] The *Tripler Case* (1875, USA v Mexico), Moore, 3 *History and Digest of the International Arbitrations to which the United States has been a Party* (1898) 2823; the *Camille Gros Case* (1876, USA v Mexico), Moore, 3 ibid 2771; the *Samuel Brannan Case* (1876, USA v Mexico), Moore, 3 ibid 2757–8; the *Campbell and Arango Case* (1879, USA v Spain), Moore, 3 ibid 2776; the *Captain Morril Case* (1890, USA v Venezuela), Moore, 3 ibid 3024; the *Gowen and Copeland Case* (1890,

On the other hand, the presiding arbitrator in the *Chattin Case* was of the view that the 'clean hands' principle did not apply to a claim brought on behalf of an alien who had acted unlawfully but had been injured by the host State. He elaborated on his view as follows:

Mexico contends that not only has Chattin, as a fugitive from justice, lost his right to invoke as against Mexico protection by the United States, but that even the latter is bound by such forfeiture of protection and may not interpose on his behalf. If this contention be sound, the American Government would have lost the right to espouse Chattin's claim, and the claim lacking an essential element required by Article 1 of the Convention signed September 8, 1923, would not be within the cognizance of this Commission. The motive for the alleged limitation placed on the sovereignty of the claimant's Government would seem to be that a government espousing such claim makes itself a party to the improper act of its national. International awards, however, establishing either the duty or the right of international tribunals to reject claims of fugitives from justice have not been found; on the contrary, the award in the *Pelletier Case* (under the Convention of May 28, 1884, between the United States and Hayti) did not attach any importance to the fact that Pelletier had escaped from an Haytian jail, nor did Secretary Bayard do so in expounding the reasons why the United States Government did not see fit to press the award rendered in its favor (Moore, at 1779, 1794,1800). In the *Roberts* and *Strother* cases (Docket Nos. 185 and 3088) this Commission virtually held that protection of a fugitive from justice should be left to the discretion of the claimant government, and it did so more explicitly in the *Massey* case (Docket No. 352; paragraph 3 of Commissioner Nielsen's opinion). A similar attitude was taken in cases in which forfeiture of the right to protection was alleged on other grounds. In paragraph 6 of its opinion in the *Macedonio J. García* case (Docket No. 607), the Commission held that the American claimant's participation in Mexican politics was not a point on which the question of the right of the United States to intervene on his behalf, and therefore the question of the Commission's jurisdiction, could properly be raised, but that the pertinency of this point could only be considered in connection with the question of the validity of the claim under the international law. In the *Francisco Mallén* case (Docket No. 2935) none of the Commissioners held that misstatements or even misrepresentations by the individual claimant could furnish a ground for the Commission to reject the claim as an unallowable one. It is true that more than once in international cases statements have been made to the effect that a fugitive from justice loses *his* right to invoke and to expect protection—either by the justice from which he fled, or by his own government—but this would seem not to imply that his government as well loses *its* right to espouse its subject's claim in its discretion. The present claim, therefore, apart from the question whether a man who leaves a jail which is thrown open may be called a fugitive from justice, should be accepted and examined.[15]

USA v Venezuela), Moore, 3 ibid 3358–9; the *Jarvis Case* (1903, USA v Venezuela), 9 UNRIAA 211–13.

[15] (1927, USA v Mexico), 4 UNRIAA 284–5. See also the '*I'm Alone*' *Case* (1935, Canada v USA), 3 UNRIAA 1617–18. Also may be mentioned a decision of the US tribunal dealing with claims against foreign States—the *Smiljanic Case* (1954), *FCSC Dec and Ann* 85–7.

Thus, while in some cases tribunals tended to regard the 'clean hands' principle as applied to the alien's conduct in an international claim by his national State as relevant to the success of the claim, the later cases treat the principle as inapplicable.

Some legal commentators, sometimes citing irrelevant or misconstrued cases or no judicial authority at all, have expressed the view that the 'clean hands' principle as applied to the conduct of an alien regardless of the national State's clean hands is relevant in cases brought by national States of aliens to prevent the exercise of diplomatic protection.[16] On the other hand, many writers question the applicability of the 'clean hands' doctrine in the circumstances being considered or sometimes generally.[17] Further, the earlier cases mentioned above as supporting the applicability of the doctrine to diplomatic protection, where the alien is alleged to have unclean hands, are susceptible of a different interpretation.

During the debate in the Sixth Committee of the General Assembly at its fifty-ninth session (2004) most delegations had made no comment on the 'clean hands' doctrine, and those that had commented had agreed that it should not be included in the draft articles on diplomatic protection.[18]

In the debate in the ILC[19] in 2005 general support was expressed for the Special Rapporteur's conclusion that the 'clean hands' doctrine should not be included in the draft articles. The doctrine had been raised primarily in the context of claims for direct State injury, which was beyond the scope of diplomatic protection, and the few cases falling within the scope of diplomatic protection did not constitute sufficient practice to warrant codification. Nor could its inclusion be justified as an exercise in the progressive development of international law. Furthermore, support was expressed for the Special Rapporteur's suggestion in his report that it was more appropriate for the doctrine to be invoked at the stage of the examination of the merits since it related to the attenuation or exoneration of responsibility rather than admissibility; and it was suggested that such a possibility could be expressly recognized in the draft articles. Another suggestion was to insert a

[16] See Cheng, *General Principles of Law as Applied by International Courts and Tribunals* (1953) 155 (citing early authority); Malanczuk, *Akehurst's Modern Introduction to International Law* (1997) 263–9 (citing no authority); Ruzié, *Droit international public* (1999) 95 (citing no authority); Combacau and Sur, *Droit international public* (2001) 596–7 (citing no authority); Carreau, *Droit international public* (2001) 467–8 (citing two misconstrued cases), the *Ben Tillett Case* (1898, UK *v* Belgium), *La Fontaine* 583, and *The Virginius* (1873, USA and Spain), ibid 592, which concerned an incident resulting in a dispute which was settled by negotiation without reference to a judicial organ. On the correct interpretation of the two latter cases referred to above see Dugard (note 9 above) 6–7.

[17] See particularly Salmon, 'Des "mains propres" comme condition de recevabilité des reclamations internationales', AFDI (1964) 225–66; Salmon, *Dictionnaire de droit international public* (2001) 677–8; Garcia Arias, 'La doctrine des "clean hands" en droit internationale public', 30 *Annuaire des anciens auditeurs de l'Academie de droit international* (1960) 14.

[18] See *Report of the ILC (2005)* 112, para 230.

[19] This summary is taken from ibid 112–14, paras 231–6.

proviso stating that the draft articles were without prejudice to the application of general international law to questions of admissibility.

Others were of the view that the Special Rapporteur had gone too far in suggesting that the 'clean hands' doctrine could lead to exoneration of responsibility at the stage of the merits, and preferred that it be limited to attenuation. It was pointed out that the application of the doctrine, or that of good faith, could yield different results in different situations, and would not necessarily deny the complaining party the right to seek in every single instance a suitable remedy, even if its own wrongful conduct had elicited the wrongful response. Reference was also made to Article 39 on Responsibility of States for Internationally Wrongful Acts.

Notwithstanding their support for the Special Rapporteur's conclusions, some members took issue with the Special Rapporteur's reasoning. For example, the Commission was cautioned against stretching the principle in the *Mavrommatis Case* that an injury to a national is an injury to the State itself too far: it would not be incongruous to consider that the 'clean hands' of the individual could constitute a precondition for diplomatic protection, exactly as the exhaustion of local remedies was up to the private individual and not the State.

In addition, some members maintained that in referring to the consular notification cases (the *La Grand Case* and the *Avena Case*), by way of illustrating the point that the 'unclean' hands of the individuals concerned played no role in diplomatic protection, the Special Rapporteur was employing too vague a conception of the clean hands doctrine because he failed to examine the relationship between the unlawful act of the individual and the internationally wrongful act of the State. The question was whether the individual who benefited from diplomatic protection was himself or herself responsible for the breach of the rule of international law that the host State was accused of violating.

In another view, the lack of practice did not necessarily preclude the adoption of some version of the doctrine by way of progressive development of the law. The key difficulty involved the proper identification of the doctrine, as there existed at least the two following different legal positions described by the same phrase: (a) where the illegality alleged would, in principle, form part of the merits, and (b) where it is invoked ex parte by a respondent State simply by way of prejudice as a principle of international public policy constituting a bar to the admissibility of the claim. Each case called for contextual analysis and careful characterization.

The Special Rapporteur observed that the clean hands doctrine was an important principle of international law that had to be taken into account whenever there was evidence that an applicant State had not acted in good faith and that it had come to court with unclean hands. It was to be distinguished from the *tu quoque* argument, which allowed a respondent State to assert that the applicant State had also violated a rule of international law, and was instead to be confined to cases in which the applicant State had acted improperly in bringing a case to court.

The evidence in favour of the application of the 'clean hands' doctrine to defeat a claim in the circumstances being discussed is, to say the least, inconclusive.

On the other hand, the more recent *Chattin Case* points in the direction of not permitting the application of a 'clean hands' doctrine. It is, therefore, difficult to disagree with the statement that:

Even within the context of diplomatic protection, the authority supporting the existence of a doctrine of 'clean hands', whether as a ground of admissibility or otherwise, is in Salmon's words, 'fairly long-standing and divided'. It deals largely with individuals involved in slave-trading and breach of neutrality, and in particular a series of decisions of the United States–Great Britain Mixed Commission set up under a Convention of 8 February 1853 for the settlement of shipowners' compensation claims. According to Salmon, in the cases were the claim was held inadmissible:

> In any event, it appears that these cases are all characterized by the fact that the breach of international law by the victim was the sole cause of the damage claimed, [and] that the cause-and-effect relationship between the damage and the victim's conduct was pure, involving no wrongful act by the respondent State. When, on the contrary, the latter has in turn violated international law in taking repressive action against the applicant, the arbitrators have never declared the claim inadmissible.[20]

Furthermore, as has been observed:

Whether the doctrine is applicable at all to claims involving diplomatic protection is highly questionable. There is no clear authority to support the applicability of the doctrine to cases of diplomatic protection. Such authority as there is is uncertain and of ancient vintage, dating mainly from the mid-nineteenth century—as the above-cited passages from Salmon demonstrate. Although some authors support the existence of the doctrine in the context of diplomatic protection, they are unsupported by authority.[21]

This solution proposed is pragmatic. It may be justified on the basis of the Vattelian theory that the right asserted by the protecting State is its own right and not that of the alien with the consequence that whatever the alien has done to dirty his hands cannot be relevant to or nullify the assertion of the national State's right to protect the alien. The solution is also in keeping with the concept of giving the individual protection rather than depriving him of it.[22]

Conclusion

The examination above of the 'clean hands' doctrine and its application shows that there are many problems to be faced both in defining it and in applying it. Even in direct inter-State cases there is uncertainty, as the precedents of the

[20] Crawford, 'Second Report on State Responsibility', (1999) 49, para 330, UN Doc A/CN.4/498/Add 2, footnotes omitted. For the citations from Salmon see loc. cit. (AFDI) note 17, 249, 261.

[21] Dugard (note 9 above) 9.

[22] The ILC has not included any provisions on 'clean hands' in its 2006 Draft Articles on diplomatic protection.

ICJ show, whether it is inexorably and automatically applicable in all cases. The approach taken by the court in the *Gabčíkovo-Nagymaros Project Case* may be interpreted to require some caution in applying the doctrine in absolute terms so that the claimant State or the *actor* must in all cases where the doctrine is applied as relevant fail without qualification. In treaty cases, at any rate, the ICJ has not been excessively keen on applying the doctrine in this absolute way. The aim of the ICJ has been in all cases to arrive at a just and fair solution as between the parties largely on a pragmatic basis, while not ignoring entirely the equitable requirement of 'clean hands', and at the same time dealing with the doctrine flexibly. That an absolute inflexible approach has been rejected is also clear from the *Arrest Warrant Case* where the court differed from the dissenting ad hoc judge and did not apply the doctrine to defeat the claimant State's claim, as the dissenting ad hoc judge did.

In any case there seem to be two points to be noted. The first is that the doctrine is not an absolute one. Clearly, because it is based on good faith, which is an important fundamental principle of international law, it has to be taken into account. But, as the practice of the ICJ shows, it is a flexible doctrine subject to adaptation. It is relevant and viable, it would seem, but only to the extent that its application promotes the cause of justice and does not result in injustice. It is also noteworthy that the ICJ, while obliquely recognizing the principle of 'clean hands', has never applied it to find that the claimant must fail. On the contrary it has avoided recognizing the applicability of the principle to the cases before it in one way or another.

The second point is that it is not clear whether the doctrine in direct inter-State cases, when it is applied, must result in dismissal of the case or could work as a source of mitigation or extenuation of offences. In principle, regarding the principle as based on good faith, there is no reason why, in order to achieve justice, it should not be applied only in mitigation or extenuation in the appropriate case. There is also the question whether, where the objection is raised that the claimant does not come to court with clean hands, it is an objection of a preliminary nature relating to admissibility of the claim or one that goes to the merits. Suffice it to note that in no case so far decided has the objection been regarded as of a preliminary nature relating to admissibility. The issue of 'clean hands' has been dealt with together with the merits.

In cases where the claimant State protecting its national comes to court with unclean hands in the context of the diplomatic protection it is exercising, it is easy to take the view that the 'clean hands' doctrine must apply, whatever is the consequence of such application. No such example of such a case has been found, however. But the view may be taken that the case falls within the category of direct inter-State cases and there should be no difficulty in applying the doctrine to the same extent and in the same way as it might be applied in such cases. This is so, even though the result would be that the individual loses protection through no fault of his own. The Vattelian conception of diplomatic protection as a right of the State, regardless that the injury is to the individual, would logically and pragmatically prevail.

Where the individual being protected has unclean hands the logical consequences of the Vattelian theory that the right asserted is that of the claimant State and not that of the individual have been applied in some cases such as the *Chattin Case*. In many cases, such as the *Brig 'Lawrence'*, the lack of clean hands on the part of the alien was regarded as a defence on the merits to the extent that the latter had breached the national law of the host State which justified the actions of the host State. The nexus between the breach of national law by the alien and the actions of the host State was clear. There was more involved in these cases than general or simple unclean hands. However, even otherwise, tribunals have entertained the absence of clean hands on the part of the individual as a defence, though the finding on the facts may have been in favour of the individual. Illogical though this may seem, taking into account the Vattelian principle, arbitral tribunals have not regarded the 'clean hands' principle as irrelevant to cases of diplomatic protection. What emerges is that a pragmatic and realistic approach has been taken leading to acknowledgement or absence of denial that the 'clean hands' doctrine is applicable to the conduct of the alien being protected. Considering that the alien is the real person being protected this seems fair although it gives him less protection.

However, there remains the question whether it is a just solution that the 'clean hands' doctrine should apply in respect of both the State protecting and the alien being protected. What seems to follow is that logic does not necessarily prevail and that the 'clean hands' doctrine may apply in respect of both State and alien, as a result of a more pragmatic and realistic approach. The protecting State and the alien, it may be asserted, are on one side and the host State is on the other. Both the former must come to court with clean hands as against the host State. The solution, it is true, happens to favour the host State but then, it may be suggested, this does not interfere with the requirements of justice. The host State is entitled to expect that diplomatic protection is exercised against it only if both parties on the other side have clean hands, regardless of the conceptual logic of the situation. This may be a situation in which conceptual logic is abandoned just as in the case of the applicability of the rule of exhaustion of local remedies and some other rules connected with nationality.

What is more disturbing is the lack of guidance in the jurisprudence of tribunals, particularly as to what amounts to the absence of 'clean hands'. There has been a reference to *iniuria* which signifies an unlawful act on the part of the party concerned but beyond that nothing is clear. For example, must the conduct be unlawful according to some norm of international law or is it to be unlawful according to the host State's national law? Must the unlawful conduct be connected with the host State's alleged violation of international law and how should it be so connected if this is a requirement? Clearly, on the other hand, 'unclean hands' signifies something less than conduct on the part of the party concerned which justifies substantively the impeached treatment of the alien by the host State. In the latter case there is a complete defence on the merits, and the defence is one which may be characterized as a lawful excuse for the violation of the law in question.

Because of the lack of guidance on the issue in the sources, it is suggested that the defence of 'unclean hands' not only is one which pertains to the merits and not to admissibility, as the few relevant cases show, but is no more than one which is to be used to secure fairness and justice for the host State where the conduct of one or the other of the other two parties involved in the case may be questionable. It would be fair to the latter parties if the conduct be unlawful according to either international law or the national law of the host State (or even that of the protecting State), though it does not afford a complete defence on the merits, and be sufficiently connected with the alleged violation of international law by the host State to raise concern that permitting the case to proceed or inflicting an unmitigated penalty would be unfair by the host State. Stated in these terms the defence of 'unclean hands' could be seen as one to admissibility where it is raised in order to secure dismissal of the case but in fact it has been treated as one to be taken up at the merits stage, regardless of when it is raised.

14

Attribution of Conduct as the Act of the State

Introduction

In a given situation in which the international responsibility of a State for an injury to an alien is invoked and in which diplomatic protection may be exercised there are several conditions which have to be fulfilled in respect of the respondent State's position. Apart from other requirements,[1] there must be an act or omission of a person or a group of persons and this must be attributable (or imputable)[2] to the respondent State. This attribution is a matter for international

[1] The conduct, consisting of acts or omissions, must be in breach of an obligation imposed by a norm of international law, which is a different question. Thus, there are two different requirements—(i) attribution of the conduct as a conduct of the State and (ii) a breach of an international obligation: see eg Starke 'Imputability in International delinquencies', 19 BYIL (1938) 106; Cheng, *General Principle of Law as Applied by International Courts and Tribunals* (1953) 170; Rousseau, *Droit International Public* (1953) 361, Ch de Visscher, 'La responsabilité des États', 2 *Bibliotheca Visseriana* (1924) 89 ff; Anzilotti , 'La Responsabilité des États', 13 RGDIP (1906) at 7 ff; and now Article 2 of the ILC Articles on State Responsibility: Crawford, *The International Law Commission's Articles on State Responsibility* (2002) 61, and commentary which reflects the *lex lata*, 83 ff. Special mention needs to be made of the work of the ILC and its Special Rapporteurs on State Responsibility in connection with the subject of this chapter: see Ago, 'Third Report on State Responsibility, Adds 1–3' 2 YBILC (Part I, 1971) 223–74; 'Fourth Report on State Responsibility, Adds 1–3' 2 YBILC (1972, Part I) 72–160, including bibliography on State Responsibility; 'Seventh Report on State Responsibility', 2 YBILC (Part I, 1978) 52–60; 'Eighth Report on State Responsibility', 2 YBILC (Part I, 1979) 4–27; 'Report of the ILC, 1973' 2 YBILC (1973) 191–8; 'Report of the ILC, 1974' 2 YBILC (Part I, 1974) 277–90; 'Report of the ILC, 1975', 2 YBILC (1975) 60–106; 'Report of the ILC, 1978', 2 YBILC (Part II, 1978), 98–106; 'Report of the ILC, 1979', 2 YBILC (Part II, 1979) 94–106; Crawford, 'First Report on State Responsibility, Adds 5, 6, and 7' UN Doc A/CN.490/Add 5, Add 6, Add 7, including additional updated bibliography; 'Second Report on State Responsibility, Add 1', UN Doc A/CN.4/498/ Add. 1; Crawford, *The International Law Commission's Articles on State Responsibility* (2002) 91–123, 145–159, which contains relevant final Articles (4–11, 16–19) of the ILC, as reported to the GA, and the commentaries thereon. The latter work by and large reflects the *lex lata* and has been used and followed extensively and unqualifiedly in this Chapter.

[2] The ILC had opted for the terms 'attribution' and 'attributable' rather than 'imputability' and 'imputable': see Article 2 of the ILC's Articles on State Responsibility and heading of Part One, Chapter II; Crawford, ibid 61, 81 ff and 91, and 'First Report on State Responsibility, Addendum 5' (ILC, 1998), UN Doc A/CN.4/490/Add. 5 3 ff. The ICJ and arbitral tribunals have, in fact, used the terms 'imputable' and 'imputed': see the *Diplomatic and Consular Staff Case,* 1980 ICJ Reports 29,41; the *Dickson Car Wheel Co Case* (1931, USA v Mexico), 4 UNRIAA 678.

law, though the internal or national law of the State may be recognized as applicable by international law. The element of attribution may be said to relate to the 'objective' capacity of the respondent State to be cited as respondent in the case and, thus, may be regarded as being of concern to the law of diplomatic protection, as pointed out in Chapter 1.

This attribution is the result of an intellectual operation necessary to bridge the gap between an individual or a group of individuals and the State,[3] and attaching given conduct (action or omission) to the State. Thus, attribution becomes a basic notion in the law of State responsibility for injuries to aliens and diplomatic protection. It is not to be confused with the basis of a State's obligation which may rest on 'fault' or 'risk' or 'strict liability', as the case may be in different situations, which considerations would be pertinent in determining only whether an act or omission in violation of international law has taken place. The notion of attribution becomes particularly important where conflicts may arise, in a given situation, between national law and international law concerning the competence of State organs or officials which can only be resolved by a clear conception of the nature of attribution (and attributability).

In the *Phosphates in Morocco Case (Preliminary Objections)* the PCIJ explicitly linked the creation of international responsibility with the existence of an 'act being attributable to the State...'[4] The ICJ has also referred to attributability on several occasions. In the *Diplomatic and Consular Staff Case*, the court pointed out that, in order to establish the responsibility of Iran, 'First it must determine how far, legally, the acts in question may be regarded as imputable to the Iranian State.'[5] In the *Bosnia Genocide Case* the court required a similar attribution to the respondent State of genocide.[6] In the *Dickson Car Wheel Company Case*, the claims tribunal noted that the condition required for a State to incur international responsibility is 'that an unlawful international act be imputed to it....'[7]

Negatively, the test of imputability is not whether the damage suffered by the alien can be said to have occurred on the territory of a particular State. The decision in the *Corfu Channel Case* shows clearly that this is not the test, even though that case dealt with damage to the property of a foreign State and not of aliens.[8]

Again, in a negative sense the State is not responsible for all the acts or omissions of all persons or individuals on its territory. Thus, normally it is not responsible for

[3] Starke (note 1 above) 105; Cheng (note 1 above) 180; Brierly, 'The Theory of Implied State Complicity in International Claims', 9 BYIL (1928) 42; also Anzilotti (note 1 above) 286; Ago, 'Le délit international', 68 Hague Recueil (1939) 459 ff; Freeman, *The International Responsibility of States for Denial of Justice* (1938) 23 ff; Diena, *Diritto internazionale púbblico* (1939); Cohn, 'La théorie de la responsabilité internationale', 68 Hague Recueil (1939) 293 ff.

[4] (1938), PCIJ Series A/B, No. 74, 28.

[5] 1980 ICJ Reports 29, 41. See also the *Nicaragua Case (Merits)*, 1986 ICJ Reports 117–18; and the *Gabčíkovo-Nagymaros Project Case*, 1997 ICJ Reports 54.

[6] 2007 ICJ Reports at 136 (<www.icj-cij.org>).

[7] (1931, USA v Mexico), 4 UNRIAA 678.

[8] 1949 ICJ Reports 4.

the wrongful acts of private persons. In the *Lovett Case* it was said by the tribunal that: 'All the authorities on international law are a unit as regards the principle that an injury done by one of the subjects of a nation is not to be considered as done by the nation itself.'[9] Calvo, among textwriters, explicitly supports this view,[10] as do others.

However, it is not the case that a State can never be responsible in connection with acts or omissions of private persons. There may be circumstances where the State is responsible for the damage resulting from such acts or omissions because it has occurred as a result of an omission by an entity and, in the circumstances, is attributable to the State. Thus, in the *Home Missionary Society Case* it was clearly affirmed that: 'It was a well established principle of international law that no government can be held responsible for the act of rebellious bodies of men committed in violation of its authority, where it is itself guilty of no breach of good faith, or of no negligence in suppressing the insurrection'.[11] What is implied is that there could have been State responsibility for a wrongful omission by the organs of the State.

In this connection the distinction is generally made between the liability of a State and its responsibility for a breach of international obligation. Where a person commits an injury against an alien, the State does not become responsible for that injury by the very fact that the injury was committed by a person on its territory. Nevertheless, it is possible that, because of the nature of the injury, international law requires that the State take some action to punish the wrongdoer and even provide a proper remedy through its courts for the injured alien. Its failure to do either of these things would result in a breach of its international obligations and in its international responsibility. It is said to be *liable* to punish the wrongdoer and provide a remedy for the injured alien, while it becomes responsible for the failure to do this. *Responsibility* is not for the wrong originally committed by the individual, and arises by the failure of an organ or individual to discharge the liability. It is this failure that is attributed to the State. This liability is to be distinguished, firstly, from the duty that a State has in respect of the prevention of wrongs, which is a different kind of obligation imposed by international law and for a breach of which a State would become responsible when an organ or individual whose acts are attributable to the State fails to perform acts in discharge of that duty.[12] Secondly, it must be distinguished from the situation where the State is responsible directly for a wrong committed by an individual

[9] (1892), Moore, 3 *International Arbitrations* (1898) 2991. See also in the same sense the *Oberlander and Messenger Case* (1897, USA v Mexico), *US Foreign Relations* (1897) 387; the *Tellini Case*, opinion of the Committee of Jurists to which in 1923 reference of the case was made by the LN Council: League of Nations, *Official Journal*, 5th Year, No 4 (April 1924) 524; the *Janes Claim* (1925), 4 UNRIAA 82.

[10] 3 *Le Droit international théorique et pratique* (1897) 134.

[11] AD (1919–1922), Case No 117, 173. See also the *Noyes Claim* (1933, USA v Panama), 6 UNRIAA 311.

[12] See the *Noyes Claim*, ibid 308.

or organ because the act constituting the wrong is attributed to the State under international law. This view of liability is supported by the decision in the *Janes Claim*, where Mexico had failed to apprehend and prosecute the murderer of Janes, an American citizen. The tribunal found Mexico responsible because it failed to discharge its liability to prosecute and punish the offences.[13]

Attribution and the substantive violation of the international law are considerations which must be dealt with separately. Also, attribution is strictly not based on the notion of vicarious responsibility.

Positively the question is, assuming that an individual or group of individuals has caused damage to an alien, which would be wrongful if attributed to the State, on what basis is that act or omission to be attributed to the State?

The concept of attribution or attributability has been explicitly accepted in Draft Codifications. Thus the Guerrero Report adopted by the LN Committee of Experts for the Progressive Codification of International Law as early as 1926 contains a conclusion that: 'A State is responsible for damage incurred by a foreigner attributable to an act contrary to international law or to an omission of an act which the State was bound under international law to perform...'[14]

The concept of attribution is essential to the law of State responsibility for injuries to aliens. In principle, attribution takes place where the individual or organ bears some special relation to the State. To establish such special relations international law invokes the doctrine of attribution on an objective basis. Furthermore, attribution for the purpose of international responsibility and diplomatic protection does not necessarily and ultimately depend on the question whether the State would be responsible for the particular act or omission according to its or any other national or internal law. The question is one for international law to decide. The ICJ in the *Bosnia Genocide Case* made a distinction between *de iure* organs, ie those that are State organs according to the State's internal law, and *de facto* organs, ie those that were, nevertheless, in reality organs of the State though not according to the internal law. It was conceded by implication that the reality was a matter for international law. Later in the same case, the court explained that the test to be applied in determining whether any persons or entities—which were not State organs according to the internal law—could be equated with State organs (in reality), was whether they were in a relationship of complete dependence on the state.[15]

[13] (1926, USA v Mexico), 4 UNRIAA 87. See also the *Putnam Claim* (1927, USA v Mexico), 4 ibid 151; *Kennedy's Claim* (1927, USA v Mexico), 4 ibid194; and Brierly (note 3 above) 42. A conflicting view which identified the State with the culprit has as a result been rejected.

[14] *League of Nations Publication V Legal* 1926, V 3 (Doc C46 M 23, 1926, V). See Article 1(1) of the 1961 Harvard Draft Convention, 55 AJIL (1961) 548; and now Article 2 of the ILC's 2001 Articles on State Responsibility.

[15] 2007 ICJ Reports at 138–40, 145. The Court held that several groups were neither *de iure* organs of Serbia and Montenegro nor *de facto* organs of that State where acts could be attributed to that State.

The Primary Principles

The general rule is that the only conduct attributed to the State at the international level is that of (i) the organs of government, or (ii) others who have acted under the direction, instigation, or control of those organs, that is, as agents of the State.[16] In principle also the State's responsibility is engaged by conduct in violation of its international obligations, irrespective of the level of administration or government at which the conduct occurs. Moreover, 'in order to attribute an act to the State, it is necessary to identify with reasonable certainty the actors and their association with the State'.[17]

Articles 4 and 7 of the ILC's 2001 Draft Articles on State Responsibility purport to focus on the primary principles involved. Article 4 states:

> 1. The conduct of any State organ shall be considered an act of that State under international law, whether the organ exercises legislative, executive, judicial or any other functions, whatever position it holds in the organization of the State, and whatever its character as an organ of the central government or of a territorial unit of the State.
>
> 2. An organ includes any person or entity which has that status in accordance with the internal law of the State.

Article 7 states:

> The conduct of an organ of a State or of a person or entity empowered to exercise elements of the governmental authority shall be considered an act of the State under international law if the organ, person or entity acts in that capacity, even if it exceeds its authority or contravenes instructions.

The Organs of the State

State organs cover all the individual or collective entities which make up the organization of the State and act on its behalf. Included is an organ or any territorial government entity within the State. It is clear that attribution takes place only when the individual or organ bears a special relationship to the State.[18]

[16] Brownlie, *System of the Law of Nations: State Responsibility (Part 1)* 1983, 132–66; Caron, 'The Basis of Responsibility: Attribution and Other Trans-Substantive Rules', in Lillich & Magraw (eds), *The Iran-United States Claims Tribunal: Its Contribution to the Law of State Responsibility* (1998) 109; Condorelli, 'L'imputation à l'État d'un fait internationalement illicite: solutions classiques et nouvelles tendances', 189 Hague Recueil (1984-VI) 9; Dipla, *La responsibilité de l'État pour violation des droits de l'homme–problèmes d'imputation* (1994); A V Freeman, 'Responsibility of States for Unlawful Acts of Their Armed Forces' 88 Hague Recueil (1956) 261; Przetacznik, 'The International Responsibility of States for Unauthorized Acts of their Organs', *Sri Lanka Journal of International Law* (1989) 151.

[17] The *Yeager Case* (1987), 17 Iran-US CTR 101–2.

[18] See for what follows on the general principle incorporated in the Article also commentary to Article 4 of the 2001 ILC's Articles, Crawford (2002) (note 1 above) 94 ff. In the *Bosnia Genocide Case* the ICJ cited with approval this Article 4 as the basis for attribution: 2007 ICJ Reports 138.

That the State is responsible for the conduct of its own organs has long been recognized in international judicial decisions. In the *Moses Case*, for example, as early as 1871, Umpire Lieber said, 'An officer or person in authority represents *pro tanto* his government, which in an international sense is the aggregate of all officers and men in authority'.[19] There have been many statements of the principle since then.[20] The replies by governments to the Preparatory Committee for the 1930 Conference for the Codification of International Law unanimously reflected the view that the actions or omissions of organs of the State must be attributed to it.[21]

The ILC's Article 4 reflects the principle of the unity of the State which entails that the acts or omissions of all its organs should be regarded as acts or omissions of the State for the purposes of international responsibility. There is no category of organs specially designated for the commission of internationally wrongful acts, and any State organ may be the author of such an act. The reference to a State organ is not limited to the organs of the central government, to officials at a high level or to persons with responsibility for the external relations of the State. It extends to organs of government of whatever kind or classification, exercising whatever functions, and at whatever level in the hierarchy, including those at provincial or even local level. Thus, in the *Salvador Commercial Company Case*, the tribunal said that:

> ... a State is responsible for the acts of its rulers, whether they belong to the legislative, executive, or judicial department of the Government, so far as the acts are done in their official capacity.[22]

The ICJ has also confirmed the rule. In the *Difference Relating to Immunity from Legal Process of a Special Rapporteur of the Commission on Human Rights Opinion*, it stated:

> According to a well established rule of international law, the conduct of any organ of a State must be regarded as an act of that State. This rule... is of a customary character...[23]

[19] (1871) Moore, 3 *International Arbitrations* 3129.

[20] The *Chiessa Claim* (1901, Italy v Peru), 15 UNRIAA 399; the *Sessarego Claim* (1901, Italy v Peru), ibid 401; the *Roggero Claim* (1901, Italy v Peru), ibid 409; the *Miglia Claim* (1901, Italy v Peru), ibid 411; the *Salvador Commercial Co. Case* (1902, USA v Salvador), ibid 477; the *Finnish Shipowners Arbitration* (1934), (GB v Finland), 3 UNRIAA 1501.

[21] League of Nations, Conference for the Codification of International Law, 3 *Bases of Discussion for the Conference Drawn up by the Preparatory Committee: Responsibility of States for Damage Caused in their Territory to the Person or Property of Foreigners* (Doc. C.75.M69, 1929, V.) 25, 41, 52; *Supplement to Volume 3: Replies made by the Governments to the Schedule of Points; Replies of Canada and the United States of America* (Doc. C.75(a)M.69(a), 1929, V.) 2–3, 6. The Third Committee of the Conference adopted unanimously an Article 1 which provided for the international responsibility of a State as a consequence of the 'failure on the part of its organs' to fulfil the international obligation of the State: see 2 YBILC (1956) 225 (Annex 3).

[22] (1902), 15 UNRIAA 477. See also the *Chattin Case*, 4 ibid (1927), 285–6; *Dispute Concerning the Interpretation of Article 79 of the Treaty of Peace* (1955), 13 ibid. 438.

[23] The *Difference Relating to Immunity from Legal Process of a Special Rapporteur of the Commission on Human Rights Opinion*, 1999 ICJ Reports 87, para. 62, referring to the Draft Articles on State Responsibility, Article 6, now reflected in Article 4.

In that case the court was principally concerned with decisions of State courts, but the same principle applies to legislative and executive acts. As the PCIJ said in the *German Interests in Polish Upper Silesia Case (Merits)*:

> From the standpoint of International Law and of the Court which is its organ, municipal laws... express the will and constitute the activities of States, in the same manner as do legal decision or administrative measures.[24]

Article 4 of the ILC Articles covers organs, whether they exercise 'legislative, executive, judicial or any other functions'. This language allows for the fact that the principle of the separation of powers is not followed in any uniform way, and that many organs exercise some combination of public powers of a legislative, executive or judicial character. Moreover, the language is one of extension, not limitation, as is made clear by the words 'or any other functions'.[25] It is also irrelevant for the purposes of attribution that the conduct of a State organ may be classified as 'commercial' or as '*actum iure gestionis*'.[26] Of course, the simple breach by a State of a contract does not as such entail a breach of international law.[27] Something further is required before international law becomes relevant, such as a denial of justice by the court of the State in proceedings brought by another contracting party. But the entry into or breach of a contract by a State organ is nonetheless an act of the State.[28]

Nor is any distinction made at the level of principle between the acts of 'superior' and 'subordinate' officials, provided they are acting in their official capacity. Acts or omissions committed by them in their official capacity are nonetheless attributable to the State. Mixed commissions after the Second World War often had to consider the conduct of minor organs of the State, such as administrators

[24] (1926), PCIJ, Series A No. 7, 19. For other cases before the World Courts, as to legislative acts, see the *German Settlers in Poland Opinion* (1923), PCIJ, Series B No. 6, 35–6; the *Phosphates in Morocco Case (Preliminary Objections)* (1939), PCIJ Series A/B, No. 74, 25–6; the *Rights of Nationals of the United States of America in Morocco Case*, 1952 ICJ Reports 193–4; as to executive acts see the *Nicaragua Case (Merits)*, 1986 ICJ Reports 14; the *ELSI Case*, 1989 ICJ Reports 158; as to judicial acts see the *'Lotus' Case* (1927), PCIJ Series A No. 10 24; the *Jurisdiction of the Courts of Danzig Opinion* (1928), PCIJ Series B No.15, 24; the *Ambatielos Case (Merits)*, 1953 ICJ Reports 21–2. Some cases involve both executive and judicial acts: see the *Guardianship of Infants Case*, 1958 ICJ Reports 65. These cases and others will be referred to below in the discussion on the organs, and the like, of States.

[25] These functions might involve, eg, the giving of administrative guidance to the private sector. Whether such guidance involves a breach of an international obligation may be an issue, but as 'guidance' it is clearly attributable to the State. See GATT, *Japan—Trade in Semi-conductors*, Panel Report of 24 March 1988 at paras 110–111; WTO, *Japan—Measures affecting Consumer Photographic Film and Paper*, Panel Report, 31 March 1998, WT/DS44, at paras 10.12–10.16.

[26] The irrelevance of the classification of the acts of State organs as *iure imperii* or *iure gestionis* was affirmed by all those members of the Sixth Committee who responded to a specific question on this issue from the Commission: see *Report of the ILC*, 1998 UN Doc. A/53/10 at para. 35.

[27] See C F Amerasinghe, *Local Remedies in International Law* (2004) chapter 5.

[28] The decision of the European Court of Human Rights in the *Swedish Engine Drivers' Union Case*, ECHR, Series A, No. 20 (1976) 14; and *Schmidt and Dahlström,* ECHR., Series A, No. 21 (1976) 15.

of enemy property, mayors, and police officers, and consistently treated the acts of such persons as attributable to the State.[29]

Likewise, the principle in Article 4 applies equally to organs of the central government and to those of regional or local units. For example in the *Heirs of the Duc de Guise Case* the Commission said:

> For the purposes of reaching a decision in the present case it matters little that the decree of 29 August 1947 was not enacted by the Italian State but by the region of Sicily. For the Italian State is responsible for implementing the Peace Treaty, even for Sicily, notwithstanding the autonomy granted to Sicily in internal relations under the public law of the Italian Republic.[30]

This principle was strongly supported during the preparatory work for the Conference for the Codification of International Law of 1930,[31] and at the Conference itself.[32]

The Commentary to the ILC's Article 4(2) explains the relevance of domestic law in determining the status of a State organ:

> Where the law of a State characterizes an entity as an organ, no difficulty will arise. On the other hand, it is not sufficient to refer to internal law for the status of State organs. In some systems the status and functions of various entities are determined not only by law but also by practice, and reference exclusively to internal law would be misleading. The internal law of a State may not classify, exhaustively or at all, which entities have the status of 'organs'. In such cases, while the powers of an entity and its relation to other bodies under internal law will be relevant to its classification as an 'organ', internal law will not itself perform the task of classification. Even if it does so, the term 'organ' used in internal law may have a special meaning, and not the very broad meaning required. For example, under some legal systems the term 'government' refers only to bodies at the highest level such as the head of State and the cabinet of ministers. In others, the police have a special status, independent of the executive; this cannot mean that for international law purposes they are not organs of the State. Accordingly, a State cannot avoid responsibility for the conduct of a body which does in truth act as one of its organs merely by denying it the status under its own law. This result is achieved by the use of the word 'includes' in paragraph 2.[33]

[29] See the *Currie Case* (1954), 14 UNRIAA, 24; the *Dispute Concerning the Interpretation of Article 79 of the Treaty of Peace* (1955), 13 UNRIAA, 431–2; the *Mossé Case* (1953), ibid 492–3. See earlier cases cited in Crawford (2002) (note 1 above) 96, fn 119 (ILC Commentary). See also the characterization of the requisition of a plant by the Mayor of Palermo in the *ELSI Case*, 1989 ICJ Reports 50.

[30] (1951) 13 UNRIAA, 161. For earlier decisions, see the *Pieri Dominique and Co Case* (1905), 10 UNRIAA, 156.

[31] League of Nations, Conference for the Codification of International Law (note 21 above) 90; *Supplement to Vol.* 3 (note 21 above) 3, 18.

[32] Governments were expressly asked whether the State became responsible as a result of acts or omissions of bodies exercising public functions of a legislative or executive character (communes, provinces, etc.). All answered in the affirmative.

[33] Crawford (2002) (note 1 above) 98.

The principle in Article 4, as applied in particular to legislative, executive, and judicial organs and functions, respectively, and some issues connected with it are discussed herein.

(a) *The Legislature*

First, the enactment of legislation or the failure to enact legislation by the legislature of a State is clearly to be attributed to the State. The State is regarded as fully responsible for acts and omissions of its legislature at international law. This responsibility is in no way dependent on the liability of the State for such legislation, according to its internal or national law.

The principle covers the ordinary legislature of a State as well as those organs of the State which together may constitute the legislative body for the purposes of constitutional change in the State.

Support for the general proposition, which is obvious, is to be found in the arbitral decision in the *Salvador Commercial Co Case*[34] and in the *German Interests in Upper Silesia Case*[35] before the PCIJ, as seen earlier.

In the *Exchange of Greek and Turkish Population Opinion* the PCIJ said:

> Un Etat qui a valablement contracté des obligations internationales est tenu d'apporter a sa legislation les modifications necessaries pour assurer l'execution des engagements pris.[36]

This statement is particularly relevant to the omissions of legislatures.

Other international jurisprudence is not lacking in examples where a State had been held responsible for the acts of its legislature which were in violation of its international obligations. In the *Affaire de L'Impôt sur les Benefices de Guerre*[37] arbitrator Ador held that France was responsible for the act of her legislature in imposing an extraordinary tax on the war profits of Spanish nationals contrary to the Convention of 1862 between France and Spain. The question has also arisen in the case of the requisition of property,[38] the virtual annulment of contract rights in violation of treaty obligations,[39] and expropriation contrary to treaty.[40]

Legal commentators have had no difficulty in acknowledging this principle. Thus, it has been stated, the State bears full international responsibility for such legislative acts of parliament as are 'contrary to International Law and have been finally incorporated as part of its Municipal Law'.[41] Rousseau explained the position further:

> (a) Il y a responsabilité *par voie d'action* dans l'hypothése de la promulgation d'une loi contraire aux obligations internationales de l'Etat;

[34] (1902), 15 UNRIAA, 477. [35] (1926), PCIJ, Series A No. 7, 19.

[36] (1925), PCIJ, Series B No. 10, 20.

[37] (1927, France v Spain), 1 UNRIAA, 302.

[38] The *Norwegian Shipowners Claim* (1922, Norway v USA), 1 UNRIAA p. 309.

[39] The *German Settlers in Poland Opinion* (1923), PCIJ, Series B No. 6.

[40] The *Chorzòw Factory Case (Merits)* (1928), PCIJ, Series A/B No. 17. For other cases decided by the PCIJ dealing in general with responsibility for legislative acts see cases cited above note 24.

[41] Oppenheim, 1 *International Law* (1955) 359 (ed H Lauterpacht).

(b) Il y a responsabilité *par voie d'omission* dans deux hypotheses: soit que l'organe legislative n'edicte pas les lois necessaries, soit qu'il negligee d'abroger une loi contraire aux obligations internationales de l'Etat.[42]

The Third Committee of the 1930 Hague Conference for the codification of International Law adopted an Article which stated:

International responsibility is incurred by a State if damage is sustained by a foreigner as a result of either the enactment of legislation incompatible with its international obligations or of the non-enactment of legislation necessary for carrying out those obligations.[43]

The revised Draft submitted by Garcia Amador to the ILC in 1961 contained an Article in which similar ideas are expressed. The notion of attribution of legislative or constitutional measures was fully accepted.[44]

The Draft prepared by the Institute de droit international in 1927 also contained an Article which mentions responsibility for acts or omissions of the legislature.[45] The 1961 Harvard Draft defines organ or agency of a State as including 'the head of state and any legislative, deliberative, executive, administrative, or judicial organ or agency of a State'.[46]

Clearly, the authorities give ample support to the general proposition of law that the acts and omissions of the legislature are attributable to the State.

(b) Administrative Organs and Officials

As already stated, the attribution of the acts or omissions of organs or officials of a State to the State does not depend entirely on the internal law of that State but also on the concepts of international law. Indeed, there may be cases in which, according to the internal law of the State concerned, the State is not liable for the wrongs of its officials even when done within their competence or apparent authority,[47] but attribution resting on international legal principles takes place. Separate problems arise in this connection relating to the characterization of administrative organs or bodies and attribution of their acts as acts of the State.

How is it to be determined, for example, that a particular individual or organ is an administrative organ of the State? Suppose an individual purports to act as a customs officer when he is not, or suppose a minister of State purports to act

[42] Cited from Rousseau (note 1 above) 370. Sibert made a careful study of the subject and admitted the proposition: 'Considérations sur certain aspects du régime juridique des emprunts internationaux', 47 RGDIP (1940) 5. See also in accord Vitta, *La Responsabilitá internazionale dello stato per atti legislativi* (1953); Musacchia, *La Responsabilitá internazionale degli stati per fatti degli organi legislativi* (1939).

[43] Article 6, Annex 3 in 2 YBILC (1956) 225. See also in accord Basis of Discussion No. 2 before the conference, cited in Annex 2, 2 ibid 223.

[44] Article 13(1), 2 *YBILC* (1961) 48.

[45] Article 1, in Annex 8, ibid 227.

[46] Article 16, 55 *AJIL* (1961) 576.

[47] *Nadaraja v The Attorney-General* (1956), 59 New L.R. 136 (Ceylon). This was the position in the UK before the Crown Proceedings Act 1947.

officially when he has not been legally appointed; is he to be regarded as an organ of the State? Or, if certain administrative organs are not regarded as organs of the State in the internal law for the purposes of delictual liability,[48] does the determination of the internal law hold good for international law?

Perhaps, the answer in the situation where a person *usurps* office is that his conduct is not attributable to the State, so that responsibility of the State for injury flowing from such conduct will arise only on the basis of the omission of the State (ie its validly appointed organs) in not preventing the usurpation. It would not be in keeping with principle that a State should be held liable for the acts of usurpers as for the acts of its proper organs or agents. Where, however, the particular internal law attributes such acts to the State there can be no doubt that this attribution will be accepted by international law.

In the situation where organs are not regarded as organs of the State by the internal law for the purpose of internal State liability, the solution is perhaps to be found in determining what organs should be regarded as the organs of a State according to an international law concept of a State's organic functions irrespective of the attitude of the internal law. Thus, for instance, it cannot be doubted that the police organ would normally be regarded as an organ of the State as would the army, navy and air force.[49] But in principle, as held by the ICJ in the *Bosnia Genocide Case*, armed forces operating in a territory may fail to qualify as an executive organ of the State because they are neither an organ according to the internal law of that State (*de iure*) nor can they be regarded as an organ de facto. They would fail to qualify as a de facto organ of the State because they were not in a relationship of complete dependence on the State which, as pointed out earlier, is the test to be applied.[50]

The basic principle of attribution is applicable to the legislative and judicial or quasi-judicial functions of administrative organs or officials just as to their administrative functions, though much of the case law deals explicitly with the latter kind of functions. In the *Fair American Case*[51] regulations confiscating property, which exceeded the power of the executive and were invalid, were made by the Mexican government. Mexico was held to be responsible for the execution of such regulations. This case illustrates the application of the principle in relation to the legislative functions of the executive, but the principle is of general application to all the functions of the executive.[52]

[48] Under the Crown Proceedings Act 1947, Section 2(b), in England, the State was not responsible for acts of the police force.

[49] Such a concept is different from the concept of State functions used in the law of sovereign immunity to distinguish between acts *iure imperii* and acts *iure gestionis*: see Sucharitkul, *State Immunities and Trading Activities* (1959) 162 ff.

[50] 2007 ICJ Reports 139–40. Among other things, the court held that the VRS in Bosnia was not an organ of the FRY.

[51] (1841, USA v Mexico), Moore, 4 *International Arbitrations* 3369.

[52] For other cases decided by the PCIJ and ICJ involving acts of the executive see above note 24.

In the case of wrongs arising from contract, the question whether a contract between alien and State has been created does raise the question of attribution, but since this is a matter for the proper law of the contract rather than international law as such, the question whether the act of an official can be regarded as creating a contractual obligation must be answered by reference to that proper law. Here again, it is not an adequate answer that the internal law of the contracting State is always determinative. It may be that in certain circumstances the internal law of the contracting State is the proper law and then the question whether a contract between State and alien had been created by an ultra vires act of an official will be determined by that law. But it has also been found that, where the law governing the formation of contract is not the internal law but general principles of law or principles of international law, the contract may come into existence on the basis of the scope of apparent authority of the official representing the State or of ratification by subsequent conduct by the government of the State, even if there is no valid contract according to the internal law of the State.[53] However, it must be noted that the doctrine of attribution of a wrongful act being here discussed really comes into operation in regard to an act which would constitute an international wrong, if it had been committed by a State. The formation of contract does not constitute a wrongful act of this kind. The wrongful act in the case of contracts of this kind normally arises when there is a judicial denial of justice in regard to remedies or, in the absence of remedies, in connection with an alleged breach or when the alleged breach involves a breach of treaty also, or when it is by legislative act amounting to unlawful expropriation.[54] It is really in regard to acts done by administrative organs or officials which amount to breaches of international law in those circumstances that the doctrine of attribution will be relevant. In such cases the doctrine of attribution as outlined above in connection with tortious acts will apply.

(c) The Judiciary

The question of attribution in regard to acts of the judiciary is important. It would seem to be reasonable that as in the case of the previous categories, the international responsibility of the State cannot depend on the internal law liability of the State. It may be that the State is not liable according to its internal law for wrongful acts of its judicial officers.[55] Perhaps, the answer is to be found in

[53] See Meron, 'Repudiation of *Ultra Vires* State Contracts and the International Responsibility of States', 6 ICLQ (1957) 278 ff. The doctrine of unjust enrichment has also been called in aid to protect an alien where the contract was initially void because the official was acting ultra vires: see the *Parker Case* (1926, USA v Mexico), 4 UNRIAA p. 35, the *General Finance Corporation Case* (1942, USA v Mexico), *U.S. Dept. of State Publication 2859, Arbitration Series 9* 546. However, in such cases the contract is held to be void and non-existent and relief is given on different grounds according to an international law standard.

[54] See C F Amerasinghe (note 2 above) 119 ff.

[55] See the position in England: Crown Proceedings Act 1947, Section 2(5).

adopting similar criteria for attribution as are applied to administrative organs and officials.

The international case law has always admitted the attributability of acts of the judiciary to the State. That the judiciary may be independent according to the constitutional law of a State does not seem to have affected these decisions. In the *Salvador Commercial Co Case* which has been referred to earlier, it was said without distinction that, 'There can be no doubt...that a State is responsible for the acts of its rulers, whether they belong to the legislative, executive or judicial department of the government, so far as the acts are done in their official capacity.'[56] In the *Way Case* it was said, 'Under international law a nation has responsibility for the conduct of judicial officers.'[57] There are several cases in which the State has been held to be internationally responsible for the wrongful acts of the judiciary, irrespective of its liability according to its internal law. Thus, in the *Chattin Case*[58] Mexico was held responsible for certain irregularities in the proceedings of trial of a an American citizen who had been arrested on a charge of embezzlement. No question was raised as to whether the acts were attributable or not, but attribution was assumed to be in accord with the law if the illegality were proved. The same notion underlay the *Dyches Case*[59] where the Mexican judiciary was held to have delayed proceedings beyond all reason and beyond periods prescribed by provisions of constitutional law and Mexico was held responsible for injury caused to an American citizen. The PCIJ and ICJ have also approved of the attribution to the state of acts of the judiciary.[60]

In the *Yuille, Shortridge and Co Case* the arbitrating Senate of Hamburg said: 'It would be altogether unjust to make the Royal Government of Portugal account for the faults committed by its tribunals.'[61] This statement cannot be taken to mean that acts of the judiciary are never to be attributed to the State, because the tribunal did hold that the judgment of the Court of Appeal of Portugal was a legitimate ground of complaint against Portugal.[62] The statement of the tribunal is, therefore, to be interpreted as meaning that there is a presumption that acts of judges are regular so that State responsibility arises only in extreme cases. The tribunal was not commenting upon attributability but upon the actual content of a State's obligations in the field of judicial activities.

The Convention Relative to the Rights of Aliens signed at the Second International Conference of American States in 1902 also contains a reference to

[56] (1902, USA v Salvador) 15 UNRIAA 477.

[57] (1928, USA v Mexico), 4 UNRIAA 400.

[58] (1927, USA v Mexico), 4 ibid. 282.

[59] (1927, USA v Mexico), 4 ibid 458. See also the *Kennedy Case* (1927, USA v Mexico), 4 ibid 19; the *John Chase Case* (1928, USA v Mexico), 4 ibid 337; the *De Galvan Case* (1927, USA v Mexico), 4 ibid 273; the *Martini Case* (1930, Italy v Venezuela), 2 ibid 975; the *El Oro Mining and Railway Co Case* (1931, UK v Mexico), 5 ibid 191.

[60] See cases referred to in footnote 24 above.

[61] (1931, GB v Portugal), Lapradelle and Politis, 2 RAI 103.

[62] Ibid 107.

responsibility for a manifest denial of justice, among other things, and, therefore, acknowledged that judicial acts are attributable to the State.[63] The Resolution on 'International Responsibility of the State' adopted at the Seventh International Conference of American States in 1933 also contains a reference to liability of the State for denial of justice by the courts.[64] Some Asian States, such as Burma, Iraq, and Japan, have in the past expressed the view that there should be no international standards governing the acts of judicial organs, but that the standard should be determined by internal law, while other States were in favour of such standards.[65] It would seem, however, there was no denial of the doctrine of attribution as applied to the acts of judicial organs.

Legal commentators are unanimous that acts of the judiciary are attributable to the State, as appears from their discussion of State responsibility for denial of justice,[66] despite the fact that there is considerable difference of opinion on the meaning of denial of justice.

Previous attempts at codification by official bodies have implicitly, if not explicitly, admitted the attributability of the acts of the judiciary.[67] Several drafts prepared by private bodies also contain references to responsibility for judicial acts.[68]

There seems to be no doubt that attribution of acts of judicial organs to the State is generally accepted.

(d) Political Subdivisions

The principle that acts or omissions of political subdivisions, federal or otherwise, should on some basis be attributable to the State is admitted in modern international relations.

It means that federal States cannot avoid responsibility for acts or omissions of organs or officials of their political components. It also means that unitary States or federal States cannot avoid responsibility for acts or omissions of such institutions as municipalities or town councils which are instruments of government, and that States cannot avoid liability for acts of protected or dependent States.

[63] Annex 5 in 2 YBILC (1956) 226.

[64] Annex 6 in ibid 226.

[65] See AALCC, *Report of the Fourth Session* (1961) 141.

[66] See especially Freeman (note 16 above) 151; Oppenheim (note 41 above) 367 and literature there cited; Briggs, *Law of Nations* (1953) 677 ff and literature there cited; also *Eustathiades, La responsibilité internationale de l'État pour les actes des organs judiciares et la problème du dèni de justice* (1936), passim.

[67] See the Guerrero Report, Paras 6 and 7, 2 YBILC (1956) 222, Annex 1; *The Basis of Discussions*, Nos. 5 and 6 of the Preparatory Committee of the 1930 Hague Codification Conference, ibid 223, Annex 2; Article 9 of the document approved by the Third Committee of the same Conference, ibid 226, Annex 3; Articles 3 and 12 of Garcia Amador's 1961 Draft for the ILC, 2 ibid (1961) 46, 67.

[68] The 1925 Draft of the American Institute of International Law, 2 ibid, (1956) 227, Annex 7; the 1927 Draft of the Institut de droit international, ibid 228, Annex 8; the 1927 Harvard Draft, ibid 229, Annex 9; the 1961 Harvard Draft, Articles 15 and 16, 55 AJIL (1961) 576.

There are some cases in which a federal State has been held responsible for the acts of courts and organs of constituent States, though the issue of attribution was not as such discussed. Thus, in the *De Galvan Case*[69] the US was held responsible for the failure of Texas courts to prosecute the murderer of a Mexican subject, the murderer having been indicted by a grand jury but not having been brought to trial for six years. It does not matter for this purpose whether the territorial unit in question is a component unit of a federal State or a specific autonomous area, and it is equally irrelevant whether the internal law of the State in question gives the federal parliament power to compel the component unit to abide by the State's international obligations. The 1875 decision in the *'Montijo' Case* is the starting point for a consistent series of decisions to this effect.[70] The France/Mexico Claims Commission in the *Pellat Case* reaffirmed 'the principle of the international responsibility... of a federal State for all the acts of its separate States which give rise to claims by foreign States' and noted specially that such responsibility 'cannot be denied, not even in cases where the federal constitution denies the central government the right of control over the separate States or the right to require them to comply, in their conduct, with the rules of international law'.[71] In the *LaGrand Case* the ICJ said:

> Whereas the international responsibility of a State is engaged by the action of the component organs and authorities acting in that State, whatever they may be; whereas the United States should take all measures at its disposal to ensure that Walter LaGrand is not executed pending the final decision in these proceedings; whereas, according to the information available to the Court, implementation of the measures indicated in the present Order falls within the jurisdiction of the Governor of Arizona; whereas the Government of the United States is consequently under the obligation to transmit the present Order to the said Governor; whereas the Governor of Arizona is under the obligation to act in confirmity with the international undertakings of the United States...[72]

The reasons for this position are reinforced by the fact that federal States vary widely in their structure and distribution of powers, and that in most cases the constituent units have no separate international legal personality of their own (however limited), nor any treaty-making power. In those cases where the constituent unit of a federation is able to enter into international agreements on its own account,[73] the other party may well have agreed to limit itself to recourse

[69] (1927, Mexico v USA), 4 UNRIAA 273.

[70] (1875) Moore, 2 *International Arbitrations* 1440. See also the *De Brissot and Others Case* (1855), 3 ibid 2970–1; the *Pieri Dominique and Co. Case* (1905), 10 UNRIAA 156–7; the *Davy Case* (1903), 9 ibid 468; the *Janes Case* (1925), 4 ibid 86; the *Swinney Case* (1925) 4 ibid 101; the *Quintanilla Case*, (1925), 4 ibid 177; the *Venable Case* (1925) 230; the *Tribolet Case* (1925), 4 ibid 601.

[71] (1929), 5 UNRIAA 356.

[72] The *LaGrand Case (Provisional Measures)*, 1999 ICJ Reports 16. See also the *LaGrand Case (Merits)*, 2001 ICJ Reports para. 81. The same issue could have arisen in the *Breard Case*, 1998 ICJ Reports (<http://www.icj-cig.org>) where the US was the respondent. The case was discontinued before it came to judgement.

[73] See Arts 56(3), 172(3) of the Constitution of the Swiss Federation, 18 April 1999.

against the constituent unit in the event of a breach. In that case the matter will not involve the responsibility of the federal State. Another possibility is that the responsibility of the federal State under a treaty may be limited by the terms of a federal clause in the treaty.[74] This is clearly an exception to the general rule, applicable solely in relations between the States parties to the treaty and in the matters which the treaty covers.

On the other hand, there are a few early cases where acts of constituent States of a federation have not been attributed to the federal States.[75] Thus, in the *Rosenstein Case* the Rumanian-German Mixed Arbitral Tribunal held that Germany was not liable for injury caused in connection with a contract concluded by a Rumanian subject with the State of Hamburg. Similarly, in the *Ransomes, Sim, and Jefferies Case*,[76] the Anglo-Turkish Mixed Arbitral Tribunal rejected a claim based on a contract made by a British subject with the Vilayet of Andrinople on the ground that Turkish Vilayets were distinct juristic persons for whose contractual obligations the Turkish government would not be held responsible.

State practice is also somewhat conflicting. In several early instances the US has denied that it was responsible for the acts of constituent States or their organs which were in contravention of international law, while at the same time it has maintained that responsibility does exist for such acts on the basis of attribution.[77] Thus, Secretary of State Stimson wrote to the Preparatory Committee of the Codification Conference of 1929:

> The Federal Government has frequently paid indemnities for the delinquencies of the States where the States have failed to furnish protection and redress...In claims against foreign States, the United States had refused to recognize the plea that the federal organization of the respondent State was not internationally responsible for the maintenance of order and the provision of effective redress in its constituent political subdivisions.[78]

Canada denied such attributability in the *Cutting Case* but later paid an indemnity for the damage suffered by Cutting.[79]

A cogent authority in favour of attributability of acts or omissions of political subdivisions or their organs is to be found in the 1961 Revised Draft prepared by Garcia Amador for the ILC, Article 14 of which states, 'The acts or omissions of political subdivisions, whatever their internal organization may be and whatever degree of legislative, judicial or administrative autonomy they enjoy, shall be imputable to the State.'[80] Attributability of acts of constituent states of

74 See Article 34 of the Convention for the Protection of the World Cultural and Natural Heritage (1972), 1037 UNTS 152.

75 (Rumania v Germany), 7 Recueil TAM 121.

76 (GB v Turkey), 8 ibid 203.

77 See Hackworth, 5 *Digest* 593 ff.

78 3 *Bases of Discussion, Supp. 10*, League of Nations Publications 1929, 21.

79 (1934, USA v Canada), Hackworth, 5 *Digest* 561.

80 2 YBILC (1961) 48.

federal States was also conceded in the Guerrero Report.[81] Such attribution is based on the principle applicable to the acts or omissions of legislative, judicial, and administrative organs or officials of the State in general.[82]

The problem was discussed by Garcia Amador in his first report to the ILC, where he referred to two considerations which have influenced the question of attribution of acts or omissions of political subdivisions, colonies, or dependencies: namely, (i) the degree of control or authority exercised by the State over the internal affairs of its political subdivisions, colony, or dependency, and (ii) the extent to which the State concerned is responsible for the international relations and representations of the entity.[83] Emphasis on the first has led to a repudiation of attribution in regard to constituent States of federations in some cases. The second principle has been applied in determining the responsibility of the protecting State for acts or omissions of protected States.

In spite of the conflict of authority, it is generally admitted now in the case of constituent States of a federation and other political subdivisions of a State, including local government bodies, the degree of control or authority exercised by the federal State or State over the member States or political subdivisions should not determine the question of attribution. There is attribution as a matter of law in these cases.[84]

In any event, if a rule relating to political subdivisions, as determined above, is to have any useful meaning it is submitted that it must be stated as follows: a State is responsible for the acts and omissions of its political subdivisions, their legislative, administrative, and judicial organs, attribution depending on the same principles as are applicable to its own respective organs.

Exclusion of Attribution—Ultra Vires Conduct

Another problem relates to the basis on which an injury to the alien done by a person or organ which may be characterized as an organ of the State or as acting as one is to be attributed as an act of the State.

[81] Paragraph 10, 2 ibid (1956) 222.

[82] Article 14(c) of Garcia Amador's draft for the ILC, 2 ibid (1961) 48. For private drafts supporting attribution see Article IX of the 1927 Draft of the Institut de droit international: 2 ibid (1956) 288, Annex 8; Article 17 of the 1961 Harvard Draft, 55 AJIL (1961) 576. The latter draft deals also with protectorates, colonies, and dependencies.

[83] 2 YBILC (1956) 187.

[84] In the case of colonies, protected States, dependencies, and trust or mandated territories, a similar principle would be applicable. The question to be determined is whether the State being impugned is responsible for the international relations of the other entity, at least to a substantial extent. This is in keeping with the observation that:

> in a case involving a protectorate or like entity . . . one must determine whether, in addition to enjoying full internal autonomy, the entity in question has a measure of international personality and whether this personality carries with it the capacity to enter directly into international commitments with other States. (per Garcia Amador, ibid.)

Clearly, where the national or internal law attributes the injury to the State no problem arises in international law. International law can accept this attribution. When the internal law does not so attribute the injury on the basis that the act was ultra vires or some other basis, the question arises how is international law to deal with such a situation? It is clearly not essential that the answer given by the internal law be followed. The matter relates to acts of the administrative organs as well as the legislative and judicial organs and of political subdivisions.

International practice shows that there are a few cases which reflect the view that ultra vires acts of administrative officials are not attributable to the State. The opinion of US Secretary of State Bayard in the *Tunstall Case* is especially important among these.[85] The same view had been expressed by US Attorneys-General[86] and *obiter* in the *Forrest Case*.[87]

However, this older view appears to have been superseded by the more modern approach. The more modern and general rule is that acts of officials are attributed to the State, even if they are ultra vires according to the internal law, provided they were committed within the 'apparent authority' of such officials. Such terms as 'general scope of authority' and 'cover of authority' are used with the same meaning. In the *Union Bridge Company Case*[88] the appropriation of neutral property by an official of the Cape Government in the mistaken belief that it was enemy property, which was, therefore, contrary to international law, was held to be attributable to the British State in spite of the fact that the act of the official was unauthorized. The official was held to have been acting within the general scope of his duty. In the *Caire Case* it was stated that to be able to admit an objective responsibility of the State for the acts committed by its officers or organs outside the limit of their competency, 'Il fait qu'ils aient agi au moins apparemment comme des fonctionnnaires ou organs competents....'[89] In *The Jessie* it was said, 'any Government is responsible for errors in judgments of its officials purporting to act within the scope of their duties'.[90]

There are numerous other cases which support this view.[91]

It also emerges from the cases that the fact that the ultra vires acts of officials were motivated by willfulness or malice does not necessarily put such acts outside the scope of their apparent authority.[92] A fortiori, honest or bonafide mistake in the exercise of power by officials does not mean that the act or omission

[85] (1885) *U.S. Foreign Relations* (1885) 451.

[86] 22 *Opinions of the Attorney General of the United States* (1990) 64, 13 ibid (1873) 553.

[87] (Undated but circa 1885, USA v Venezuela), Moore, 3 *International Arbitrations* 2946.

[88] (1924, USA v GB), 6 UNRIAA 138.

[89] (1929, France v Mexico), 5 ibid 530.

[90] (1921, GB v USA), 6 ibid 58.

[91] See for a full survey of the cases Meron, 'International Responsibility of States for Unauthorized Acts of Their Officials', 35 BYIL (1957) 93 ff.

[92] *The Arménie* (1895, France v Turkey), 2 *RGDIP* (1895) 623; the *Baldwin Case* (1842, USA v Mexico), Moore, 4 *International Arbitrations* 3235; *The Industry* (1842, USA v Mexico), Moore, 3 ibid 3045.

necessarily falls outside the scope of their apparent authority. Thus, in *The Wanderer* the seizure of a British vessel by US revenue officers acting in violation of US legislation was held to be attributable to the USA even though the officers may have been bonafide or the statutory provisions may have constituted a likely cause of error.[93]

The conclusion has also been reached that the cases do not support the view that attribution of acts done within the scope of 'apparent authority' further depends on whether the official is a superior official as opposed to a minor one but is of general application to all officials,[94] since the defence based on the inferior rank of the official has often been rejected.[95] The cases which have been cited as authority for the contrary view are all explicable on the basis that local remedies had not been exhausted,[96] so that the question whether the ultra vires acts of minor officials done within the scope of their apparent authority were not to be attributed to the State did not arise at all.

It would appear that whether an act or omission of an official is within the scope of his 'apparent authority' must be determined by international law by reference to the facts of each case and by analogy with decided cases just as, for example, in private law the concept of the 'scope of employment' of a servant is largely dependent on similar factors.[97]

Moreover, according to the international case material, tribunals have attributed responsibility to States even where the official has acted outside the scope of his apparent authority, provided the commission of the act was made possible through means put at the official's disposal by the State and it was not possible that the alien could, in consequence of the apparent lack of authority of the official, have avoided the damage. It is also necessary that the alien, notwithstanding the apparent illegality of the act, was unable to prevent it and thus avoid the damage. This view of the law was affirmed in the *Caire Case* where it was said that, in order that unauthorized acts of officials be attributed to the State, they should have acted within the scope of their apparent authority or '*en agissant, ils usé de pouvoirs ou de moyens propres a leur qualité officielle*'.[98] There are several

[93] (1921, GB v USA, 6 UNRIAA 68; see also the *Union Bridge Co. Case*, 6 ibid 141, *The Favourite* (1921, GB v USA), 6 ibid 82. *The Jessie* (1921, GB v USA), 6 ibid 58.

[94] Meron (note 91 above) 97. See also Eagleton, *The Responsibility of States in International Law* (1928) 47 ff. Contra Borchard, *Diplomatic Protection of Citizens Abroad* (1915) 185 ff. The views of Eagleton and Meron are more accurate.

[95] See particularly the *Roper Case* (1927, USA v Mexico), 4 UNRIAA 145; the *Massey Case* (1927, USA v Mexico), 4 ibid 157, 159 and the *Stephens Case* (1927, USA v Mexico), 4 ibid 267.

[96] The *Bensley Case* (1850, USA v Mexico), Moore, 3 *International Arbitrations* 3016; the *Blumhardt Case* (1875, USA v Mexico), 3 ibid 3146; the *Slocum Case* (1876, USA v Mexico), Moore, 3 ibid 3140.

[97] See the early literature cited in C F Amerasinghe, 'Imputability in the Law of State Responsibility for Injuries to Aliens' 22 *Revue Egyptienne de droit international* (1966) fns 53 and 37, 106 and 103.

[98] (1929, France v Mexico), 5 UNRIAA 580.

other cases which support the rule.[99] The application is further illustrated by the *Mallen Case*.[100] Two maliciously motivated assaults were made on the Mexican consul in Texas by the local deputy constable. In the course of the first assault, the deputy constable, having met the consul in a street at night, slapped his face. This was regarded by the tribunal as the act of a private individual and not of an official. The second assault occurred when the consul had been arrested and imprisoned by the deputy constable who then made use of his official badge and pistol. This second attack was held to have been made possible only through the abuse of governmental means and was attributed to the US.[101] The question whether the commission of the act causing the injury was made possible through means or powers put at the disposal of the official by the State and it was not possible for the alien to avoid the damage in spite of the apparent lack of authority must be answered according to international law.

As for the views of publicists, a few of them have taken the view that attribution cannot be allowed at all for ultra vires acts.[102] The most prominent of these were Calvo[103] and Bluntschli.[104] But most writers now admit that States are responsible for the acts of their officials acting within the apparent or general scope of authority, although they may differ as to the doctrinal bases upon which they found such responsibility.[105] At the other extreme, Eagleton bases State responsibility on the 'exclusive territorial control' of the State and, therefore, argues that, since the State 'puts the agent into a position which he may abuse, and since no other State may invade its territorial jurisdiction, it must accept responsibility for the protection of other States against its agents whether within their powers or not'.[106] There is no limitation in terms of 'apparent scope of authority'.

[99] The *Mages Case* (1874, GB v Guatemala), BFSP (1873–1874) 875; the *Speyers Case* (undated, but circa 1868, USA v Mexico), Moore, 3 *International Arbitrations* 2868; the *Youmans Case* (1926, USA v Mexico), 4 UNRIAA 110; the *Munroe Case* (1926, USA v Mexico) 4 ibid 538; *The Panther* (1906, Brazil v Germany), 13 RGDIP (1906) 200; the *Way Case* (1928, USA v Mexico), 4 UNRIAA 391; the *Quintanilla Case* (1926, Mexico v USA), 4 ibid 101; and generally Meron (note 91 above) 107 ff.

[100] (1927, Mexico v USA), 4 UNRIAA 173.

[101] In the *Gordon Case* an American was accidentally wounded by a shot fired by a Mexican army doctor who was practising target-shooting with a new pistol privately acquired by one of the soldiers. Although Mexican army regulations required daily target practice it was held that the target practice engaged in was not that prescribed by the regulations but was of an absolutely different character instituted as the result of the private purchase of the pistol. The basis of the decision was that the practice was neither within the scope of the apparent authority of the official nor was it made possible by the use of governmental means (1930, USA v Mexico), 4 ibid 586.

[102] See authorities collected in Soldati, *La Responsibilté Internationale des États dans le Droit International* (1934) 55.

[103] 3 *Le Droit international théoretique et pratique* (1896) 120.

[104] *Das Moderne Völkerrecht der Civilisierten Staaten als Rechtsbuch Dargesteldz* (1878) 261.

[105] Décencière—Férrandière, *La résponsibilté internationale des états à raison des dommages subis par des étrangers* (1925) 67; Ago (note 3 above) 459; Cohn (note 3 above) 293; Starke (note 1 above) 109; Briggs, *Law of Nations* (1953) 516; Bustamante, 2 *Derecho internacional publico* (1936) 495; Anzilotti, 1 *Corso di Diritto Internazionale* (1928) 289 ff; Ch. De Visscher (note 1 above) 92; Eagleton (note 94 above) 213.

[106] Ibid.

Official attempts at codification also display a variety of views.[107]

Drafts formulated by private bodies contain references to the concept of 'scope of function'.[108]

States have also expressed opinions on this point. Among Asian and African nations in 1961 some were of the view that a State should not be held liable for the ultra vires acts of a government official when such wrongs were committed on his own initiative and in excess of his authority, while some have expressed the view that States become liable even in such cases.[109] On the other hand, in the controversy concerning the Panama Star and Herald and the La Estrella de Panama Co Ltd—where the Governor of Panama, a Colombian State, illegally suspended the publication of an American newspaper even after contrary orders were given by the president of Colombia, because he was maliciously motivated—at first Colombia denied responsibility on the ground that only the personal

[107] The Guerrero Report took the narrowest view of attributability. It did not go so far as explicitly to deny that the wrong could be attributed to the State where the official had acted outside his competence according to the national law, but where attribution was allowed in such situations the conduct had to be characterized by specific conditions or circumstances—though the latter almost equated the position to that of acts or omissions of private individuals where there is no real attribution. These conditions were enumerated as follows:

(a) If the Government, having been informed that an official is preparing to commit an illegal act against a foreigner, does not take timely steps to prevent such act;
(b) If, when the act has been committed, the Government does not with all due speed take such disciplinary measures and inflict such penalties on the said official as the laws of the country provide;
(c) If there are no means of legal recourse available to the foreigner against the offending official, or if the municipal courts fail to proceed with the action brought by the injured foreigner under the national laws (cited in Annex 1 in 2 YBILC (1956) 222).

The Preparatory Committee of the 1930 Hague Conference allowed for attribution, where the official was acting within his competence, or, if acting outside his competence, purported to act within the scope of his authority: *Bases of Discussion* Nos. 12 and 13, Annex 2, 2 YBILC (1956), 223. The Third Committee of the Hague Codification Conference in Article 8 accepted these basic ideas, although the term used to represent the idea of 'within the scope of apparent authority' was 'under cover of their official character': Annex 3 in ibid 226. Garcia Amador's 1961 Revised Draft for the ILC predicated attribution on the notion that, even if the officials or organs exceeded their competence, they, nevertheless, 'purported to be acting in their official capacity', Article 12(c), 2 ibid (1961) 47. The Draft also explicitly stated that there can be no liability where the 'act exceeding the competence of the officials or organs concerned was by its nature totally outside the scope of their functions and powers, even though they may to some extent have used the means at their disposal by reason of that position' (Article 12(3), ibid 48) or where the act or omission was 'so manifestly outside the competence of the organ or official concerned that the alien should have been aware of the fact and could, in consequence, have avoided the injury' (Article 12(4), ibid 48).

[108] Article 7 of the 1929 Harvard Draft makes liability of the State rest on the acts or omissions 'being within the scope of the office or function' of the authority concerned but makes a distinction between higher officials and minor officials and requires an additional factor in the case of the latter: Annex 9 in 2 ibid (1956) 229. The 1961 Harvard Draft, however, in Article 15 sheds this distinction and adopts the test of 'scope of function or actual or apparent authority' as determining attributability: Article 15 in 55 AJIL (1961) 576.

[109] Burma, Ceylon, India, and Indonesia espoused the former view while Japan and the UAR took the latter; see AALCC, *Report of the Fourth Session* (1961) 141.

responsibility of the Governor was involved. But later, after diplomatic negotiations, it conceded its responsibility for an ultra vires act done by abuse of official means put at the disposal of the Governor by the State.[110]

This survey of the sources shows that there has been considerable conflict in the views expressed on the basis for attributing ultra vires acts or omissions of administrative organs or officials. That there must be some attributability seems to be the modern view.

The older view that there should be no attribution where an official acts ultra vires—which is also virtually expressed in the Guerrero Report and has been supported by some Asian and African States—is untenable in the face of stronger authority. If attribution arises only where the State concerned is vicariously responsible according to its internal law for acts or omissions of officials causing injury in violation of international law, attribution would depend entirely on the internal law. Then it would be possible for a State to avoid responsibility for the acts or omissions of its officials, where the law of the State does not contemplate State liability for acts or omissions of its officials, or by reference to express legislation preventing such liability. Either of the above alternatives would leave aliens entirely at the mercy of the State concerned and would not secure an adequate balance of interests between the State and the alien. It would seem that some measure of protection against the State itself beyond that which may possibly be afforded by the internal law of the State should be available to an alien against acts or omissions of officials. Hence, some criterion which goes beyond the internal law, where the internal law is inadequate, is required as the basis of attribution.

It is equally clear that the apparently unqualified view of Eagleton that a State is responsible for all acts or omissions of officials on the basis of 'exclusive territorial control' is too extreme and is not generally accepted in State practice nor in the international case decisions, nor by legal commentators generally, nor by draft conventions.

The better view seems to be that ultra vires acts or omissions of officials and organs are to be attributed to the State, if they are within the scope of the apparent authority of the official or organ. Also the cases and some State practice go further and support the proposition that even where the acts or omissions are outside the scope of the apparent authority of the official or organ they may be attributed to the State provided the perpetration of the acts or omissions was made possible through means put at the disposal of an official or organ by the State and it was not possible that the alien could, in consequence of the apparent lack of authority of the official or organ, have avoided the damage. Legal commentators and draft conventions generally do not refer to such a possibility nor do they expressly deny it. The better view, however, favours the proposition. Further, it seems clear that no derogation from these principles is permitted where the official is a minor official.

[110] See *US Foreign Relations* (1886) 168, ibid (1888) 423; ibid (1890) 260, 272, ibid (1899) 218.

The above two principles represent good law. It cannot be said that they conflict with the policies behind the law of alien treatment by giving too much emphasis to the interests of the alien and his State. The law as it stands on this point may be stated in the form of four propositions:

(i) An act or omission of an administrative organ or official of a State is attributable to the State, if the State is responsible for the act or omission according to the internal law of such State.
(ii) An act or omission of an administrative organ or official of a State is to be attributed to the State, where the State is not responsible for the act or omission according to its internal law if it or he was acting within the scope of its or his apparent authority.
(iii) An act or omission of an administrative organ or official of a State is to be attributed to the State, even if the act or omission is outside the scope of its or his apparent authority, if the commission of the act or omission was made possible through means put at the disposal of the organ or official by the State and the alien could not, in consequence of its or his apparent lack of authority, have avoided the damage.
(iv) An act or omission of an administrative organ or official of a State is not to be attributed to the State, if it falls outside rules (i), (ii), (iii).

The conclusions reached above make for clarity and are supported by authority. They differ somewhat from the content of Article 7 of the ILC's Articles on State responsibility, which states that what is required is that 'the organ, person or entity acts in that capacity'. The meaning is not entirly clear, *pace* the commentary.[111]

An issue which had not received very much attention is whether a State is responsible for the internally unlawful acts or omissions of its legislature. The 1961 Harvard Draft appears to contain the notion that such acts or omissions are attributable if they fall within the scope of the actual or apparent authority or the function of the legislature. If this means that any invalid legislation must be subjected to the test of whether it was within the apparent authority of the legislature, in order to determine attribution, it would leave room for situations where the State would not be responsible for acts of the legislature, for instance, where it is obvious that the legislature has acted unconstitutionally. There is room for the view, however, that a State is absolutely responsible for legislative acts of its legislature, because legislation is a function of statehood which is particularly involved with its sovereignty. The power deriving from the legislative function of the legislative organs is so great that it would not be laying too much of a burden on the State to make all legislative acts of such organs absolutely attributable to the State. There are cases, in which a State had been held responsible for ultra

[111] See Crawford (2002) (note 1 above) 106 ff.

vires legislation. In *Peabody's Case*[112] imposition of taxes under an invalid law was held attributable to Mexico. Although in that case the legislation was that of a State within the Federation, the principle holds good generally.

With regard to acts of judicial organs, a qualification in terms of 'apparent authority' appears to have been acknowledged by the 1961 Harvard Draft and in the *Salvador Commercial Co Case*, though it had not been hitherto fully discussed. Such a qualification is in order. Clearly, the State cannot be made responsible for all the acts of its judicial officers. Thus, the State cannot be held responsible for the act of a judge who causes injury to an alien in his private capacity, for instance, while building a house. While this particular qualification may appear to be easily admissible, the question may be raised whether there should not be attribution, even if the act or omission is outside the scope of apparent authority of the judicial officer provided the commission of the act or omission was made possible through means put at the disposal of the officer by the State and the alien could not, in consequence of the apparent lack of authority, have avoided the damage. Thus, a judge might give a decision against an alien which is manifestly beyond his jurisdiction but may, nevertheless, employ the means afforded him by the State in his capacity as a judicial officer to give and enforce that decision, thereby causing damage to an alien which the latter cannot avoid. Should the State not then be responsible for this act? It is proper to apply by analogy the principles stated earlier and applicable to the attribution of acts or omissions of administrative organs and officials, because the policies governing the two situations are similar. On this basis there would be attribution to the State in the above circumstances. It may be concluded that the principles applicable to the attribution of the conduct of judicial organs and officers are the same as those applicable to the attribution of acts or omissions of administrative organs or officials.

Attribution of the ultra vires conduct of the different kinds of organs of political subdivisions will be on the same basis, *mutatis mutandis*, as the attribution of ultra vires conduct of similar organs of the State.

Conduct of an Insurrectional or Other Movement

Article 10 of the 2001 ILC Articles on State Responsibility deals with the special case of attribution to a State of conduct of an insurrectional or other movement which subsequently becomes the new government of the State or succeeds in establishing a new State. It states:

1. The conduct of an insurrectional movement which becomes the new government of a State shall be considered an act of that State under international law.

[112] (1942, USA v Mexico), *US Dept. of State Publication* 2859, *Arbitration Series* 9 (1942) 475.

2. The conduct of a movement, insurrectional or other, which succeeds in establishing a new State in part of the territory of a pre-existing State or in a territory under its administration shall be considered an act of the new State under international law.[113]

At the outset, the conduct of the members of the movement presents itself purely as the conduct of private individuals. It can be placed on the same footing as that of persons or groups who participate in a riot or mass demonstration and it is likewise not attributable to the State. Once an organized movement comes into existence as a matter of fact, it will be even less possible to attribute its conduct to the State, which will not be in a position to exert effective control over its activities. The general principle in respect of the conduct of such movements, committed during the continuing struggle with the constituted authority, is that it is not as such attributable to the State under international law unless for some other reason.

Ample support for this general principle is found in arbitral jurisprudence. International mixed claims commissions[114] and arbitral tribunals[115] have uniformly affirmed what Commissioner Nielsen in the *Solis Case* described as a 'well-established principle of international law', that no government can be held responsible for the conduct of rebellious groups committed in violation of its authority, where it is itself guilty of no breach of good faith, or of no negligence in suppressing insurrection.[116] Diplomatic practice is remarkably consistent in recognizing the same principle. This can be seen, for example, from the preparatory work for the 1930 Codification Conference. Replies of governments to point IX of the request for information addressed to them by the Preparatory Committee indicated substantial agreement that: (a) the conduct of organs of an insurrectional movement could not be attributed as such to the State; and (b) only conduct engaged in by organs of the State in connection with the injurious acts of the insurgents could be attributed to the State.[117]

The general principle is premised on the assumption that the structures and organization of the insurrectional or other movement are and remain independent of those of the State. This will be the case where the State successfully puts

[113] The Article also states that what is stated in paragraphs 1 and 2 is without prejudice to the attribution to a State of any conduct, however related to that of the movement concerned, which is to be considered an act of the State by virtue of other Articles (Articles 4 to 9). What follows on Article 10 reflects closely the commentary of the ILC.

[114] See the decision of the various mixed commissions: the *Zuloaga and Miramon Governments Case*, Moore, 3 *International Arbitrations* 2873; the *McKenney Case*, Moore, 3 ibid 2881; the *Confederate States Case*, Moore, ibid 2886; the *Confederate Debt Case*, Moore, ibid 2900; the *Maximilian Government Case*, Moore, ibid 2928–9.

[115] The *British Claims in the Spanish Zone of Morocco Case* (1925), 2 UNRIAA 642; the *Several British Subjects (Iloilo Claims) Case* (1925), 6 UNRIAA 159–60.

[116] (1928), 4 UNRIAA 361 (referring to *Home Missionary Society Case* (1920), 6 UNRIAA 42, also the *Sambiaggio Case* (1903) 10 UNRIAA 524.

[117] *League of Nations, Conference for the Codification of International Law*, (note 21 above) 108; *Supplement to Volume III:* (note 21 above) 3, 20.

down the revolt. In contrast, where the movement achieves its aims and either installs itself as the new government of the State or forms a new State in part of the territory of the pre-existing State or in a territory under its administration, the new regime or new State could not avoid responsibility for conduct earlier committed by it. In these circumstances, Article 10 provides for the attribution of the conduct of the successful insurrectional or other movement to the State. The basis for this attribution lies in the continuity between the movement and the new government or State as such. It does not flow from the individual acts of members of the movement, acting in their own capacity.

Where the insurrectional movement, as a new government, replaces the previous government of the State, the continuity which exists between the new organization of the State and that of the insurrectional movement leads naturally to the attribution to the State of conduct which the insurrectional movement may have committed during the struggle. In such a case, the State does not cease to exist as a subject of international law. It remains the same State despite the changes which may occur in its institutions. Moreover, it is the only subject of international law to which responsibility can be attributed. The situation requires that acts committed during the struggle for power by the apparatus of the insurrectional movement should be attributable to the State, alongside acts of the then established government.

Where the insurrectional or other movement succeeds in establishing a new State, either in part of the territory of the pre-existing State or in a territory which was previously under its administration, the attribution to the new State of the conduct of the insurrectional or other movement is again justified by the virtue of the continuity in the organization of the State to which the success of the movement has given rise. Furthermore the predecessor State cannot be held responsible for that conduct.

Article 10(1) covers the scenario in which the insurrectional movement, having triumphed, has substituted its structures for those of the previous government of the State in question. However, the rule in Article 10(1) should not be pressed too far in the case of governments of national reconciliation, formed following an agreement between the existing authorities and the leaders of an insurrectional movement. The State should not be made responsible for the conduct of a violent opposition movement merely because, in the interests of an overall peace settlement, elements of the opposition are drawn into a reconstructed government. Thus, the criterion of application of Article 10(1) is that of a real and substantial continuity between the former insurrectional movement and the new government it has succeeded in forming.

Article 10(2) of Article 10 addresses the second scenario, where the structures of the insurrectional or other revolutionary movement become those of a new State, constituted by secession or decolonization in part of the territory which was previously subject to the sovereignty or administration of the predecessor State. The expression 'or in any other territory under its administration' is included in order to take account of the differing legal status of different dependent territories.

A comprehensive definition of the types of groups encompassed by the term 'insurrectional movement' as used in Article 10 is made difficult by the wide variety of forms which insurrectional movements may take in practice, according to whether there is relatively limited internal unrest, a genuine civil war situation, an anti-colonial struggle, the action of a national liberation front, revolutionary or counter-revolutionary movements, and so on. Insurrectional movements may be based in the territory of the State against which the movement's actions are directed, or on the territory of a third State. Despite this diversity, the threshold for the application of the laws of armed conflict contained in Additional Protocol II of 1977 may be taken as a guide.[118] Article 1(1) of that protocol refers to 'dissident armed forces or other organized armed groups which, under responsible command, exercise such control over part of [the relevant State's] territory as to enable them to carry out sustained and concerted military operations and to implement this Protocol', and it contrasts such groups with 'situations of internal disturbances and tensions, such as riots, isolated and sporadic acts of violence and other acts of a similar character' (Article 1(2)). This definition of 'dissident armed forces' reflects, in the context of the Protocols, the essential idea of an 'insurrectional movement'. As compared with Article 10(1), the scope of the attribution rule articulated by Article 10(2) is broadened to include 'insurrectional or other' movements. The existence of a greater variety of movements whose actions may result in the formation of a new State is, thus, reflected. However, the actions of a group of citizens advocating separation or revolution, where these are carried out within the framework of the predecessor State, are not encompassed. Nor is the situation covered where an insurrectional movement within a territory succeeds in its agitation for union with another State. This is essentially a case of succession and outside the scope what is being discussed here, whereas Article 10 focuses on the continuity of the movement concerned and the eventual new government or State, as the case may be.

No distinction should be made for the purposes of Article 10 between different categories of movements on the basis of any international 'legitimacy' or of any illegality in respect of their establishment as government.[119] From the standpoint of the formation of rules of law governing State responsibility and diplomatic protection it is unnecessary and undesirable to exonerate a new government or a new State from responsibility for the conduct of its personnel by reference to considerations of legitimacy or illegitimacy of its origin.[120]

[118] Protocol Additional to the Geneva Conventions of 12 August 1949, and Relating to the Protection of Victims of Non-international Armed Conflicts (Protocol II), 8 June 1977, 1125 UNTS 609.

[119] See Atlam, 'International Liberation Movements and International Responsibility' in Simma and Spinedi (eds), *United Nations Codification of State Responsibility* (1987) 35.

[120] As the ICJ said in the *Namibia (South West Africa) Opinion*, 'Physical control of a territory, and not sovereignty or legitimacy of title, is the basis of State liability for acts affecting other States': 1971 ICJ Reports 54.

Arbitral decisions, together with State practice and legal commentators, indicate a general acceptance of the two positive attribution rules in Article 10. The international arbitral decisions, eg those of the mixed commissions established in respect of Venezuela (1903) and Mexico (1920–30), support the attribution of conduct by an insurrectional movement where the movement is successful in achieving its revolutionary aims. For example, in the *Bolivar Railway Company Case* the principle is stated in the following terms: 'The nation is responsible for the obligations of a successful revolution from its beginning, because in theory, it represented *ab initio* a changing national will, crystallizing in the finally successful result.'[121]

The tribunal in the *French Company of Venezuelan Railroads Case* emphasized that the State cannot be held responsible for the acts of revolutionaries 'unless the revolution was successful', since such acts then involve the responsibility of the State 'under the well-recognized rules of public law'.[122]

Likewise the possibility of holding the State responsible for the conduct of a successful insurrectional movement was reflected in the request for information addressed to governments by the Preparatory Committee for the 1930 Codification Conference.[123] On the basis of replies received from a number of governments, the Preparatory Committee of the Conference drew up the following Basis of Discussion: 'A State is responsible for damage caused to foreigners by an insurrectional party which has been successful and has become the government to the same degree as it is responsible for damage caused by acts of Government *de jure* or its officials or troops.'[124]

Other Situations

Now Articles 5, 8, 6, 9, and 11 of the 2001 ILC Articles on State Responsibility and the Commentary thereto purport to address a few other issues.[125] Apart from these Articles, there are two other situations to be considered below.

[121] (1903), 9 UNRIAA 453. See also the *Puerto Cabello and Valencia Railway Company Case* (1903), 9 ibid 513.

[122] (1902), 10 ibid 354. See also *Dix Case* (1902), 9 ibid 119; and the *Pinson Case* (1928), 5 ibid 353.

[123] *League of Nations, Conference for the Codification of International Law* (note 21 above) 116; reproduced in 2 YBILC (1956) 224.

[124] Basis of Discussion No. 22(c), *League of Nations, Conference for the Codification of International Law* (note 21 above) 118; reproduced in 2 YBILC (1956) 224. Perhaps, also, a more precise approach would require the application to the conduct of the legislative, administrative, and judicial organs of the revolutionaries, if these are identifiable as such organs, the rules discussed above which are applicable to the attribution to the State of the conduct of similar organs of the State; if not, the principles applying to the conduct of administrative organs and officials of the State are applicable.

[125] Where appropriate, the contents of this section, dealing with other situations, reflect the Commentaries of the ILC's Articles on State Responsibility on Articles 5, 8, 6, 9 and 11.

Where conduct of persons or entities not as such organs of the State are attributable to the State for some reason (see eg Articles 6 and 8 and the sections on aiding and assisting, and coercing), it is understood that the State to whom the conduct is attributed would have to be aware of the circumstances or facts which make the conduct a violation of its international obligations, if the conduct was its conduct. However, it must also be pointed out that this is not a matter connected with attribution but is part of the substantive mental element (*mens rea*, so to speak) for the existence of a violation of international obligations. Attribution as such should, nevertheless, take place. The respondent State may raise the defence that the 'mental' element is absent.

(i) **Articles 5 and 8**

Article 5 reads:

> The conduct of a person or entity which is not an organ of the State under article 4 but which is empowered by the law of that State to exercise elements of the governmental authority shall be considered an act of the State under international law, provided the person or entity is acting in that capacity in the particular instance.

Article 8 states:

> The conduct of a person or group of persons shall be considered an act of a State under international law if the person or a group of persons is in fact acting on the instructions of, or under the direction or control of, that State in carrying out the conduct.

Article 5 deals with the attribution to the State of conduct of bodies which are not State organs according to the internal law but which are nonetheless authorized to exercise governmental authority. The Article is intended to take account of the increasingly common phenomenon of para-statal entities, which exercise elements of governmental authority in place of State organs, as well as situations where former State corporations have been privatized but retain certain public or regulatory functions.

There is a wide variety of bodies which, though not organs, may be empowered by the law of a State to exercise elements of governmental authority. They may include public corporations, semi-public entities, public agencies of various kinds, and even, in special cases, private companies, provided that in each case the entity is empowered by the law of the State to exercise functions of a public character normally exercised by State organs and the conduct of the entity relates to the exercise of the governmental authority concerned. For example, in some countries private security firms may be contracted to act as prison guards and in that capacity may exercise public powers such as powers of detention and discipline pursuant to a judicial sentence or to prison regulations. Private or State-owned airlines may have delegated to them certain powers in relation to immigration control or quarantine. In one case before the Iran-US Claims Tribunal,[126] an autonomous

[126] The *Hyatt International Cooperation Case* (1985), 9 Iran-US CTR 88–94.

foundation established by the State held property for charitable purposes under close governmental control; its powers included the identification of property for seizure. It was held that it was a public and not a private entity, and therefore within the tribunal's jurisdiction; with respect to its administration of allegedly expropriated property, it would in any event have been covered by Article 5.

The fact that an entity can be classified as public or private according to the criteria of a given legal system, the existence of a greater or lesser State participation in its capital, or, more generally, in the ownership of its assets, the fact that it is not subject to executive control—these are not decisive criteria for the purpose of attribution of the entity's conduct to the State. Instead, Article 5 refers to the true common feature, *namely that these entities are empowered, if only to a limited extent or in a specific context, to exercise specified elements of governmental authority.*

Para-statal entities may be considered a relatively modern phenomenon, but the principle embodied in Article 5 has been recognized for some time. For example the replies to the request for information made by the Preparatory Committee for the 1930 Codification Conference indicated strong support from some governments for the attribution to the State of the conduct of autonomous bodies exercising public functions of an administrative or legislative character. The German government, for example, asserted that:

> when, by the delegation of powers, bodies act in a public capacity, e.g., police an area... the principles governing the responsibility of the State for its organs apply with equal force. From the point of view of international law, it does not matter whether a State polices a given area with its own police or entrusts this duty, to a greater or less extent, to autonomous bodies.[127]

The Preparatory Committee accordingly prepared the following Basis of Discussion, though the Third Committee of the Conference was unable in the time available to examine it:

> A State is responsible for damage suffered by a foreigner as the result of acts or omissions of such... autonomous institutions as exercise public functions for a legislative or administrative character, if such acts or omissions contravene the international obligations of the State.[128]

The justification for attributing to the State under international law the conduct of 'para-statal' entities lies in the fact that the internal law of the State has conferred on the entity in question the exercise of certain elements of the governmental authority. If it is to be regarded as an act of the State for purposes of international responsibility, the conduct of an entity must accordingly concern

[127] *League of Nations, Conference for the Codification of International Law* (note 21 above) 90. The German Government noted that these remarks would extend to the situation where 'the State, as an exceptional measure, invests private organizations with public powers and duties or authorities [sic] them to exercise sovereign rights, as in the case of private railway companies permitted to maintain a police force'; ibid.

[128] Ibid 92.

governmental activity and not other private or commercial activity in which the entity may engage. Thus, for example, the conduct of a railway company to which certain police powers have been granted will be regarded as an act of the State under international law if it flows from the exercise of those powers, but not if it concerns other activities (eg the sale of tickets or the purchase of rolling-stock).

Article 5 does not attempt to identify precisely the scope of 'governmental authority' for the purpose of attribution of the conduct of an entity to the State. Beyond a certain limit, what is regarded as 'governmental' depends on the particular society, its history and traditions. Of particular importance will be not just the content of the powers, but the way they are conferred on an entity, the purposes for which they are to be exercised, and the extent to which the entity is accountable to the government for their exercise. These are essentially questions of the application of a general standard to varied circumstances.

The formulation of Article 5 clearly limits it to entities which are empowered by internal law to exercise governmental authority.[129] For the purposes of Article 5, an entity is covered even if its exercise of authority involves an independent discretion or power to act; there is no need to show that the conduct was in fact carried out under the control of the State. On the other hand, Article 5 does not cover, for example, situations where internal law authorizes or justifies certain conduct by way of self-help or self-defence; ie where it confers powers upon or authorizes conduct by citizens or residents generally. The internal law in question must specifically authorize the conduct as involving the exercise of public authority; it is not enough that it permits activity as part of the general regulation of the affairs of the community. Article 5, accordingly, relates to a narrow category.

Article 8 deals with a different problem.[130] As a general principle, the conduct of private persons or entities is not attributable to the State under international law. Circumstances may arise, however, where such conduct is, nevertheless, attributable to the State because there exists a specific factual relationship between the person or entity engaging in the conduct and the State. Article 8 deals with two such circumstances. The first involves private persons acting on the *instructions* of the State in carrying out the wrongful conduct. The second deals with a more general situation where private persons act under the State's *direction or control*.[131] Because of the important role played by the principle of effectiveness in international law, it is necessary to take into account in both cases the existence of a real link between the person or group performing the act and the State machinery.

[129] Article 9, discussed later herein, covers specifically the case in which an entity or group seizes and exercises power in the absence of State organs, but in situations where the exercise of governmental authority is demanded.

[130] See commentary to Article 8 of the ILC's Articles: Crawford (2002) (note 1 above) 110–13.

[131] Separate issues are raised where one State engages in internationally wrongful conduct at the direction or under the control of another State: see below.

The attribution to the State of conduct in fact 'authorized' by it is widely accepted in international jurisprudence.[132] In such cases it does not matter that the person or persons involved are private individuals nor whether their conduct involves 'governmental activity'. Most commonly cases of this kind will arise where State organs supplement their own action by recruiting or instigating private persons or groups who act as 'auxiliaries' while remaining outside the official structure of the State.

More complex issues arise in determining whether conduct was carried out 'under the direction or control' of a State. Such conduct will be attributed to the State only if it directed or controlled the specific operation and the conduct complained of was an integral part of that operation. The principle does not extend to conduct which was only incidentally or peripherally associated with an operation and which escaped from the State's direction or control.

The degree of control which must be exercised by the State in order for the conduct to be attributable to it was a key issue in the *Nicaragua Case (Merits).*[133] The question was whether the conduct of the *contras* was to be attributed to the US so as to hold the latter generally responsible for breaches of international humanitarian law committed by them. This was analysed by the court in terms of the notion of 'control'. On the one hand, it held that the US was responsible for the 'planning, direction and support' given by the US to Nicaraguan operatives.[134] But it rejected the broader claim of Nicaragua that all the conduct of the *contras* was attributable to the US by reason of its control over them. It concluded that:

> despite the heavy subsidies and other support provided to them by the United States, there is no clear evidence of the United States having actually exercised such a degree of control in all fields as to justify treating the *contras* as acting on its behalf...All the forms of United States participation mentioned above, and even the general control by the respondent State over a force with a high degree of dependency on it, would not in themselves mean, without further evidence, that the United States directed or enforced the perpetration of the acts contrary to human rights and humanitarian law alleged by the applicant State. Such acts could well be committed by members of the *contras* without the control of the United States. For this conduct to give rise to legal responsibility of the United States, it would in principle have to be proved that that State had effective control of the military or paramilitary operations in the course of which the alleged violations were committed.[135]

Thus, while the US was held responsible for its own support for the *contras*, only in certain individual instances were the acts of the *contras* themselves held

[132] *The 'Zafiro'* (1925) 6 UNRIAA 160; the *Stephens Case* (1927), 4 ibid 267; the *Lehigh Valley Railroad Company, and Others Case*: *'Black Tom' and 'Kingsland' Incidents* (1930, USA v Germany), 8 ibid 84 and (1939, USA v Germany), 8 ibid 458.

[133] 1986 ICJ Reports 14.

[134] Ibid 51.

[135] Ibid 62 and 64–5. See also the concurring opinion of Judge Ago, ibid 189.

attributable to it, based upon actual participation of, and directions given by the US. The court confirmed that a general situation of dependence and support would be insufficient to justify attribution of the conduct to the State.

The Appeals Chamber of the ICTY has also addressed similar issues.[136] In the *Tadić Case*, the tribunal stressed that:

> The requirement of international law for the attribution to States of acts performed by private individuals is that the State exercises control over the individuals. The *degree of control* may, however, vary according to the factual circumstances of each case. The Appeals Chamber fails to see why in each and every circumstance international law should require a high threshold for the test of control.[137]

The Appeals Chamber held that the requisite degree of control by the Yugoslavian authorities over these armed forces required by international law for considering the armed conflict to be international was '*overall control* going beyond the mere financing and equipping of such forces and involving also participation in the planning and supervision of military operations'.[138] In the course of its reasoning the majority considered it necessary to disapprove the ICJ's approach in the *Nicaragua Case (Merits)*. However, it must be pointed out that the legal issues and the factual situation in that case were different from those facing the ICJ in the *Nicaragua Case (Merits)*. The tribunal's mandate is directed to issues of individual criminal responsibility, not State responsibility, and the question in that case concerned not responsibility but the applicable rules of international humanitarian law.[139] In any event it is a matter for appreciation in each case whether particular conduct was or was not carried out under the control of a State, to such an extent that the conduct controlled should be attributed to it.[140]

In the more recent *Bosnia Genocide Case* the ICJ distinguished the *Tadić Case*, citing Article 8 of the 2001 ILC Articles with approval as reflecting the law, and said, while approving of the court's approach and statement of the law in the *Nicaragua Case (Merits)*:

> 399. This provision (Article 8) must be understood in the light of the Court's jurisprudence on the subject, particularly that of the 1986 Judgement in the case concerning *Military and Paramilitary Activities in and against Nicaragua (Nicaragua v United States of*

136 Case IT-94-1, *Prosecutor v Tadić* (1999) 38 ILM 1518. For the judgment of the Trial Chamber (1997), see 112 ILR 1.

137 Case IT-94-1, *Prosecutor v Tadić* (1999) 38 ILM 1541 (emphasis in original).

138 Ibid 1546 (emphasis in original).

139 See the explanation given by Judge Shahabuddeen, ibid 1614–15.

140 The problem of the degree of State control necessary for the purposes of attribution of conduct to the State has also been dealt with, for example, by the Iran-US Claims Tribunal: the *Yeager Case* (1987) 17 Iran-US CTR 103 (see also the *Starrett Housing Corp. Case* (1983) 4 ibid 143; and by the European Court of Human Rights, *Loizidou v Turkey (Merits)*, ECHR Reports, 1996-VI 2235-6. See also ibid 2234 and the decision on the preliminary objections: ECHR, Series A, No. 310 (1995) 62).

America)... In that Judgement the Court, as noted above, after having rejected the argument that the *contras* were to be equated with organs of the United States because they were 'completely dependent' on it, added that the responsibility of the Respondent could still arise if it were proved that it had itself 'directed or enforced the perpetration of the acts contrary to human rights and humanitarian law alleged by the applicant State' (*ICJ Reports 1986*, p. 64, para 115); this led to the following significant conclusion:

For this conduct to give rise to legal responsibility of the United States, it would in principle have to be proved that State had effective control of the military or paramilitary operations in the course of which the alleged violations were committed. (*Ibid.*, p.65)

400. The test thus formulated differs in two respects from the test... to determine whether a person or entity may be equated with a State organ even if not having that status under internal law. First, in this context it is not necessary to show that the persons who performed the acts alleged to have violated international law were in general in a relationship of 'complete dependence' on the respondent State; it has to be proved that they acted in accordance with that State's instructions or under its 'effective control'. It must however be shown that this 'effective control' was exercised, or that the State's instructions were given, in respect of each operation in which the alleged violations occurred, not generally in respect of the overall actions taken by the persons or groups of persons having committed the violations.

401. The Applicant has, it is true, contended that the crime of genocide has a particular nature, in that it may be composed of a considerable number of specific acts separate, to a greater or lesser extent, in time and space. According to the Applicant, this particular nature would justify, among other consequences, assessing the 'effective control' of the State allegedly responsible, not in relation to each of these specific acts, but in relation to the whole body of operations carried out by the direct perpetrators of the genocide. The Court is however of the view that the particular characteristics of genocide do not justify the Court in departing from the criterion elaborated in the Judgement in the case concerning *Military and Paramilitary Activities in and against Nicaragua (Nicaragua v United States of America)*. The rules for attributing alleged internationally wrongful conduct to a State do not vary with the nature of the wrongful act in question in the absence of a clearly expressed *lex specialis*. Genocide will be considered as attributable to a State if and to the extent that the physical acts constitutive of genocide that have been committed by organs or persons other than the State's own agents were carried out, wholly or in part, on the instructions or directions of the State, or under its effective control. This is the state of customary international law, as reflected in the ILC Articles on State Responsibility.

402. The Court notes however that the Applicant has further questioned the validity of applying, in the present case, the criterion adopted in the *Military and Paramilitary Activities* Judgment. It has drawn attention to the Judgment of the ICTY Appeals Chamber in the *Tadić* case (IT-94–1-A, Judgment 15 July 1999). In that case the Chamber did not follow the jurisprudence of the Court in the *Military and Paramilitary Activities* case: it held that the appropriate criterion, applicable in its view to imputing the acts committed by Bosnian Serbs to the FRY under the law of State responsibility, was that of the 'overall control' exercised over the Bosnian Serbs by the FRY; and further that criterion was satisfied in the case (on this point, *ibid*, para 145).

404. . . . [T]he ICTY presented the 'overal control' test as equally applicable under the law of State responsibility for the purpose of determining—as the Court is required to do in the present case—when a State is responsible for acts committed by paramilitary units, armed forces which are not among its official organs. In this context, the argument in favour of that test is unpersuasive.

406. It must next be noted that the 'overall control' test has the major drawback of broadening the scope of State responsibility well beyond the fundamental principle governing the law of international responsibility: a State is responsible only for its own conduct, that is to say the conduct of persons acting, on whatever basis, on its behalf. That is true of acts carried out by its official organs, and also by persons or entities which are not formally recognized as official organs under internal law but which must nevertheless be equated with State organs because they are in a relationship of complete dependence on the State. Apart from these cases, a State's responsibility can be incurred for acts committed by persons or groups of persons—neither State organs nor to be equated with such organs—only if, assuming those acts to be internationally wrongful, they are attributable to it under the rule of customary international law reflected in Article 8 cited above (paragraph 398). This is so where an organ of the State gave the instructions or provided the direction pursuant to which the perpetrators of the wrongful act acted or where it exercised effective control over the action during which the wrong was committed. In this regard the 'overall control' test is unsuitable, for it stretches too far, almost to breaking point, the connection which must exist between the conduct of a State's organs and its international responsibility.

407. Thus it is on the basis of its settled jurisprudence that the Court will determine whether the Respondent has incurred responsibility under the rule of customary international law set out in Article 8 of the ILC Articles on State Responsibility.[141]

On the basis of the law as explained, the Court found that the respondent State did not, as required by Article 8, instruct, direct, or control the armed groups in issue which were not its organs. As pointed out by the Court, where control is the test for attribution, it is effective and not overall control that matters.

Questions arise with respect to the *conduct of companies or enterprises which are State-owned and controlled.* If such corporations act inconsistently with the international obligations of the State concerned the question arises whether such conduct is attributable to the State. In discussing this issue it is necessary to recall that international law acknowledges the general separateness of corporate entities at the national level, except in those cases where the 'corporate veil' is a mere device or a vehicle for fraud or evasion.[142] The fact that the State initially establishes a corporate entity, whether by special law or otherwise, is not a sufficient basis for the attribution to the State of the subsequent conduct of that entity.[143] Since corporate entities, although owned by and in that sense subject to the control of

[141] 2007 ICJ Reports 143 ff.

[142] The *Barcelona Traction Co Case, Second Phase,* 1970 ICJ Reports 39.

[143] The Worker's Councils considered in the *Schering Corporation Case* (1984), 5 Iran-USCTR 361; the *Otis Elevator Co Case* (1987), 14 ibid 283; the *Eastman Kodak Co Case* (1987), 17 ibid 153.

the State, are considered to be separate, prima facie their conduct in carrying out their activities is not attributable to the State unless they are exercising elements of governmental authority within the meaning of Article 5. This was the position taken, for example, in relation to the de facto seizure of property by a State-owned oil company, in a case where there was no proof that the State used its ownership interest as a vehicle for directing the company to seize the property.[144] On the other hand, where there was evidence that the corporation was exercising public powers,[145] or that the State was using its ownership interest in or control of a corporation specifically in order to achieve a particular result,[146] the conduct in question has been attributed to the State.[147]

It is clear, then, that a State may, either by specific directions or by exercising control over a group, in effect assume responsibility for the latter's conduct. Each case will depend on its own facts, in particular those concerning the relationship between the instructions given or the direction or control exercised and the specific conduct in issue. In Article 8, the three terms 'instructions', 'direction', and 'control' are disjunctive; it is sufficient to establish any one of them. At the same time, it is made clear that the instructions, direction, or control must relate to the conduct which is said to have amounted to an internationally wrongful act.

Where a State has authorized an act, or has exercised direction or control over it, questions can arise as to the State's responsibility for actions going beyond the scope of the authorization. For example, questions might arise if the agent, while carrying out lawful instructions or directions, engages in some activity which contravenes both the instructions or directions given and the international obligations of the instructing State. Such cases can be resolved by asking whether the unlawful or unauthorized conduct *was really incidental to the mission or clearly went beyond it.* In general a State, in giving lawful instructions to persons who are not its organs, does not assume the risk that the instructions will be carried out in an internationally unlawful way. On the other hand, where persons or groups have committed acts under the effective control of a State the condition for attribution will still be met, even if particular instructions may have been ignored.

Article 8 covers the conduct of a group lacking separate legal personality but acting on a de facto basis. Thus, while a State may authorize conduct by a legal entity such as a corporation, it may also deal with aggregates of

[144] The *SEDCO Inc Case* (1987), 15 ibid 23. See also the *International Technical Products Corp Case* (1985) 9 ibid 206; the *Flexi-Van Leasing Inc Case* (1986), 12 ibid 349.

[145] The *Phillips Petroleum Co Iran Case* (1989), 21 ibid 79; the *Petrolane Inc Case* (1991), 27 ibid 64.

[146] The *Foremost Tehran Inc Case* (1986), 10 ibid 228; the *American Bell International Inc Case* (1986), 12 ibid 170.

[147] See also *Hertzberg et al v Finland,* decision of 2 April 1982, *GAOR, Thirty-fifth Session, Supplement No. 40,* (A/37/40) 161, para. 9.1; *X v Ireland* (App. 4125/60) (1971), 14 *Yearbook* ECHR 198; *Young, James and Webster v United Kingdom,* ECHR, Series A, *No. 44* (1981).

individuals or groups that do not have legal personality but are nonetheless acting as a collective.

(ii) Article 6

Article 6 of the ILC Articles also deals with characterization of acts of an organ so as to render them attributable to the State. It states:

> The conduct of an organ placed at the disposal of a State by another State shall be considered an act of the former State under international law if the organ is acting in the exercise of elements of the governmental authority of the State at whose disposal it is placed.

This Article[148] deals with the limited and precise situation in which an organ of a State is effectively put at the disposal of another State so that the organ may temporarily act for its benefit and under its authority. In such a case, the organ, originally that of one State, acts exclusively for the purposes of and on behalf of another State and its conduct is attributed to the latter State alone.

The notion of an organ 'placed at the disposal of' the receiving State—which is an essential condition—is a specialized one, implying that the organ is acting with the consent, under the authority of, and for the purposes of the receiving State. Not only must the organ be appointed to perform functions appertaining to the State at whose disposal it is placed. In performing the functions entrusted to it by the beneficiary State, the organ must also act in conjunction with the machinery of that State and under its exclusive direction and control, rather than on instructions from the sending State. Thus, the Article is not concerned with ordinary situations of inter-State cooperation or collaboration, pursuant to treaty or otherwise.[149]

Examples of situations that could come within this limited notion of a State organ 'placed at the disposal' of another State might include a section of the health service or some other unit places under the orders of another country to assist in overcoming an epidemic or natural disaster, or judges appointed in particular cases to act as judicial organs of another State. On the other hand, mere aid or assistance offered by organs of one State to another on the territory of the latter is not covered. For example, armed forces may be sent to assist another State in the exercise of the right of collective self-defence or for other purposes. Where the forces in question remain under the authority of the sending State, they exercise elements of the governmental authority of that State and not of the receiving

[148] What follows are the explanation and commentary in the 2001 ILC Articles on State Responsibility: Crawford (2002) (note 1 above) 103–5.

[149] Thus conduct of Italy in policing illegal immigration at sea pursuant to an agreement with Albania was not attributable to Albania: *Xhavara & Others v Italy & Albania* (Application Nos. 39473–98), ECHR, decision of 11 January 2001. Conversely conduct of Turkey taken in the context of the EC–Turkey customs union was still attributable to Turkey: see WTO, *Turkey—Restrictions on Imports of Textile and Clothing Products*, Panel Report, 31 May 1999, WT/DS34/R, paras 9.33–9.44.

State. Situations can also arise where the organ of one State acts on the joint instructions of its own and another State, or there may be a single entity which is a joint organ of several States. In these cases, the conduct in question would be attributable to both or all the States.

What is crucial for the purposes of Article 6 is the establishment of a functional link between the organ in question and the structure or authority of the receiving State. Excluded is the case of State organs, sent to another State for the purposes of the former State or even for shared purposes, which retain their own autonomy and status: for example, cultural missions, diplomatic or consular missions, foreign relief or aid organizations. Also excluded are situations in which functions of the 'beneficiary' State are performed without its consent, as when a State placed in a position of dependence, territorial occupation, or the like is compelled to allow the acts of its own organs to be set aside and replaced to a greater or lesser extent by those of the other State.[150]

There are two further criteria that must be met in this connection. First, the organ in question must possess the status of an organ of the sending State; and secondly its conduct must involve the exercise of elements of the governmental authority of the receiving State. The first of these conditions excludes the conduct of private entities or individuals which have never had the status of an organ of the sending State. For example, experts or advisors placed at the disposal of a State under technical assistance programs usually do not have the status of organs of the sending State. Under the second condition there will only be an act attributable to the receiving State where the conduct of the loaned organ involves the exercise of the governmental authority of that State. By comparison with the number of cases of cooperative action by States in fields such as mutual defence, aid and development, Article 6 covers only a specific and limited notion of 'transferred responsibility'. Yet, in State practice the situation is not unknown.

In the *Chevreau Case*,[151] a British consul in Persia, temporarily placed in charge of the French consulate, lost some papers entrusted to him. On a claim being brought by France, Arbitrator Beichmann held that 'the British government cannot be held responsible for negligence by its Consul in his capacity as the person in charge of the Consulate of another Power'.[152] It is implicit in the arbitrator's finding that the agreed terms on which the British Consul was acting contained no provision allocating responsibility for the consul's acts. If a third State had brought a claim, the proper respondent in accordance with Article 6 would have been the State on whose behalf the conduct in question was carried out.

[150] For the responsibility of a State for directing, controlling or coercing the internationally wrongful act of another see Articles 17 and 18 and commentaries of the 2001 ILC Articles on State Responsibility: Crawford (2002) (note 1 above) 64, 152 ff, and below.

[151] (1931, France v GB), 2 UNRIAA 1113.

[152] Ibid 1141.

Similar issues were considered by the EComHR in a case relating to the exercise by Swiss police in Liechtenstein of 'delegated' powers.[153] At the relevant time Liechtenstein was not a party to the European Convention, so that if the conduct was attributable only to Liechtenstein no breach of the Convention could have occurred. The Commission held the case admissible, on the basis that under the treaty governing the relations between Switzerland and Liechtenstein of 1923, Switzerland exercised its own customs and immigration jurisdiction in Liechtenstein, albeit with the latter's consent and in their mutual interest. For that reason the police were not 'placed at the disposal' of the receiving State.[154]

Similar questions could also arise in the case of organs of international organizations placed at the disposal of a State and exercising elements of that State's governmental authority. This is even more exceptional than the inter-State cases to which the Article is limited. It also raises difficult questions of the relations between States and international organizations. Article 6 also does not concern those cases where, for example, accused persons are transferred by a State to an international institution pursuant to treaty.[155] In cooperating with international institutions in such a case, the State concerned does not assume responsibility for their subsequent conduct.

(iii) Article 9

Article 9 of the ILC's Articles states:

> The conduct of a person or group of persons shall be considered an act of a State under international law if the person or group of persons is in fact exercising elements of the governmental authority in the absence or default of the official authorities and in circumstances such as to call for the exercise of those elements of authority.

This Article[156] deals with the exceptional case of conduct in the exercise of elements of the governmental authority by a person or group of persons acting in the absence of the official authorities and without any actual authority to do so. The exceptional nature of the circumstances envisaged in the article is indicated by the phrase 'in circumstances such as to call for'. Such cases occur only rarely, such as during revolution, armed conflict or foreign occupation, where the regular authorities dissolve, are disintegrating, have been suppressed, or are for

[153] *X and Y v Switzerland*, 1977 (Joined Apps. 7289/75 and 7349/76), 20 *Yearbook* ECHR 402–6.

[154] See also *Drozd and Janousek v France and Spain*, (1992), ECHR., *Series A, No. 240* (1992) paras 96, 110. See also *Comptroller and Auditor-General v Davidson* (1996), 104 ILR 536–7, 574–6 (Court of Appeal, New Zealand). An appeal to the Privy Council on other grounds was dismissed: 108 ILR 622.

[155] The Rome Statute of the International Criminal Court (1998), A/CONF.183/9, Article 89.

[156] What follows on Article 9 is taken from the commentary on the Article in the 2001 ILC's Articles of State Responsibility: see Crawford (2002) (note 1 above) 114 ff.

the time being inoperative. They may also cover cases where lawful authority is being gradually restored, eg, after foreign occupation.

The principle underlying Article 9 owes something to the old idea of the *levee en masse*, the self-defence of the citizenry in the absence of regular forces:[157] in effect it is a form of agency of necessity. Instances continue to occur from time to time in the field of State responsibility. Thus, the position of the Revolutionary Guards or 'Komitehs' immediately after the revolution in the Islamic Republic of Iran was treated by the Iran-United States Claims Tribunal as covered by the principle expressed in Article 9. The *Yeager Case* concerned, inter alia, the action of performing immigration, customs, and similar functions at Tehran airport in the immediate aftermath of the revolution. The tribunal held the conduct attributable to Iran, on the basis that, if it was not actually authorized by the government, then the Guards:

> at least exercised elements of governmental authority in the absence of official authorities, in operations of which the new Government must have had knowledge and to which it did not specifically object.[158]

Article 9 establishes three conditions which must be met in order for conduct to be attributable to the State: first, the conduct must effectively relate to the exercise of elements of the governmental authority; secondly, the conduct must have been carried out in the absence or default of the official authorities; and thirdly, the circumstances must have been such as to call for the exercise of those elements of authority.

As regards the first condition, the person or group acting must be performing governmental functions, though they are doing so on their own initiative. It must also be stressed that the private persons covered by Article 9 are not equivalent to a general de facto government. The cases envisaged by Article 9 presuppose the existence of a government in office and of State machinery whose place is taken by irregulars or whose action is supplemented in certain cases. A general de facto government, on the other hand, is itself an apparatus of the State, replacing that which existed previously. The conduct of the organs of such a government is covered by Article 4 rather than Article 9.[159]

In respect of the second condition, both the situation of a total collapse of the State apparatus as well as cases where the official authorities are not exercising

[157] This principle is recognized as legitimate by Article 2 of the 1907 Hague Regulations Respecting the Laws and Customs of War on Land: J B Scott (ed), *The Proceedings of The Hague Peace Conferences: The Conference of 1907* (1920) 623; and by Article 4, paragraph A (6), of the 1949 Geneva Convention on the Treatment of Prisoners of War, 75 UNTS 135.

[158] (1987), 17 Iran-USCTR 104.

[159] See the award by Arbitrator Taft in the *Tinoco Case* (1923), 1 UNRIAA 381–2. On the responsibility of the State for the conduct of *de facto* governments, see also Frowein, *Das de facto-Regime im Völkerrect* (1968) 70–71. Conduct of a government in exile might be covered by Article 9, depending on the circumstances.

their functions in some specific respect, for instance, in the case of a partial collapse of the State or its loss of control over a certain locality are covered.

The third condition for attribution under Article 9 requires that the circumstances must have been such as to call for the exercise of elements of the governmental authority by private persons. Some exercise of governmental functions such as police functions must be called for in the absence of constituted authority, though not necessarily the conduct in question. There is a form of agency which distinguishes these situations and creates an exception to the normal principle that conduct of private parties, including insurrectionary forces, is not attributable to the State.[160]

(iv) Article 11

Article 11 of the ILC's Articles states:

> Conduct which is not attributable to a State under the preceding articles shall nevertheless be considered an act of that State under international law if and to the extent that the State acknowledges and adopts the conduct in question as its own.

The Article[161] provides for the attribution to a State of conduct that was not or may not have been attributable to it at the time of commission, but which is subsequently acknowledged and adopted by the State as its own.

In many cases the conduct which is acknowledged and adopted by a State will be that of private persons or entities.

Article 11 acknowledges the principle that purely private conduct cannot be attributed to a State but recognizes that conduct is to be considered as an act of State 'if and to the extent that the State acknowledges and adopts the conduct in question as its own'. Instances of the application of the principle can be found in judicial decisions and State practice. For example, in the *Lighthouses Arbitration*, a tribunal held Greece liable for the breach of a concession agreement initiated by Crete at a period when the latter was an autonomous territory of the Ottoman Empire, partly on the basis that the breach had been 'endorsed by [Greece] as if it had been a regular transaction . . . and eventually continued by her, even after the acquisition of territorial sovereignty over the island . . .'.[162] In the context of State succession, it is unclear whether a new State succeeds to any State responsibility of the predecessor State with respect to its territory.[163] However, if the successor State, faced with a continuing wrongful act on its territory, endorses and

[160] *The Sambiaggio Case* (1904), 10 UNRIAA. See further above on Article 10 of the 2001 ILC's Articles on State Responsibility.

[161] For what follows see commentary to Article 11 of the 2001 ILC's Articles on State Responsibility: Crawford (2002) (note 1 above) 121–3.

[162] (1956), 12 UNRIAA 198.

[163] The matter is reserved by Article 39, Vienna Convention on Succession of States in Respect of Treaties, (1978) 1946 UNTS 3.

continues that situation, the inference is to be readily drawn that it has assumed responsibility for it.

Outside the context of State succession, the *Diplomatic and Consular Staff Case*[164] provides a further example of subsequent adoption by a State of particular conduct. There the court drew a clear distinction between the legal situation immediately following the seizure of the United States embassy and its personnel by the militants, and that created by decree of the Iranian State which expressly approved and maintained the situation. The court said:

> The policy thus announced by the Ayatollah Khomeini, of maintaining the occupation of the Embassy and the detention of its inmates as hostages for the purpose of exerting pressure on the United States Government was complied with by other Iranian authorities and endorsed by them repeatedly in statements made in various contexts. The result of that policy was fundamentally to transform the legal nature of the situation created by the occupation of the Embassy and the detention of its diplomatic and consular staff as hostages. The approval given to these facts by the Ayatollah Khomeini and other organs of the Iranian State, and the decision to perpetuate them, translated continuing occupation of the Embassy and detention of the hostages into acts of that State.[165]

In that case it made no difference whether the effect of the 'approval' of the conduct of the militants was merely prospective, or whether it made the Islamic Republic of Iran responsible for the whole process of seizure of the embassy and detention of its personnel *ab initio*. Iran had already been held responsible in relation to the earlier period on a different legal basis, viz its failure to take sufficient action to prevent the seizure or to bring it to an immediate end.[166] Sometimes no such prior responsibility will exist. Where the acknowledgement and adoption is unequivocal and unqualified there is good reason to give it retroactive effect, which is what the tribunal did in the *Lighthouses Arbitration*.[167] This is consistent with the position established by Article 10 for the insurrectional movements and avoids gaps in the extent of responsibility for what is, in effect, the same continuing act.

As regards State practice, the capture and subsequent trial in Israel of Adolf Eichmann may provide an example of the subsequent adoption of private conduct by a State. On 10 May 1960, Eichmann was captured by a group of Israelis in Buenos Aires. He was held in captivity in Buenos Aires in a private home for some weeks before being taken by air to Israel. Argentina later charged the Israeli government with complicity in Eichmann's capture, a charge neither admitted nor denied by the Israeli Foreign Minister, Ms. Meir, during the Security Council's discussion of the complaint. She referred to Eichmann's captors as a 'volunteer

[164] 1980 ICJ Reports 3.
[165] Ibid 35.
[166] Ibid 31–3.
[167] (1956), 12 UNRIAA 197–8.

group'.[168] Security Council resolution 138 of 23 June 1960 implied a finding that the Israeli government was at least aware of, and consented to, the successful plan to capture Eichmann in Argentina. It may be that Eichmann's captors were 'in fact acting on the instructions of or under the direction or control of' Israel, in which case their conduct was more properly attributed to the State under Article 8. But where there are doubts about whether certain conduct falls within Article 8, these may be resolved by the subsequent adoption of the conduct in question by the State.

Acknowledgement and adoption are to be distinguished from cases of mere support or endorsement.[169] The Court in the *Diplomatic and Consular Staff Case* used phrases such as 'approval', 'endorsement', 'the seal of official governmental approval', and 'the decision to perpetuate [the situation]'.[170] These were sufficient in the context of that case, but as a general matter, conduct will not be attributable to a State under Article 11 where a State merely acknowledges the factual existence of conduct or expresses its verbal approval of it. In international controversies States often take positions which amount to 'approval' or 'endorsement' of conduct in some general sense but do not involve any assumption of responsibility. The language of 'adoption', on the other hand, carries with it the idea that the conduct is acknowledged by the State as, in effect, its own conduct. Indeed, provided the State's intention to accept responsibility for otherwise non-attributable conduct is clearly indicated, Article 11 may cover cases where a State has accepted responsibility for conduct of which it did not approve, which it had sought to prevent, and which it deeply regretted. However, it is clear that what is required is something more than a general acknowledgement of a factual situation. Rather the State must identify the conduct in question and make it its own.

The principle established by Article 11 governs the question of attribution only. Where conduct has been acknowledged and adopted by a State, it will still be necessary to consider whether the conduct was internationally wrongful. The international obligations of the adopting State are the criterion for wrongfulness. The conduct may have been lawful so far as the original actor was concerned, or the actor may have been a private party whose conduct in the relevant respect was not regulated by international law. By the same token, a State adopting or acknowledging conduct which is lawful in terms of its own international obligations does not thereby assume responsibility for the unlawful acts of any other person or entity. Such an assumption of responsibility would have to go further and amount to an agreement to indemnify for the wrongful act of another.

[168] *S.C.O.R., Fifteenth Year*, 865th Mtg, 22 June 1960, 4.

[169] The separate question of aid or assistance by a State to internationally wrongful conduct of another State is dealt with in Article 16 of the 2001 ILC's Articles on State Responsibility: see below.

[170] 1980 ICJ Reports 3.

A State might acknowledge and adopt conduct only to a certain extent, ie a State may elect to acknowledge and adopt only some of the conduct in question. Moreover, the act of acknowledgement and adoption, whether it takes the form of words or conduct, must be clear and unequivocal.

The conditions of acknowledgement and adoption are cumulative. The order of the two conditions indicates the normal sequence of events in cases in which reliance on them is placed. Acknowledgement and adoption of conduct by a State might be express (as for example in the *Diplomatic and Consular Staff Case*), or it might be inferred from the conduct of the State in question.

(v) Aiding or Assisting[171]

Where a State provides aid or assistance to a person or entity with a view to facilitating the commission of an act which would be an internationally wrongful act if committed by that State, there is a responsibility on the part of the former. Such a situation arises where a State voluntarily assists or aids such person or entity in carrying out conduct which violates the international obligations of the State, for example, by knowingly providing an essential facility or financing the activity in question. Examples include facilitating the abduction of persons on foreign soil, or assisting in the destruction of property belonging to nationals of another State. The person or entity acts or conducts itself, and the assisting State has only a supporting role. The two examples given above are of concern to diplomatic protection. The assisting State will only be responsible to the extent that its own conduct has caused or contributed to the internationally wrongful act.

The scope of responsibility for the aid or assistance may be limited in two ways. First, the aid or assistance must be given with a view to facilitating the commission of that act, and must actually do so. Secondly, the completed act must be such that it would have been wrongful had it been committed by the assisting State itself.

The situation is limited to those cases where the aid or assistance given is clearly linked to the conduct which is objectively wrongful. A State is not responsible for aid or assistance, unless the relevant State organ intended, by the aid or assistance given, to facilitate the occurrence of what constitutes the wrongful conduct and what is the internationally wrongful conduct is actually committed by the aided or assisted person or entity. There is no requirement that the aid or assistance should have been essential to the performance of what becomes the internationally wrongful act of a State; it is sufficient if it contributed significantly to that act.

It is a necessary requirement for the responsibility of an assisting State that the conduct in question, if attributable to the assisting State, would have constituted a breach of its own international obligations.

[171] This section, and the next, are based on considerations which use by anology the principles relating to the attribution to one State of the conduct of another State.

There is really no State practice on this issue in relation to diplomatic protection but it is reasonable to accept the law as stated above. The ILC has not dealt with this situation.

An illustration of this kind of attribution is that of a State incurring responsibility, if it provides material aid to a person or entity that uses the aid to commit human rights violations. Where the allegation is that the assistance of a State had facilitated human rights abuses, the particular circumstances of each case must be carefully examined to determine whether the aiding State by its aid was aware of and intended to facilitate the commission of what becomes the internationally wrongful conduct. The facilitation of human rights abuses may easily result in injuries to aliens precipitating diplomatic protection against the facilitating State.

In general it is required that the assistance not be only an incidental factor in the commission of the primary act, and that it may have contributed in more than a minor degree, if at all, to the injury suffered. By assisting or aiding a person or entity to commit what would be an internationally wrongful act, if committed by a State, a State should not necessarily be held to indemnify the victim for all the consequences of the act, but only for those which flow from its own conduct and only to the extent that its asistance contributed to the injury to the victim.

(vi) Coercion

Where a private person or entity for whose conduct a State may not usually be responsible by attribution of conduct to the State is coerced into conduct which would be a breach of the State's international obligations vis-á-vis an alien, if engaged in by it, the conduct would be attributed to the State as its conduct and the State would be internationally responsible for it.

The concern here is with the specific problem of coercion deliberately exercised in order to procure the breach of one State's obligation to another State. In such a case the responsibility of the coercing State with respect to the other State derives not from its act of coercion, but rather from the wrongful conduct resulting from the action of the coerced person or entity. The coercing State is responsible vis-á-vis the victim of the coerced act, in particular another State, which is injured through its national as a result.

In order that there be coercion, nothing less than conduct which forces the will of the person or entity concerned will suffice, giving him or it no effective choice but to comply with the wishes of the coercing State. It is not sufficient that compliance with the obligation is made more difficult or onerous. Moreover, the coercing State must coerce the very act which is internationally wrongful.

Though coercion may be narrowly defined, thus, it is not limited to unlawful coercion. Indeed, coercion could possibly take various forms, eg serious economic pressure, provided that it is such as to deprive the person or entity involved of any possibility of avoiding the impeached conduct. A State which sets out to procure by coercion a breach of its own obligations to another State in respect of the latter's nationals will be held responsible to the other State for the consequences. The ILC has not elaborated on the situation considered in this sub-section.

Conduct of Individuals and Other Entities as such

Acts or omissions of individuals, bodies, groups, or organs which fall outside those categories discussed above are not as such attributable to the State.[172] Responsibility of the State in connection with such acts or omissions will arise only as a result of the omission of the State or the acts or omissions of persons whose acts or omissions are to be attributed to the State in relation thereto. It will have to be shown in such cases that damage has been suffered as a result of an act or omission directly causing the damage. Thus, where a thief steals the property of an alien, the State is not responsible for the damage. However, if because of the negligence of police officers the thief is not punished and the property recovered, then this act of negligence is attributable to the State, because it is the omission of an executive organ of the State and the State becomes responsible for the loss occasioned by it.

Of course, the responsibility of the State will depend in each case on whether there has been a violation of international law by an organ whose conduct is attributable to the State and this will depend on the substantive law defining a State's obligations towards aliens. In terms of the doctrine of attribution, however, the above is the proper way of explaining how a State incurs responsibility in connection with acts of individuals, bodies, groups, or organs which do not fall within the categories discussed herein.

Attribution to a State of Conduct of Another State

As an addendum to the matters considered above which may be described as concerning the direct attribution of conduct, whether acts or omissions, to a State, the issue will be discussed at this point of attribution to State A of the conduct of State B for the purpose of establishing the international responsibility of State A. The rules of attribution in this regard in cases of diplomatic protection, ie resulting from injuries to nationals, are no different from those applicable to State responsibility in general.[173] Such rules relate in both cases to

[172] There is a considerable literature dealing with the obligations of a State in respect of acts of this nature, though not in connection with the doctrine of attribution: see particularly authorities referred to in C F Amerasinghe, *Studies in International Law* (1969) 244, note 125.

[173] The subject has been discussed in detail as one of considerable complexity by two rapporteurs of the ILC: see Ago, 'Seventh Report on State Responsibility' 2 YBILC (1978), Part I 52–60, and 'Eighth Report on State Responsibility' 2 YBILC (1979), Part I 4–27; Crawford, 'Second Report on State Responsibility, Addendum' (ILC, 1999) UN Doc. A/CN. 4/ 498/ Add. 1, 2–23. However, a much simplified approach is taken in the Articles on Responsibility of States for Internationally Wrongful

objective or passive aspects of responsibility in the sense described earlier in the Chapter, while being inextricably connected to the law of diplomatic protection. Much of the law discussed here is connected with State responsibility in general, while it applies as such to the case of diplomatic protection.

The parameters established for the discussion of such attribution include both mere 'incitement' by State A of State B to commit an act or omission which is a violation of international law and conduct on the part of State A adopting as its own, viz., as an 'accessory after the fact', the act or omission committed by State B after the commission of such act or omission by State B. The latter case has been discussed earlier in this Chapter in connection with attributable conduct of persons or entities. It is clear also that apart from specific treaty obligations, there is no customary law dictating as such that States must cooperate in suppressing the internationally wrongful conduct of another State which may have already occurred. In the case of incitement to wrongful conduct, it is generally agreed that this is insufficient by itself to warrant attribution which will give rise to responsibility on the part of the inciting State,[174] though there can be specific treaty provisions making incitement unlawful,[175] in which case incitement would be a breach of treaty and a violation of international law.

Put succinctly, the State's conduct under discussion would consist of (i) *aiding* or *assisting* another State in the commission of an internationally wrongful act, or (ii) *instructing* or *directing and controlling* another State in the commission of an internationally wrongful act, or (iii) *coercing* another State to commit an act which but for the coercion would be an internationally wrongful act. In the first two situations the attribution of the conduct of the perpetrating State and responsibility for it to the other State results in 'derivative' responsibility as opposed to independent responsibility which attaches to the perpetrating State. In the third situation, because the coerced State is not responsible for its conduct on account of duress or *force majeure*, the responsibility of the coercing State is an independent responsibility.

Acts of the ILC adopted on second reading and submitted in 2001 to the GA of the UN (Articles 16 to 19 and commentary thereto, which reflect the *lex lata*). The problems surrounding the subject have been discussed more recently in Padelletti, *Pluralità di Stati nel Fatto Illecito Internazionale* (1990); Brownlie, *State Responsibility. Part I* (1983) 189–192; Quigley, 'Complicity in International Law: A New Direction in the Law of State Responsibility' 57 BYIL (1986) 77; Noyes & Smith, 'State Responsibility and the Principle of Joint and Several Liability' 13 Yale Journal of International Law (1988) 225; Graefrath, 'Complicity in the Law of International Responsibility' 29 RBDI (1996) 370; and also earlier in Brierly, 'The Theory of Implied State Complicity in International Claims' 9 BYIL (1928) 42. Reference may also be made to the Reports of the ILC in 2 YBILC, Part II (1978) 98–106, and 2 YBILC, Part II (1979) 94–106. In this section the Commentary to Articles 16, 17 and 18 of the ILC's Articles on State Responsibility has been relied on *in extenso*.

[174] See the opinion of the US-French Commissioners in the *French Indemnity of 1831 Case*, Moore, 5 *International Arbitrations* 4473–75; and the *Nicaragua Case (Merits)*, 1986 ICJ Reports 129, and the dissenting opinion of Judge Schwebel, ibid 259.

[175] Art. III (c) of the Convention on the Prevention and Punishment of the Crime of Genocide, (1948), 78 UNTS 277; Art. 4 of the International Convention on the Elimination of All Forms of Racial Discrimination, (1966), 660 UNTS 195.

Two situations involving direct or independent responsibility must be distinguished. First, internationally wrongful conduct may often result from the collaboration of several States rather than of one State acting alone.[176] This may involve independent conduct by several States, each playing its own role in carrying out an internationally wrongful act, or it may be that a number of States act through a common organ to commit a wrongful act. Internationally wrongful conduct can also arise out of situations where a State acts on behalf of another State in carrying out the conduct in question. Moreover, various forms of collaborative conduct can co-exist in the same case. Thus, three States, Australia, New Zealand, and the UK, together constituted the Administering Authority for the Trust Territory of Nauru. In the *Certain Phosphate Lands in Nauru Case* proceedings were commenced against Australia alone in respect of acts performed on the 'joint behalf' of the three States.[177] The acts performed by Australia involved both 'joint' conduct of several States and day-to-day administration of a territory by one State acting on behalf of the other States as well as on its own behalf. There would have been independent responsibility on the part of all three States in this case. In cases of collaborative conduct by States responsibility will be determined according to the principle of independent responsibility not of derivative responsibility.

The second case to be distinguished is the case where the wrongfulness of a State's conduct depends on the independent action of another State. A State may engage in conduct in a situation where another State is involved and the conduct of the other State may be relevant or even decisive in assessing whether the first State has breached its own international obligations and incurs, nevertheless, a direct independent responsibility and not a derivative one. For example, in the *Soering Case* the ECHR held that the proposed extradition of a person to a State not party to the European Convention on Human Rights where he was likely to suffer inhuman or degrading treatment or punishment involved a breach of Article 3 of the Convention by the extraditing State.[178] A similar case of independent responsibility arises where a State is secured by its own international obligations to prevent certain conduct by another State, or at least to prevent the harm that would flow from such conduct. Thus, the basis of responsibility in the *Corfu Channel Case* was Albania's failure to warn the UK of the presence of mines in Albanian waters which had been laid by a third State.[179] Albania's responsibility in the circumstances was original and independent and not derived from the wrongfulness of the conduct of any other State.

[176] See the articles cited in footnote 173 above.

[177] *Certain Phosphate Lands in Naura Case* 1992 ICJ Reports 258. See also the separate opinion of Judge Shahabuddeen, ibid 284.

[178] ECHR Series A, No. 161 (1989) 33–6. See also the *Cruz Varas Case*, ECHR Series A, No. 201 (1991) 28; The *Vilvarajah Case*, ECHR, Series A, No. 215 (1991) 37.

[179] *Corfu Channel Case (Merits)*, 1949 ICJ Reports 22.

Apart from these two kinds of cases, there are cases where conduct of the organ of one State, not acting as an organ or agent of another State, is nonetheless attributable to the latter State, and this may be so even though the wrongfulness of the conduct lies, or at any rate primarily lies, in a breach of the international obligations of the former. These are the three cases referred to earlier in this section. Such cases have all arisen, as far as the sources go, in the post-1914 era.

(i) Aiding or Assisting

Article 16 of the ILC's Articles on State Responsibility states:

> A State which aids or assists another State in the commission of an internationally wrongful act by the latter is internationally responsible for doing so if:
>
> (a) that State does so with knowledge of the circumstances of the internationally wrongful act; and
> (b) the act would be internationally wrongful if committed by that State.

As explained earlier in connection with attribution to a State of the conduct of persons or entities, where aid or assistance is provided, the content of Paragraph (a) is properly not relevant to attribution as such. This element is, therefore, not discussed here.

Where one State provides aid or assistance to another with a view to facilitating the commission of an internationally wrongful act by the latter, there is a derivative responsibility on the part of the former.[180] Such situations arise where a State voluntarily assists or aids another State in carrying out conduct which violates the international obligations of the latter, for example, by knowingly providing an essential facility or financing the activity in question. Other examples include providing means for the closing of an international waterway, facilitating the abduction of persons on foreign soil, or assisting in the destruction of property belonging to nationals of a third country. The State primarily responsible in each case is the acting State, and the assisting State has only a supporting role. The last two examples are of concern to diplomatic protection. The situation of aid or assistance is to be distinguished from that of co-perpetrators or co-participants in an internationally wrongful act. The assisting State will only be responsible to the extent that its own conduct has caused or contributed to the internationally wrongful act. Thus in cases where that internationally wrongful act would clearly have occurred in any event, the responsibility of the assisting State will not extend to compensating for the act itself.

The scope of responsibility for the aid or assistance requires that the aid or assistance be given with a view to facilitating the commission of the impugned act, and must actually do so; and that the completed act must be such that it would have been wrongful had it been committed by the assisting State itself.

[180] See Crawford (2002) (note 1 above) 148 ff.

The fact that the aid or assistance must be given with a view to facilitating the commission of the wrongful act, and must actually do so limits the application of the Article to those cases where the aid or assistance given is clearly linked to the subsequent wrongful conduct. A State is not responsible for aid or assistance, unless the relevant State organ intended, by the aid or assistance given, to facilitate the occurrence of the wrongful conduct and the internationally wrongful conduct is actually engaged in by the aided or assisted State. There is no requirement that the aid or assistance should have been essential to the performance of the internationally wrongful act; it is sufficient if it contributed significantly to that act.

Moreover, the aid or assistance must result in the breach of obligations by which the aiding or assisting State is itself bound. An aiding or assisting State may not deliberately procure the breach by another State of an obligation by which both States are bound; a State cannot do by another what it cannot do by itself. On the other hand, a State is not bound by obligations of another State vis-à-vis third States.[181] Correspondingly, a State is free to act for itself in a way which is inconsistent with obligations of another State vis-à-vis third States. Any question of responsibility in such cases will be a matter for the State to whom assistance is provided vis-à-vis the injured State. Thus, it is a necessary requirement for the responsibility of an assisting State that the conduct in question, if attributable to the assisting State, would have constituted a breach of its own international obligations.

The meagre State practice that there is supports assigning international responsibility to a State which deliberately participates in the internationally wrongful conduct of another through the provision of aid or assistance, in circumstances where the obligation breached is equally opposable to the assisting State. For example, in 1984 Iran protested against the supply of financial and military aid to Iraq by the United Kingdom, which allegedly included chemical weapons used in attacks against Iranian troops, on the ground that the assistance was facilitating acts of aggression by Iraq. The British government denied both the allegation that it had chemical weapons and that it had supplied them to Iraq.[182] In 1998, a similar allegation surfaced that Sudan had assisted Iraq to manufacture chemical weapons by allowing Sudanese installations to be used by Iraqi technicians for steps in the production of nerve gas. The allegation was denied by Iraq's representative to the United Nations.[183]

[181] See Articles 34 and 35 of the Vienna Convention on the Law of Treaties, 1155 UNTS 331, which reflect this principle.

[182] See *New York Times*, 5 March 1984, A3, col. 1 and ibid., 6 March 1984, A1, col. 1.

[183] See ibid, Aug. 26, 1998, A8, col. 1. See also 20 *ZAORV* (1960) 663–4. In the 1986 Tripoli bombing incident involving US armed action against Libya, the UK had allowed several of its air bases to be used for the launching of US fighter planes to attack Libyan targets. The UK was accused by Libya of being 'partly responsible' for having 'supported and contributed in a direct way' to the raid. The UK denied responsibility on the basis that the raid by the US was lawful as an act of self-defence against Libyan terrorist attacks on American targets. A proposed SC resolution concerning

Another example is that of a State incurring responsibility, if it provides material aid to a State that uses the aid to commit human rights violations. In this respect, the UNGA has called on member States in a number of cases to refrain from supplying arms and other military assistance to countries found to be committing serious human rights violations.[184] Where the allegation is that the assistance of a State had facilitated human rights abuses by another State the particular circumstances of each case must be carefully examined to determine whether the aiding State by its aid was aware of and intended to facilitate the commission of the internationally wrongful conduct. The facilitation of human rights abuses may easily result in injuries to aliens precipitating diplomatic protection against the facilitating State.

In accordance with Article 16, the assisting State is responsible for its own act in deliberately assisting another State to breach an international obligation by which they are both bound. It is not responsible, as such, for the act of the assisted State. In some cases this may be a distinction without a difference: where the assistance is a necessary element in the wrongful act in absence of which it could not have occurred, the injury suffered can be concurrently attributed to the assisting and the acting State. In other cases, however, the difference may be very material: the assistance may have been only an incidental factor in the commission of the primary act, and may have contributed only to a minor degree, if at all, to the injury suffered. By assisting another State to commit an internationally wrongful act, a State should not necessarily be held to indemnify the victim for all the consequences of the act, but only for those which flow from its own conduct and only to the extent that its assistance contributed to the injury to the victim.[185]

(ii) Direction and Control

Article 17 of the ILC's Articles on State Responsibility states:

> A State which directs and controls another State in the commission of an internationally wrongful act by the latter is internationally responsible for that act if:
>
> (a) that State does so with the knowledge of the circumstances of the internationally wrongful act; and
>
> (b) the act would be internationally wrongful if committed by that State.

the attack was vetoed but the UNGA issued a resolution condemning the 'military attack' as 'a violation of the Charter of the United Nations and of international law', and calling upon all States 'to refrain from extending any assistance or facilities for perpetrating acts of aggression against the Libyan Arab Jamahiriya': on this incident and its sequel in the UN see USA, *Department of the State Bulletin*, No. 2111, June 1986, 8; the statement of Ambassador Hamed Houdeiry, Libyan People's Bureau, Paris, *The Times*, 16 April 1986, 6, col. 7; the statement of Mrs Margaret Thatcher, Prime Minister, UK, cited in 57 BYIL (1986) 638; GA Rs. 41/38 of 20 Nov. 1986, paras 1, 3.

[184] See Report of the Economic and Social Council, Report of the Third Committee of the General Assembly, Draft Rs. XVII, Dec. 14, 1982, UN Doc. A/ 37/ 745, 50.

[185] See Article 47 of the ILC's Articles on State Responsibility (2001), Crawford (2002) (note 1 above) 70–1, 272–5.

A State which directs and controls another in the commission of an internationally wrongful act is responsible for the act itself, since it controlled and directed the act in its entirety.[186] As pointed out in the previous sub-section in the case of aid and assistance, the element of knowledge is not relevant to attribution as such.

Some examples of international responsibility flowing from the exercise of direction and control over the commission of a wrongful act by another State are now largely of historical significance. International dependency relationships such as 'suzerainty' or 'protectorate' warranted treating the dominant State as internationally responsible for conduct formally attributable to the dependent State. For example, in the *Rights of Nationals of the United States in Morocco Case*,[187] France commenced proceedings under the Optional Clause of the ICJ Statute in respect of a dispute concerning the rights of the US nationals in Morocco under French protectorate. The United States objected that any eventual judgment might not be considered as binding upon Morocco, which was not a party to the proceedings. France confirmed that it was acting both in its own name and as the protecting power over Morocco, with the result that the court's judgment would be binding both on France and on Morocco,[188] and the case proceeded on that basis.[189] The court's judgment concerned questions of the responsibility of France in respect of the conduct of Morocco which were raised both by the application and by the US counter-claim.

Now, however, older dependency relationships have generally been terminated. Such links that there are do not involve a legal right to direct and control. In cases of representation the represented entity remains responsible for its own international obligations, even though diplomatic communications may be channeled through another State. The representing State in such cases does not, merely because it is the channel through which communications pass, assume any responsibility for their content. Even earlier, in the *British Claims in the Spanish Zone of Morocco Case* the arbitral tribunal affirmed that 'the responsibility of the protecting State…proceeds from the fact that the protecting State alone represents the protected territory in its international relations', and that the protecting State is answerable 'in place of the protected State'.[190] The principal concern in the arbitration was to ensure that, in the case of a protectorate which put an end to direct international relations by the protected State, international responsibility for wrongful acts committed by the protected State was not erased to the detriment of third States injured by the wrongful conduct. The acceptance

[186] In the case of aiding and assisting, the State which aids and assists, by contrast, incurs international responsibility only to the extent of the aid or assistance.

[187] 1952 ICJ Reports 176.

[188] 1 *ICJ Pleadings, Rights of Nationals of the United States in Morocco* 235; 2 ibid 431–3. The US thereupon withdrew its preliminary objection: 2 ibid 434.

[189] 1952 ICJ Reports 179.

[190] (1925), 2 UNRIAA 649, 648.

by the protecting State to answer in place of the protected State was viewed as an appropriate means of avoiding that danger.[191] The justification for such an acceptance was not based on the relationship of 'representation' as such but on the fact that the protecting State was in virtually total control over the protected State. It was not merely acting as a channel of communication.

Other relationships of dependency, such as dependent territories, fall entirely outside the scope of this Article, which deals only with the responsibility of one State for the conduct of another State. In most relationships of dependency between one territory and another, the dependent territory, even if it may possess some international personality, is not a State. Even in cases where a component unit of a federal State enters into treaties or other international legal relations in its own right (and not by delegation from the federal State), the component unit is not itself a State in international law.[192]

Nonetheless, instances exist or can be envisaged where one State exercises the power to direct and control the activities of another State, whether by treaty or as a result of a military occupation or for some other reason. For example, during the belligerent occupation of Italy by Germany in the Second World War, it was generally acknowledged that the Italian police in Rome operated under the control of the occupying Power. Thus the protest by the Holy See in respect of wrongful acts committed by Italian police who forcibly entered the Basilica of St Paul in Rome in February 1944 asserted the responsibility of the German authorities.[193] In such cases the occupying State is responsible for acts of the occupied State which it directs and controls.

The Article is limited to cases where a dominant State actually directs and controls conduct which is a breach of an international obligation of the dependent State. International tribunals have consistently refused to infer responsibility on the part of a dominant State merely because the latter may have the power to interfere in matters of administration internal to a dependent State, if that power is not exercised in the particular case. In the *Robert E Brown Case*, for example, the arbitral tribunal held that the authority of Great Britain, as suzerain over the South African Republic prior to the Boer War, 'fell far short of what would be required to make her responsible for the wrong inflicted upon Brown'.[194] It went on to deny that Great Britain possessed power to interfere in matters of internal administration and continued that there was no evidence 'that Great Britain ever did undertake to interfere in this way'.[195] Accordingly the relation of suzerainty

[191] Ibid.

[192] The federal State above is the international person responsible internationally for the conduct of its component units which have no international personality: see the *La Grand Case (Provisional Measures)*, 1999 ICJ Reports 16.

[193] See Ago, 'L'occupazione bellica di Roma e il Trattato lateranense' 2 *Comunicazioni e studi* (1949) 167–8.

[194] (1923, USA v GB), 6 UNRIAA 130.

[195] Ibid 131.

'did not operate to render Great Britain liable for the acts complained of'.[196] In the *Heirs of the Duc de Guise Case*, the Franco-Italian Conciliation Commission held that Italy was responsible for a requisition carried out by Italy in Sicily at a time when it was under Allied occupation. Its decision was not based on the absence of Allied power to requisition the property, or to stop Italy from doing so. Rather the majority pointed to the absence in fact of any 'intermeddling on the part of the Commander of the Occupation forces or any Allied authority calling for the requisition decrees'.[197] The mere fact that a State may have *power* to exercise direction and control over another State in some field is not by itself a sufficient basis for attributing to it any wrongful acts of the latter State in that field.[198]

It has been pointed out that:

> In the formulation of Article 17, the term 'controls' refers to cases of domination over the commission of wrongful conduct and not simply the exercise of oversight, still less mere influence or concern. Similarly the word 'directs' does not encompass mere incitement or suggestion but rather connotes actual direction of an operative kind. Both direction and control must be exercised over the wrongful conduct in order for a dominant State to incur responsibility. The choice of the expression, common in English, '*direction and control*', raised some problems in other languages, owing in particular to the ambiguity of the term '*direction*' which may imply, as is the case in French, complete power, whereas it does not have this implication in English.[199]

As is reflected in the Article, it has also to be shown that the completed act would have been wrongful had it been committed by the directing and controlling State itself. The essential principle is that a State should not be able to do through another what it could not do itself. Further, it is no excuse for the directing State to show that the directed State was a willing or even enthusiastic participant in the internationally wrongful conduct, if in fact the conditions laid down in the Article are met.

(iii) Coercion of Another State

The third case of derived responsibility is that of coercion of one State by another. The concern here is with the specific problem of coercion deliberately exercised in order to procure the breach of one State's obligation to a third State. In such a case the responsibility of the coercing State with respect to the third State derives

[196] Ibid.

[197] (1951), 13 UNRIAA 161. See also, in another context, *Drodz & Janousek v France & Spain*, ECHR, Series A, No. 240 (1992) and *Iribarne Pérez v France*, ECHR, Series A, No. 325-C (1995) 62–63.

[198] It may be that the fact of the dependence of one State upon another is relevant in terms of the burden of proof, since the mere existence of a formal State apparatus does not exclude the possibility that control was exercised in fact by an occupying Power; see the *Restitution of Household Effects Belonging to Jews Deported from Hungary Case* (1965), 44 ILR 340–342, an action brought in a German court.

[199] Crawford (2002) (note 1 above) 154 (commentary Article 17).

not from its act of coercion, but rather from the wrongful conduct resulting from the action of the coerced State. On the one hand, responsibility for the coercion itself is that of the coercing State vis-à-vis the coerced State. On the other hand, the coercing State is responsible vis-à-vis the victim of the coerced act, in particular a third State which is injured as a result. It is to be noted that in this case the responsibility of the coercing State is not dependent on the responsibility of the coerced State, though it is described as derived. It is a derived responsibility in that it is indirect.

In order that there be coercion, nothing less than conduct which forces the will of the coerced State will suffice, giving it no effective choice but to comply with the wishes of the coercing State. It is not sufficient that compliance with the obligation is made more difficult or onerous, or that the acting State is assisted or directed in its conduct. Moreover, the coercing State must coerce the very act which is internationally wrongful. It is not enough that the consequences of the coerced act merely make it more difficult for the coerced State to comply with the obligation.

Though coercion may be narrowly defined, thus, it is not limited to unlawful coercion. As a practical matter, now most cases of coercion meeting the requirements will be unlawful, eg because they involve a threat or use of force contrary to the Charter of the United Nations, or because they involved intervention, ie coercive interference, in the affairs of another State. However, coercion could possibly take other forms, eg serious economic pressure, provided that it is such as to deprive the coerced State of any possibility of conforming with the obligation breached.

Coercion is equated to *force majeure* which is a defence to State responsibility. This means that in cases of coercion under consideration the responsibility of the coerced State will be precluded vis-à-vis the injured third State. Therefore, the act perpetrated by the coerced State cannot be described as an internationally wrongful act by that State. Although the coerced State commits no international wrong, the coercing State does so. It is doubtful whether coercion not amounting to *force majeure* can create a derived responsibility for the coercing State or release the 'coerced' State from responsibility.

A State which sets out to procure by coercion a breach of another State's obligations to a third State will be held responsible to the third State for the consequences, regardless of whether the coercing State is also bound by the obligation in question. If this were not so, the injured State would potentially be deprived of any redress, because the acting State can rely on *force majeure* as a circumstance precluding wrongfulness. Thus, in the case of coercion there is no allowance for an exemption from responsibility for the act of the coerced State in circumstances where the coercing State itself is not bound by the international obligations as such.

State practice lends some support to the principle that a State bears responsibility for the internationally wrongful conduct of another State which it coerces, though mostly in a negative manner. In the *Romano-Americana Case*, the claim of the US government in respect of the destruction of certain oil storage and other facilities owned by an American company on the orders of the Romanian government during the First World War was originally addressed to the British government. At the time the facilities were destroyed, Romania was at war with Germany, which was preparing to invade the country, and the US claimed that the Romanian authorities had been *compelled* by Great Britain to take the measures in question. In support of its claim, the US government argued that the circumstances of the case revealed 'a situation where a strong belligerent for a purpose primarily its own arising from its defensive requirements at sea, compelled a weaker Ally to acquiesce in an operation which it carried out in the territory of that Ally'.[200] The British government denied responsibility, asserting that its influence over the conduct of the Romanian authorities 'did not in any way go beyond the limits of persuasion and good counsel as between governments associated in a common cause'.[201] The point of disagreement between the governments of the US and of Great Britain was not as to the responsibility of a State for the conduct of another State which it has coerced, but rather the existence of *coercion* in the particular circumstances of the case.[202]

Article 18 of the ILC's Articles on State Responsibility thus states:

> A State which coerces another State to commit an act is internationally responsible for that act if:
>
> (a) the act would, but for the coercion, be an internationally wrongful act of the coerced State; and
>
> (b) the coercing State does so with knowledge of the circumstances of the act.

In this case also, the issue of knowledge does not affect attribution, though it is relevant to responsibility.

(iv) Caveats

The law as considered in the three preceding subsections does not dispense with the responsibility of the State which has committed the internationally wrongful act, albeit with the aid or assistance, under the instruction or direction and control, or subject to the coercion of another State under the general law. International responsibility attributed to an assisting, directing, or coercing State does not preclude the responsibility of the assisted, directed, or coerced State, as such. The law is, thus, without prejudice to any other basis for establishing the responsibility of the assisting, directing, or coercing State under any rule of international law defining particular conduct as wrongful. Moreover,

[200] Note from the US Embassy in London, 1925, in Hackworth, 5 *Digest* 702.

[201] Note from the British Foreign Office, dated July 5, 1928, Hackworth, 5 ibid 704.

[202] For a different example involving the coercion of a breach of contract in circumstances amounting to a denial of justice see Bouvé, 'Russia's liability in tort for Persia's breach of contract' 6 *AJIL* (1912) 389.

the responsibility of any other State than the States involved in the impeached conduct, to whom the internationally wrongful conduct might also be attributable under other provisions of the law, is preserved. Any contrary inference in respect of responsibility which may arise from primary rules, precluding certain forms of assistance or from acts otherwise attributable to any State under the law is to be avoided. This is so for both the implicated and the acting State. The law of attribution considered in this section is concerned only with situations in which the act lying at the origin of the wrong is an act committed by one State and not by the other. If both States can be shown to have committed the act, then that situation would fall within the realm of co-perpetration, and there would be no derived or indirect responsibility.[203]

[203] See Article 19 of the ILC's Articles on State Responsibility.

15

Remedies

As a consequence of a State's violation of international law in respect of an alien, the alien's national State may take a course of action in response. This course of action may involve asserting rights by way of remedy which do not directly impose the obligation to act on the part of the responsible State. Thus, for example, if the violation of international law is a material breach of treaty which specifies obligations of the host State in respect of the alien, the national State of the alien may as a legal consequence terminate or suspend the treaty in whole or in part.[1] As another example of action by the national State may be mentioned the exercise of the right of reprisal or retaliation short of the use of force. Acts of reprisal or retaliation (countermeasures) could be in other circumstances a violation of the host State's rights but, when they result upon a wrong done by the host State, it is a remedial action permitted by the law. The law governing such countermeasures is based on the same principles as govern countermeasures in the general law of State responsibility. Reference is made to the law relating to such countermeasures later in this chapter.

Such courses of action aside, the international wrong committed by the responsible or host State generates an international responsibility which causes the legal relationship between it and the national State of the alien to change, so that the latter could require the responsible or host State to take certain remedial measures. These remedial measures stem from State responsibility and are reflected in the general law of State responsibility. It is to be noted in this context that the ILC does not deal with remedial measures as such in its Articles on Diplomatic Protection but has left these as to be found in its Draft Articles on State Responsibility, even though much of the material considered relevant to remedies in the law of State responsibility in general is to be found in cases of diplomatic protection. However, there are some special matters of interest to diplomatic protection of aliens which will be discussed later in this Chapter. Suffice it here to deal generally with the remedies available to the national State of the alien vis-à-vis the host or responsible State. Certain general principles applicable to State responsibility in general are relevant to diplomatic protection as a result of the violation of international rules relating to the treatment of aliens.

[1] 1969 Vienna Convention on the Law of Treaties, Article 60: see 1155 UNTS 331.

Continuing Duty of Performance, Cessation, and Non-repetition

The first set of general principles are those relating to (i) the continuing duty of the respondent or host State (the responsible State) to perform the obligation breached regardless of other legal consequences of the internationally wrongful act;[2] (ii) the obligation of the responsible State to cease the wrongful act if it is continuing;[3] and (iii) the obligation of the responsible State to offer appropriate assurances and guarantees of non-repetition, if circumstances so require.[4]

As to (i), the principle is that the legal consequences of an internationally wrongful act do not affect the continuing duty of the responsible State to perform the obligation which has been breached. A result of the violation of international law is that a new set of legal relations is established between the responsible State and the national State of the alien. However, the new relationship does not wipe out the pre-existing legal relation established by the primary norms. Even if the responsible State complies with the principles that it must cease the wrongful conduct and must make full reparation for the injury, it is not relieved thereby of performing the obligation breached, as long as the breach of the primary

[2] Article 29 of the ILC's Articles on State Responsibility (2001): Crawford, *The International Law Commission's Articles on State Responsibility* (2002) 67, 194–5.

The ILC's Articles on State Responsibility and the commentary thereto, where relevant, have been relied on extensively and generously in this chapter, because the reasoning in them is sensible, and they reflect and clarify the current *lex lata*, or interpret it, in an acceptable manner.

The work of the UNCC cited in what follows relates to damage to property by an invading State in time of war. It is relevant where it incorporates general principles of law, especially concerning valuation of property, which are applicable in the areas of remedies in the law of (diplomatic) protection of nationals abroad as such.

The reports of two Special Rapporteurs of the ILC, Arangio-Ruiz and Crawford, on remedies in the law of State responsibility, may also be mentioned in particular: see especially Arangio-Ruiz, 'Preliminary Report on State Responsibility', 2 YBILC (1988) 11–43 (UN Doc A/CN.4/416 and Add 1), and 'Second Report on State Responsibility', 2 YBILC (1989) 3–56 (UN Doc A/CN.4/425 and Add 1); Crawford, 'Third Report on State Responsibility', UN Doc A/CN.4/507 (2000) 3 ff. These reports deal with important matters relating to remedies other than countermeasures. Countermeasures are discussed in Arangio-Ruiz, 'Third Report on State Responsibility', 2 YBILC (1991) at 11–36 (UN Doc A/CN.4/440 and Add 1), and 'Fourth Report on State Responsibility', 2 YBILC (1992) 6–42 (UN Doc A/CN.4/444 and Add 1–3); Crawford, 'Fourth Report on State Responsibility', UN Doc A/CN.4/517 (2001) 21–9. Reference may also be made on remedies in particular to the *Report of the ILC (1991),* Chapter VII; *Report of the ILC (1992),* Chapter III; *Report of the ILC (1993),* 54–83; *Draft Articles on State Responsibility Adopted by the ILC on First Reading* (1996); Crawford, op cit at the beginning of this footnote, Articles 41–50, 358–61, *The ILC's Articles on the Responsibility of States for Internationally Wrongful Acts* (2002), Crawford, ibid, Articles 28–39, 49–53, with commentary, 192–241, 284–301.

[3] See Article 30(a) of the ILC's Articles on State Responsibility (2001): Crawford, ibid 67, 196 ff.

[4] See Article 30(b) of the ILC's Articles on State Responsibility (2001): Crawford, ibid 67, 196, 198 ff.

obligation does not put an end to the obligation itself.[5] On this first principle the authorities are agreed.[6]

The other two principles which are linked relate to the cessation of the wrongful conduct and the offer of assurances and guarantees of non-repetition by the responsible State, if circumstances so require. Both responses are aspects of the restoration and repair of the legal relationship affected by the breach. Cessation is, as it were, the negative aspect of future performance, concerned with securing an end to continuing wrongful conduct, whereas assurances and guarantees serve a preventive function and may be described as a positive reinforcement of future performance. The continuation in force of the underlying obligation is a necessary assumption of both, since if the obligation has ceased following its breach, the question of cessation does not arise and no assurances and guarantees can be relevant.

Cessation is relevant to all wrongful acts extending in time regardless of whether the conduct of a State is an act or omission, because there may be cessation consisting in abstaining from certain actions, as there is cessation consisting in performance of actions.[7] In the *Rainbow Warrior* the arbitral tribunal emphasized that there were two essential conditions for the existence of the need to cease wrongful conduct, namely that the wrongful act has a continuing character and that the violated rule is still in force at the time at which the order of the tribunal is issued.[8] Cessation of conduct in breach of an international obligation is the first requirement in eliminating the consequences of wrongful conduct. With reparation, it is one of the two general consequences of an act or omission which is a violation of international law.

As with regard to State responsibility in general so also with diplomatic protection there is an obligation upon the responsible State to offer appropriate assurances and guarantees of non-repetition, *if circumstances so require* and the injured State so requests. Assurances and guarantees are concerned with the restoration of confidence in a continuing relationship, although they involve much more flexibility than cessation and are not required in all cases. They are most commonly sought when the injured State has reason to believe that the mere restoration of the pre-existing situation does not protect it satisfactorily. Assurances are normally given verbally, while guarantees of non-repetition involve something more—for example, preventive measures to be taken by the responsible State designed to avoid repetition of the breach. With regard to the kind of guarantees that may be requested international practice is not uniform. In the case of wrongful acts affecting its nationals, what the injured State normally

[5] The breach of a primary obligation may result in the termination of that obligation, as where the injured State elects to terminate a treaty for material breach.

[6] See discussion in the commentary to Article 29 of the ILC's Articles: ibid 194 ff.

[7] See the *Rainbow Warrior* (1990), 20 UNRIAA 270, para 113.

[8] Ibid, para 114.

demands are assurances of better protection of persons and property.[9] There is, however, other conduct, such as the giving of specific instructions, which the injured State may require and may be appropriate.[10]

It may also be noted that the responsible State may not rely on its internal law as justification for failure to comply with the obligations discussed above.[11]

Reparation

The second general obligation of the responsible State relating to remedies is to make full reparation upon the commission of an internationally wrongful act. In the *Chorzów Factory Case (Jurisdiction)* which concerned the alleged violation of a treaty as a result of the confiscation of property belonging to the complainant State's national, the general principle of the consequences of the commission of an internationally wrongful act was stated by the PCIJ as follows:

> It is a principle of international law that the breach of an engagement involves an obligation to make reparation in an adequate form. Reparation therefore is the indispensable complement of a failure to apply a convention and there is no necessity for this to be stated in the convention itself.[12]

The Court later specified in more detail in the *Chorzów Factory Case (Merits)* the content of the obligation of reparation, stating:

> The essential principle contained in the actual notion of an illegal act—a principle which seems to be established by international practice and in particular by the decisions of arbitral tribunals—is that reparation must, so far as possible, wipe out all the consequences of the illegal act and reestablish the situation which would, in all probability, have existed if that act had not been committed. Restitution in kind, or, if this is not possible, payment of a sum corresponding to the value which a restitution in kind would bear; the award, if need be, of damages for loss sustained which would not be covered by restitution in kind or payment in place of it, such are the principles which should serve to determine the amount of compensation due for an act contrary to international law.[13]

In this statement, the court, first, gave a general definition of reparation, emphasizing that its function was the re-establishment of the situation affected

[9] See the *Doane* incident (1886), Moore, 6 *Digest* (1906) 345–6.

[10] For cessation and assurances and guarantees in general see the discussion in the commentary to Article 30 of the ILC's Articles on State Responsibility: Crawford (2002) (note 2 above) 196 ff.

[11] See Article 32 of the ILC's Articles on State Responsibility.

[12] (1927), PCIJ Series A, No 9 21.

[13] (1928), PCIJ Series A, No 17 47. The two judgments of the PCIJ in the *Chorzòw Factory Case* insofar as they deal with reparations as a general principle are the *locus classicus* for the explanation of the principle of reparation.

by the breach; secondly, it dealt with that aspect of reparation encompassed by 'compensation' for an unlawful act, namely restitution or the value of restitution, and in addition damages for loss sustained as a result of the wrongful act. The obligation placed on the responsible State[14] is to make full reparation in this sense. The responsible State must endeavour to wipe out all the consequences of the illegal act and re-establish the situation which would, in all probability, have existed if that act had not been committed through the provision of one or more of the forms of reparation discussed below. The general obligation of reparation arises automatically upon commission of an internationally wrongful act and is not, as such, contingent upon a demand or protest by any State, even if the form which reparation should take in the circumstances may depend on the response of the injured State.

The responsible State's obligation to make full reparation relates to the 'injury' caused by the internationally wrongful act. 'Injury' includes any damage caused by that act and, in particular, covers any material or moral damages caused thereby. 'Material' damage here refers to damage to property or other interests of the State and its nationals which is assessable in financial terms. 'Moral' damage includes such matters as individual pain and suffering, loss of loved ones, or personal affront associated with an intrusion into one's home or private life.

As a corollary there is no general requirement, over and above any requirements laid down by the relevant primary obligation, that a State should have suffered material harm or damage before it can seek reparation for a breach. The existence of actual damage will be relevant to the form and quantum of reparation. But there is no general requirement of material harm or damage for a State to be entitled to seek reparation. In the *Rainbow Warrior* arbitration it was initially argued that 'in the theory of international responsibility, damage is necessary to provide a basis for liability to make reparation', but the parties subsequently agreed that, 'Unlawful action against non-material interests, such as acts affecting the honor, dignity or prestige of a State, entitle the victim State to receive adequate reparation, even if those acts have not resulted in a pecuniary or material loss for the claimant State'.[15]

The identification of injury resulting from an unlawful act is essentially a 'legal' process and not merely a historical or causal process. The legal process and the problems faced in such process, which relates to the remoteness or proximity of damage, are described in the commentary to Article 31 of the ILC's Articles on State Responsibility as follows:

Various terms are used to describe the link which must exist between the wrongful act and the injury in order for the obligation of reparation to arise. For example, reference

[14] See commentary to Article 31 of the ILC's Articles on State Responsibility: Crawford (2002) (note 2 above) 202. See also P-M Dupuy, 'Le fait générateur de la responsibilité internationale des États', 188 Hague Recueil (1984) 94.

[15] (1990), 20 UNRIAA 267, para 109.

may be made to losses attributable to the wrongful act 'as a proximate cause'[16] or to damage which is 'too indirect, remote, and uncertain to be appraised'[17] or to 'any direct loss, damage, including environmental damage and the depletion of natural resources, or injury to foreign Governments, nationals and corporations as a result of' the wrongful act.[18] Thus causality in fact is a necessary but not a sufficient condition for reparation. There is a further element, associated with the exclusion of injury that is too 'remote' or 'consequential' to be the subject of reparation. In some cases, the criterion of 'directness' may be used,[19] in others 'foreseeability'[20] or 'proximity'.[21] But other factors may also be relevant: for example, whether State organs deliberately caused the harm in question, or whether the harm caused was within the ambit of the rule which was breached, having regard to the purpose of that rule.[22] In other words, the requirement of a causal link is not necessarily the same in relation to every breach of an international obligation.[23]

In international law as in national law remoteness or proximity of damage is not a part of the law which can be satisfactorily based on a single verbal formula.

The duty on the part of the claimant to mitigate damage is a factor which may affect the scope of reparation. This duty does not itself give rise to responsibility but it is rather that a failure to mitigate by the claimant or injured party may preclude recovery to that extent. Even the wholly innocent victim of unlawful conduct is expected to act reasonably in order to reduce the extent of damage

[16] See United States-Germany Mixed Claims Commission, *Administrative Decision No II* (1923), 7 UNRIAA 30. See also the *Dix Case* (1902), 9 UNRIAA 121, and the Canadian statement of claim following the disintegration of the *Cosmos 954* Soviet nuclear-powered satellite over its territory in 1978: 18 ILM (1979) 907, para 23.

[17] See the *Trail Smelter Case* (1938, 1941), 3 UNRIAA 1931. See also A Hauriou, 'Les dommages indirects dans les arbitrages internationaux', 31 RGDIP (1924) 209, citing the *Alabama Arbitration* as the most striking application of the rule excluding 'indirect' damage.

[18] Security Council Resolution 687 (1991), para 16. This was a Chapter VII resolution, but it is expressed to reflect Iraq's liability 'under international law... as a result of its unlawful invasion and occupation of Kuwait'. The United Nations Compensation Commission and the Governing Council have provided some guidance on the interpretation of the requirements of directness and causation under para 16. See eg *Recommendations Made by the Panel of Commissioners Concerning Individual Claims for Serious Personal Injury or Death (Category "B" Claims)*, 14 April 1994, S/AC.26/1994/1, reproduced in 109 ILR 127, approved by Governing Council Decision 20, 26 May 1994, S/AC.26/Dec 20, reproduced in 109 ibid 622; *Recommendations Made by the Panel of Commissioners Appointed to Review the Well Blowout Control Claim*, 15 November 1996, S/AC.26/1996/5/Annex, paras 66–86, reproduced in 109 ibid 506–11, approved by Governing Council Decision 40, 17 December 1996 S/AC.26/Dec.40, reproduced in 109 ibid 669.

[19] As in Security Council Resolution 687 (1991), para 16.

[20] The *Naulilaa Case* (1928), 2 UNRIAA 1031.

[21] For comparative reviews of issues of causation and remoteness see eg Hart & Honoré, *Causation in the Law* (2nd edn, 1985); Honoré, 'Causation and Remoteness of Damage', in Tunc, (ed), 9 *International Encyclopedia of Comparative Law*, (1983) Part 1, Chap VII, 156; Zwiegert and Kötz, *Introduction to Comparative Law* (3rd edn. trans J A Weir, 1998), 601–27 (esp 609 ff); Markesinis, 2 *The German Law of Obligations. The Law of Torts: A Comparative Introduction* (3rd edn, 1997), 95–108, with many references to the literature.

[22] See eg the decision of the Iran-United States Claims Tribunal in *Islamic Republic of Iran v United States of America* (Cases A15(IV) and A24) (1996), 32 Iran-US CTR 115.

[23] Crawford (2002) (note 2 above) 204. The footnote numbers in this quotation are not the same numbers that occur in the original text. The content of the footnotes, save the numbers, on the other hand, corresponds to that of the footnotes in the original text.

when confronted with the injury; in a case concerned with State responsibility in general the ICJ explained what mitigating damage involved:

Slovakia also maintained that it was acting under a duty to mitigate damages when it carried out Variant C. It stated that 'It is a general principle of international law that a party injured by the non-performance of another contract party must seek to mitigate the damage he has sustained.' It would follow from such a principle that an injured State which has failed to take the necessary measures to limit the damage sustained would not be entitled to claim compensation for that damage which could have been avoided. While this principle might thus provide a basis for the calculation of damages, it could not, on the other hand, justify an otherwise wrongful act.[24]

The situation could arise where an identifiable element of injury can properly be allocated to one of several concurrently operating causes. In such a case, unless some part of the injury can be shown to be severable in causal terms from that attributed to the responsible State, the latter is held responsible for all the consequences, which are not too remote, of its unlawful conduct. Moreover, in the '*Zafiro*' *Case*, involving concurrent causes, the tribunal in effect placed the onus on the responsible State to show what proportion of the damage was not attributable to its conduct. The tribunal stated:

We think it clear that not all of the damage was done by the Chinese crew of the *Zafiro*. The evidence indicates that an unascertainable part was done by Filipino insurgents, and makes it likely that some part was done by the Chinese employees of the company. But we do not consider that the burden is on Great Britain to prove exactly what items of damage are chargeable to the *Zafiro*. As the Chinese crew of the *Zafiro* are shown to have participated to a substantial extent and the part chargeable to unknown wrongdoers can not be identified, we are constrained to hold the United States liable for the whole. In view, however, of our finding that a considerable, though unascertainable, part of the damage is not chargeable to the Chinese crew of the *Zafiro*, we hold that interest on the claims should not be allowed.[25]

Furthermore, a State may not invoke its internal law as a justification for failure to comply with obligations of reparation.[26] Although practical difficulties may arise for a State organ confronted with an obstacle to compliance posed by the rules of the internal legal system under which it is bound to operate, the State is not entitled to oppose its internal law or practice as a legal barrier to the fulfilment of an international obligation of reparation. However, the principle may be qualified by the relevant primary rule, or by a *lex specialis*. An example of this exception in the human rights field is Article 41 of the European Convention on Human Rights, which provides for just satisfaction in lieu of full reparation, 'if the internal law of the said Party allows only partial reparation to be made'.[27] The

[24] The *Gabčíkovo-Nagymaros Project Case*, 1997 ICJ Reports 55.

[25] (1925), 6 UNRIAA 164–5.

[26] See Article 32 of the ILC's Articles on State Responsibility and commentary thereto.

[27] See 213 UNTS 221. Other examples from the law of State responsibility in general are Article 32 of the Revised General Act for the Pacific Settlement of Disputes of 23 April 1949, 72 UNTS

principle that a responsible State may not rely on the provisions of its internal law as justification for failure to comply with its obligations of reparation arising out of the commission of an internationally wrongful act is supported both by State practice and international decisions in relation to State responsibility in general, including responsibility for the mistreatment of aliens. For example, in the *Peter Pázmány University Case* the PCIJ specified that the property to be returned should be 'freed from any measure of transfer, compulsory administration, or sequestration'.[28] The general principle is that international law does not recognize that the obligation of a responsible State to provide reparation is subject to the State's internal legal system nor does it allow internal law to count as an excuse for non-performance of the obligation of reparation.

The form of full reparation is commonly defined as 'restitution, compensation and satisfaction, either singly or in combination'.[29] In the *Chorzów Factory Case (Merits)* the injury was a material one and the PCIJ dealt only with two forms of reparation, namely restitution and compensation.[30] In certain cases, satisfaction may be called for as an additional form of reparation. Thus, full reparation may take the form of restitution, compensation, and satisfaction, as required by the circumstances. Also full reparation may only be achieved in particular cases by the combination of different forms of reparation. For example, re-establishment of the situation which existed before the breach may not be sufficient for full reparation because the wrongful act has caused additional material damage (eg injury flowing from the loss of the use of property wrongfully seized). Compensation may additionally be required. Wiping out all the consequences of the wrongful act may thus require some or all forms of reparation to be provided, depending on the type and extent of the injury that has been caused. In cases of restitution not involving the return of persons or property of nationals of the injured State, the notion of reverting to the *status quo ante* has to be applied with care. Restitution should not in any case give the injured State more than it would have been entitled to if the obligation had been performed.

The forms of reparation may also be affected by any valid election that may be made by the injured State as between different forms of reparation. For example, in most circumstances the injured State is entitled to elect to receive compensation rather than restitution. The forms of reparation referred to herein are ways of giving effect to the underlying obligation or reparation. It must be noted that there are not, as it were, separate secondary obligations of restitution, compensation and satisfaction. Some flexibility is shown in practice in terms of the appropriateness of requiring one form of reparation rather than another, subject to the

101, and Article 30 of the 1957 European Convention for the Peaceful Settlement of Disputes, 30 UNTS 243.

[28] (1933), PCIJ Series A/B No 61, 249.

[29] Article 34 of the ILC's Articles on State Responsibility. See also the commentary to this Article for what follows.

[30] (1928), PCIJ Series A, No 17, 47.

requirement of full reparation for the violation of international law.[31] To the extent that one form of reparation is dispensed with or is unavailable in the circumstances, others, especially compensation, will be correspondingly more important. There may also be limitations, such as proportionality, within each aspect of reparation which need to be recognized.

Restitutio in Integrum

Article 35 of the ILC's Articles on State Responsibility states:

> A State responsible for an internationally wrongful act is under an obligation to make restitution, that is, to re-establish the situation which existed before the wrongful act was committed, provided and to the extent that restitution:
> (a) is not materially possible;
> (b) does not involve a burden out of all proportion to the benefit deriving from restitution instead of compensation.[32]

Restitution (*restitutio in integrum*) is the first of the forms of reparation available to a State injured by any internationally wrongful act in general and in respect of its nationals in particular. What applies to State responsibility in general holds true for State responsibility arising from an injury to one of a State's nationals. Restitution involves the re-establishment as far as possible of the situation which existed prior to the commission of the internationally wrongful act, to the extent that any changes that have occurred in that situation may be traced to that act. In its simplest form, this involves such conduct as the release of persons wrongly detained or the return of property wrongly seized. In other cases, restitution may be a more complex act.

Restitution is not only a form of reparation, but it is the chief form of reparation. Its must be ordered by a tribunal and the complainant is entitled to it, unless the complainant does not request it or gives up his or its right to it, or circumstances make it difficult to implement it. On the other hand, restitution may be inadequate to remedy the damage caused. Then there will be an entitlement to compensation in addition.

The concept of restitution is not uniformly defined. According to one definition, restitution consists in re-establishing the *status quo ante*, ie the situation that existed prior to the occurrence of the wrongful act. Under another definition, restitution is the establishment or re-establishment of the situation that would have existed if the wrongful act had not been committed. The former definition is the narrower one; it does not extend to the compensation which may be

[31] For example, in the *Mélanie Lachenal Case* (1954), 13 UNRIAA 130–1, compensation was accepted in lieu of restitution originally decided upon, the Franco-Italian Conciliation Commission having agreed that restitution would require difficult internal procedures.

[32] Crawford (2002) (note 2 above) 68, 213. What is written herein follows closely the commentary to Article 35: ibid 213 ff. Article 35 and the commentary thereto accurately reflect the *lex lata*.

due to the injured party for loss suffered, for example for loss of the use of goods wrongfully detained but subsequently returned. The latter definition absorbs into the concept of restitution other elements of full reparation and tends to conflate restitution as a form of reparation and the underlying obligation of reparation itself. Article 35 of the ILC Articles adopts the narrower definition which has the advantage of focusing on the assessment of a factual situation and of not requiring a hypothetical inquiry into what the situation would have been if the wrongful act had not been committed. Restitution in this narrow sense may, of course, have to be complemented by compensation in order to ensure full reparation for the damage caused. Nonetheless, because restitution most closely conforms to the general principle that the responsible State is bound to wipe out the legal and material consequences of its wrongful act by re-establishing the situation which existed before the wrongful act had been committed, it comes first among the forms of reparation. The primacy of restitution was clearly asserted by the PCIJ in the *Chorzów Factory Case (Merits)*. It said that the responsible State was under 'the obligation to restore the undertaking and, if this be not possible, to pay its value at the time of the indemnification, which value is designed to take the place of restitution which has become impossible'.[33] The Court added that 'The impossibility, on which the Parties are agreed, of restoring the Chorzów factory could therefore have no other effect but that of substituting payment of the value of the undertaking for restitution.'[34] It can be seen in operation in the cases where tribunals have considered compensation only after concluding that, for one reason or another, restitution could not be effected.[35] Despite the difficulties restitution may encounter in practice, States have often insisted upon claiming it in preference to compensation. Where a peremptory norm is violated in the treatment of an alien, eg one relating to personal liberty, restitution may be required as an aspect of compliance with the primary obligation.

However, there are often situations where restitution is not available or where its value to the injured State is so reduced that other forms of reparation take priority. But quite apart from valid election by the injured State or other entity, the possibility of restitution may be practically excluded, eg because the property in question has been destroyed or fundamentally changed in character or because the situation cannot be restored to the *status quo ante* for some reason. Indeed, in some cases tribunals have inferred from the terms of the *compromis* or the positions of the parties what amounts to a discretion to award compensation rather than restitution. For example, in the *Walter Fletcher Smith Case*, the arbitrator, while maintaining that restitution should be appropriate in principle, interpreted the *compromis* as giving him a discretion to award compensation and did so in

[33] (1928), PCIJ Series A No. 17, 48.

[34] Ibid.

[35] The *British Claims in the Spanish Zone of Morocco Case* (1925), 2 UNRIAA 621–5, 651–742; the *Religious Property Expropriated by Portugal Case* (1920), 1 UNRIAA 7; the *Walter Fletcher Smith Case* (1929), 2 UNRIAA 918; the *Heirs of Lebas de Courmont Case* (1957), 13 UNRIAA 764.

'the best interests of the parties, and of the public'.[36] In the *Aminoil Case* the parties agreed that restoration of the *status quo ante* following the annulment of the concession by the Kuwaiti decree would be impracticable.[37]

Restitution may take the form of material restoration or return of property, or the reversal of some juridical act, or some combination of them. Examples of material restitution include the release of detained individuals, the handing over to a State of an individual arrested in its territory,[38] the return of ships,[39] or other types of property[40] including documents, works of art, share certificates, etc.[41] The term 'juridical restitution' is sometimes used where restitution requires or involves the modification of a legal situation whether within the legal system of the responsible State or in its legal relations with the injured State. Such cases include the revocation, annulment, or amendment of a constitutional or legislative provision enacted in violation of a rule of international law, or the rescinding or reconsideration of an administrative or judicial measure unlawfully adopted in respect of the person or property of a foreigner.[42] In some cases, both material and juridical restitution in the above sense may be required.[43] In others, an international court or tribunal can, by determining the legal position with binding force for the parties, award what amounts to restitution under another form.[44] The term 'restitution' for the purpose of reparation has a broad meaning,

[36] (1929), 2 UNRIAA 918. In the *Greek Telephone Company Case*, the arbitral tribunal, while ordering restitution, asserted that the responsible State could provide compensation instead for 'important State reasons': see Wetter and Schwebel, 'Some Little Known Cases on Concessions', 40 BYIL (1964) 221.

[37] See the *Aminoil Arbitration* (1982), 66 ILR 533.

[38] Examples of material restitution involving persons include the *Trent* (1861) and *Florida* (1964) incidents, both involving the arrest of individuals on board ships: Moore, 7 *Digest* (1906) 768, 1090–1; and the *Diplomatic and Consular Staff Case* in which the ICJ ordered Iran immediately to release every detained US national: *1980* ICJ Reports 44–5.

[39] The *Giaffarieh* incident (1886) which originated in the capture in the Red Sea by an Egyptian warship of four merchant ships from Massawa under Italian registry: Società Italiana per l'Organizzazione Internazionale Consiglio Nazionale delle Ricerche, 2 *La prassi italiana di diritto internazionale* (1st series, 1970) 901–2.

[40] See also the *Hôtel Métropole Case* (1950), 13 UNRIAA 219; the *Ottoz Case* (1950), 13 ibid 240; the *Hénon Case* (1951), 13 ibid 249.

[41] In the *Buzau-Nehoiasi Railway Case*, an arbitral tribunal provided for the restitution to a German company of shares in a Romanian railway company: (1939), 3 UNRIAA 1839.

[42] Eg, the *Martini Case* (1930), 2 UNRIAA 973.

[43] Thus the PCIJ held that Czechoslovakia was 'bound to restore to the Royal Hungarian Peter Pázmány University of Budapest the immovable property claimed by it, freed from any measure of transfer, compulsory administration, or sequestration, and in the condition in which it was before the application of the measures in question': the *Peter Pázmány University Case* (1933), PCIJ Series A/B, No 61, 249.

[44] In the *Legal Status of Eastern Greenland Case*, the PCIJ decided 'that the declaration of occupation promulgated by the Norwegian Government on July 10th, 1931, and any steps taken in this respect by that Government, constitute a violation of the existing legal situation and are accordingly unlawful and invalid' (1933) PCIJ Series A/B No 53 75. In the *Free Zones of Upper Savoy and the District of Gex Case* the PCIJ decided that France 'must withdraw its customs line in accordance with the provisions of the said treaties and instruments; and that this regime must continue in force so long as it has not been modified by agreement between the Parties': (1932),

encompassing any action that needs to be taken by the responsible State to restore the situation resulting from its internationally wrongful act, in respect of an alien or aliens.

What may be required in terms of restitution will often depend on the content of the primary obligation which has been breached. Restitution, as the first of the forms of reparation, is of particular importance where the obligation breached is of a continuing character, and even more so where it arises under a peremptory norm of general international law.

The obligation to make restitution is not unlimited. In particular, restitution is required 'provided and to the extent that' it is neither materially impossible nor wholly disproportionate. The phrase 'provided and to the extent that' makes it clear that restitution may be only partially excluded, in which case the responsible State will be obliged to make restitution to the extent that this is neither impossible nor disproportionate. Under Article 35(a) restitution is not required if it is 'materially impossible'. This would apply where property to be restored has been permanently lost or destroyed, or has deteriorated to such an extent as to be valueless. On the other hand, restitution is not impossible merely on the grounds of legal or practical difficulties, even though the responsible State may have to make special efforts to overcome these. As pointed out earlier, the wrongdoing State may not invoke the provisions of its internal law as justification for the failure to provide full reparation, and the mere fact of political or administrative obstacles to restitution do not amount to impossibility. Material impossibility is not limited to cases where the object in question has been destroyed, but can cover more complex situations. In the *Forests of Central Rhodope Case* the claimant was entitled to only a share of the forestry operations and no claims had been brought by other participants. The forests were not in the same condition as at the time of their wrongful taking, and detailed inquiries would have been necessary to determine their condition. Moreover, since the taking, third parties had acquired rights to them. For a combination of these reasons, restitution was denied.[45] The case supports a broad understanding of the impossibility of granting restitution. However, it concerned questions of property rights within the legal system of the responsible State.[46] The position may be different where the rights and obligations in issue arise directly on the international plane. In the latter context restitution plays a particularly important role. In certain cases, the position of third parties may have been taken into account in considering whether restitution is materially possible. This was true in the *Forests of Central Rhodope Case*, referred to above. But whether the position of a third party will preclude restitution will

PCIJ Series A/B No 46, 172. These cases do not deal with diplomatic protection but state principles which are relevant to restitution in cases of diplomatic protection.

[45] (1933), 3 UNRIAA 1432.

[46] For restitution in cases of transnational State contract arbitration see the *BP Arbitration* (1974), 53 ILR 354; the *Texaco Arbitration* (1977), 53 ILR 507–8, para 109; the *LIAMCO Arbitration* (1977), 62 ILR 200.

depend on the circumstances, including whether the third party at the time of entering into the transaction or assuming the disputed rights was acting in good faith and without notice of the claim to restitution.

A second exception, dealt with in Article 35(b), involves those cases where the benefit to be gained from restitution is wholly disproportionate to its cost to the responsible State. Specifically, restitution may not be required if it would 'involve a burden out of all proportion to the benefit deriving from restitution instead of compensation'. This should apply only where there is a grave disproportionality between the burden which restitution would impose on the responsible State and the benefit which would be gained, either by the injured State or by any person who is a victim of the breach. It is thus based on considerations of equity and reasonableness,[47] although with a preference for the position of the injured State in any case where the balancing process does not indicate a clear preference for compensation as compared with restitution. The balance will invariably favour the injured State in any case where the failure to provide restitution in a case involving its national would jeopardize its political independence or economic stability.[48]

Restitution is a form of specific performance and covers any specific performance required to achieve the *restitutio in integrum*.

Compensation

Compensation will be payable for damage caused by an internationally wrongful act, to the extent that such damage is not made good by restitution. This damage may be material or moral. Compensation covers any financially assessable damage and may include loss of profits so far as this is established in the given case.[49] Compensation for an affront or injury caused by a violation of rights not associated with actual damage to property or persons is not included. This is properly the subject matter of satisfaction. What is covered by satisfaction is moral damage to a State as such, as will be seen later.

Of the various forms of reparation, compensation is perhaps the most commonly sought in international practice, particularly in connection with the diplomatic protection of aliens. In the *Gabčíkovo-Nagymaros Project Case*, the ICJ stated in general terms: 'It is a well-established rule of international law that

[47] See for this idea Verzijl, *International Law in Historical Perspective*, Part VI (1973), 744.

[48] In State responsibility, in general, it may be suggested that the balance will invariably favour the injured State, where the failure to provide restitution would jeopardize its political independence or economic stability.

[49] Thus, Article 36 of the ILC's Articles on State Responsibility states:

1. The State responsible for an internationally wrongful act is under an obligation to compensate for the damage caused thereby, insofar as such damage is not made good by restitution.
2. The compensation shall cover financially assessable damage including loss of profits insofar as it is established.

an injured State is entitled to obtain compensation from the State which has committed an internationally wrongful act for the damage caused by it.'[50] This applies in diplomatic protection as well as in other areas. In the *Chorzów Factory Case (Merits)* which involved the protection of alien property, albeit under an international agreement between the claimant State and the respondent State, the PCIJ said that it was 'a principle of international law that the reparation of a wrong may consist in an indemnity'.[51] Moreover, an international court or tribunal which has jurisdiction with respect to a claim of State responsibility in general, has, as an aspect of that jurisdiction, the power to award compensation for damage suffered. *Restitutio in integrum*, despite its primacy as a matter of legal principle, is frequently unavailable or inadequate. It may be partially or entirely excluded either on the basis of the exceptions required in law[52] or because the injured State prefers compensation or for other reasons. Moreover, even where restitution is made, it may be insufficient to ensure full reparation. The role of compensation then is to fill in gaps so as to ensure full reparation for damage suffered.[53] As was outlined by the PCIJ, 'Restitution in kind, or, if this is not possible, payment of a sum corresponding to the value which a restitution in kind would bear; the award, if need be, of damages for loss sustained which would not be covered by restitution in kind or payment in place of it—such are the principles which would serve to determine the amount of compensation due for an act contrary to international law.'[54] Entitlement to compensation in monetary terms for such losses is supported by extensive case law, State practice, and the writings of jurists.

Compensation is different from satisfaction. As compared with satisfaction the function of compensation is to address the actual losses incurred as a result of the internationally wrongful act. Compensation corresponds to the financially assessable damage suffered by the injured State and its nationals. Its object is not to punish the responsible State nor does it have an exemplary character.[55] Thus, compensation generally consists of a monetary payment, though it may sometimes

[50] 1997 ICJ Reports 81.

[51] (1928), PCIJ Series A No 17, 27. See also the *Chorzòw Factory Case (Jurisdiction)*, (1927), PCIJ Series A No 9, 21, and in general the *Nicaragua Case (Merits)*, 1986 ICJ Reports 142.

[52] See Article 35(a) and (b) of the ILC's Articles on State Responsibility (2001).

[53] The *Chorzòw Factory Case (Merits)*, (1928), PCIJ Series A No 17, 47–8.

[54] Ibid 147. See also the *Lusitania Case* where it was said: 'The fundamental concept of "damages" is... reparation for a *loss* suffered; a judicially ascertained *compensation* for wrong. The remedy should be commensurate with the loss, so that the injured party may be made whole' (1923), 7 UNRIAA 39 (emphasis in original).

[55] In the *Velásquez Rodríguez (Compensation) Case* the Inter-American Court of Human Rights held that international law did not recognize the concept of punitive or exemplary damages: IACHR Series C No 7 (1989) 52. See also *Re Letelier and Moffit* (1992), 88 ILR 727, concerning the assassination in Washington by Chilean agents of a former Chilean Minister: the *compromis* excluded any award of punitive damages, despite their availability under United States law. On punitive damages see also Jorgensen, 'A Reappraisal of Punitive Damages in International Law', 68 BYIL (1997) 247; Wittich, 'Awe of the Gods and Fear of the Priests: Punitive Damages in the Law of State Responsibility', 3 Austrian Review of International and European Law (1998) 131.

take the form, as agreed, of other forms of value. It is true that monetary payments may be called for by way of satisfaction but they perform a function distinct from that of compensation. Monetary compensation is intended to offset, as far as may be, the damage suffered by the injured State through its nationals as a result of the breach of law. Satisfaction is concerned essentially with non-material injury, specifically non-material injury to the State, on which a monetary value can be put only in a notional and highly approximate way. However, compensation could involve payment for moral damage to the individual, ie for an abstraction which is given a monetary value.

The responsible State has an obligation to provide reparation for the consequences flowing from the commission of an internationally wrongful act. This obligation is confined to financially assessable damage, that is, any damage which is capable of being evaluated in financial terms. Financially assessable damage covers in any situation damage suffered by the State itself (to its property or personnel or in respect of expenditures reasonably incurred to remedy or mitigate damage flowing from an internationally wrongful act) as well as damage suffered by nationals, whether natural or legal persons, in respect of whom the State is exercising diplomatic protection.

The PCIJ and the ICJ have both dealt with claims for compensation in the exercise of diplomatic protection. Other tribunals which have done so include, more recently, the Iran-US Claims Tribunal.[56] Compensation claims have also been settled by agreement, normally on a 'without prejudice' basis, the payment of substantial compensation being a term of the agreement. The general rules applied in these cases in assessing compensation are in accord with those stated above.

As to the appropriate heads of compensatable damage and the principles of assessment to be applied in quantification, these will vary. They depend upon the content of particular primary obligations, an evaluation of the respective behaviour of the parties and, more generally, a concern to reach an equitable and acceptable outcome.[57]

As an illustration of how compensation is assessed, where there has been injury to a ship and its crew, may be taken the recent *M/V Saiga (No 2) Case*. Saint Vincent and the Grenadines sought compensation from Guinea following the wrongful arrest and detention of a Saint Vincent and the Grenadines' registered vessel, the *Saiga*, and its crew. The ITLOS awarded compensation of US $2,123,357 with interest. The heads of damage compensated included, inter alia, damage to the vessel, including costs of repair, losses suffered with respect

[56] See on this tribunal which has developed a recognizable jurisprudence on the assessment and the valuation of property, eg Aldrich, *The Jurisprudence of the Iran-United States Claims Tribunal* (1998), Chapters 5, 6, and 12; Brower and Brueschke, *The Iran-United States Claims Tribunal* (1998), chapters 14–18; C F Amerasinghe, 'Issues of Compensation for the Taking of Alien Property in the Light of Recent Cases and Practice', 41 ICLQ (1992) 22.

[57] See on the treatment of aliens, eg Aldrich (note 56 above) 242.

to charter hire of the vessel, costs related to the detention of the vessel, and damages for the detention of the captain, members of the crew, and others on board the vessel. Saint Vincent and the Grenadines had also claimed compensation for the violation of its rights in respect of ships flying its flag occasioned by the arrest and detention of the *Saiga*. However, the Tribunal considered that its declaration that Guinea acted wrongfully in arresting the vessel in the circumstances, and in using excessive force, constituted adequate reparation. Claims regarding the loss of registration revenue due to the illegal arrest of the vessel and for the expenses resulting from the time lost by officials in dealing with the arrest and detention of the ship and its crew were also unsuccessful. In respect of the former, the tribunal held that Saint Vincent and the Grenadines failed to produce supporting evidence. In respect of the latter, the tribunal considered that such expenses were not recoverable, because they were incurred in the exercise of the normal functions of a flag State.[58]

In a number of cases payments have been directly negotiated between injured and injuring States following wrongful attacks on ships causing damage or sinking of the vessel, and in some cases, loss of life and injury among the crew.[59] Similar payments have been negotiated where damage is caused to aircraft of a State, such as the 'full and final settlement' agreed between Iran and the US following a dispute over the destruction of an Iranian aircraft and the killing of its 290 passengers and crew.[60]

(a) Personal injury cases

Appropriate compensation has been awarded for personal injury to nationals, in addition to any compensation for direct injury which a State may itself have suffered in relation to the same event. Compensatable personal injury covers not only associated material losses, such as loss of earnings and earning capacity, medical expenses, and similar losses, but also non-material or moral damage suffered by the individual. Moral damage is capable of financial assessment and may be the subject of a claim of compensation as was emphatically stated in the *Lusitania Case*.[61] It was said that international law offers compensation

58 ITLOS, Judgment of I July 1999, paras 176–7, <http://www.itlos.org>.

59 See the payment by Cuba to the Bahamas for the sinking by Cuban aircraft on the high seas of a Bahamian vessel, with loss of life among the crew, 85 RGDIP (1981), 540; the payment of compensation by Israel for an attack in 1967 on the USS *Liberty*, with loss of life and injury among the crew, 85 ibid (1981) 562; and the payment by Iraq of $27 million for the 37 deaths which occurred in May 1987, when Iraqi aircraft severely damaged the USS *Stark*, 83 AJIL (1989) 561. The last two cases, albeit involving aliens, related to direct injuries to the State.

60 The *Aerial Incident of 3 July 1988 Case*, 1996 ICJ Reports 9 (order of discontinuance following settlement). For the settlement agreement itself, see the General Agreement between Iran and the US on the Settlement of Certain ICJ and Tribunal Cases of 9 February 1996, which was made an *Award on Agreed Terms* by order of the Iran-US Claims Tribunal, dated 22 February 1996: 32 Iran-US CTR 213.

61 (1923), 7 UNRIAA 32. Pecuniary compensation has been granted by international tribunals in several cases for moral injury to aliens: eg, the *Chevreau Case* (1923), 2 UNRIAA 1113; the

for mental suffering, injury to feelings, humiliation, shame, degradation, loss of social position, or injury to credit and reputation, which were very real injuries, and that 'the mere fact that they are difficult to measure or estimate by money standards makes them none the less real and affords no reason why the injured person should not be compensated…'.[62] International courts and tribunals have in many cases made assessments of compensation for personal injury. For example, in the *M/V Saiga Case*, referred to earlier, the ITLOS held that Saint Vincent and the Grenadines' entitlement to compensation included damages for injury to the crew, their unlawful arrest, detention, and other forms of ill-treatment.

Historically compensation for personal injury suffered by the nationals of a State was dealt with mainly by mixed claims commissions associated with the exercise of diplomatic protection resulting from State responsibility for injury to aliens. Compensation was awarded for personal injury in cases of both wrongfully causing death and deprivation of liberty. Where claims were made in respect of wrongful death, compensation by way of damages was calculated by evaluating the damage to the surviving heirs or successors on the basis of the formula expressed by Umpire Parker in the *Lusitania Case*, under which an estimate is made of

> the amounts (a) which the decedent, had he not been killed, would probably have contributed to the claimant, add thereto (b) the pecuniary value to such claimant of the deceased's personal services in claimant's case, education, or supervision, and also add (c) reasonable compensation for such mental suffering or shock, if any, caused by the violent severing of family ties, as [the] claimant may actually have sustained by reason of such death. The sum of these estimates reduced to its present cash value, will generally represent the loss sustained by claimant.[63]

In cases of deprivation of liberty, arbitrators sometimes awarded a particular amount for each day spent in detention.[64] Awards were often increased when abusive conditions of confinement accompanied the wrongful arrest and imprisonment, resulting in particularly serious physical or psychological injury.[65]

Compensation for personal injury has also been awarded by human rights bodies, in particular the European and Inter-American Courts of Human Rights. Awards of compensation encompass material losses (loss of earnings, pensions, medical expenses, etc) and non-material or moral damage (pain and suffering, mental anguish, humiliation, loss of enjoyment of life, and loss of companionship or consortium), the latter usually being quantified on the basis of an equitable assessment. Hitherto, amounts of compensation or damages, especially for

Gage Case (1903), 10 UNRIAA 226; the *Di Caro Case* (1903), 10 UNRIAA 597; the *Heirs of Jean Maninat Case* (1903), 10 UNRIAA 55.

62 (1923), 7 UNRIAA 40.

63 (1923), ibid 35.

64 Eg the *Topaze Case* (1903), 9 UNRIAA 389; the *Faulkner Case* (1926), 4 UNRIAA 71.

65 Eg the *William McNeil Case* (1931), 5 UNRIAA 168.

moral injury, awarded or recommended by these bodies have been modest.[66] These decisions of human rights bodies on compensation clearly call in aid principles recognized by general international law.[67]

(b) Property claims

There are a large number of lump-sum compensation agreements covering multiple claims involving property.[68] These have been negotiated and do not in general reflect principles of compensation while clearly only partial compensation was made. Apart from these, property claims of nationals arising out of an internationally wrongful act have been adjudicated by a wide range of ad hoc and standing tribunals, with reported cases spanning over two centuries. The adjudicating bodies are diverse and, therefore, awards are varied. While property claims may not always nor necessarily involve the taking of property, most cases deal with the latter. Damage caused by injury to property other than by a taking of property is, however, compensated. The approach in property cases is to give a value in monetary terms to the loss suffered by the claimant whose property rights have been infringed. This loss is usually assessed by reference to specific heads of damage relating to (a) compensation for capital value, (b) compensation for loss of profits (*lucrum cessans*),[69] and (c) compensation for consequential damage (*damnum emergens*), including incidental expenses.

A breach of contract by a State is not per se a violation of international law.[70] There needs generally to be an additional 'denial of justice' by the State. Thus, when claims are made in relation to a contractual breach, in addition to damage (both *damnum emergens* and *lucrum cessans*) resulting from the breach of contract, the denial of justice is in principle also subject to compensation. However, most of the cases involving pure breaches of contract which tribunals or courts have dealt with have concentrated entirely on the breach of contract by itself in assessing damages. The reasons are that, where the cases have been referred to truly international tribunals, claimants have omitted to claim damages for a denial of justice, or the reference to adjudication has been negotiated on the understanding that contract claims are to be decided as contract claims, even where there has been no reference to judicial settlement by the host State, and that denial of justice in respect of local remedies after resort to them had been sought was not

[66] Shelton, *Remedies in International Human Rights Law* (1999), Chapters 8 and 9; Randelzhofer and Tomuschat (eds), *State Responsibility and the Individual: Reparation in Instances of Grave Violations of Human Rights* (1999), passim.

[67] Eg *Velásquez Rodríguez v Honduras* (1989), IACHR Series C No 4 26–7, 30–1; *Papamichalapoulos v Greece* (1995), ECHR Series A No 330-B at para 36.

[68] On these settlements see Lillich and Weston, *International Claims: Their Settlement by Lump Sum Agreements* (1975), and Weston, Lillich, and Bederman, *International Claims: Their Settlement by Lump Sum Agreements, 1975–1995* (1999).

[69] Article 36(2) of the ILC's Articles on State Responsibility (2001) states that lost profits must be included in compensation.

[70] See C F Amerasinghe, *Local Remedies in International Law* (2004), Chapter 5.

a requirement, as is the case with the cases before the Iran-US Claims Tribunal. In some contract cases decided by tribunals which are not truly international tribunals (in the sense of being created by States in the exercise of diplomatic protection or in lieu of diplomatic protection but are in reality a substitute for the local tribunals of the host State) such transnational tribunals have also awarded compensation (or damages) on the basis of breach of contract.

Compensation (or damages) for an unlawful taking or destruction of property is to be distinguished and kept separate from the amount required to be paid as compensation in order that an expropriation which is in other respects lawful may not become unlawful for failure to provide appropriate compensation. The PCIJ in the *Chorzów Factory Case (Merits)*[71] clearly drew the distinction between lawful and unlawful takings in regard to the amount of compensation or damages to be awarded. What is in issue here is compensation for unlawful takings or injury to property and not the measure of compensation for lawful expropriations.

That having been said, it is noteworthy that there has been a certain amount of confusion between lawful and unlawful takings of property both in the cases and among the authorities. First, there are decided cases in which tribunals have overtly ruled in favour of including lost profits (*lucrum cessans*) in the award of damages where the taking has been treated as unlawful. This was the situation in the *Amoco Case* decided by the Iran-US Claims Tribunal.[72] Then, there are cases in which no palpable distinction was drawn between the lawfulness and unlawfulness of the taking.[73] Lost profits were overtly included in the award of damages in some of these cases.

What is of interest in these cases, where the issue of lawfulness or unlawfulness of the taking of property became relevant, is that in all of them no compensation at all had been offered or paid by the host State for the expropriation; nor was there a procedure provided by the host State available for the affected alien to seek appropriate compensation. The claimant, whether national State or alien, did not always clearly claim that the taking was unlawful, *because there was no compensation paid or available*, as should have been done for the claim to immediately become one for compensation or damages for an unlawful taking. Instead the tribunals appear to have addressed the problem without definition and sometimes awarded compensation on the basis that the taking without compensation was unlawful. But sometimes also it was not clear whether the compensation was not being awarded apparently on the basis that the taking, even though without compensation initially, was lawful. What can be said of the cases so far decided

[71] (1928), PCIJ Series A No 17, 47.

[72] (1987), 15 Iran-US CTR 246. There are transnational arbitrations between aliens and host States as substitutes for local remedies in which damages including lost profits were awarded on the basis of the takings being unlawful: see the *LIAMCO Arbitration* (1982), 62 ILR 202–3 (Libya being the respondent); the *Aminoil Arbitration* (1982), 66 ILR 600 (Kuwait being the respondent).

[73] The *Phillips Petroleum Co Iran Case* (1989), 21 Iran-US CTR 122; the *Starrett Housing Corp Case* (1987), 16 ibid 201 ff.

by tribunals in which compensation for the taking of property (expropriation) has been an issue is that in none of them has the host State initially offered or made possible appropriate compensation. Hence, in all these cases the taking was strictly unlawful. Thus, claims should have been made for compensation for unlawful expropriations and damages or compensation should have been awarded as for unlawful takings.

(i) Capital value

To revert to takings or destruction of property in violation of international law proper, there seems to be no doubt that the capital value of the property for the purpose of compensation or damages is generally assessed on the basis of 'fair market value' of the property concerned. In the *American International Group Inc Case* the Iran-US Claims Tribunal stated that under general international law 'the valuation should be made on the basis of the fair market value of the shares'.[74] As for the application of the 'fair market principle', in the *Starrett Housing Corp Case* the same tribunal accepted its expert's concept of fair market value 'as the price that a willing buyer could pay to a willing seller in circumstances in which each had good information, each desired to maximize his financial gain, and neither was under duress or threat'.[75]

However, there are variations in the methods used to assess 'fair market value' which must depend on the nature of the asset concerned. Each case must be considered on its own and there may be difficulties associated with the process of establishing 'fair market value'.

There is some case law, to be found mainly in the jurisprudence of the Iran-US Claims Tribunal, dealing with the establishment of 'full' value generally, in the context of the taking of property as expropriation. 'Full' value covers the concept of 'fair market value', whether the taking being considered is lawful or unlawful.[76]

To deal with the transnational awards first, in the *LIAMCO Arbitration*[77] the sole arbitrator dealt differently with physical assets—plant and equipment—and contractual rights under the concession expropriated. Under the former the value given to current assets at market rates was accepted, while for other assets the 'market value' given by the investor was accepted. The value of seventy oil wells was based on the original cost as shown on the books adjusted for variation in construction costs by application of the appropriate international Middle East construction index. Reductions were made for current liabilities as for income tax. The acceptance of these amounts was also referred to the terms of the concession contract. The claim for the loss of the concession rights to exploit oil wells which

[74] (1983), 4 ibid 106.

[75] (1987), 16 ibid 201.

[76] The establishment of full value does not affect the question whether full value is always due for a lawful taking of property as contrasted with an unlawful taking.

[77] (1977), 62 ILR 208–15.

entailed an estimate of lost profits was based on an evaluation of production over the period of the concession determined by reference to the official market price of crude oil for July 1976, without heeding any probable future increase, less costs, expenditures, taxes, etc. But because the arbitrator had decided that only an 'equitable' amount should be awarded for lost profits, taking into account certain other variables, the claimant's estimate of $193,770,000 was reduced in the award to $66,000,000. From the point of view of valuation methods what is important there is that (a) for physical assets the original cost, as shown on the books of the claimant adjusted for variation in construction costs by the appropriate index less actual liabilities and as claimed by the claimant, was accepted for the calculation of market value; (b) for current assets the claimant's estimate of their value market rates was accepted; and (c) for lost profits the value of crude oil at the market price on a fixed day in the past on the basis of the claimant's reasonable estimate of volume determined by past experience was not accepted as the true estimate of lost profits, because there was a discrepancy between the claim and an estimate which could have been made the basis of the Libyan partner's share of the possible profits from the operation of the concessions. Separately the arbitrator awarded an 'equitable' amount to cover lost profits. In the *Aminoil Arbitration* the tribunal accepted a joint report by the respective accountants of the parties as the basis for its award, taking the mean of the two totals reached and modifying this by reference to certain other factors in respect of which it did not posses any data as numerically worked out as those included in the joint report.[78] The accounting was based on the 'going concern value' of the enterprise, the anticipated profits on a reasonable basis being reckoned over the relevant period of years and discounted at an annual rate of interest and the depreciated replacement value of the fixed assets (not the net book value) being added to that.[79] From this amount was deducted liabilities. The original cost could not be used as a basis for the valuation of fixed assets in this case, as it might have been, if the investment had been a recent one. It should be observed that in this case the parties produced figures based on the principles of valuation accepted by the tribunal and it was only because there was a discrepancy in the results that the solution of adopting the mean was accepted.

The Iran-US Claims tribunal, as an international tribunal, has had to determine the full value of expropriated property on several occasions. With regard to land and tangible assets, whether their value has been claimed as part of the going concern value of a business or by themselves, the tribunal has accepted a variety of valuation methods, depending largely on the proposals put forward by the claimants. In the *Sedco Inc Case*[80] the claim was for the value of land and tangible assets per se. The claimant proposed that two parcels of land be valued but in different

[78] (1982), 66 ILR 518, 611.
[79] Ibid 608, 612–13.
[80] (1987), 15 Iran-US CTR 23.

ways. For one parcel of land, while it was alleged by the claimant that prices had risen in the past year, the historic cost of the land based on the price paid for a similar parcel of land one year earlier was awarded as the fair market value. In the other the value was determined by means of current cost accounting. This involved: '(1) increasing the historical or book cost of an asset through application of an appropriate price index to arrive at an estimate of "current cost new" of the asset, and (2) subtracting from the "current cost new" a "current depreciation" amount derived by application of the same price index to the book depreciation of the asset.'[81] In the absence of substantiated argument against the figures proposed by the claimant, the tribunal awarded the sums claimed. In addition the value of tangible assets, oil rigs, equipment, and warehouse stock was claimed. The claimant proposed that the 'liquidation value' be accepted on the assumption that the affairs of the enterprise had been wound up and its assets disposed of on the open market but presumably with no discount from this value as might occur in actual distress liquidation circumstances. The tribunal accepted this criterion. In order to prove the value of the assets on the open market the claimant produced evidence, including data as to comparable sales and appraisals, the value placed on oil rigs in its insurance policies, what it would have cost in 1979 to replace the rigs, the rigs' current net book value on the books of account of the company, and the appraisal of an expert. The respondent contested the amount claimed on this basis, giving a value of less than half that amount. The tribunal held that the respondent's figures were based on several incorrect assumptions and awarded about 79 per cent of the amount claimed, having adjusted the figure downward on the basis of its own analysis of the relationship between the claimant's net book value and actual value. In another aspect of the case the tribunal awarded as a part of what it described as *damnum emergens* lost profits for the use of oil rigs for nine months—the time considered necessary to procure and assemble replacement rigs.[82] The tribunal had decided to include this element in *damnum emergens* in the second interlocutory award in that case.[83] In this case, the tribunal proceeded on the basis that full compensation, including its conception of *damnum emergens*, had to be paid.[84]

There were four other cases in which tangible assets were valued in the awards made. These may be summarized in the following manner.[85] In the *Sola Tiles Inc Case*[86] the value of the physical assets and inventory of a luxury building tiles business was fixed by a determination of the market value of the assets on the basis of an appraisal that had been performed by an interested investor approximately

[81] Ibid 50, para 304.

[82] Ibid 53, para 315.

[83] (1986), 25 ILM (1987) 632, 635.

[84] Ibid 634.

[85] See Westberg, 'Compensation in Cases of Expropriation and Nationalization: Awards of the Iran-United States Claims Tribunal', 5 ICSID Law Review (1990) 288–9.

[86] (1987), 14 Iran-US CTR, paras 36–60.

one year before the business was expropriated. In the *Computer Sciences Corporation Case*[87] the tribunal awarded net book value of office equipment and furniture as had been requested by the claimant, but in the *Dames and Moore Case*[88] in which the claimant requested US $354,924 as the actual purchase price of vehicles, office equipment, instruments, and other equipment, the tribunal awarded an estimated value of US $100,000 in the absence of evidence of the relationship between the purchase price and the value on the date the assets were expropriated. Similarly, in the *William L Pereira Associates Inc Case*[89] the tribunal awarded 1,000,000 Rials for office equipment and a company car, citing likely depreciation and nominal resale value for small items, although the claimant had asked for 5,455,990 Rials as the actual purchase price.

In the three so-called 'nationalization' cases, where the tribunal purported to award full compensation by whatever route it took in interpreting the law, different methods were used for ascertaining the value of the property. In the *INA Corporation Case*[90] (nationalization of an insurance company), which was the simplest in this regard, the tribunal proceeded to award the claimant the full amount which it had invested in the enterprise approximately one year before the nationalization took place. In the *American International Group Inc Case*,[91] where also an insurance company was nationalized, the award indicated that full compensation in this case meant fair market value of the claimant's share interests (35 per cent) in the enterprise as a going concern, including goodwill and likely future profitability. The court went on to say that any effects of the nationalization or subsequent events should not be considered in arriving at that value,[92] but that the impact of changes in the political, economic, and social conditions as a result of events which took place prior to the nationalization should be included in measuring that value. The technique of valuation used by the tribunal was that of 'approximation' based on evidence produced by the parties. The claimant produced the reports of two independent actuaries, one Swedish and one British. The respondent produced two reports of experts, one of which showed the book value of the company, while the other gave the value of the entire company. The latter was between four and five per cent of the figure quoted by the claimant's experts. The valuations were widely disparate. The tribunal, therefore, made 'an approximation of that value, taking into account all relevant circumstances in the case'.[93] This sum (US $10,000,000) was about five or six times the highest value proposed by the respondents and about 25 per cent of the value requested by the claimant. In the third case, the *Phillips Petroleum Company of Iran Case*,[94]

[87] (1986), 10 ibid, paras 275, 302, 304.
[88] (1983), 4 ibid 223–4.
[89] (1984), 5 ibid 227.
[90] (1985), 8 ibid 373.
[91] (1983), 4 ibid 96.
[92] Ibid 106–9.
[93] Ibid 109.
[94] (1989), 21 ibid 79.

the tribunal's *terminus ad quem* was also the establishment of the fair market value of the enterprise. The respondent argued in favour of the net book value as the amount of compensation, while the claimant presented a claim based on the discounted cash flow (DCF) method. The tribunal, noting that there was no active and free market, declared that it was necessary to resort to various analytical methods to construct the market value and to consider all factors relevant to the valuation, not merely those which were components of particular methods of valuation.[95] The tribunal adverted also to the 'underlying asset valuation method' as being useful for its purposes, in addition to mentioning the DCF method. The 'underlying asset valuation' method was described as taking as a starting point previous investment and determining future profitability on the basis of historical performance. The tribunal disagreed with several factors used in the claimant's DCF calculation and also took the view that it was not an exclusive method of analysis, though it did say that the method could make a relevant contribution to the evidence of market value. Finally, it awarded the claimant about 32 per cent of what had been claimed on the basis of the DCF method, after itself reducing the figure reached on its own calculations based on the method of valuation preferred by it. Presumably, this was the tribunal's notion of full value.

In the cases where interests in business enterprises had been expropriated a variety of valuation methods have been accepted by the tribunal. In two cases, the *Tippetts, Abbett, McCarthy, Stratton Case* and the *Sedco Inc Case*,[96] the tribunal made determinations on the basis of the dissolution value of the businesses expropriated, because the claimants requested this. The dissolution value was described in the former case as the value of the enterprise after the collection of all assets and the discharge of all obligations.[97]

In the case of ongoing business enterprises the approach was different. In the *Starrett Housing Corp Case*[98] compensation payable was taken to be the fair market value of the claimant's interest in the business as a going concern. The fair market value was defined as the price the willing buyer would pay a willing seller in circumstances in which each had good information, each desired to maximize his financial gain, and neither was under duress or threat, the willing buyer being a reasonable business man.[99] The tribunal found that the DCF method had been highly emphasized by the expert to whom they had referred the matter and the respondent had not objected to the use of the method. The tribunal ultimately questioned some of the expert's judgments on key elements and awarded less than one-third of the original amount claimed. This seems to be the only case in

[95] Ibid, paras 111–12. A technique was developed in this case to construct, in the absence of actual transactions, hypothetical values representing what a willing buyer and a willing seller might agree.
[96] (1984), 6 ibid 219 and (1987), 15 ibid 23, respectively.
[97] (1984), 6 ibid 226.
[98] (1987), 16 ibid 112.
[99] Ibid, para 277.

which the claimant's use of the DCF method was totally accepted as a means of establishing the market value, even though the claim was drastically reduced.

In the *Phelps Dodge Corporation Case*[100] the going concern value was rejected as a measure of value of the business because the business was not a going concern on the date of expropriation. It was also found that the business of the enterprise was likely to have been diminished as a result of the Iranian Revolution, and that there was no market for that kind of business or shares in the business. The respondent offered net book value but this the tribunal did not accept as a fair value of the business. Instead the tribunal awarded the amount of the claimant's original investment which had been made not long before the property was expropriated. In the *Sola Tiles Inc Case*[101] the going concern value was rejected in respect of a business involving the import and distribution of tiles for luxury housing, because the business had operated for only two years and there had been a loss in the first year and a small profit in the second and the demand for luxury tiles would have diminished as a result of the revolution. This meant that no value would be assigned to goodwill or future profitability. On the other hand, it was recognised that the business did have some market value which should be the basis of the award of compensation. On the basis of evidence produced by the claimant the tribunal placed a value on what it saw as the elements of the business which covered the value of the physical assets including inventory and a reasonable estimate of accounts receivable. It awarded less than 20 per cent of what had been claimed. In both these cases going concern value was rejected on the facts.[102]

The *Thomas Earl Payne Case*[103] concerned a business for the distribution of motion picture films, sales representation, and technical laboratory services. The enterprise had been operating at a substantial profit level for several years before it was expropriated. The claimant proposed that the business should be valued as a going concern by taking a multiple of ten times the net average earnings of the three years preceding the taking. The respondent contended that only the net book value which showed a negative net worth should be considered. The tribunal conceded that the going concern value should be awarded. However, it found, upon considering the effects of the revolution upon the kind of business conducted by the enterprise and other factors which had affected the level of business, that it must make an approximation of the value of the interest expropriated. It awarded less than one-third the amount claimed. In the more recent *CBS Inc Case*[104] the tribunal found that because of the effects of the revolution upon the nature of the business which had been expropriated the enterprise had a negative net worth at the time of expropriation. A valuation based

[100] (1986), 10 ibid 121.
[101] (1987), 14 ibid 223.
[102] See also Khan, *The Iran-United States Claims Tribunal* (1990) 244–5.
[103] (1986), 12 Iran-US CTR 3, paras 34–7.
[104] Award No 486–197-2 of 28 June 1990.

on past net profits or on an estimate of profits which induced the investment was therefore rejected and no compensation awarded.

An important contribution was made by the *Amoco International Finance Corp Case*[105] in which the DCF method of establishing going concern or fair market value was not adopted as such. The business involved the building and operating of a plant for the production and marketing of sulphur and various kinds of gas. The tribunal was of the view that a lawful expropriation demanded 'just' compensation in the sense of the full equivalent of the property taken, which meant, inter alia, that extraneous factors such as excessive past profits or the rate of return on the initial investment should not be considered.[106] Market value, on the other hand, was said to be ambiguous when 'an open market does not exist for the expropriated asset or for goods identical or comparable to it'.[107] In this case the claimant valued the property taken according to the DCF method and arrived at a value of $183,232,986. The respondent argued for the net book value of the property and arrived at a figure of $14,650,000. The tribunal seems to have had some concerns about the relevance of lost future profits as a major element in the calculation of the market value on the ground that they could be too speculative.[108] While it acknowledged that the DCF method could provide useful information about profitability, it, nevertheless, felt that it could be applied in such a way that *lucrum cessans* became the sole element of compensation, which was not acceptable. A distinction was made between profitability as an intangible that could be included in the value of total assets whose net value would be payable when an expropriation was lawful and the value of revenues that the owner would have earned if the expropriation had not taken place which was only relevant in the case of an unlawful expropriation.[109] Having concluded that neither the DCF method nor the net book value was per se appropriate in the case, the tribunal ordered that the parties provide additional information to the tribunal in order to make the determination of the exact amount of the award which must represent the going concern value of the expropriated interest, also stating that:

> 264. Going concern value encompasses not only the physical and financial assets of the undertaking, but also the intangible valuables which contribute to its earning power, such as contractual rights (supply and delivery contracts, patent licenses and so on), as well as goodwill and commercial prospects. Although those assets are closely linked to the profitability of the concern, they cannot and must not be confused with the financial capitalization of the revenues which might be generated by such a concern after the transfer of property resulting from the expropriation (*lucrum cessans*).

[105] (1987), 15 Iran-US CTR 189.
[106] Ibid, para 208.
[107] Ibid, para 219.
[108] Ibid, paras 217–26.
[109] Ibid, paras 227–32.

265. The value of a going concern—of Khemco in this case—is 'made up of the values of the various components of the undertaking separately considered, and of the undertaking itself considered as an organic totality or going concern—therefore as a unified whole, the value of which is greater than that of its component parts', to take the words of the award in the *Aminoil Case*... The arbitral tribunal in that case added that account should also be taken 'of the legitimate expectations of the owners'. This last remark, however, has to be understood in relation to a previous finding of that tribunal, which noted that this concept of 'legitimate expectations' had been used by the parties in their contractual relations with a specific meaning. In the present Case, the legitimate expectations of the Parties can only be deduced from the history of the concern and from its various components, as well as from the terms of the Khemco Agreement, taking into account the circumstances prevailing at the time of the taking. Finally, the liabilities of Khemco at the valuation date have to be deducted from the total value so determined.[110]

The precedents discussed above show a variety of approaches to establishing full compensation. As for methods of valuation, there is certainly no rule of thumb or magic in any particular method. Much depends on the nature of the property or interest taken as well as on the circumstances of the taking. Different approaches may be demanded for tangible assets and business concerns. Even so there is no single accepted method of valuing either of those categories, as has been seen.

As for the valuation of interests in business concerns, it is not always the case that 'going concern value' is the criterion. This depends on the circumstances of the case—was the business in fact a going concern? Whether the business was

[110] Ibid paras 264–5. See also on the DCF method of valuation the *Ebrahimi (Shahin Shaine) Case* (1994), 30 ibid 170. Since 1945, valuation techniques have been developed to factor in different elements of risk and probability. See, for example, the detailed methodology developed by the UNCC for assessing Kuwaiti corporate claims (*Report and Recommendations Made by the Panel of Commissioners Concerning the First Instalment of 'E4' Claims*, 19 March 1999, S/AC.26/1999/4, paras 32–62) and claims filed on behalf of non-Kuwaiti corporations and other business entities, excluding oil sector, construction/engineering and export guarantee claims (*Report and Recommendations Made by the Panel of Commissioners Concerning the Third Instalment of 'E2' Claims*, 9 December 1999, S/AC, 26/1999/22). The discounted cash flow (DCF) method has gained some favour, especially in the context of calculations involving income over a limited duration, as in the case of wasting assets. Although developed as a tool for assessing commercial value, it can also be useful in the context of calculating value for compensation purposes. But difficulties can arise in the application of the DCF method to establish capital value in the compensation context. The method analyses a wide range of inherently speculative elements, some of which have a significant impact upon the outcome (eg discount rates, currency fluctuations, inflation figures, commodity prices, interest rates and other commercial risks). This has led tribunals to adopt a cautious approach to the use of the method. Hence, although income-based methods have been accepted in principle there has been a preference rather for asset-based methods, as have been described earlier in this chapter. In the context of claims for lost profits there is a corresponding preference for claims to be based on past performance rather than forecasts. For example, the UNCC guidelines on valuation of business losses in Decision 9, S/AC.26/1992/9, para 19 states: 'The method of a valuation should therefore be one that focuses on past performance rather than on forecasts and projections into the future.' A particular concern is the risk of double-counting which arises from the relationship between the capital value of an enterprise and its contractually based profits (eg the *Ebrahimi (Shahin Shaine) Case* (1994), 30 Iran-US CTR, para 159). For the above views, see the Commentary to Article 36(1) of the ILC's Articles on State Responsibility, para 26: Crawford (2002) (note 2 above) 227.

a going concern or not, the method of valuation may vary. In the event that the business is held to be a going concern, still there is no single accepted method of valuation that tribunals have applied. The DCF method, for instance, was fully accepted only in one of the many cases concerning businesses which the Iran-US Claims Tribunal decided, though even so the valuation based on that method was drastically reduced in the award. Further, the respondent virtually agreed to the use of this method in the case by not objecting to it. It was also rejected outright in one such case. Another factor which may be of some importance in determining the approach a tribunal may take are the methods of valuation used by the parties. If the parties are in agreement on the method, the tribunal may be inclined to adopt the method agreed upon as at least the basis for an award. If the parties disagree, the tribunal may or may not use the claimant's method but will be more ready to find a third way or a compromise.

There are a few more observations to be made. Net book value as a method of establishing full compensation is not generally accepted, especially for going concerns,[111] although it has been used on one or two occasions, where the circumstances have been very special and it has been fancied, particularly by the respondent. It may be noted in this connection that in the *Amoco International Finance Corp Case* the view was taken that the doctrine of unjust enrichment, even if relevant to the calculation of compensation payable, did not require that only net book value be paid.[112]

Future profitability and goodwill which are different from actual profits may well be elements to be considered in the assessment of full value regardless of whether lost profits must be compensated. This principle emerges particularly from the *Amoco International Finance Corp Case*, where it was understood that the *Chorzów Factory Case* did not permit the inclusion of *lucrum cessans* or probable future profits in the value of the undertaking as such.[113]

To sum up the methods used to establish the value of property and the problems associated with the process the commentary to Article 31 of the ILC's Articles on State Responsibility may be cited:[114]

[111] In the *Banco Nacional de Cuba Case* (1981), 658 F 2d, 875 (2d 1981), however, net value was awarded.

[112] (1987), 15 Iran-US CTR 267–8. Net book value (ie the difference between the total assets of the business and total liabilities as shown on its books) as a method of valuation for capital loss had advantages and limitations. Its advantages are that the figures can be determined by reference to market costs, they are normally drawn from a contemporaneous record, and they are based on data generated for some other purpose than supporting the claim. Accordingly, net book value (or some variant of this method) has been employed to assess the value of businesses. The limitations of the method lie in the reliance on historical figures, the use of accounting principles which tend to undervalue assets, especially in periods of inflation, and the fact that the purpose for which the figures were produced does not take account of the compensation context and any rules specific to it. The balance sheet may contain an entry for goodwill, but the reliability of such figures depends on their proximity to the moment of an actual sale. On this see the Commentary on Article 36(1) of the ILC's Articles on State Responsibility, para 26: Crawford (2002) (note 2 above) 226–7.

[113] (1987), 15 Iran-US CTR 269–71.

[114] See Crawford (2002) (note 2 above) 226.

(22)... Where the property in question or comparable property is freely traded on an open market, value is more readily determined. In such cases, the choice and application of asset-based valuation methods based on market data and the physical properties of the assets is relatively unproblematic, apart from evidentiary difficulties associated with long outstanding claims.[115] Where the property interests in question are unique or unusual, for example, art works or other cultural property,[116] or are not the subject of frequent or recent market transactions, the determination of value is more difficult. This may be true, for example, in respect of certain business entities in the nature of a going concern, especially if shares are not regularly traded.[117]

(23) Decisions of various *ad hoc* tribunals since 1945 have been dominated by claims in respect of nationalised business entities. The preferred approach in these cases has been to examine the assets of the business, making allowance for good will and profitability as appropriate. This method has the advantage of grounding compensation as much as possible in some objective assessment of value linked to the tangible asset backing of the business. The value of goodwill and other indicators of profitability may be uncertain, unless derived from information provided by a recent sale or acceptable arms-length offer. Yet, for profitable business entities where the whole is greater than the sum of the parts, compensation would be incomplete without paying due regard to such factors.[118, 119]

[115] Particularly in the case of lump sum settlements, agreements have been concluded decades after the claims arose. See eg the USSR-UK Agreement of 15 July 1986 concerning claims dating back to 1917 and the China-UK Agreement of 5 June 1987 in respect of claims arising in 1949. In such cases, the choice of valuation method was sometimes determined by availability of evidence.

[116] See *Report and Recommendations Made by the Panel of Commissioners concerning Part Two of the First Instalment of Individual Claims for Damages above US$100,000 (Category 'D' Claims)*, 12 March 1998, UN Doc S/AC.26/1998/3, paras 48–9, where the UNCC considered a compensation claim in relation to the taking of the claimant's Islamic art collection by the Iraqi military personnel.

[117] Where share prices provide good evidence of value, they may be utilized, as in the *INA Corporation Case* (1985), 8 Iran-US CTR 373.

[118] Early claims recognized that even where a taking of property was lawful, compensation for a going concern called for something more than the value of the property elements of the business. The Mexican-American Claims Commission in rejecting a claim for lost profits in the case of a lawful taking stated that payment for property elements would be 'augmented by the existence of those elements which constitute a going concern': the *Wells Fargo & Company Case (Decision No 22-B)*, American-Mexican Claims Commission (1926) 153. See also *Propositions and Conclusions on Compensation for Business Losses: Types of Damages and their Valuation*, Decision 9 of the UNCC Governing Council, 6 March 1992, UN Doc S/AC.26/1992/9, para 16.

The footnote numbers in footnotes 115 to 118 are mine reflecting footnotes 584 to 587 in the Commentary on Article 36(1) of the ILC's Articles on State Responsibility.

[119] As pointed out earlier, the valuation of property, as such, and the establishment of value require similar techniques, whether the taking is lawful or unlawful.

Valuation of business enterprises and tangible assets is done on the basis of valuation principles which are accepted in the more sophisticated business world. Such principles are associated with accounting techniques. None of them are as scientific as the formulas for the law of gravity, as in virtually all of them there is a discretionary element involved. Below are given the meanings in general use and in general terms of some of the concepts which have been used in the application of valuation terms, particularly with reference to the discussion which follows in the text:

1. *Fair market value*. The price a willing buyer would pay a willing seller in circumstances in which each had good information, each deserved to maximize his financial gain, and neither was under duress or threat, the willing buyer being a reasonable businessman. It is to be noted that there are, nevertheless, questions as to what market is to be used, if, indeed, there is a

(ii) Lost profits

In certain cases compensation for loss of profits (*lucrum cessans*) may be appropriate.[120] International and transnational tribunals have in fact included awards

market, and whether the willing buyer is always a stereotype who will use a particular standard of valuation.
2. *Going concern value.* Value of a business as a functioning enterprise, not about to be liquidated or dissolved.
3. *Net book value.* The value on the books of account of the owner's equity in an enterprise, which is the amount that remains after deducting the total liabilities from the total assets of an enterprise (company) in the amounts that these items appear on the company's book of account. There may be some variation depending on accounting principles employed for keeping the books.
4. *Net worth.* This term generally has the same meaning as 'net book value'.
5. *Historic cost.* This term is based on the purchase price or starting cost of assets and liabilities after depreciation and improvement have been accounted for and approximates to net book value. It is used especially in connection with tangible assets such as real estate.
6. *Depreciated replacement value.* The value of recreating the entire business in terms of its tangible assets, after such assets have been depreciated for years of use. This concept does not take into account intangibles and the earning power of the business. However, it is applied frequently to land, buildings, and tangible assets.
7. *Reproduction cost.* A term which is similar to the previous term, while being based on reproduction of the elements of a business.
8. *Liquidation value.* Value upon dissolving the operation, selling the assets piecemeal and converting them into cash, the liabilities having been accounted for in the process.
9. *Dissolution value.* This term is similar to the previous one.
10. *Good will.* This term represents an intangible asset or a collection of such assets, which according to most authorities defies clear definition. It is generally regarded as representing excess earnings but this usage is not uniform. Sometimes it is used to denote simply the ability to make a profit.
11. *Discounted cash flow (DCF) method.* This method of valuation briefly involves the following steps:
    (a) making a forecast of the income and cash flow of the enterprise into the future for a given number of years and then calculating for each year the present value of the cash flow by using a discount factor or figure, which takes into account the perceived risks;
    (b) adding up the values of all the assets of the enterprise which are expected to be present at the end of the projected period (the residual assets) and calculating the present value of that figure;
    (c) adding up the present values of the cash flows for each year (see (a) above) and the present value of the assets expected to remain at the end of the whole period (see (b) above) and then deducting any debts or other liabilities expected to remain at the end of the period.

As will readily be realised, there are many discretionary choices which have to be made in using this method.

For more information of a basic nature on valuation concepts and principles reference should be made to such accounting and valuation books as Horn, *Business Valuation Manual* (1987); Smith, *Corporate Valuation: A Business and Professional Guide* (1988); and Davidson and Weil, *Handbook of Modern Accounting* (1983). Some assistance may also be gained from Weigel and Weston, 'Valuation upon the Deprivation of Foreign Enterprises: A Policy Oriented Approach to the Problem of Compensation Under International Law' in Lillich (ed), 1 *The Valuation of Nationalized Property in International Law* (1972) 3 and especially 16–23; Goldman and Paxman, 'Real Property Valuation in Argentina, Chile and Mexico' in Lillich (ed), 2 ibid (1973) 129 and especially 146–63.

[120] See Article 36(2) of the ILC's Articles on State Responsibility which recognizes this: Crawford (2002) (note 2 above) 218. This section on lost profits as compensation follows closely the commentary to Article 36(2) of the ILC's Articles on State Responsibility: Crawford, ibid 228 ff.

for loss of profits in assessing compensation: eg in the *Cape Horn Pigeon Case*,[121] the *Delagoa Bay Railway Case*,[122] the *William Lee*,[123] the *Yuille Shortridge and Co Case*,[124] and the *Sapphire International Petroleum Ltd Case*.[125] Loss of profits was featured in the *Chorzów Factory Case* itself, when the PCIJ decided that the claimant should receive the value of property by way of damages not as it stood at the time of expropriation but at the time of indemnification.[126] Awards for loss of profits as such have also been made in respect of contract-based lost profits in the *LIAMCO Arbitration*[127] and in some ICSID arbitrations.[128] Such cases illustrate the principle that lost profits may be payable as compensation. Nevertheless, lost profits have not as commonly been awarded in practice as compensation for accrued losses. Tribunals have been reluctant to provide compensation for claims with inherently speculative elements. According to the arbitrator in the *Shufeldt Case*,[129] 'the *lucrum cessans* must be the direct fruit of the contract and not too remote or speculative'. In the ICSID *Amco Asia Corp and Others Case*, on the other hand, it was stated that 'non-speculative profits' were recoverable.[130]

The UNCC also stressed the requirement for claimants to provide 'clear and convincing evidence of ongoing and expected profitability'.[131] In assessing claims for lost profits of construction contracts, Panels of the UNCC have generally required that the claimant's calculation take into account the risk inherent in the project.[132] When compared with tangible assets, profits (and intangible assets which are income-based) are relatively vulnerable to commercial and political risks, and increasingly so the further into the future projections are made. In cases where lost future profits have been awarded, it has been where an anticipated income stream has attained sufficient attributes to be considered a legally protected interest of sufficient certainty to be compensatable. In considering claims for future profits the UNCC Panel dealing with certain claims stated that in

[121] (1902), 9 UNRIAA 63, where lost profits resulting from the seizure of an American whaler were assessed and awarded.

[122] (1900), Moore, 2 *International Arbitrations* 1865.

[123] (1863), Moore, 4 ibid 3405.

[124] (1861), de Lapradelle and Politis, 2 RAI 78.

[125] (1963), 35 ILR 187, 189.

[126] (*Merits*, 1928) PCIJ Series A No 17 47–8, 53.

[127] (1977), 62 ILR 140.

[128] The *Amco Asia Corp and Others Case*, First Arbitration (1984), Annulment (1986), Resubmitted Case (1990), 1 ICSID Reports 377; the *AGIP Spa Case* (1999), 1 ibid 306. In the *Sedco Inc Case* (1987), 15 Iran-US CTR 23, what were lost profits in fact were assessed as *damnum emergens*.

[129] (1930), 2 UNRIAA 1099.

[130] Resubmitted Case (1990), 1 ICSID Reports 569.

[131] *Report and Recommendations Made by the Panel of Commissioners Concerning the First Instalment of 'E3' Claims* (17 December 1998), UN Doc S/AC.26/1998/13 para 147.

[132] See ibid para 157, and *Report and Recommendations Made by the Panel of Commissioners Concerning the Fourth Instalment of 'E3' Claims* (30 September 1999), UN Doc S/AC.26/1998/14 para 126.

order for such claims to warrant recommendation, 'it is necessary to demonstrate by sufficient documentary and other appropriate evidence a history of successful (ie profitable) operation, and a state of affairs which warrants the conclusion that the hypothesis that there would have been future profitable contracts is well founded'.[133] This has normally been achieved by virtue of definite contractual arrangements or, in some cases, a well-established history of dealings.[134]

In some cases lost profits have been excluded on the basis that they were not sufficiently established as a legally protected interest. In the *Oscar Chinn Case* a monopoly was not accorded the status of an acquired right.[135] In the *Asian Agricultural Products Case*, a claim for lost profits by a newly established business was rejected for lack of evidence of established earnings.[136] Needless to say, claims for lost profits are also subject to the usual limitations on the recovery of damages, such as causation, remoteness, evidentiary requirements, and accounting principles, which seek to discount speculative elements from projected figures.

There are several categories of loss of profits which may be distinguished. First, for example, lost profits may be from income-producing property during a period in which there has been no interference with title as distinct from temporary loss of use. This category involves claims for loss of profits due to the temporary loss of use and enjoyment of the income-producing asset. In these cases there is no interference with title and hence in the relevant period the loss compensated is the income to which the claimant was entitled by virtue of undisturbed ownership. Many of the early cases concern vessels seized and detained. In *The Montijo* an American vessel was seized in Panama. The umpire in the arbitration allowed a sum of money per day for loss of the use of the vessel.[137] In *The Betsey*, compensation was awarded not only for the value of the cargo seized and detained, but also for demurrage for the period representing loss of use.[138]

The second category of claims relates to the unlawful taking of income-producing property which results in lost profits between the date of taking away of title and adjudication. In such cases lost profits have been awarded for the period up to the time of adjudication. In the *Chorzów Factory Case (Merits)* this took the form of re-invested income, representing profits from the time of taking to the time of adjudication.[139] In the *Norwegian Shipowners Claim* lost profits were similarly not awarded for any period beyond the date of adjudication.[140] Once the capital value of income-producing property has been restored through

[133] Ibid para 140.

[134] Whiteman, 3 *Damages* 1837 states: 'in order to be allowable, prospective profits must not be too speculative, contingent, uncertain and the like. There must be proof that they were *reasonably* anticipated; and that the profits anticipated were probable and not merely possible.'

[135] (1934), PCIJ Series A/B No 63.

[136] (1990), 4 ICSID Reports 245.

[137] (1875), Moore, 2 *International Arbitrations* 1421.

[138] (1794), Moore, 5 *International Adjudications* 113.

[139] (1928), PCIJ Series A No 17.

[140] (1922), 1 UNRIAA 307.

the mechanism of compensation, funds paid by way of compensation can once again be invested to re-establish an income stream. Although the rationale for the award of lost profits in these cases is less clearly articulated, it may be attributed to a recognition of the claimant's continuing beneficial interest in the property up to the moment when potential restitution is converted to a compensation payment.[141] This category is most commonly associated with the deprivation of property, as opposed to wrongful termination of a contract or concession. If restitution were awarded, the award of lost profits would be analogous to cases of temporary dispossession. If restitution is not awarded, as in the two cases referred to above, lost profits may be awarded up to the time when compensation is made available as a substitute for restitution.

The third category of claims for loss of profits arises in the context of concessions and other contractually protected interests. Here the profits anticipated and lost after the date of adjudication are awarded. Awards of lost future profits have been made in the context of a contractually protected income stream, as in the *Amco Asia Corp Case*, rather than on the basis of the taking of income-producing property.[142] In the UNCC's *Report and Recommendations made by the Panel of Commissioners Concerning the Second Installment of 'E2' Claims*, dealing with reduced profits, the Panel found that losses arising from a decline in business were compensatable even though tangible property was not affected and the businesses continued to operate throughout the relevant period.[143] In such cases lost future income has been compensated. In some cases, lost profits were not awarded beyond the date of adjudication, though for reasons unrelated to the nature of the income-producing property. In the *Robert May Case*, for instance, the concession had expired.[144] In other cases, circumstances giving rise to *force majeure* had the effect of suspending contractual obligations.[145] In the *Delagoa Bay Railway Case*[146] and in the *Shufeldt Case*[147] lost profits were awarded in respect of concessions which had been terminated. In the *Sapphire International Petroleum Ltd Case*,[148] and the *LIAMCO Arbitration*[149] (both transnational arbitrations) and in the *Amco Asia Corp and Others Case*[150] (an ICSID arbitration) awards of lost profits were also sustained on the basis of contractual relationships. In the case

[141] For the approach of the UNCC in dealing with loss of profits claims associated with the destruction of businesses following the Iraqi invasion of Kuwait, see *Report and Recommendations Made by the Panel of Commissioners Concerning the First Instalment of 'E4' Claims*, 19 March 1999, UN Doc S/AC.26/1999/4, paras 184–7.

[142] First Arbitration (1984), Annulment (1986), Resubmitted Case (1990), 1 ICSID Reports 377.

[143] 19 March 1999, UN Doc S/AC.26/1999/6.

[144] (1900), Whiteman, 3 *Damages* 1704, 1860.

[145] The *Gould Marketing Inc Case* (1984), 6 Iran-US CTR 272; the *Sylvania Technical Systems Case* (1985), 8 Iran-US CTR 298.

[146] (1900), Moore, 2 *International Arbitrations* 1865.

[147] (1930), 2 UNRIAA 1079.

[148] (1963), 35 ILR 136.

[149] (1977), 62 ILR 140.

[150] First Arbitration (1984), Annulment (1986), Resubmitted Case (1990), 1 ICSID Reports 377.

of contracts, it is the future income stream which is compensated, up to the time when legal recognition of entitlement ends. In some contracts this is immediate, eg where the contract is determinable at the instance of the State,[151] or where some other basis for contractual termination exists, or it may arise from some future date dictated by the terms of the contract itself.[152]

(iii) *Damnum emergens*, including incidental expenses

It is well established on the basis of a general principle of law that *damnum emergens*, ie consequential damage subject to absence of remoteness and such, is compensatable. This includes incidental expenses which are reasonably incurred to repair damage and otherwise mitigate loss arising from the violation of international law. Such damages may be associated with, for example, the displacement of staff or the need to sell or store undelivered products at a loss. Compensation for such damages has been awarded by the UNCC, where compensation was awarded for evacuation and relief costs, repatriation, termination costs, renovation costs, and expenses in mitigation.[153] In the *General Electric Company Case* the Iran-US Claims Tribunal awarded compensation for items resold at a loss and for storage costs.[154]

(c) Interest

The award of interest on compensation awarded has been appropriately dealt with in Article 38 of the ILC's Articles on State Responsibility. The general principles applicable are the same for cases of diplomatic protection as for cases between States per se. Article 38 states:

1. Interest on any principal sum payable under this Chapter shall be payable when necessary in order to ensure full reparation. The interest rate and mode of calculation shall be set so as to achieve that result.

2. Interest runs from the date when the principal sum should have been paid until the date the obligation to pay is fulfilled.[155]

Furthermore, what is said in the commentary to this Article correctly reflects the state of the law.[156]

Interest is not an autonomous form of reparation, nor is it a necessary part of compensation in every case. The principal sum awarded in compensation may, however, be supplemented by an award of interest, depending on the circumstances of the case. An award of interest may be required in some cases in order to provide full reparation for the injury caused by an internationally wrongful act

151 See the *Sylvania Technical Systems Case* (1985), 8 Iran-US CTR 298.

152 On the connection between lost profits and interest see the section below on *Interest*.

153 *Report and Recommendations on the First Instalment of 'E2' Claims*, 3 July 1998, UN Doc S/AC.26/1998/7, paras 133, 153, 249, 228, 214, 225, and 183, respectively.

154 (1991), 26 Iran-US CTR 165–7, 168–9.

155 See Crawford (2002) (note 2 above) 68 and 235.

156 Crawford, ibid 235 ff. What follows here borrows from the commentary.

and it is normally the subject of separate treatment both in claims for reparation and in the awards of tribunals. Support for a general rule favouring the award of interest as an aspect of full reparation is found in international jurisprudence. For example, awards of interest were made in the *Illinois Central Railroad Case*[157] and the *Lucas Case*.[158] An award of interest was also dealt with in *Administrative Decision No. III*[159] by the United States-Germany Mixed Claims Commission. In *The SS Wimbledon*, the PCIJ awarded simple interest at 6 per cent as from the date of judgment, on the basis that interest was only payable 'from the moment when the amount of the sum due has been fixed and the obligation to pay has been established'.[160] As a general principle, an injured State is entitled to interest on the principal sum representing its loss, if that sum is quantified as at an earlier date than the date of the settlement of, or judgment or award concerning, the claim and to the extent that it is necessary to ensure full reparation. Thus, interest may not be allowed where the loss is assessed in current value terms as at the date of the award.[161]

Issues concerning the award of interest have frequently arisen before international tribunals, both in cases where the underlying claim involved injury to private parties and where the injury was to the State itself. Thus, in the *M/V Saiga (No 2) Case* the ITLOS awarded interest at different rates in respect of different categories of loss.[162] In *Islamic Republic of Iran v United States of America (Case No A-19)*, the Iran-US Claims Tribunal acting as the full tribunal held that its general jurisdiction to deal with claims included the power to award interest, but declined to lay down uniform standards for the award of interest on the ground that this fell within the jurisdiction of each Chamber and related 'to the exercise... of the discretion accorded to them in deciding each particular case', further explaining on the principle involved that:

> claims for interest are part of the compensation sought and do not constitute a separate cause of action requiring their own independent jurisdictional grant. This Tribunal is required by Article V of the Claims Settlement Declaration to decide claims 'on the basis of respect for law'. In doing so, it has regularly treated interest, where sought, as forming an integral part of the 'claim' which it has a duty to decide. The Tribunal notes that the Chambers have been consistent in awarding interest as 'compensation for damages suffered due to delay in payment'... Indeed, it is customary for arbitral tribunals to award interest as part of an award for damages, notwithstanding the absence of any express reference to interest in the *compromis*. Given that the power to award interest is

157 (1926), 4 UNRIAA 134.

158 (1966), 30 ILR 220.

159 (1923), 7 UNRIAA 66.

160 (1923), PCIJ Series A, No 1, 32. The Court recognized the French claim for an interest rate of 6 percent as fair, having regard to the existing financial situation of the world and the conditions prevailing for public loans.

161 See the *Lighthouses Case* (1956), 12 UNRIAA 252–3.

162 *Saint Vincent and the Grenadines v Guinea*), Judgment of 1 July 1999 para 173, <http://www.itlos.org>.

inherent in the Tribunal's authority to decide claims, the exclusion of such power could only be established by an express provision in the Claims Settlement Declaration. No such provision exists. Consequently, the Tribunal concludes that it is clearly within its power to award interest as compensation for damage suffered.[163]

This tribunal has not awarded interest in certain cases, eg where a lump-sum award was considered as reflecting full compensation and where other special circumstances existed.[164]

Decision 16 of the Governing Council of the UNCC dealt with the question of interest. It provided that:

1. Interest will be awarded from the date the loss occurred until the date of payment, at a rate sufficient to compensate successful claimants for the loss of use of the principal amount of the award.

2. The methods of calculation and of payment of interest will be considered by the Governing Council at the appropriate time.

3. Interest will be paid after the principal amount of awards.[165]

The provision favours the award of interest where necessary, to compensate a claimant. At the same time it allows for flexibility. Clearly, interest as a form of compensation is regarded as a secondary element subordinated to the principal amount of the claim. This is so, though an important point is that an injured State or alien is not automatically entitled to the payment of interest. The trend of international decisions and practice is towards greater availability of interest as an aspect of full reparation. It is clear that the awarding of interest depends on the circumstances of each case essentially in terms of whether an award of interest is necessary in order to ensure full reparation. This approach of international tribunals reflects a general principle of law which emerges from the practice of various legal systems.

As regards compound interest as opposed to simple interest, the general view of international courts and tribunals has been against the award of compound interest, even though they may hold claimants to be normally entitled to compensatory interest. For example, the Iran-United States Claims Tribunal has consistently denied claims for compound interest, even where the claimant had suffered losses through compound interest charges on indebtedness associated with the claim. In the *RJ Reynolds Tobacco Co Case* the tribunal failed to find

any special reasons for departing from international precedents which normally would allow the awarding of compound interest. As noted by one authority, '[t]here are few rules within the scope of the subject of damages in international law that are better settled than the one that compound interest is not allowable'... Even though the term 'all sums' could be construed to include interest and thereby to allow compound interest, the Tribunal,

[163] (1987), 16 Iran-US CTR 289–90.

[164] See the detailed analysis in the *McCollough & Co Inc Case* (1986), 11 Iran-US CTR 26–31, Chamber Three.

[165] *Award of Interest*, Decision 16, 4 January 1993, UN Doc S/AC.26/1992/16.

due to the ambiguity of the language, interprets the clause in the light of the international rule just stated, and thus excludes compound interest.[166]

Consistent with this approach the same tribunal has gone behind contractual provisions appearing to provide for compound interest, in order to prevent the claimant gaining a profit 'wholly out of proportion to the possible loss that [it] might have incurred by not having the amounts due at its disposal'.[167] Thus, the weight of authority supports the view of Arbitrator Huber in the *British Claims in the Spanish Zone of Morocco Case* that:

> the arbitral case law in matters involving compensation of one State for another for damages suffered by the nationals of one within the territory of the other... is unanimous... in disallowing compound interest. In these circumstances, very strong and quite specific arguments would be called for to grant such interest... [168]

It has been argued that the principle should show greater flexibility on the ground that 'compound interest reasonably incurred by the injured party should be recoverable as an item of damage'.[169] Indeed, arbitral tribunals have supported this view in some cases.[170] But in terms of the preponderant precedents in international law it cannot be said that there is any entitlement to compound interest in the absence of special circumstances which justify some element of compounding as an aspect of full reparation.

The actual calculation of interest on any principal sum payable by way of reparation raises complex issues concerning the starting date (date of breach,[171] date on which payment should have been made, date of claim or demand), the terminal date (date of settlement or award, date of actual payment) as well as the applicable interest rate (rate current in the respondent State, in the applicant State, international lending rates). In fact, there is no uniform approach, internationally, to questions of quantification and assessment of amounts of interest payable. In practice the circumstances of each case and the conduct of the parties strongly affect the outcome. As the Iran-United States Claims Tribunal has observed, such matters, if the parties cannot resolve them, must be left 'to the

[166] (1984), 7 Iran-US CTR 191–2. The tribunal cited Whiteman, 3 *Damages* 1997.

[167] The *Anaconda-Iran, Inc. Case* (1986), 13 Iran-US CTR 235. See also Aldrich (note 56 above) 477–8.

[168] (1924), 2 UNRIAA 650. However, in the *Aminoil Arbitration* (1982), 66 ILR 613, para 178(5), a transnational arbitration, the interest awarded was compounded for a period without any reason being given. This interest compounded accounted for more than half of the total final award.

[169] Mann, 'Compound Interest as an Item of Damage in International Law', in *Further Studies in International Law* (1990) 383.

[170] The *Compañía des Desarrollo de Santa Elena SA Case* (2000), 5 ICSID Reports 177 ff, paras 103–5, Award of 1 Feb. 2000.

[171] Using the date of the breach as the starting date for calculation of the interest term is problematic as there may be difficulties in determining that date, and many legal systems require a demand for payment by the claimant before interest will run. The date of formal demand was taken as the relevant date in the *Russian Indemnity Case* (1921), 11 UNRIAA 242, by analogy with the general position in European legal systems. In any case, failure to make a timely claim for payment is relevant in deciding whether to allow interest.

exercise...of the discretion accorded to [individual tribunals] in deciding each particular case'.[172] On the other hand, it is to be noted that the present international practice is somewhat unsettled. Article 38 of the ILC's Articles on State Responsibility chooses a solution indicating that the date from which interest is to be calculated is the date when the principal sum should have been paid, while interest runs from that date until the date the obligation to pay is fulfilled. As for the interest rate and mode of calculation, they must be set so as to achieve the result of providing full reparation for the injury suffered as a result of the internationally wrongful act.

Where a sum for loss of profits is included as part of the compensation for the injury caused by a wrongful act, an award of interest will be inappropriate if the injured State would thereby obtain double recovery. A capital sum cannot be earning interest and be notionally employed in earning profits at one and the same time. Thus, interest may not be awarded on profit-earning capital over the same period of time. However, interest may be due on the profits which would have been earned but which have been withheld from the original owner.[173]

(d) Compensation and the national State

Because the international wrong is construed as have been suffered by the national State of the alien, strictly speaking reparation—particularly compensation—is to benefit the national State. Nevertheless, there is also the alien who is involved at the receiving end of the wrong. Thus, restitution, for example, would primarily benefit the alien.

However, it is an accepted rule that the damage for which reparation must be made is the damage to the alien's national State which is not identical with that which its national has suffered, so that the reparation ordered in a given case need not be simply equivalent to the loss suffered by the alien.[174] Yet it is a fact that it is the damage to the alien which constitutes the measure of reparation. It is a

[172] *Islamic Republic of Iran* v *United States of America (Case No A-19)* (1987), 16 Iran-US CTR 290.

[173] Awards of interest have also been envisaged by international human rights courts and tribunals, even though the compensation practice of these bodies is relatively cautious and the claims are almost always unliquidated. Interest is awarded, for example, to protect the value of an award of damages payable by instalments over time: the *Velásquez Rodríguez Case (Compensation),* IACHR, Series C, No 7 (1990), para 57; and the *Papamichalapoulos* v *Greece* (1995), ECHR Series A, No 330-B, para 39, where interest was payable only in respect of the pecuniary damages awarded; see further Shelton (note 66 above) 270–2.

In their more recent practice, it would appear, national compensation commissions and tribunals have also generally allowed for interest in assessing compensation. However in certain cases of partial lump-sum settlements, claims have been expressly limited to the amount of the principal loss, on the basis that with a limited fund to be distributed, claims to principal should take priority. See eg the Foreign Compensation (People's Republic of China) Order 1987 (UK), section 10, giving effect to a Settlement Agreement of 5 June 1987, UKTS No 37 (1989). Some national court decisions have also dealt with issues of interest under international law: *McKesson Corporation* v *Islamic Republic of Iran* (2000), 116 F supp 2d 13 (District Court, DC). However, more often questions of interest are dealt with as part of the law of the forum.

[174] The *Chorzów Factory Case* (*Merits*, 1928), PCIJ Series A, No 17 28.

mixed bag. The injury suffered by the alien is used as a scale for the calculation of damages. Although the ultimate reparation may involve more than the actual loss to the alien,[175] the damage suffered by the alien is the basis for the award of reparation. Such damages awarded may include both damages for material loss and for moral injury suffered by the alien. Although the economic assets of an individual may, by a fiction, be regarded as part of the wealth of his national State, international law does not really treat such assets as being actually the property of the national State. As regards damage through personal injury including moral suffering, it would be difficult to regard the national State as having suffered such damage even by a legal fiction.

Another feature is that the national State has complete control over the disposition of the proceeds of a claim and is not even obliged to hand them to the individual or individuals whose claims it has espoused.[176] This is because the claim has a public character based on the interests of the national State. It must be stressed that this is the rule, though in reality States do distribute the proceeds of the awards or settlements on the basis that the individual suffering the injury has an interest in reparation.[177]

There is also a rule that the national State may waive, compromise, or discontinue the presentation of the claim irrespective of the wishes of the alien.[178] This rule reflects the interests of the national State as the beneficiary of reparation.

Such rules reflect the basic principle that the State does not appear as a representative or on behalf of the alien whose claim it espouses, but defends its own rights. However, a particular practice which has developed reveals that both national States and host States (respondents) regard the aliens as the proper claimants in cases where aliens have been injured. From the early nineteenth century to the present States have by agreement established Claims Commissions and Claims Tribunals which adjudicate on claims brought by the aliens themselves against the wrongdoing State. Because the wrongdoing State is a party to the agreements establishing such tribunals, this is an acknowledgment that reparation is due to the alien rather than to his national State. In turn the national State by being a

[175] The *Chorzów Factory Case (Merits)*, (1928), ibid.

[176] *Frelinghuysen v US ex rel Key*, 110 US 63 (1884); *US ex rel Boynton v Blaine*, 139 US 306 (1891); *Heirs of Oswald v Swiss Government*, 3 AD (1925–6) 244; *US v La Abra Silver Mining Co*, 175 US 423 (1899); *Great Western Insurance Co v US*, 19 Ct Cl 206 (1884); Hackworth, 5 *Digest* 763 ff, and Feller, *The Mexican Claims Commissions* (1935) 84 and the authorities there cited at note 6.

[177] In *Administrative Decision No V* (1924), 7 UNRIAA 152, the umpire recognized this rule while stating that in reality States distribute the proceeds of awards on the basis that the interests of individuals are involved. The rule is recognized in international agreements between States covering lump-sum settlements of the claims of aliens: see Bederman, 'Lump Sum Agreements and Diplomatic Protection' in ILA, *Report of the Seventieth Conference* (2002) 237. If there is a duty incumbent upon the alien's national State to transfer the compensation received to the extent of what covers the injury to the alien, the issue would arise, as in the case of a duty to protect, to whom this duty is owed.

[178] Moore, 6 *Digest* 1012 ff; Borchard, *The Diplomatic Protection of Citizens Abroad* (1915) 366 ff; and Whiteman, 1 *Damages* 282.

party to such agreements resigns its right to have reparation made to itself and acknowledges that providing full reparation to its national alone is a complete discharge of the wrongdoing State's obligation of providing reparation. It is true that this turn of events is based on specific agreements but it is an inroad into the rule that injury is to the national State.

Claims tribunals which have been established include those between the USA and European States, Latin American States, tribunals such as the Iran-US Claims Tribunal and the ICSID tribunals. One of the consequences of the establishment of such tribunals is that, where the agreement is construed to do so or explicitly does so, as in the case of the ICSID Convention and the agreement setting up the Iran-US Claims Tribunal, certain claims (such as contract claims which have not matured into claims based on international wrongs after the commission of a denial of justice) become subject to the jurisdiction of the tribunals. But this is a matter of interpretation of the agreement establishing the tribunal. Certain nineteenth century Claims Commissions have taken the view that under the instruments creating them contract claims as such were not within their jurisdiction, unless they were based on a violation of international law in addition to there being a simple breach of contract.[179]

The ILC in Article 19 of its Articles on Diplomatic Protection of 2006 included a recommendation, though not a rule of law, that any compensation obtained for an injury to a national by a responsible State should be transferred to the injured person, subject to any reasonable deductions.[180] The commentary provided by the ILC on this recommendation which is in Article 19(c) is quoted here at length in order that the reasoning of the ILC, with which it is difficult to disagree, may be seen more clearly.

(5) Subparagraph (c) provides that States should transfer any compensation received from the responsible State in respect of an injury to a national to the injured national. This recommendation is designed to [encourage] discourage the widespread perception that States have an absolute discretion in such matters and are under no obligation to transfer moneys received for a claim based on diplomatic protection to the injured national. This perception has its roots in the *Mavrommatis* rule and a number of judicial pronouncements. In terms of the *Mavrommatis Palestine Concessions* dictum a State asserts its own right in exercising diplomatic protection and becomes 'the sole claimant'.[181] Consequently, logic dictates that no restraints are placed on the State, in the interests of the individual, in the settlement of the claim or the payment of any compensation received. That the State has 'complete freedom of action' in its exercise of diplomatic protection is confirmed by the *Barcelona Traction* case.[182] Despite the fact that the logic of *Mavrommatis* is

[179] See C F Amerasinghe (note 70 above) chapter 5, for a discussion of the requirement of a breach of international law in contract claims.

[180] *Report of the ILC (2006)*, UN Doc A/61/10, 2006, 94 (see <http://www.un.org>). The footnotes in the quotation which follow (181–92) are footnotes 277 to 288 in the original and are only renumbered, while their context and form are as they appear in the ILC's Report.

[181] (1924), PCIJ, Series A No 2, 2.

[182] 1970 ICJ Reports 344.

undermined by the practice of calculating the amount of damages claimed on the basis of the injury suffered by the individual,[183] which is claimed to be a rule of customary international law,[184] the view persists that the State has an absolute discretion in the disposal of compensation received. This is illustrated by the dictum of Umpire Parker in the US-German Mixed Claims Commission in *Administrative Decision V*:

> In exercising such control [the nation] is governed not only by the interest of the particular claimant but by the larger interests of the whole people of the nation and must exercise an untrammelled discretion in determining when and how the claim will be presented and pressed, or withdrawn or compromised and the private owner will be bound by the action taken. *Even if payment is made to the espousing nation in pursuance of the award, it has complete control over the fund so paid to and held by it and may, to prevent fraud, correct a mistake or protect the national honour, at its election return the fund to the nation paying it or otherwise dispose of it.*[185]

Similar statements are to be found in a number of English judicial decisions,[186] which are seen by some to be an accurate statement of international law.[187]

(6) It is by no means clear that State practice accords with the above view. On the one hand, States agree to lump sum settlements in respect of multiple individual claims which in practice result in individual claims receiving considerably less than was claimed.[188] On the other hand, some States have enacted legislation to ensure that compensation awards are fairly distributed to individual claimants. Moreover, there is clear evidence that in practice States do pay moneys received in diplomatic claims to their injured nationals. In *Administrative Decision V*, Umpire Parker stated:

> ... But where a demand is made on behalf of a designated national, and an award and payment is made on that specific demand, the fund so paid is not a national fund in the sense that the title vests in the nation receiving it entirely free from any obligation to account to the private claimant, on whose behalf the claim was asserted and paid and who is the real owner thereof. Broad and misleading statements susceptible of this construction are found in cases where lump-sum awards and payments have been made to the demanding nation covering numerous claims put forward by it and where the tribunal making the award did not undertake to adjudicate each claim or to allocate any specified amount to any designated claim. It is not believed that any case can be cited in which an award has been made by an international tribunal in favour of the demanding nation on behalf of its designated national in which the nation receiving payment of such award has, in the absence of fraud or mistake, hesitated to account to the national designated, or those claiming under him, for the full amount of the award

[183] *Chorzów Factory Case (Merits)*, (1928), PCIJ Series A, No 17, 28.

[184] See Bolleker-Stern, *Le Préjudice dans la Théorie de la Responsibilité Internationale* (1973).

[185] 7 UNRIAA, 119, 152 (emphasis added).

[186] *Civilian War Claimants Association v R* [1932] AC 14; *Lonrho Exports Ltd v Exports Credit Guarantee Department* [1996] 4 All ER, 687.

[187] American Law Institute, *Restatement of the Law*, Third, Foreign Law of the United States (1987) at §902, 348–9; *Distribution of the Aslop Award*, Opinion of J Reuben Clark, Department of State, cited in Hackworth, 5 *Digest of International Law*, 766, B Bollecker-Stern (note 184 above) 108.

[188] Geck 'Diplomatic Protection' in 1 EPIL (1992) 1058; Bederman, 'Interim Report on Lump Sum Agreements and Diplomatic Protection', ILA, *Report of the Seventieth Conference (2002)* 230; Lillich 'The United States-Hungarian Claims Agreement of 1973', 69 AJIL (1975) 534; R Lillich and Weston, *International Claims: Their Settlement by Lump-Sum Agreements* (1975).

> received. So far as the United States is concerned it would seem that the Congress has treated funds paid the nation in satisfaction of specific claims as held 'in trust for citizens of the United States or others'.[189]

That this is the practice of States is confirmed by scholars.[190] Further evidence of the erosion of the State's discretion is to be found in the decisions of arbitral tribunals which prescribe how the award is to be divided.[191] Moreover in 1994 the European Court of Human Rights decided in *Beaumartin* v. *France*[192] that an international agreement making provision for compensation could give rise to an enforceable right on the part of the injured persons to compensation.

(7) Subparagraph (c) acknowledges that it would not be inappropriate for a State to make reasonable deductions from the compensation transferred to injured persons. The most obvious justification for such deductions would be to recoup the costs of State efforts to obtain compensation for its nationals, or to recover the cost of goods or services provided by the State to them.

(8) Although there is some support for curtailing the absolute right of the State to withhold payment of compensation received to the injured national in national legislation, judicial decisions and doctrine, this probably does not constitute a settled practice. Nor is there any sense of obligation on the part of States to limit their freedom of disposal of compensation awards. On the other hand, public policy, equity and respect for human rights support the curtailment of the States discretion in the disbursement of compensation. It is against this background that draft article 19, subparagraph (c), has been adopted. While it is an exercise in progressive development it is supported by State practice and equity.[193]

There are questions, the answers to which are not clear. To whom is the duty owed internationally in regard to the payment of compensation ie apart from any duty under internal law which would be owed to the individual? Who may enforce the obligation at international law? The answers may very well be that the duty is owed to the international community at large, ie *erga omnes*, and any member of the international community may enforce it. This is, however, a very controversial position.

Satisfaction

The ILC Articles on State Responsibility state in Article 37:

Satisfaction

1. The State responsible for an internationally wrongful act is under an obligation to give satisfaction for the injury caused by that act insofar as it cannot be made good by restitution or compensation.

[189] 7 UNRIAA, 119, 152.

[190] Geck (note 188 above) 1057; Garcia-Amador, Sohn and Baxter, *Recent Codification of the Law of the State Responsibility for Injuries to Aliens* (1974), 151.

[191] See Bollecker-Stern (note 184 above) 109.

[192] Case No 15287/89, [1994] ECHR 40.

[193] *Report of the ILC to the GA (2006)*, UN Doc A/61/10, 2006, 97–100 (see <http://www.un.org>). For the pure practice of States, mainly the USA, in distributing lump sums received under international agreements see Bederman (note 177 above) 237 ff.

2. Satisfaction may consist in an acknowledgement of the breach, an expression of regret, a formal apology or another appropriate modality.

3. Satisfaction shall not be out of proportion to the injury and may not take a form humiliating to the responsible State.[194]

Satisfaction is the third form of reparation which the responsible State may have to provide in discharge of its obligation to make full reparation for the injury caused by an internationally wrongful act. It is not a standard form of reparation, in the sense that in many cases the injury caused by an internationally wrongful act of State may be fully repaired by restitution and/or compensation. As Article 37 states, satisfaction is required 'insofar as [the injury] cannot be made good by restitution or compensation'. It is only in those cases where those two forms have not provided full reparation that satisfaction may be required.

The injury for which a responsible State is obliged to make full reparation covers 'any damage, whether material or moral, caused by the internationally wrongful act of a State'. Material and moral damage resulting from an internationally wrongful act will normally be financially assessable and hence covered by the remedy of compensation. Satisfaction, on the other hand, is the remedy for those injuries, not financially assessable, which amount to an affront to the State. These injuries are frequently of a symbolic character, arising from the very fact of the breach of the obligation, irrespective of its material consequences for the State concerned.

The availability of the remedy of satisfaction for injury of this kind is well-established in international law. The point was made, for example, by the tribunal in the *Rainbow Warrior Case*:

> There is a long established practice of States and international Courts and Tribunals of using satisfaction as a remedy or form of reparation (in the wide sense) for the breach of an international obligation. This practice relates particularly to the case of moral or legal damage done directly to the State, especially as opposed to the case of damage to persons involving international responsibilities.[195]

Satisfaction may consist of an acknowledgement of the breach, an expression of regret, a formal apology, or another appropriate modality. The forms of satisfaction listed in the Article are only examples. The appropriate form of satisfaction will depend on the circumstances of the case.

One of the most common modalities of satisfaction provided in the case of moral or non-material injury to the State is a declaration of the wrongfulness of the act by a competent court or tribunal. The utility of declaratory relief as a form of satisfaction in the case of non-material injury to a State was affirmed by the ICJ in the *Corfu Channel Case (Merits)* where the court, after finding unlawful

[194] See Crawford (2002) (note 2 above) 68 and 231, and the commentary which follows: ibid 231 ff.

[195] (1990), 20 UNRIAA 272–3, para 122.

a mine-sweeping operation (Operation Retail) carried out by the British Navy after an explosion, said:

to ensure respect for international law, of which it is the organ, the Court must declare that the action of the British Navy constituted a violation of Albanian sovereignty. This declaration is in accordance with the request made by Albania through her Counsel, and is in itself appropriate satisfaction.[196]

Another form of satisfaction is an apology, which may be given verbally or in writing by an appropriate official or even the head of State. Expressions of regret or apologies were required or offered in several cases in order to provide for satisfaction.[197]

Excessive demands may be made under the guise of 'satisfaction'. Thus, there is a need to impose a limit on the measures that can be sought by way of satisfaction to prevent abuses, inconsistent with the principle of the equality of States. Satisfaction is not intended to be punitive in character, nor does it include punitive damages. Article 37(3) places limitations on the obligation to give satisfaction by setting out two criteria: first, the proportionality of satisfaction to the injury; second, the requirement that satisfaction should not be humiliating to the responsible State.

The decided cases and past international incidents do not concern diplomatic protection as such, though aliens may have been involved. However, there is no reason why the general principles applicable to satisfaction should not apply to appropriate cases of diplomatic protection. For example, discriminatory harming of aliens, where a particular nationality is targeted, may require satisfaction to the national State of the alien on the basis that there has been an affront to such State. At the same time it must be acknowledged that the injury to the State must be over and above the injury to the individuals involved.

Contribution to the Injury

Article 39 of the ILC's Articles on State Responsibility states:

In the determination of reparation, account shall be taken of the contribution to the injury by wilful or negligent action or omission of the injured State or any person or entity in relation to whom reparation is sought.[198]

[196] 1949 ICJ Reports 35, 36. For a similar declaration by the way of satisfaction, see now the *Bosnia Genocide Case*, 2007 ICJ Reports, para. 469 (<http://www.icj-cij.org>), where it was stated that, by way of satisfaction the Court would include in the judgment's operative clause a declaration that the respondent had failed to comply with the Court's order indicating provisional measures. Operative clause 7 of the judgment contained the required declaration.

[197] The *I'm Alone Case* (1935), 3 UNRIAA 1609; the *Kellet Case* (1897), Moore, 5 *Digest* 43; the *Rainbow Warrior* (1990), 20 UNRIAA 217; the *Consular Relations Case (Provisional Measures)*, 1998 ICJ Reports 248; the *La Grand Case (Provisional Measures)*, 1999 ICJ Reports 9, and the *La Grand Case (Merits)*, 2001 ICJ Reports, para 123, <http://www.icj-cij.org>.

[198] See Crawford (2002) (note 2 above) 68, 240. See also for the commentary on this Article: ibid 240 ff, which explains the application of the Article, inter alia, to diplomatic protection.

This principle is applicable in the case of reparation for injuries to aliens. The principle deals with the situation where damage has been caused by an internationally wrongful act of a State, which is accordingly responsible for the damage but where the injured State, or the individual victim of the breach, has materially contributed to the damage by some wilful or negligent act or omission. Its focus is on situations which in national law systems are referred to as 'contributory negligence', 'comparative fault', 'faute de la victime', etc.[199] It recognizes that the conduct of the injured State, or of any person or entity in relation to whom reparation is sought, should be taken into account in assessing the form and extent of reparation. This is consonant with the principle that full reparation is due for the injury—but nothing more—arising in consequence of the internationally wrongful act. It is also consistent with fairness as between the responsible State and the victim of the breach. In the *La Grand Case (Merits)* the ILC recognised that the conduct of the claimant State could be relevant in determining the form and amount of reparation. There Germany had delayed in asserting that there had been a breach and in instituting proceedings. The court noted 'that Germany may be criticised for the manner in which these proceedings were filed and for their timing', and stated that it would have taken this factor, among others, into account 'had Germany's submission included a claim for indemnification'.[200] This was not a direct case of diplomatic protection but the general principle is illustrated by it. The relevance of the injured State's contribution to the damage in determining the appropriate reparation is widely recognized in the literature[201] and in State practice.[202] While questions of an injured State's contribution to the damage arise most frequently in the context of compensation, the principle is also relevant to other forms of reparation.

Not every action or omission which contributes to the damage suffered is relevant for this purpose. Only those actions or omissions may be taken into account which can be considered as wilful or negligent, ie which manifest a lack of due care on the part of the victim of the breach for his or her own property or rights. While the notion of negligent action or omission is not qualified, eg by a requirement that the negligence should have reached the level of being 'serious' or 'gross', the relevance of any negligence to reparation will depend upon the degree to which it has contributed to the damage as well as the other circumstances of the case.

199 von Bar, 2 *The Common European Law of Torts* (2002) 517–40.

200 2001 ICJ Reports paras 57, 116, <http://www.icj-cij.org>.

201 Graefrath, 'Responsibility and Damage Caused: Relations between Responsibility and Damages', 185 Hague Recueil (1984) 95; Bollecker-Stern (note 184 above) 265–300.

202 In the *Delagoa Bay Railway Case* (1900), the arbitrators noted that: 'All the circumstances that can be adduced against the concessionaire company and for the Portuguese Government mitigate the latter's liability and warrant...a reduction in reparation': Moore, 2 *International Arbitrations* 1865. This was a case of diplomatic protection. For other cases in general see Gray, *Judicial Remedies in International Law* (1987) 23 ff.

The wilful or negligent action or omission which contributes to the damage may be that of the injured State or any person or entity in relation to whom reparation is sought. The situation where a State claims on behalf of one of its nationals in the field of diplomatic protection is clearly covered.

Countermeasures

As already stated, the principles applicable to countermeasures[203] in the law of diplomatic protection of nationals abroad are the same as for the law of State responsibility in general. For that reason, suffice it here to summarize the present law which is also reflected in Articles 49 to 53 of the Articles of the ILC on State Responsibility dealing with countermeasures.[204] There is no reason to consider the matter in greater detail. The commentary on these articles contains a full discussion of the law.

It is to be emphasized that the object of countermeasures taken by the injured State, in the present case the national State of the alien, is to induce the responsible State to comply with its international obligations in regard to the treatment of the former's national and, in the appropriate case, to provide reparation for the wrong. That purpose underlies the system of countermeasures. Moreover, the countermeasures envisaged in connection with the *diplomatic* protection of a national do not include the use of force and are confined to peaceful means.

On that basis, countermeasures are limited to the non-performance for the time being of international obligations of the State taking the measures towards the responsible State and must, as far as possible, be taken in such a way as to permit the resumption of performance of the obligations relating to the injured alien in question. However, the countermeasures taken do not affect obligations of the national State relating to the protection of fundamental human rights, obligations of a humanitarian character which may not be violated by way of reprisal, and other obligations under peremptory norms of international law. A State taking countermeasures is not relieved from fulfilling its obligations under any dispute settlement procedure applicable between it and the responsible State and to respect the inviolability of diplomatic or consular agents, premises, archives, and documents.

Most importantly, countermeasures must be commensurate with the injury suffered, taking into account the gravity of the internationally wrongful act and the violated rights in question.[205] Furthermore, before taking countermeasures, an injured State must call on the responsible State to fulfil its international

[203] The term used previously was 'reprisals'.
[204] See Crawford (2002) (note 2 above) 281–301.
[205] On proportionality see the *Naulilaa Case* (1928), 2 UNRIAA 1028.

obligations relating to remedies which have allegedly not been observed and notify the responsible State of any decision to take countermeasures and offer to negotiate with that State. Notwithstanding these limitations however, the injured State may take such urgent countermeasures as are necessary to preserve its rights. Countermeasures may not be taken, and if already taken must be suspended without undue delay, if the internationally wrongful act has ceased and the dispute is pending before a court or tribunal which has the authority to make decisions binding on the parties. But this prohibition does not apply, if the responsible State fails to implement the dispute settlement procedures in good faith. Countermeasures must be terminated as soon as the responsible State has complied with its secondary obligations in relation to the internationally wrongful act.[206]

[206] These obligations are reflected in Part II of the ILC's Articles on State Responsibility and relate to remedial measures becoming applicable upon the commission of an international wrong in respect, in the present case, of an alien. These measures are those discussed earlier in this Chapter.

16

Influence of the Law of Human Rights Protection—Parallels

The remedial law of human rights protection may have an influence on the law of diplomatic protection in certain areas, particularly that of the exhaustion of local remedies. Parallels from the law of human rights protection may apply to diplomatic protection. There have been developments in the application of the rule of domestic remedies to human rights protection, albeit under conventional law, which could affect the application of the rule in the diplomatic protection of aliens. This feature is discussed here, because it reveals a novel aspect of the rule of local remedies inextricably involved with the impact of human rights law and hitherto not properly or fully addressed.

It must be recognized that the so-called *domestic* remedies rule is not an invention of international human rights law. Not only do the relevant instruments generally refer to 'general international law' (which obviously means the law of diplomatic protection in particular), but (i) human rights organs, particularly those operating judicially or under judicial control, invoke general international law; (ii) there is no substantial evidence that, in the event that there is a customary law applying the rule to human rights law as such, the rule applicable would not be based on the rule in diplomatic protection as is the case with the conventional law and that applied by human rights organs mentioned above. Consequently, it would be foolhardy to postulate differences as a basic assumption, rather than to recognize that human rights law starts with an awareness of the relevance of the principles of the general international law of diplomatic protection[1] and proceeds to use them, while at the same time implementing the law with refinements (and even, perhaps, differences) where such are called for by the particular circumstances of human rights protection. This pragmatic approach appears to be the one taken by all human rights organs virtually without exception. They do not, as the evidence shows, take the view that the rule as applied to diplomatic protection is 'rigid', as opposed to 'flexible', as such, or that the rule as applied to human rights protection is original and has an existence of its own or that

[1] The local remedies rule as applied to diplomatic protection is examined in Chapter 11 above.

they must ignore the principles found in the law of diplomatic protection.[2] It may be possible to identify a narrowing of scope or broadening of limitations, for example, especially in applications to particular situations when legitimate comparisons are possible, but that is not to say that basic approaches, whether of principle or conceptual content, or of contextual applications, are fundamentally and always different, or can never be similar or comparable, or that comparison and analogies are irrelevant.[3]

It must be emphasized that there is a difference between changing or not recognizing a *principle,* in this case as applied to diplomatic protection, and giving the principle development (ie of conceptual content) which may be different. When the latter takes place, the principle remains, though the conceptual development may be narrower. Indeed, conceptual concretizations cannot be characterized as narrower or different, unless identical or, at least, similar contextual situations are being considered. When a situation has not been encountered in the law of diplomatic protection but has been in the law of human rights protection, it is not appropriate to say that there has been a narrower development or application of the *principle,* or, still less, that the *principle* is different or has been changed. What is taking place is a development in application. That having been said, where principles or their conceptual development or contextual application are different from those recognized in the law of diplomatic protection, this must be recognized.

The above distinctions and realities are noted because there are what are properly termed specific contextual applications as well as what are properly characterized as differences of principle, and differences of conceptual content, in the implementation of the rule of domestic remedies by human rights organs. It will be apparent, though, that the incidence of differences in principle is much less than the incidence of conceptual development or contextual applications, though sometimes these phenomena are confused or, at least, not kept distinct by legal commentators.[4] Furthermore, while differences or similarities in broad principle are easy to identify, it is often not easy to distinguish conceptual development

[2] Cançado Trindade disagrees in effect with this approach, believing virtually that the rule as applied to human rights protection has a total life of its own. This is the burden of his argument in 'Book Review', 86 AJIL (1992) 626, passim. In any case, 'flexibility' and 'rigidity' are relative terms—relative to the point of view being used. What is flexibility from the respondent State's angle is rigidity from the individual's point of view and vice versa. This is so, even though, as has become apparent, some human rights organs and bodies do use this terminology, obviously with a bias against States and in favour of individuals. It makes sense and accords more with reality to talk, for instance, in terms of expansion or narrowing of the scope of, and narrowing or expansion of the limitations on, the rule.

[3] On the specific application of the rule in conventional human rights protection see C F Amerasinghe, *Local Remedies in International Law* (2004), Chapter 13.

[4] Cançado Trindade (note 2 above) 626, does not keep these distinctions separate. The working of conceptual development is explained in greater detail by me in my treatise, *Principles of the Institutional Law of International Organizations* (2005), Chapter 6.

from contextual application, but making such a distinction is the appropriate manner in which to approach the matter.[5]

It is evident that in principle human rights organs have implicitly accepted that the starting point is the law of diplomatic protection. This is evidenced by their recognition of such basic principles, broad and conceptually indeterminate in a sense though they may be, such as, for example, those relating to ordinary and extraordinary remedies, to full exhaustion, to unavailability, inaccessibility and inefficacy of remedies, to undue delay, to repetition of injury, and to waiver and estoppel.

What has happened in the law of human rights protection in most areas is that (i) general concepts included in principles have already been filled out and given narrower definition (eg full exhaustion, use of ordinary or extraordinary remedies, including alternative remedies, and inaccessibility); and (ii) there has been application of principle and general concepts included in them to situations which have not been encountered at all in the law of diplomatic protection (eg inaccessibility).

It is unnecessary here to examine in detail where the law of human rights protection differs from or is similar to the law of diplomatic protection with regard to the rule of local or domestic remedies. Suffice it to say that there are considerable differences between the approach of human rights bodies and the law of diplomatic protection to the conceptual content of effectiveness of a remedy.

However, it is equally important to recognize that just as there are clear similarities of principle in other areas, eg availability of remedies and undue delay, there are also (i) areas, such as inaccessibility, in which there has been further conceptual development in the experience of human rights bodies; and (ii) areas, such as extraordinary remedies and alternative remedies, in which there have been new and contextual applications to situations which have not been encountered in the law of diplomatic protection. In both of these categories, the proper and useful approach is to regard the approach of human rights bodies as a possible source for the development of the law relating to local remedies in diplomatic protection. Thus, for instance, the application in human rights law of the concept of inaccessibility to the situation where in a given social context the legal profession is virtually coerced into not advising an individual is a development which can inform the law of diplomatic protection. That development also highlights to some extent the possibility that inaccessibility may result not only from

[5] Cançado Trindade is obsessed with 'flexibility' and 'adjustment' at the expense of recognizing new applications of the rule: see (note 2 above) 631, and Cançado Trindade, 'The Inter-American Human Rights System at the Dawn of a New Century', in Harris and Livingstone (eds), *The Inter-American System of Human Rights* (1998) 401. A more helpful and objective, and less dogmatic and less assumptive, approach to the implementation of the American Convention is taken by Cerna, 'The Inter-American Commission on Human Rights', in ibid 85–92, and Vivanco and Bhansali, 'Procedural Shortcomings in the Defence of Human Rights', in ibid 429–32.

conduct or situations attributable to the respondent State but also from societal phenomena.

In the same way as for conceptual development, the application of principles to new fact situations could inform the law of diplomatic protection. The approach taken by human rights bodies to extraordinary and alternative remedies is a good example of this. It is not being suggested that there should or can be a wholesale and indiscriminate importation to the law of diplomatic protection of developments in these senses in the law of human rights protection. What is necessary is that a close look be taken at the developments referred to above, in the context of diplomatic protection, before they are accepted as being relevant or rejected as being irrelevant.

That there are differences between the law of human rights protection and the law of diplomatic protection in certain areas of the application of the rule of local remedies must also be recognized. It is not suggested that it is always desirable that the gap be bridged. Nevertheless, the lessons learned in one area may be useful in the other area. A good example is the conceptual development of inaccessibility to include the indigence of the individual who is the victim as a factor to be considered. In some early cases in the law of diplomatic protection, impecuniosity or indigence of the alien was regarded as a factor which was not relevant to the issue of inaccessibility. It may be possible that the irrelevance of indigence in these cases depended on the circumstances of each case. A similar treatment of indigence is to be found in the jurisprudence under the European Convention and in the practice of the UN Human Rights Committee. However, the advisory opinion of the IACHR has now indicated that indigence is a factor which *in principle* is relevant (to inaccessibility) for the purposes of the rule of domestic remedies. This precedent is clearly one that could inform the law of diplomatic protection which was apparently in principle interpreted differently. Here is an instance where current apparent differences could result in a closer look being taken at the conceptual content of principle even to the extent of changing it or its approach.[6]

The important point is that, though it is possible that there be differences in the content or application of the rule in the two areas, which must exist because of the possible differences that there may be in the perception of the rule as it is relevant to the two areas, there is no need to regard the development of the rule in the two areas as incurably separate. Nor is there a justification for such an approach in the light of the bases of the rule as applied in the two areas. While

[6] The issue of indigence and impecuniosity in relation to the limitations (based on inaccessibility) on the rule of local remedies, both in diplomatic protection and in human rights protection, is discussed at length in C F Amerasinghe, 'Indigence and Inaccessibility as Limitations on the Rule of Local Remedies', in *Hacia un Nuevo Orden Internacional y Europeo, Estudios en Homenaje al Profesor Don Manuel de Velasco* (1993) 57. See also C F Amerasinghe (note 3 above) 327 ff.

valid differences must be accepted, there is every reason why the experience in one area could inform the development of the law in the other.[7]

That having been said, it is also clear that the development of conceptual content in like principles and the contextual application of such principles are subject to the influence of several different factors which become relevant on account of the diverse phenomena in modern international society. These include factors such as the existence of tyrannical dictatorships opposed to truly just democracies or other polities, of endemic judicial inefficiency and corruption even in democracies or polities of whatever kind, and of a distinction made in conventional human rights law between non-derogable and derogable rights, though there are no absolute and invariable conclusions to be reached because of such differences. That this is the position in the context of international human rights protection is easily conceded.[8] On the other hand, there is no reason why similar factors which may exist could not have an impact on the rule of local remedies in diplomatic protection.

It has been pointed out recently by the IAComHR that the Inter-American system (under the American Convention particularly) of providing an 'international remedy' is subsidiary compared to the primary role of national courts.[9] The Commission made clear that, where petitioners can litigate before domestic courts and do have access to justice, they must do so in compliance with the rule of domestic remedies. This is an unequivocal admission that the domestic remedies rule has a significance in the context of human rights protection just as it does in the law of diplomatic protection. There is no implication that domestic remedies may be side-stepped at the drop of a coin or that the object of the human rights protection system is to get the matter at any cost to an international forum, simply because international human rights dispute settlement procedures are available. This view of the international remedy may be applicable in diplomatic protection as well. The point being made is that the general principles are still valid that the rule of domestic remedies applicable in human rights law *derives* from the rule of local remedies of the law of diplomatic protection and bears a significant resemblance to the latter, and that the development of the rule in the two areas are interconnected and need not *necessarily* be different.[10]

[7] In the light of the above analysis, the implication is open to question that generally recognized rules of international law relating to the application of the rule in diplomatic protection must 'suffer adjustment or adaptation' in the context of the law of human rights protection in general and necessarily, resulting in unbridgeable and consolidated *differences*. This implication is found in Cançado Trindade (note 2 above).

[8] See Vivanco and Bhansali (note 5 above) 429–31.

[9] *Marzioni v Argentina* (1996), Report No 39/96, Case 11 673, paras 50–2.

[10] On the exhaustion of domestic remedies in connection with human rights law, particularly under the European Convention on Human Rights, see now Schermers, 'Exhaustion of Domestic Remedies', in 2 *Liber Amicorum Judge Shigera Oda* (2002) 947–75.

17

The Effect of Investment Treaties and of International Investment Law

The foreigner who does business abroad also now has new and alternative remedies available to him. The Convention on the Settlement of Investment Disputes between States and Nationals of Other States of 1965[1] enables natural or juridical persons to seek arbitration in investment disputes against a State party to the convention before the International Centre for Settlement of Investment Disputes, provided both the defendant (host) State and the national State of the person and also the parties to the dispute, ie the host State and the national of the other State, have consented to this procedure. Article 26 of the ICSID Convention waives the application of the rule of local remedies, unless it is incorporated in the arrangements between the host State and the foreigner. Article 27 waives the right of the national State to exercise diplomatic protection until a certain point in the settlement of an investment dispute—the refusal of the host State to honour an award in a dispute given by an ICSID Tribunal. ICSID procedures for the settlement of disputes have been and are frequently used in investment disputes since the inception of ICSID and provide an alternative to diplomatic protection favoured by national States and their nationals.

A phenomenon peculiar to the aftermath of the Second World War is the bilateral investment treaty (BIT).[2] Investment treaties may also be multilateral.[3] There have been drafts of model multilateral and bilateral treaties relating to

[1] 4 ILM (1965) 352.

[2] The records show that the first post-Second World War so-called BIT was signed in 1959. Between 1959 and 2001, there have been 837 BITs signed: ICSID, *Investment Promotion and Protection Treaties*, Release 2001–3 (2001). All these treaties with the exception of one (between Germany and Greece in 1961) have been between developed countries, on the one hand, and less developed countries, on the other. A few of these treaties have been between two less developed countries (eg Malaysia and Vietnam (1992), Singapore and Sri Lanka (1980), and Israel and Romania (1991)). Clearly, the BIT is directed at less developed countries and is an instrument to secure special protection, vis-à-vis these countries, for investments made in them by nationals of developed states. On the impact of BITs on the rule of local remedies see C F Amerasinghe, *Local Remedies in International Law* (2004) 267 ff, from which the material in this Chapter is taken. See also on the subject of investment treaties and their relationship to, and effect on, diplomatic protection: Kokott, 'The Role of Diplomatic Protection in the Field of the Protection of Foreign Investment' in ILA, *Report of the Seventieth Conference* (2002) 259.

[3] Perhaps NAFTA would qualify for this description.

foreign investment in one way or another by, inter alia, the OECD, the AALCC and the UNCTC.[4] The modern BIT is European in origin. The first was between the Federal Republic of Germany and Pakistan (1959). In 1967, the OECD finalized a Draft Convention on the protection of Foreign Property. However, the draft was never opened for signature. There are some developed States, such as the US, Switzerland, and Denmark, which have model agreements. To reflect the particular interests of developing States in the face of such activity by developed States, the AALCC produced a model treaty with two variants in 1984.

A trend among BITs is to include several different possible forms of arbitration for the settlement of investor-State disputes. Several treaties refer to different kinds of arbitration to which parties may agree. They also provide that in the absence of agreement between the parties on this matter the dispute shall be settled by arbitration according to a particular one of the mentioned forms.[5] Other treaties, for example those concluded by the US, give the host State's advance consent to each of the mentioned forms of arbitration, thus in effect giving the investor the choice.[6] References are common to ICSID, to arbitration under the UNCITRAL rules, and, to a lesser extent, ICC arbitration. There is comparatively little uniformity in this particular area of treaty practice. While the inclusion of an investor-State arbitration clause has become a common feature of BITs, there is variety in the choice of arbitration methods.

Basically, whether an investment treaty (or for that matter any relevant international dispute settlement treaty) includes a waiver, express or implied, of the local remedies rule, where it would otherwise be applicable, is strictly a matter of interpreting the treaty. There is no hard and fast rule that BITs, for instance, by their very nature imply a general waiver of the rule. On the contrary, the correct presumption may be the opposite—that no waiver may have taken place unless express provision is made for it. The view of the ICJ, as pointed out, is that the rule is an important one whose waiver cannot lightly be presumed. Express waivers, total or partial, have appeared in BITs. More difficult is the answer to the question when a waiver may be implied where express provision is not made for it. The issue being addressed relates to the incidence of a waiver of the rule.

Where the BIT incorporates ICSID arbitration either as the only dispute settlement procedure[7] or as one alternative,[8] and says no more, it is clear that by virtue of Article 26 of the ICSID Convention the rule of local remedies is waived

[4] For the OECD, see 7 ILM 117 (1968); for the AALCC, see 23 ILM 254 (1984); and for the UNCTC, see UN Doc E/1990/94, Annex.

[5] Article 8 of the UK BIT with Czechoslovakia (1990), and Article 10 of the UK BIT with Ghana (1989).

[6] Article VI(4) of the US BIT with Armenia (1992), and Article VII(4) of the US BIT with Argentina (1991).

[7] See the BITs between the UK and Nigeria (1990) and the UK and Congo (1989), and between the Netherlands and Paraguay (1992).

[8] See the BITs between the UK and Ghana (1989), the UK and Ukraine (1990), the UK and Argentina (1990), Switzerland and Paraguay (1992), and Switzerland and Ghana (1991).

where it otherwise would apply in circumstances where ICSID arbitration is the relevant means of dispute settlement. A reference to ICSID arbitration as such would involve a waiver of the rule subject to an express and appropriate statement or acceptance of its applicability.

Sometimes the BIT may specifically invoke the local remedies rule or a modified form of it, even where ICSID arbitration is the arbitration procedure chosen. In that case, the provisions of Article 26 are expressly excepted, a possibility which Article 26 itself contemplates. An example of such an occurrence is the provision in Article 9 of the BIT between the Netherlands and Jamaica (1991) which states:

> 2. If such a dispute has not been settled amicably within a period of three months from the date on which either party to the dispute requested amicable settlement, either party may pursue local remedies for the settlement of that dispute.
>
> 3. If the dispute has not been settled within a period of eighteen months from its submission to a competent body for the purpose of pursuing local remedies, then for the purpose of Article 36 of the Convention on the Settlement of Investment Disputes between States and Nationals of other States opened for signature at Washington on 18 March 1965 (the Convention) the Contracting Party hereby gives its consent to the submission of the dispute to arbitration under that Article.

The provision retains an obligation on the part of the investor to accept a reference to local remedies within limits before ICSID arbitration is invoked.[9]

BITs which incorporate other arbitration procedures, such as ad hoc arbitration, whether under the UNCITRAL Rules or not, or ICC arbitration, and exclusively so as an alternative, sometimes make no reference at all to the exhaustion or invocation of local remedies as a pre-condition for arbitration. This is the case with such BITs as that between Switzerland and Lithuania of 1992 (Article 9). In such circumstances, the question whether the rule of local remedies has been impliedly waived becomes one of construction of the BIT. The answer is not crystal clear. It is arguable that, because the host State has agreed to arbitration which is international, being under a treaty, the procedure provided for is in effect the exercise of diplomatic protection by the investor's national State; therefore, in keeping with the established line of authority discussed earlier, even though the investor is given standing per se before the international forum, he has such standing by virtue of the treaty, and the local remedies rule applies in the absence of express waiver. The contrary argument is that because the host State has agreed to arbitration, even though it is set up by an act of the host State and the investor and not by a direct act of the host State and the investor's national State (the other party to the BIT) and although the arbitration flows from an international treaty, it is to be compared to such private arbitrations as took place in the *LIAMCO* and *Elf Aquitaine* arbitrations which imply the exclusion of the rule's application as being substitutes for remedies at the national level. It may

[9] See also the BIT between Switzerland and Argentina (1991).

be observed that the argument flowing from the conception of the arbitration procedure as one instituted in the exercise of diplomatic protection has considerable force. However, both arguments referred to above are still to be tested in circumstances where, in an arbitration set up by the host State and the investor under the BIT, the objection to admissibility is raised based on the rule of local remedies.

A situation may arise where the BIT provides for the rule of local remedies by the investor as an alternative to or prior to the institution of arbitration under the treaty. An example of this is the provision in the BIT of 1991 between Argentina and the US which states:

> 2. In the event of an investment dispute, the parties to the dispute should initially seek a resolution through consultation and negotiation. If the dispute cannot be settled amicably, the national or company concerned may choose to submit the dispute for resolution:
> (a) to the courts or administrative tribunals of the Party that is a party to the dispute; or
> (b) in accordance with any applicable, previously agreed dispute settlement procedures; or
> (c) in accordance with the terms of paragraph 3.
>
> 3. (a) Provided that the national or company concerned has not submitted the dispute for resolution under paragraph 2(a) or (b) and that six months have elapsed from the date on which the dispute arose, the national or company concerned may choose to consent in writing to the submission of the dispute for settlement by binding arbitration...

It is clear that it is the investor who is given the option of resorting to local remedies. Once this option is exercised, the import of the provision would seem to be that local remedies must be exhausted. Failure to exhaust them would then certainly result in the inadmissibility of an international claim based on diplomatic protection, if such a claim were made. Whether such a claim is available is not clear at all from the express terms of the treaty but there is no reason why it should not be.

Where the investor does not exercise the option of referring the dispute to the local courts, it would appear to be implied that arbitration instituted by the investor and the host State under the provision would not be subject to the prior exhaustion of local remedies. Unless this interpretation were given to the text, the provision would not make consistent sense.[10]

There are BITs which provide for submission to arbitration after the investor has exercised an option available to him to have recourse to the local courts. For example, the BIT of 1992 between Switzerland and Paraguay provides in Article 9(2) and (3) that:

> (2) Si estas consultas no permitieran solucionar la controversia en un plazo de seis meses, a partir de la fecha de solicitud de arreglo de la diferencia, el inversionista puede sorneter

[10] See also Article 8(2) and (3) of the BIT between France and Argentina (1991) and Article IX(2) of the BIT between Norway and Indonesia (1991), which are similar.

la disputa tanto a la jurisdiccion nacional de la Parte Contratante, en cuyo territorio se realizo la inversion o al arbitraje internacional. En este ultimo caso el inversionista tiene las siguientes opciones:

(a) el Centro Internacional de Arreglo de Diferencias Relativas a Inversiones (CIADI), creado por la Convención relativa al arreglo de diferencias entre Estados y nacionales de otros Estados, abierto a la firma en Washington, DC, el 18 de marzo de 1965;

(b) un tribunal ad hoc, que salvo otro paracer acordado entre las partes de la controversia, será establecido bajo las reglas de arbitraje de la Comisión de las Nacionas Unidas sobre Derecho Mercantil Internacional (CNUDMI).

(3) En caso de que el inversionaita haya sometido la divergencia a la jurisdicción nacional, él no puede apelar a uno de los tribunales arbitrales mencionados en el párrafo (2) del presente Artículo, salvo en el caso que luego de un período de 18 meses no haya una sentencia final del tribunal nacional competente.[11]

Firstly it is clear that the rule of local remedies as such has impliedly been supplanted by different rules expressly referred to in the treaty. Secondly, while local remedies are relevant, and even then only if the investor chooses to submit to them, resort to them as a prior condition for arbitration is subject to the express terms of paragraph (3) of the Article. These terms either do not necessarily require an exhaustion of local remedies as such or local remedies are to be regarded as inadequate and ineffective on the basis of undue delay in their implementation.

Provisions which clearly imply a waiver of the rule of local remedies in relation to the arbitration provided for are to be found in such BITs as the 1989 treaty between France and Bulgaria which states in Article 8:

1. Tout différend entre l'une des Parties contractantes et un investisseur de l'autre Partie contractante relatif aux investissements est autant que possible réglé a l'amiable entre les deux parties au différend.

2. Si un tel différend n'a pas pu être réglé dans un délai de six mois partir du moment où il a été soulevé par l'une ou l'autre des Parties au différend, il peut ètre soumis aux juridictions compétentes de la Partie contractante qui est partie au différend et sur la territoire ou dans les zones maritimes de laquelle l'investissement est réalisé.[12]

It is noteworthy that three important international instruments which concern foreign investment and offer models for dispute settlement, though they are not binding treaties, do not jettison the rule of local remedies. Surprisingly, perhaps, the OECD Draft Convention on the Protection of Foreign Property of 1967 uses language in Article 7 (b) which preserves the exhaustion of local remedies as a condition precedent to arbitration insofar as it states:

(b) A national of a Party claiming that he has been injured by measures in breach of this Convention may, without prejudice to any right or obligation he may have to

[11] See also Article 8(1) and (2) of the BIT between the UK and Argentina (1990) and Article 10(1) to (3) of the BIT between the Netherlands and Argentina (1992) for similar provisions.

[12] See for similar provisions Article 9 of the BIT between Switzerland and Cape Verde (1991), and Article 12(1) and (2) of the BIT between Switzerland and Ghana (1991).

resort to another tribunal, national or international, institute proceedings against any other Party responsible for such measures before the Arbitral Tribunal referred to in paragraph (a)...[13]

One of the two 1984 AALCC Model Draft Agreements for Promotion and Protection of Investments provides clearly in Articles 9 and 10 for the requirement of exhaustion of local remedies, whether before diplomatic protection is exercised or before arbitration is instituted at the request of the host State. Those Articles state:

Article 9
Access to courts and tribunals

(Alternative 1)
The nationals, companies or State entities of one Contracting Party shall have the right of access to the courts, tribunals, both judicial and administrative, and other authorities competent under the laws of the other Contracting Party for redress of his or its grievances in relation to any matter concerning an investment including judicial review of measures relating to nationalisation or expropriation, determination of compensation in the event of nationalisation or expropriation of losses suffered and any restrictions imposed on repatriation of capital or returns. The local remedies shall be exhausted before any other step or proceeding is contemplated.

[(Alternative 2)
Any difference or dispute between the investor and the host State in relation to any matter concerning an investment including those relating to nationalisation or expropriation, determination of compensation in the event of nationalisation or expropriation or losses suffered and any restrictions imposed on repatriation of capital and returns shall be settled through recourse to appropriate courts and tribunals, judicial or administrative and other authorities competent under the local laws of the host State. Neither contracting Party shall pursue through diplomatic channels any such matter until the local remedies have been exhausted.]

Article 10
Settlement of investment disputes

(i) Each Contracting Party consents to submit any dispute or differences that may arise out of or in relation to investments made in its territory by a national, company or State entity of the other Contracting Party for settlement through conciliation or arbitration in accordance with the provisions of this Article.

(ii) If any dispute or differences should arise between a Contracting Party and a national, company or State entity of the other Contracting Party, which cannot be resolved within a period of ___________through negotiations, either party to the dispute may initiate proceedings for conciliation or arbitration after the local remedies have been exhausted.[14]

[13] 7 ILM 132 (1968).
[14] 23 ILM 263–4 (1984).

The provisions on dispute settlement of the Code of Conduct on Transnational Corporations of 1989 formulated by the UNCTC emphasizes the primacy of national courts and tribunals, thus retaining the requirement of resort to and exhaustion of local remedies, while it states in Article 59 that, where the parties so agree, disputes may be referred to other mutually acceptable dispute settlement procedures.[15]

The approach taken in the drafting of BITs without exception, as the examples discussed above show, is based on the assumption that, even if arbitration instituted by the host State and investor is agreed upon in the BIT as a dispute settlement procedure, it does not per se imply a waiver of the rule of local remedies as a pre-condition to such arbitration. It is only if there is an express waiver or a waiver must necessarily be implied in the interpretation of the treaty that the application of the rule may be excluded.[16]

BITs generally provide also for the settlement of disputes between the two States parties to the particular BIT. Generally, such provisions refer to disputes relating to 'the application or interpretation' of the treaty. An example of a provision for the settlement of such disputes is Article 10 of the 1989 BIT between France and Bulgaria, which states:

1. Les différends rélatifs à l'application et à l'interprétation du présent Accord sont réglés par voie de négociation entre les Parties contractantes.
2. Si le différend n'est pas réglé dans un délai de six mois a partir dù moment ou il a été soulevé par l'une ou l'autre des Parties contractantes et sauf accord contraire de ces dernières sur la fixation d'un nouveau délai, il est soumis à la demande de l'une ou l'autre des Parties contractantes à un cour d'arbitrage.

Two questions arise with regard to such disputes which under such provisions are subject to settlement ultimately by arbitration. The first is whether the investor's national State could use these provisions to have disputes settled in the direct exercise of diplomatic protection. The second is whether the inter-State arbitration provided for, if permissible in the exercise of diplomatic protection, is subject to the exhaustion of local remedies by the investor. The answers to both questions depend naturally on the interpretation of the provisions of the particular BIT.

As to the first question, the reference to 'application and interpretation' of the BIT in the provisions cited above, for example, clearly covers the interpretation and application of the treaty to the relationship between investor and the host State. Consequently, the provision must enable the national State of the investor

[15] See CTC, 'Code of Conduct on Transnational Corporations: Report of the Secretary General', Doc E/C.10/1989/1.

[16] There is an additional question which may arise in relation to BITs in regard to international dispute settlement arrangements. That is whether breaches of contract by in particular the host State itself, which are not per se violations of international law, are in fact submitted to arbitral settlement under these treaties. Clearly, the answer depends on the interpretation of the particular treaty. The discussion above is of the incidence of the rule of local remedies which relates to exhaustion of remedies, where there has been a violation of international law, and not merely to the resort to or use of local remedies which is usually required before there can be a violation of international law in contract cases.

to bring a dispute which involves the application and interpretation of the treaty to arbitration under the provision, even though it may do so in the exercise of diplomatic protection.[17] The only problem is that the treaty specifically provides for the settlement of disputes between investor and host State by specific means. Such express terms, however, do not necessarily imply that provisions such as the one being discussed which refer to disputes between the host State and the investor's national State, must exclude disputes the solution of which is sought in the exercise of diplomatic protection directly involving the two States parties to the treaty, provided they concern the application and interpretation of the treaty. It is possible that recourse to diplomatic protection involving the two States in those circumstances is left as a possible alternative to the settlement procedures designed to involve the investor directly. On the other hand, it would be reasonable to infer that, once the procedures directly involving the investor are invoked, the treaty does not permit the resort to diplomatic protection directly with the involvement in arbitration of the investor's national State; otherwise, the settlement procedures provided for would duplicate rather than simplify the procedures for the settlement of disputes which would not be a logically consistent result. The interpretation of the BIT given here, while conceding that the settlement procedures directly involving the investor effectively substitute for the execution of diplomatic protection, also recognizes that Article 10 in addition affords an alternative procedure that can be applied in the exercise of diplomatic protection.

On the assumption that the exercise of diplomatic protection actively and directly involving the investor's State is possible as an alternative to the settlement procedures afforded the investor directly, the next issue is whether such protection by resort to inter-State arbitration procedures is subject to the exhaustion of local remedies by the investor or whether the requirement of such exhaustion has been waived. The answer again depends on the interpretation of the specific provisions of the BIT concerned. Article 10 of the BIT between France and Bulgaria, for instance, does not contain an express waiver of the application of the rule of local remedies in the appropriate circumstances nor does it necessarily imply that the application of the rule has been waived in such circumstances by the host State. The reference to negotiation as a pre-condition for arbitration is a reference to what is required of the parties to the BIT. It does not affect what is required of the investor, if a party to the treaty wishes directly to exercise diplomatic protection. This interpretation of Article 10 is not inconsistent with the provisions of the treaty nor is it illogical. On the contrary, it flows from the importance attached to the rule of local remedies in the settlement of disputes through the exercise of diplomatic protection which was recognized by the ICJ.[18]

[17] 'Application' of the BIT undoubtedly covers remedies consequent upon such application which could be included in a claim based on diplomatic protection involving the two States directly.

[18] To conclude, it may be observed in passing that bilateral investment treaties do have an impact on the substantive law regarding the treatment of alien investment, insofar as they include provisions on the subject. Such provisions may add to or subtract from the rights of investors deriving from the international minimum standard, depending on their content.

18
Concluding Observations

The law relating to the diplomatic protection of nationals abroad may be said to have crystallized in the nineteenth century with the advent perhaps of the industrial revolution in Europe and the assertion of their independence by the European colonies in Latin America. However, it was not till well into the twentieth century that the development of the law could be said to have reached its maturity. This progressive development and application of the law in the latter part of the twentieth century was spurred on, promoted, and accelerated by the ease and speed of travel for individuals between States and the formal approval and imprimatur given to the need for foreign investments in order to facilitate the economic development of the former colonies whose independence had been recognized, particularly after the Second World War. It may be observed that just as the newly won independence of States and their active assertion of this independence in their international relations from the early nineteenth century gave initial impetus to the application and development of and special interest in the law of diplomatic protection of nationals (and their property) abroad, the securing of independence of the European colonies particularly in the post-Second World War era of the twentieth century was the catalyst for the maturing of that law and for interest in making the law clearer, its codification, and its application to a variety of new situations.

That having been said, it must be conceded that the roots of the law, beginning with the Vattelian concept of injury to the State in the person of its nationals, dies hard. This is so, although there had been an attempt on the part of the more developed States and some committed international lawyers to push to the forefront the realization that it is really and unqualifiedly the national abroad, whether in his person or his property, that requires protection and is being protected. Thus, diplomatic protection as an institution still survives, particularly because of the theory that it is the State that is the owner of rights in international law and not the individual. The theory has not been abandoned, even though there have been important developments in the last half century both in conventional and in the common international law (customary law and general principles of law) which have led to the recognition of substantive human rights law. As a result individuals have come to be recognized as the subjects of international law in whom rights have been vested. Thus, on the substantive side it may not be possible any more to deny that the alien has rights and that the international minimum standard for the treatment of aliens has been fused with the basic human rights of individuals.

What has intervened in the progressive development of the international law of the rights of the alien individual in relation both to his person and his property, then, is only an absence of a general instituted and established international procedure, outside of the functioning human rights systems, for him to assert these rights before international fora without the espousal of his cause by his national State or, at any rate, a State. Hence, the need to develop and systematize the prevailing institution of diplomatic protection. Efforts generally to afford individuals as such procedural and remedial rights before international fora have not completely borne fruit, though there is evidence, supplied especially by the human rights arrangements which exist, that the international community may be moving towards such a conclusion. In the twenty-first century, then, it is still necessary to work with the institution of diplomatic protection as a means of affording protection to a certain class of individuals and their property.

It must be emphasized, however, that the law of diplomatic protection, as it has been developed, is not based on a logical conceptual system flowing from the idea that it is a State that has been injured and that it is such State that must assert its rights to a remedy. There have been many areas in which the reality of injury to the individual shows up, as has been seen in the analysis in some of the earlier chapters and particularly from the discussion of the real underpinnings of the law in Chapter 7. Thus, an approach must always be taken which does not attempt to rationalize the law or to give it a logical structure but rather which makes it possible to resolve the conflict of interests underlying the law in the most suitable manner, given that emphasizing one or the other of those interests in a particular situation would lead to different results. It is with these considerations in mind that the exposé and the discussion in the preceding chapters have been undertaken.

It must also be observed that particularly in the areas of remedies for the violation of the rules relating to the treatment of aliens via the route of diplomatic protection and the objective attribution of acts to the respondent State, there is an overlap between the law of State responsibility in general and the law of diplomatic protection. Thus, as far as the work of the ILC goes, these areas in particular which were examined by it in connection with the general law of State responsibility relate also to the law of diplomatic protection which has been separately and particularly studied by it. Indeed, it would not be wrong to maintain that at a minimum the totality of the law of State responsibility, as it has now been stated by the ILC, is relevant and applicable to the protection of nationals abroad via diplomatic protection.

The discussion in this book and the work of the ILC on the two subjects show that in the area of the peaceful and diplomatic protection of nationals abroad much of the *lex lata* still remains justified and there is little room for development or change of the law. A word of caution may, however, be spoken. The temptation to over-emphasize the interests of the individual and to ignore those of the respondent State, on the basis that it is the alien (or the national abroad) that requires as much protection as he can get or protection at any cost, is to be avoided.

The proper manner in which fundamental changes may be made is by providing, obviously by global agreement, an international forum or international fora for nationals abroad to pursue in person their remedies against States violating the law of alien treatment, just as now there are some multilateral human rights conventions which afford anyone, nationals and non-nationals alike, international fora for asserting their human rights. But until such time as this status is achieved in the international system, nationals abroad may have to rely on diplomatic protection by their national States in order to assert their remedial rights. Furthermore, sometimes that a State takes up the cause of an alien individual against another State gives that individual complainant a better chance of success than were he to contest the case by himself.

The conclusion, then, is that diplomatic protection as a remedial process must continue to exist and be used. This, however, is not a reason for eliminating from consideration in the formulation of the law of diplomatic protection the interests of the respondent wrongdoing State—which have been respected in the development hitherto of the law—in order to give the national abroad more protection. Nor is it a reason for emphasizing or giving absolute priority to the interests of the national abroad (alien) as against the interests of the respondent State. To do either would be to disregard entirely the fundamentals of the law as it has developed and to change its very nature. Too much tinkering with the institution of diplomatic protection, in order to protect the interests of the individual, would change its nature. As said earlier, the proper way of dealing with the problem of the perceived absence of adequate protection for the individual, in this case the alien, is to replace diplomatic protection as a remedial means of asserting rights with an appropriate international forum or appropriate international fora to which aliens would have access. To make changes in the law of diplomatic protection with the result that its character is erased would be to get rid of the institution. This may be desirable but should be done in the appropriate manner. There may be a justification, in this era of developed human rights law, to do just that but that is the way to make the change.

It is with these considerations in mind that it has been suggested, for example, that the better view of the law supported by authority now is that an alien's national State may not normally espouse a claim against a State of which the alien is also a national, regardless of whether he is more closely connected with the State exercising diplomatic protection. In short, a claim in respect of an injured person cannot be filed against a national State of that person by another State of which that person is also a national unless there are exceptional circumstances. The more possession of the nationality of the latter state is not adequate by itself to found such an action. This is giving the respondent State's interest primacy but the development of the law has more or less clearly made this assumption. It does not seem to be an answer that the individual would, perhaps, then have no recourse to a remedy. It is his keeping a particular nationality that has led to this result and he must take the consequences. Why penalize the respondent national State in these circumstances?

On the other hand, such suggestions which have been made to have the national State of the injured individual give proper consideration to the possibility of exercising diplomatic protection and consult his interests before rejecting a claim to protection, and pay him appropriate compensation where the national State secures a monetary award against the wrongdoing State, may be welcome and accepted. Here the interests affected are both on the side of entities involved in making the claim. The lifting of the veil, so to speak, in order to give the individual the protection which he may be regarded as deserving is acceptable. It is not a case of a true conflict of interests. Such suggestions are to be entertained, even though there is a problem connected with the question to whom the obligations involved are owed at an international level, so that they can be enforced if necessary.

The rule requiring the exhaustion of local remedies before a claim may be espoused by an alien's national State has also been interpreted and developed in particular by reducing the element of hardship to the individual while at the same time recognizing that the purpose of the rule is to give the respondent State a fair opportunity to redress grievances. The establishment of areas or situations in which the rule is inapplicable demonstrates that the law does take into account the interests of the alien, though the core rule itself is based on recognizing the interests of the respondent State.

The aggregate of rules built around the institution of diplomatic protection as such which have been considered in this work makes sense and justifies the continued reliance on the institution of diplomatic protection as a means of protecting nationals abroad. At the same time there are more rules connected with State responsibility in general which apply equally in the area of the protection of aliens. Such matters as lawful excuses have not been included in the present survey because they, among others, are to be found in the general law of State responsibility. Among other things the rules pertaining to those matters have been considered by the ILC in its 2001 Articles on State Responsibility and in these areas much is undisputed *lex lata*, as those Articles show.

Special note must be taken of the impact or possible impact of human rights conventional law and investment treaties and law, which has been discussed in Chapters 16 and 17 respectively. Undoubtedly, human rights law can have a beneficial and exemplary effect on the development and application of the local remedies rule, especially in connection with limitations on its application that is *pace* the latest approach of the ILC in its 2006 Draft Articles. The example of human rights law should work in favour of avoiding undue hardship being placed on the alien.

As for investment treaties and law, while there is no rigid and unqualified disclaimer or rejection of the local remedies rule, there are signs that choices have been made available with regard to the exhaustion of local remedies. Arbitration, which becomes international because it is provided for in a treaty between States, may replace as an alternative the resort to and exhaustion of local remedies. This is so whether the arbitration is pursuant to the ICSID Convention or directly under a bilateral investment treaty. It remains to be seen whether in the future the model with regard to arbitration provided by investment treaties will be adopted in treaties of friendship and the like in the context of protecting nationals abroad.

It is hoped that what has been presented in this book as the law relating to diplomatic protection in the areas examined constitutes a vibrant set of rules which to a large extent protect nationals abroad, while not prejudicing respondent States. The landscape presented of the law, as it has been, and may be, developed, is an adequate reflection of the delicate balancing of interests which has taken place in the past and yet takes place in the modern era. The discussion in the preceding chapters has been geared not only to elucidating and stating the law but also to improving it.

Finally, an important point must be made. It is clear, as the recent judgment of the ICJ dealing with the preliminary objections in the *Diallo Case*[1] shows, that the institution of diplomatic protection, as it has developed, is alive and well. The ICJ held that some objections to the admissibility of the case could not be upheld resulting in its having jurisdiction to decide the merits in regard to some of the claims made by the applicant State. Other objections based on the requirement of nationality for incorporated bodies were upheld, thus preventing claims brought by substitution of a shareholder for the incorporated bodies from being examined on the merits. What is important, inter alia, is that the court proceeded on the understanding that diplomatic protection was a given, while the mechanics of its application as relevant to the case had necessarily to be determined and put in place. The court does not, on the one hand, in the cases like the *Diallo Case* which relate to diplomatic protection, question the usefulness or viability of the institution. On the other, it does try to refine and fine tune the rules relating to diplomatic protection which it applies.

As a parting shot, it is asserted that as long as the alien as an individual, whether a natural or judicial person, does not, as a given and automatically, widely have standing before an international tribunal to make claims against a wrongdoing State, on the basis that he, as a subject of international law, has been injured (as a result of a violation of international law in regard to him), diplomatic protection as an institution must remain the only recourse available. However, that it may, as a result of its history, have limitations and an imperfect structure as not providing the most desirable protection to aliens, may at the same time have to be acknowledged. Also some development in the right direction may now be provided by the 2006 draft Articles of the ILC on Diplomatic Protection.

[1] Judgment of May 24, 2007: 2007 ICJ Reports, see <http://www.icj-cij.org>. The judgment on the preliminary objections dealt almost entirely with objections related to diplomatic protection.

Index

The manufacturer's authorised representative in the EU for product safety is Oxford University Press España S.A. of el Parque Empresarial San Fernando de Henares, Avenida de Castilla, 2 – 28830 Madrid (www.oup.es/en or product.safety@oup.com). OUP España S.A. also acts as importer into Spain of products made by the manufacturer.

www.ingramcontent.com/pod-product-compliance
Lightning Source LLC
LaVergne TN
LVHW011907200926
848484LV00002B/556
* 9 7 8 0 1 9 9 2 1 2 3 8 5 *